The Comprehensive Guide
to Tracking Skills

The Comprehensive Guide to Tracking Skills

*How to Track Animals and Humans by Using
All the Senses and Logical Reasoning*

by

Cleve Cheney

Safari Press Inc.

The trademark Safari Press® is registered with the U.S. Patent and Trademark Office and with government trademark and patent offices in other countries.

Cheney, Cleve

Second edition

Safari Press

2013, Long Beach, California

ISBN 978-1-57157-427-5

Library of Congress Catalog Card Number: 2012931139

10 9 8 7 6 5 4 3 2 1

Printed in China

PHOTO CREDITS: A. Brackskovski (pp. 197); M. Cowell (pp. 324, 325, 328, 329, 334, 340, 345); N. Larsen (p. 358); Ogrish.com (p. 312); B. Rossouw (pp. 278, 346, 368); B. Smuts (p. 332)

Readers wishing to receive the Safari Press catalog, featuring many fine books on big-game hunting, wingshooting, and sporting firearms, should write to Safari Press, P.O. Box 3095, Long Beach, CA 90803, USA. Tel: (714) 894-9080 or visit our Web site at www.safaripress.com.

*This book is dedicated in humble thanks to
the Creator of heaven and earth.*

*To my dear family:
my wife, Bernice; son Hunt;
and daughters Jess, Tamaryn, and Ami;
sons-in-law Rudi, George, and Earle;
daughter-in-law Lizanne; and my grandchildren
Ben, Ethan, and Bella.
You give meaning to life.
I love you all dearly.*

TABLE OF CONTENTS

ACKNOWLEDGMENTS

I wish to thank my wilderness trail brothers for their companionship. We lived and shared the good years. Two great trackers who were better than I will ever be inspired me: Ozias Cubai, who passed away in September 2011, and Ringane. They were my ranger colleagues, mentors, and friends. This book is a tribute to them both. I will always fondly remember

and cherish the years we spent in the bush together. Thank you for teaching me all I know about practical tracking in the wilds of Africa, for your patience with a slow learner, and for sharing your skills. I will always be truly grateful. Without you two this book would never have happened.

Ringane

I want to say a special thank you to Ringane for the unforgettable days we shared as we walked side by side through thousands of kilometers of bush—a country that we both love so

Author and Ozias Cubai

dearly. I still see you in my mind's eye as you stand resolutely next to me, unmovable and dependable, as we faced charges time and again from some of Africa's most feared wild animals. I think back with nostalgia to the hundreds of campfires we shared with quiet companionship. Thank you for being my teacher and friend.

CHAPTER 1

WHAT IS TRACKING?

Introduction

Tracking principles are universal. Because they are consistent, the principles you will learn in this book can be applied anywhere in the world. The species of animals might differ, but the way that soils, substrate, and vegetation responds will be the same. All animals have behaviour patterns—they mark territories, they vocally advertise their presence, they use shelter, and they utilize game paths. Birds, invertebrates, and mammals of any given system interact with one another; therefore, the one can give clues about the other.

To make good observations and draw sound conclusions in the natural environment, one must be very familiar with what is "normal" in the particular natural system where one is operating. Deviations from the normal are then easier to detect.

Aims and Objectives

What Is Tracking?

Tracking can best be described as learning to use all your senses to monitor your surroundings and to make logical and realistic deductions from what you have observed

Simply put, it is observing "signs" with your senses—sight, taste, touch, smell, and hearing—and interpreting what is observed using sound reasoning and previously learned knowledge. There is also what could best be described as a "gut feel" component that goes beyond the five senses. It is an ability acquired by experienced trackers with advanced skills.

There has always been an air of mystery associated with tracking. The uninitiated stand awestruck at a tracker's ability to "read" sign and draw significant conclusions from what appears to be very scant and inconsequential evidence.

It is the express purpose of this work to unravel some of the mystery and to reveal the logic of tracking skills. This book will help put at least a modicum of ability within the reach of every individual prepared to expend the time and energy in learning the principles of tracking and then putting these ideas into practice.

The aims and objectives of tracking are to recognize and interpret sign for some practical purpose.

Practical Applications

Tracking can be broadly classified into activities associated with wildlife and those aspects relating to the tracking of the human species.

Wildlife Tracking

Tracking is most often associated with something to do with wildlife. The term "wildlife" should not be mistakenly understood as pertaining only to animals. The term must be understood in its broadest context to encompass all components of the natural system both living (mammals, birds, insects, reptiles, plants, etc.) and nonliving (water, soil, climate).

People who lived prior to the modern technological age were very dependent on tracking skills to survive in the environment of the hunter/gatherer. The whereabouts and type of game that provided food, clothing, and implements had to be established before it could be trapped or hunted. To do this successfully the hunter/gatherer had to have an intimate knowledge of the local wildlife. Hunts often involved following up on animals that had been wounded or poisoned. The skill to track also provided the individual with the ability to recognize and avoid danger and to find the things necessary for sustaining life in a natural environment. The list necessary for life included not only food but also water, shelter, and medicinal plants. A tracker's skill is directly related to his knowledge of all aspects of the natural environment.

In the modern context, wildlife tracking is associated with hunting, guiding, and conservation activities.

Hunters either have to learn tracking skills themselves or have to make use of "trackers" during hunting activities. Tracking in the modern hunting context revolves primarily around the identification of mammal tracks and scat (droppings) and the follow-up of wounded animals. This often involves following blood spoor.

Professional guides are called upon to interpret natural sign on a far wider scale to clients with the aim of familiarizing people with natural phenomena and with monitoring the environment for safety reasons. This can encompass a wide variety of interpretive skills. These include the identification of calls and tracks of birds, mammals, amphibians, insects, reptiles, and arachnids (spiders and scorpions); the identification of plants (especially edible and medicinal plants); recognition and interpretation of animal behaviour; and an understanding of how weather and geology (soils) have an effect on plant and animal distribution. Professional nature guides are also frequently called upon to track animals so that visual sightings can be obtained.

In the conservation field, tracking skills are utilized to identify sign that can assist in establishing the presence, behaviour, movements, and habitat preference of wildlife (again in the broadest context) species. Tracking skills are also required to follow-up wounded or injured animals. Tracking skills are also important in locating animals that have run off after having been darted during chemical immobilization operations. The ability to recognize and interpret natural signs also enables the individual to be aware of and avoid possible danger.

Trackers involved in some aspect of "wildlife" tracking are intensely aware of the interrelatedness of all components that collectively make up what is referred to as the ecosystem. They need to

have a broad-based understanding and knowledge of all aspects of the natural world.

Man Tracking

Human presence and activity, like that of animals, presents or leaves behind evidence. It is possible, therefore, to also identify and interpret human sign for some specific purpose.

> Man tracking is the identification, interpretation, and follow-up of signs present or left behind by the human.

In this context man tracking would be included in military activities, antipoaching operations, criminal investigations, and in searching for fugitives or lost persons.

In the military context, trackers are sometimes also referred to as scouts, "recces," or "point men." It is their responsibility to search for, identify, and interpret signs left behind by the enemy to warn of their presence, help locate their whereabouts, establish what they are up to, and in some instances to avoid the enemy or to make it difficult for the enemy to follow.

Criminal tracking would include all aspects of forensic investigations at crime scenes as well as following signs left behind by a criminal intending to evade capture. This can include the physical tracking of a suspect or escaped fugitive from the law.

Antipoaching operations incorporate aspects of both military and criminal tracking but because of its specific nature can be regarded as a field of its own. Antipoaching tracking involves all aspects relating to the identification and interpretation of signs associated with poaching activities as well as follow-up operations aimed at apprehending poachers.

The third type of man tracking is the one associated with the search for missing persons.

It must be understood that although one makes a distinction between wildlife and man tracking and also between different types of man tracking, there are commonalities as well as differences.

CHAPTER 2

TEACHING YOURSELF TO TRACK

Sensory Optimization and Logical Reasoning

We evaluate what is going on around us through sensory input. If we do not regularly exercise our muscles, they atrophy and become weak. The same can happen if we do not train our senses. They can become lazy and operate at suboptimal levels. This will mean that we will not be as aware of what is going on around us as is possible, and we will lose a lot of potentially valuable, even lifesaving, information.

Sensory optimization means learning to train your senses so that they are used to best effect.

As a tracker, you want to assimilate (take in) as much sensory information as possible. The sorting of this information will take place at a cognitive level. This means that you will use your brain to integrate (bring together) information gathered by your senses and your powers of reasoning to make logical deductions and establish an order of priorities as to how you will respond.

Logical reasoning is the capacity to sort and interpret incoming information to best effect.

The fundamental foundation of good tracking skills is vested in your ability to use your information-gathering systems (sight, hearing, smell, taste, and touch) to best effect and then correctly interpret information from signs. Correct interpretation of signs also depends heavily on the knowledge bank you have accumulated over time.

What Is Sign?

The tracker's source of information is sign. What is sign? Wild creatures live in association with, not in isolation of, their environment. As they are going about their daily activities, they are constantly leaving behind evidence of having been there.

A sign includes anything that can be produced or left behind by living creatures and that can be perceived by our five senses.

We could, therefore, list signs as things that can be perceived by our sense of sight, those that we can hear, and those that we can smell, touch, feel, or taste.

Visual Sign

A visual sign is one that can be detected using eyesight. There are many examples.

Tracks

A track or spoor refers to impressions left by feet, paws, claws, hands, or other body parts (e.g., an elephant's trunk dragging) on the substrate. See Figure CCCH.02.02.01.

A lot of information can be obtained from tracks: when the track was registered, the age of the animal (adult/subadult/young), the group composition (single/pair/herd), the size, the speed, and direction of travel, the condition of the animal, the sex, and the activity.

Excretions

This refers to scat (droppings/feces), urine, and saliva. See Figure CCCH.02.02.02.

Scat and urine can also provide useful information. By determining the age of the sign, it is possible to figure out how long ago the animal was there. The scat's shape, colour, and configuration can identify the species. The content and consistency of the scat can indicate the diet and often also the condition of the animal. The distribution pattern can show whether the species is territorial or not.

The way the scat is deposited can also give an indication of the species involved and the gait of the animal at the time the droppings

Figure CCCH.02.02.01: Tracks are important sources of information to the tracker.

Figure CCCH.02.02.02: A scat is a source of very useful information.

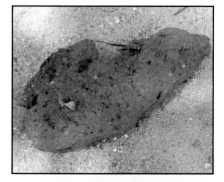

Figure CCCH.02.02.03: Flies (top right) and dung beetles (bottom right) can draw the trackers' attention to scat in the vicinity.

were deposited. Is it spread out (the animal was moving), broken up and scattered (hippo, black rhino), in a pile (the animal was stationary), or buried with soil (steenbok)?

Scat and urine are often indicated by the presence of flies and the noisy flight of dung beetles. The presence of flies and dung beetles will indicate to the tracker that fresh scat is close-by. See Figure CCCH.02.02.03.

The relative position of urine to the scat can sometimes indicate the sex of an animal. See Figure CCCH.02.02.04.

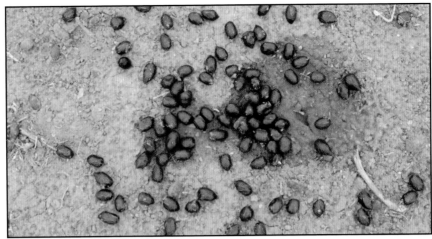

Figure CCCH.02.02.04: In this photograph the relative position of the scat pellets to the patch of urine indicates that a female impala deposited it.

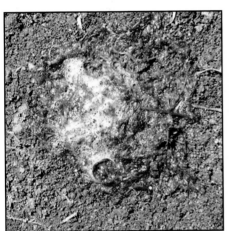  

Figure CCCH.02.02.05: Examples of a feeding sign are when cud was dropped from the mouth of an herbivore during rumination (left), seeds were dropped by feeding vervets (middle), and broken vegetation was left behind by feeding elephants (right).

Figure CCCH.02:02.06: Places where animals drink can usually supply the tracker with a lot of information.

Figure CCCH.02.02.07: Some animals such as elephants and rhinos will dig for water in dry riverbeds.

Feeding and Drinking Sign

Animals leave signs when they feed. See Figure CCCH.02.02.05.

Scat content that can indicate whether the animal is a browser, grazer, mixed feeder, carnivore, omnivore, or insectivore. Scat will also give evidence of how the food was procured, handled, and disposed of, and it can indicate the species involved, preferred habitat and diet, and when the animal was there.

Examples of feeding signs include saliva, gnawing marks on trees, a clearly defined browse line in preferred habitat of resident browsers, cud (chewed vegetation) dropped from the mouth, the remains of animals killed by predators, grass cropped close to the ground by grazing animals, broken vegetation, stripped bark, and so on. Places where animals drink are a mine of information. See Figure CCCH.02.02.06. Many animals will dig for water in dry riverbeds. See Figure CCCH.02.02.07 and Figure CCCH.02.02.08. Smaller

Figure CCCH.02.02.08: Elephants digging for water in a dry riverbed.

Figure CCCH.02.02.09: (above) Preorbital glands can be clearly seen on this gray duiker.

Figure CCCH.02.02.10: (top right) The tarsal glands are located in the tuft of black hair on an impala's hind feet.

Figure CCCH.02.02.11: (right) The parallel scrape marks of a territorial white rhino bull can be clearly seen.

species will then make use of these "wells." Drops of water can spill from an animal whilst it is drinking or moving away from a watering point. Sometimes the evidence of feeding is obvious; often it is more subtle and requires greater powers of observation.

Scent and Territorial Marking

Scent plays an extremely important role in the lives of animals. Depending on the species, scent-producing glands may be found at the anus, on the face below the eyes, on the forehead, below the eye, on the feet above the hock, or between the toes. Scent is

Figure CCCH.02.02.12: The impala ram is horning a bush to rub off facial secretions (left). On the right is a paper-bark acacia that has had a good rubbing.

Figure CCCH.02.02.13: This nyala bull is horning the ground and will leave clear sign of having done so.

Figure CCCH.02.02.14: A white rhino midden (left) and an impala midden (right).

Figure CCCH.02.02.15: Animals wallow to help cool themselves and to help rid themselves of external parasites. Buffalo wallowing (left) and warthog (right).

also incorporated in urine and scat. See Figure CCCH.02.02.09 and Figure CCCH.02.02.10.

Some animals define territorial boundaries by marking or by depositing dung, urine, or some form of secretion on the ground or on surrounding vegetation.

This can be observed as scrapes on the ground (e.g., white rhino). See Figure CCCH.02.02.11. An animal will also paste, meaning it will wipe anal secretions onto vegetation by straddling it (e.g., civet and hyena). Then there is shrub horning (e.g., impala and kudu—see Figure CCCH.02.02.12) and horning the ground (e.g., nyala and bushbuck—see Figure CCCH.02.02.13). Animals will also deposit scat in piles called middens or latrines (e.g., some antelopes and rhino). See Figure CCCH.02.02.14.

Figure CCCH.02.02.16: Dislodged ticks are evident in the mud rubbed off onto this tree.

Wallows and Dust Baths

A number of animal species enjoy wallowing in mud. They are so partial to this pastime that they sometimes take on the colour of the local soils. Thus, it's not unusual to see a "red" white rhino (if the soils of the area are reddish in colour) or a "white" black rhino (if the soils are light in colour).

Why do they wallow? Well, for a number of reasons but mainly for the pure enjoyment of it! Next time

Figure CCCH.02.02.17: A recently vacated mud wallow used by a white rhino.

you see a warthog heading for a mud wallow, take the time to stop and watch. It will be most entertaining. Watch as it slithers this way and that in the oozing, gooey, sticky mud. You will almost feel so inclined as to want to join in the fun. Animals wallow also as a means of thermoregulation, which is a means of controlling body temperature. Most species that wallow are dark-skinned. Buffaloes, rhinos, blue wildebeests, elephants, and warthogs are addicted to wallowing. See Figure CCCH.02.02.15.

Figure CCCH.02.02.18: Signs left behind from an animal walking away from a mud wallow include bits of mud on the ground. The amount of mud sign decreases the farther the animal moves away from the wallow. On the right, notice how the mud was scraped off onto a bush as the animal walked past.

Because they are dark-skinned, they tend to absorb radiant (light) energy, and this can cause them to overheat when temperatures hit the midthirties (Celsius) or higher. Rolling in mud cools the skin and helps to keep an animal's body temperature within normal limits.

Thirdly, when mud hardens, it entraps external parasites. When the animal rubs this mud off onto trees, rocks, or termite mounds, the entrapped parasites are dislodged. See Figure CCCH.02.02.16.

Certain wallows become very popular, and their long-term use can cause them to deepen and develop into semipermanent water holes. Each time an animal wallows in a water hole, it becomes deeper because some mud adheres to and is carried off by the animal.

From a tracking perspective, following mud sign is exciting and fun. It is fairly easy to follow and find an animal that has been wallowing.

It is fairly obvious to see when a mud wallow has recently been used. See Figure CCCH.02.02.17. It will be churned up and the exit point will be quite obvious. The body of the animal often leaves an impression in the mud, making it easy to identify which animal has been wallowing. Muddy footprints will lead away from the wallow and bits of mud will begin dropping off the animal as it moves away into the bush. See Figure CCCH.02.02.18.

Not only will bits of mud drop off, but mud will be scraped off on surrounding vegetation as well. The trail left behind is fairly easy to follow, but the amount of mud sign decreases the farther the animal moves away from the wallow. See Figure CCCH.02.02.18. The amount of moisture retained in mud can also give the tracker a good indication of how far behind the animal he is.

Mud tracking is a good opportunity for someone learning to track because it is relatively easy to follow, and the tracker is often rewarded with a sighting of the animal being tracked. Following an animal that has been wallowing is fairly simple even on substrate where other signs (such as tracks) do not show up well.

The height of the mud adhering to vegetation when passing by or when rubbing will indicate the size of the animal and the degree of moisture retention the age of the sign. See Figure CCCH.02.02.19 and Table 2.1.

Figure CCCH.02.02.19: The height of mud scraped or rubbed off will give an indication of the type of animal: an elephant rub on tree (top) and warthog rub on a small termite mound (above).

Table 2.1

SPECIES	HEIGHT OF RUB
Elephant	2.5–3.4 m
White rhino	1.8 m
Black rhino	1.6 m
Buffalo	1.4 m
Warthog	65 cm

Figure CCCH.02.02.20: A zebra dust bath (left) and a favourite dust bath area used after a shower of rain (right).

Rolling in sand or dust is also a grooming activity often practiced by zebras and wildebeests. This is usually seen as a dusty, bare patch where the substrate has been disturbed. See Figure CCCH.02.02.20.

Figure CCCH.02.02.22: Rubs are convenient objects against which animals will rub themselves to relieve an itch. This photo illustrates where a buffalo (left) and a warthog (right) have rubbed themselves against tree trunks.

Figure CCCH.02.02.21: Because animals will seek out shade and cover, these are good areas in which to look for sign.

Shade and Cover

Animals will seek out shade during hot weather and cover during cold or inclement weather. The tracker will, therefore, look in these places for additional signs such as bedding areas (which might still feel warm if recently vacated), cud falling from the mouth of ruminants, and scat. See Figure CCCH.02.02.21.

Rubs and Bark Stripping

Animals will sometimes use objects such as trees, fallen logs, and rocks on which to rub themselves to relieve an itch or scrape off mud during grooming. Figures

Figure CCCH.02.02.23: A buffalo uses a convenient branch to relieve an itch.

CCCH.02.02.22 and CCCH.02.02.23. Warthogs are very partial to this activity as are rhinos and elephants. Elephants strip bark from trees to supplement their diets. See Figure CCCH.02.02.24.

Paths

Game paths are usually most distinct around water holes and favourite feeding areas. Well-utilized paths often have a layer of fine soil covering them as a result of hoofs breaking down coarser soil. This is conducive to leaving distinct spoor impressions that can help to identify which species were present.

Active game paths can have a wide variety of tracks and sign, both fresh and old. The super imposition of tracks upon one another can also give an indication of sequence of events and the age of tracks. Figure CCCH.02.02.25.

Bedding Areas, Burrows, Nests, and Shelters

Some animals will be continually on the move choosing different resting and sleeping sites. Others will make use of holes or burrows to which they will return on a regular or irregular basis. The species that make use of underground burrows include porcupines, aardvarks, aardwolfs, warthogs, springhares, dwarf mongooses, wild dogs, bat-eared foxes, Cape foxes, and

Figure CCCH.02.02.24: During the dry season, elephants will often strip and eat tree bark to supplement dietary needs.

black-backed jackals. Figure CCCH.02.02.26. An occupied burrow will usually have some sign of occupation, such as the presence of flies, bones scattered around the entrance, spoor leading into and out of the hole, freshly excavated soil, and so on. The shelters or bedding sites of animals, which do not use burrows, will often be seen

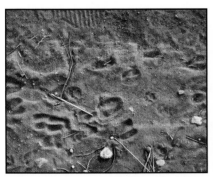 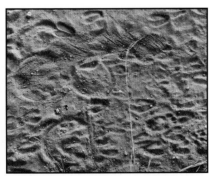

Figure CCCH.02.02.25: Game paths are a source of much information.

Figure CCCH.02.02.26: A variety of species use underground burrows for nesting and for shelter: a warthog burrow (left) and a hyena den (right).

Figure CCCH.02.02.27: Note how the vegetation in this bedding area is flattened. The size and shape of the bedding area can also give an indication of the type of animal or bird.

as flattened grass or vegetation, or body impressions left on soft substrate. See Figure CCCH.02.02.27. These bedding areas will usually be found in shade or areas providing cover from the elements.

Blood Sign

The ability to follow and correctly interpret blood sign is an important tracking skill.

The colour and amount of blood can indicate whether bleeding is from an artery, vein, or capillary. Figure CCCH.02.02.28. The clotting process of blood can give the tracker a good indication as to the age of the blood sign. Following a blood trail is important when trying to locate a wounded animal or human.

Skeletal Signs or Carcasses

Skeletal remains can indicate the presence of a particular species in a given area and can also indicate the presence of predators. Figure CCCH.02.02.29. Carcasses and skeletal signs may be present as a result of death by natural causes, death by accident, or death by disease.

Interpreting Visual Sign

The modern city dweller has, to a large degree, lost the ability to observe signs correctly in the bush. Small signs escape their notice and even large animals like elephants and buffaloes are sometimes not seen, even at short range. Figure CCCH.02.02.30. The city eye looks for complete objects. When looking for a kudu, for example, the unpracticed eye will look for the whole animal. The bush-wise and skillful tracker will know to look for "parts" of the animal—part of a leg sticking out from under a bush, a glint of sunlight off a horn, the rounding of a rump showing through dense vegetation. Another trick is to learn to look "through" vegetation and not "at" it. If one allows the focal point to shift from "at" to "beyond" an intervening object, the tracker is able to see and observe much more acutely.

Figure CCCH.02.02.28: Blood sign can assist the tracker in determining the severity of a wound and the time the animal was there. It can help lead the tracker to an injured animal or human.

Figure CCCH.02.02.29: Skeletal signs (bottom) and carcasses (top) can supply the tracker with information on the presence of a species, predator activity, or diseases.

Figure CCCH.02.02.30: The tracker must learn to look through vegetation instead of at it. If you looked at the bush in this photo, you would miss seeing the elephant standing behind it (top). At first it might be easy to miss seeing the two kudus in the photo on the bottom.

Olfactory Sign

Olfactory sign is that which can be detected using our sense of smell. Some animals have a very characteristic smell and emit odours specific to the particular species. An example is an elephant in musth. The author, as an exercise, once tracked a bull elephant in musth for about two kilometers by following the lingering smell of musth in the air and surrounding vegetation. Another example is the buffalo, which have the typical bovine odour of cattle. Then there is the goatlike odour of waterbuck, which can sometimes be smelled from a distance. Dung and urine also have characteristic odours. The smell of smoke can warn the tracker of an oncoming bushfire, or the presence of a poacher's camp. The smell of rain in the distance can give the tracker warning of a possible flash flood, giving him time to move out of drainage lines.

Sound Sign

Most emphasis is placed on the visual aspects of tracking. That is logical because we make the most use of sight to search for visual clues or sign.

> Sound, an extremely important aspect of tracking, does not always receive the attention it deserves.

The bush is filled with sound that can vary with intensity depending on the time of day and prevailing weather conditions. At times the bush can also be profoundly silent, and this, too, tells a story.

Just think for a moment of all the possible sources of sound. Animals, amphibians, and birds all possess vocal cords and are capable of vocalizing. They can also generate noise by their footfalls, brushing up against vegetation, or breaking branches. Snakes do not possess vocal cords but can hiss or make a rasping sound by rubbing scales together. Many insects are equipped with anatomical features that enable them to generate a wide variety of sounds: They buzz, whine, rasp, vibrate, whistle, squeak, and hum. Weather is also a source of sound. The wind can rustle, moan, sigh, shriek, or howl. One can hear the swishing sound of approaching rain or the rush and roar of turbulent water. Water movement can also be described as bubbling, gurgling, or growling. Thunder can crash, crack, or rumble in the distance.

Sound can be used to create a mental picture of what is going on around you.

Animals, frogs, toads, and birds vocalize for a number of reasons. Alarm calls warn of danger, communication calls bring individuals together and help to maintain group cohesion, and advertisement calls help to demarcate, proclaim, or establish territories. Distress calls can summon assistance. Comforting sounds make young feel secure. Animals make sounds that can indicate aggression and the intent to attack.

When the tracker learns to identify wildlife calls, it enables him not only to identify the creature specifically making the sound but he can often draw logical conclusions about what the animal is communicating. Is it advertising territory or warning of danger? Is it summoning its young or giving a distress call? The information from sounds is extremely valuable to a tracker. Literally thousands of examples can be given; here are a few to illustrate the point.

An adult lioness utters the low *umpf* sound to call her cubs; by recognizing this sound, the tracker will be warned that there are cubs close-by—a dangerous situation to be avoided. The guttural bark of the kudu is a deep bellow; that of the bushbuck is higher pitched. Both can warn of the presence of predators. The well-known *kwêêê* of the go-away bird (gray lourie) can warn the tracker of the presence of other humans. The high pitched hissing call of red-billed oxpeckers can tell the tracker that there could be buffalo, white rhino, giraffe, or impala in the vicinity.

Calls of water birds, double-banded sand grouse, and frogs can lead a thirsty tracker to water. The sound of heavy thunder can urge the tracker to move out of dry riverbeds (the danger of flash floods), off high ground and away from tall objects (the places lightning is most likely to strike).

Sounds can inform the tracker that "all is well" like the soft chinking of guinea fowl. When the same birds give their strident alarm calls or when frogs suddenly become silent, these sounds say "there is something not right."

The chattering of a group of birds in a tree can tell the tracker that there is possibly a snake close-by. A puff adder will warn you of its presence by hissing before you step on it. A cracking branch could give away the position of the wounded buffalo you are tracking.

And so we could go on and on. There is an inexhaustible amount of auditory information available to the tracker that can keep him well informed of "goings-on" around him. How does one learn to identify wildlife sounds? There are a number of options available.

Audio tapes and CDs are available of the calls of animals, birds, and frogs. By listening to these sound recordings, you can learn to identify the call and the animal, bird, or frog making it. It takes time and effort to learn these sounds, but there are no shortcuts to becoming a proficient tracker. It helps to have a picture to look at of the specific animal, bird, or frog while listening to the sound; your brain then establishes a connection between the two.

A second option is to look at videos or DVDs of wildlife, paying specific attention to the sounds made by the animals and birds. The third and best option is to go out into the bush and observe wildlife firsthand. Take careful note of the sounds and calls they make and learn to interpret what an animal or bird is trying to communicate.

Take the time and make the effort when an opportunity presents itself to sit somewhere quietly in the bush and concentrate on what you can hear. Close your eyes or blindfold yourself to cut out the strong visual input that could distract you.

Another exercise that will assist you in sharpening your sense of hearing is to blindfold yourself and put earplugs in your ears. After about twenty minutes, remove the earplugs but retain the blindfold. Your sense of hearing will now be intensified, and you will hear things you were not aware of before.

Remember that tracking is an integration of all your senses, and sound is one of the most important. Always bear in mind that sound has a context and, therefore, contains meaningful information that goes beyond the sound itself. Sound has a cause and an effect. Animals, birds, reptiles, amphibians, and frogs communicate for effect. They have a reason for communicating, and as you learn to identify not only the call itself but learn to interpret what is being communicated, you will become a better tracker.

> **The ability to analyze what you are hearing makes up a vital component of the skill of tracking, and next to sight it is the sense most used when tracking.**

The sense of hearing is probably used second only to that of sight. To magnify sound, face toward the source and cup your ears, which will act as antennae to catch more sound waves. Listening with your mouth slightly open can also increase sound input. Sometimes the tubes from the pharynx to the ears (Eustachian tubes) are blocked by air pressure. They can be "unblocked" by opening the mouth slightly, and thus improving hearing. Hearing is also improved by closing one's eyes whilst concentrating on sound.

Behaviour of Other Animals and Birds

The behaviour of other inhabitants of the bush can often be of assistance to the tracker, and sometimes a hindrance. Birds like red-billed oxpeckers and cattle egrets can warn you of the presence of animals such as impalas, buffaloes, giraffes, elands, kudus, and rhinos. See Figure CCCH.02.02.31. They can also warn these animals of your presence. Even if you are not tracking these species in particular, it is important for the tracker from a safety perspective to be aware of the presence of these animals.

Ground birds such as francolin, quail, and guinea fowl, flushing up from under the feet of animals can warn you of their presence and whereabouts. Francolin and guinea fowl are often very vocal and noisy when flushed and can be heard a long way off. Fork-tailed drongos frequently hang around grazing animals. As the animals move along, they flush up insects from the grass. The drongos then swoop down to catch the insects. Gray louries emit a raucous call when observing humans and predators. Other bird species such as double-banded sand grouse can lead you to water. See Figure CCCH.02.02.32.

Carrion-eating birds such as vultures can lead the tracker to sites of kills or warn them of the presence of large predators. Vultures, kites, marabou storks, and some eagles are

Figure CCCH.02.02.31: Cattle egrets (top) and red-billed oxpeckers (above) can indicate the presence of animals, including dangerous species such as buffaloes, rhinos, and hippos.

Figure CCCH.02.02.32: The behaviour of birds such as fork-tailed drongos (left), guinea fowl (centre), and double-banded sand grouse (right) can warn of danger or the presence of animals, humans, and snakes. They can also help the tracker find food or water.

quick to spot dead animals from their position aloft. By carefully watching them and understanding their behaviour, a tracker can glean a lot of information. In a survival situation, it can lead you to food and warn you of the presence of predators. Figure CCCH.02.02.33.

By observing animal behaviour, you can sometimes be warned of the presence of other animals close-by. Figure CCCH.02.02.34. An animal staring intently at a specific point, giving warning snorts or barks, or challenging a competitor for territory are just a few more examples of signs the tracker will be looking for and listening to. Remember, many of these warning signs work both ways. Oxpeckers, francolin, and flushed animals can just as easily betray your presence to the quarry you are tracking.

Figure CCCH.02.02.33: Raptors and scavenging birds can warn of the presence of carnivores and lead the tracker to kills, a potential source of food.

Incidental Sign

This category includes any other sign not covered above. Signs such as quills, tufts of hair, feathers,

Figure CCCH.02.02.34: In the picture the impala are staring intently at something. A tracker will be warned by this behaviour. It might only be a rival male impala. It could also be a predator like a lion or leopard.

a piece of material, and so on that may, or may not be associated with the species you are tracking are included in this category. It can also be weather-related information. See Figure CCCH.02.02.35.

Premonition (Gut Feel) and Prediction

A skilled tracker sometimes works on "gut feel" based largely on an intimate understanding of the habits and behaviour of the animal he is tracking. The tracker learns to "think" like the animal and can predict where the animal is going to go and what it is going to do.

It can be seen that tracking is a complex art and science that is based on a sound knowledge of natural history, animal behaviour, acute observational skill, and the ability to interpret what is observed through deductive reasoning. We now also know that tracking involves looking, listening, touching, smelling, and tasting. We also know now that there are many signs that can be taken into account and that can help you to be a successful tracker.

Figure CCCH.02.02.35: There is always an abundance of incidental signs that give indirect evidence of all different types of information. Some examples include (top left) flotsam high up in a tree indicates flood levels next to a riverbed. A spider's web (top right) built into what would, at first appearances, look like a very fresh impala track. Looks can be deceiving. A porcupine quill (lower left) betrays the presence of this species. You might not have seen the guinea fowl, but a feather (lower right) tells you they are around.

Tracker Awareness

The teaching methodology of "primitive" trackers was simple but profound. Their state of awareness enabled them to observe with acute and detailed intensity. They knew that distracted thought processes could get in the way of one's ability to be totally aware. They developed, therefore, the uncanny ability to navigate between distracted thought and awareness without the one getting in the way of the other yet allowing each to function at optimum intensity.

To give some practical examples of this: Have you sometimes been reading a book, but your thoughts were elsewhere, and suddenly you realize that you don't know what you have just read? Has it ever happened that you have been deep in thought when someone suddenly says, "Did you see that"? You didn't because your thoughts were occupied elsewhere. Focused thought and awareness go together. You ask yourself what am I seeing, hearing, smelling, tasting, touching . . . why, how, and when? What do these things mean? Your thought is now focused on what you are observing and the two processes are working together. But if you are thinking about something totally unrelated to what you are observing, then thought and awareness become mutually exclusive. Our thought processes powerfully influence what we see or think we see.

Many people find it difficult to isolate incoming sensory information because their senses are telling them something different from what their brains are trying to tell them (thought). We might recognize an object but fail to take note of its colour or texture. Unless we keep our thought processes in check, we can lose incoming sensory information. Our eyes can and do fool us into seeing something that is not actually true, and our eyes can also miss seeing things that are there. Most times the culprit is reduced awareness caused by distracted thought.

There are very few people in this modern day and age who are afforded the opportunity of being taught the art and science of tracking by a master. I was incredibly favoured during my twenty years of service in the Kruger National Park as a wilderness guide and ranger, to be mentored by some of the best. Incredibly gifted men, unsung heroes, who were never given the recognition they so deserved. One such man was my tracker and ranger colleague, Albino Ringane, standing on the far right in Figure CCCH.02.03.01. The photo was taken on the trail in the Olifants wilderness area of the Kruger National Park. A quietly spoken and humble man with the most mischievous grin you can imagine, he had tracking skills that went beyond the mere reading of signs observed by the five senses. It is only now, with the twenty/twenty vision of hindsight, that I realize how privileged I was to have had him as my teacher and friend.

Ringane's unbelievable patience as a skilled tracker, his powers of observation, his keen use of all the senses, and his astute deductions and reasoning often left me speechless with admiration and humbled at my own lack of ability. Yet never did he mock my ineptitude. With painstaking patience he would point out, time and again, the subtle and not-so-subtle signs I was failing to see, hear, smell, or feel. He found no pleasure in my failures; indeed, he was delighted at my all too infrequent successes—the hallmark of a good teacher.

Figure CCCH.02.03.01: Ringane, my teacher and friend.

TEACHING YOURSELF TO TRACK

Ringane grew up in the wild areas of Mozambique, and he followed in his father's footsteps when, as a young man, he became a ranger in Kruger National Park. Tracking was as natural to Ringane as breathing. Living in the bush was what he had done all his life, and tracking was nothing mystical to him—it was just something he did every day of his life. This book is dedicated to Ringane, the man who taught me that no sign is too small to be insignificant.

Each nuance of colour, every whiff of scent, the tiniest disturbance in the soil, all are significant and all tell a story. Learning to track is a lifelong pursuit. Master trackers are a dying breed. I wish I could say I am a master tracker, but I am not. Perhaps there was a time when I was tracking almost every day of my life that I was on the right path to becoming one, but I never reached that status. Politics in conservation got in the way, and I left Kruger National Park in 1996. Now I get much less opportunity to track in practice and a fading skill set is a reality. I would probably class as a very mediocre tracker at this point in time.

Tracking skills have never been recognized as being of much value in an industrialized and material-driven society. There has not been much incentive to hone or pursue these skills and so, sadly, they are being lost. We must not allow this to happen. How then can we keep these ancient skills alive if there is no one left to teach us? A valid question but one for which there is thankfully an answer. Teach yourself!

"How? I don't know the first thing about tracking," you reply.

Read on and find out. This is what this book is all about. Before we go on to learn how to reawaken our senses let us look for a moment at "tracker awareness." When it comes to tracker training, the African bushman and the North American Apache Indian stand out as master teachers. It might be also said of many people who live in the wilds and whose knowledge of tracking is tantamount to their very survival. Without looking back in the book, can you recall what animals were visible three pages back? You see what I mean?

Your thoughts were on the content of what you were reading and you were anxious to page ahead, and so you forgot to observe. Your distracted thoughts got in the way of awareness. As I said earlier, focused thought and awareness go together. You must ask yourself: What am I seeing, hearing, smelling, tasting, touching? Why is this so, how did this happen, and when did it occur? What do these things mean? Your thought is now focused on what you are observing, and the two processes are working together. But if you are thinking about something totally unrelated to what you are observing, then thought and awareness become mutually exclusive. Our thought processes powerfully influence what we see or think we see, hear, smell, touch, or taste.

When tracking, we must focus our thoughts on the job. If there are other things on our minds, we must take "time out" to think about these things so that they do not interfere with our levels of tracking awareness.

One aspect of tracking awareness that is often overlooked is the ability to track silently. If we are tracking an animal or a person with the intention of catching up to them, tracking in silence is critical. Let's try a simple experiment that will bring home the importance of tracking silently. Once again the lesson is learned with simple tools, yet the truth is brought home forcibly.

Go to a quiet pool of water somewhere on a calm, peaceful day. The water on the surface of the lake or pond should be mirror smooth. Take a pebble and throw it into the water. What do you observe?

Radiating outward from a source, sound sends ripples much like the stone sent ripples on the water. As the ripples spread out on the water, they became smaller and smaller until they eventually faded out completely. The farthest point to which the ripples on the water reach could be described as the perimeter of splash. The farthest point to which sound will reach can be referred to as the perimeter of sound. See Figure CCCH.02.03.02. What's important to remember is this: As you track through the bush, sound radiates out from you like the ripples moving out from the splash caused by the stone.

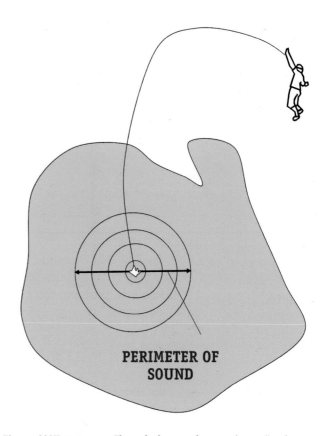

PERIMETER OF SOUND

Figure CCCH.02.03.02: The splash spreads, creating a "perimeter of sound."

Now let's briefly look at how sight is related to this. From any given point, you have a perimeter of vision concentrated mostly in a 120-degree arc in front of you.

Objects such as trees, hills, bush, fog, rain, and so on obscure your limit of vision. You will see only those objects that are within your perimeter of vision. See Figure CCCH.02.03.03.

Now look how these two relate to one another and tracking. If you are tracking an animal with the purpose of getting up close to it, your perimeter of vision must never be exceeded by your perimeter of sound; otherwise, you will never find the animal. The animal will hear you coming (perimeter of sound) and move off long before you see it (your perimeter of vision). You will fail to get close to it if this happens. Figures CCCH.02.03.04 and CCCH.02.03.05.

Bearing this in mind, the importance of stealth and silence becomes obvious, yet few people understand this. Reverse the situation and you will significantly increase the likelihood of actually catching up to your quarry. Figure CCCH.02.03.04

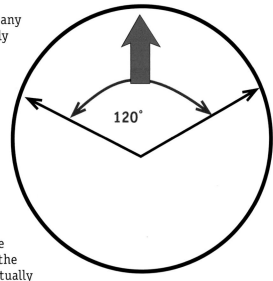

Figure CCCH.02.03.03: Our perimeter of vision limits what we see.

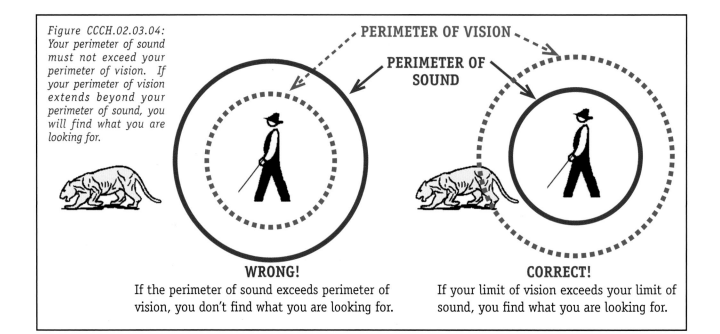

Figure CCCH.02.03.04: Your perimeter of sound must not exceed your perimeter of vision. If your perimeter of vision extends beyond your perimeter of sound, you will find what you are looking for.

PERIMETER OF VISION

PERIMETER OF SOUND

WRONG!
If the perimeter of sound exceeds perimeter of vision, you don't find what you are looking for.

CORRECT!
If your limit of vision exceeds your limit of sound, you find what you are looking for.

Figure CCCH.02.03.05: Silence is one of the keys to successful tracking.

The **RED CIRCLE** marks the perimeter of sound. If the amount of noise you make whilst tracking exceeds your limit of vision, you will never find what you are looking for.

This **BLUE CIRCLE** marks your limit of visibility. You must be able to approach to within this distance to see the animal.

Your scent wafts out far ahead of you, clinging to vegetation and permeating every part of the bush.

Each footprint and every place you touch has left a cloying, clinging, and lingering scent trail along the game path you are walking on.

WIND DIRECTION

Figure CCCH.02.03.06: If you walk with the wind blowing from behind you, your scent will waft ahead of you and warn animals of your approach. If this happens, don't expect to see many animals.

> **To track successfully, your perimeter of sound must never extend beyond your perimeter of vision.**

Thought, awareness, sound, sight . . . what else must we pay close attention to when tracking? The answer is scent. Our body odour is not only very disagreeable to most wild creatures but also very easily detected, even if we take all the necessary precautions. Our most powerful sensory ability is sight; in the animal world the most powerful sensory receptor in animals is smell. The sense of smell in most animals is forty to fifty times more acute than in humans.

One could say, in a manner of speaking, that animals smell like we see and see like we smell. Now, to understand the effect that your scent has, imagine a visible vapour being released from your body as you walk through the bush. This is a sticky, neon-green type of vapour that not only sticks to everything you touch but also blows into the surroundings, announcing your presence. See Figure CCCH.02.03.06.

If you look down a game path you have traversed, there will be neon-green blotches everywhere you have stepped and everywhere you have touched. The longer you stay in one spot, the brighter the glow of your neon sign. This is, in effect, what an animal smells—long after you have gone or before you have arrived if the wind is not in your favour. Scent oozes from your body. If you were in your bedroom with the door closed, your scent drifts from you into each corner of the room; it wafts under the door

and glides down the passage and into other parts of the house like little glowing particles of "you." We are not aware of this because our sense of smell is, compared to those in the animal world, poor.

In the bush the same thing happens; your scent is dispersed far and wide. Depending on certain factors, the smell of your body odour, clothing, shoes, or wherever you have touched will linger for a long while after you have passed. The two most important factors determining how long your smell will linger before finally dissipating are humidity and ambient temperature. High humidity and cool to warm (not hot) temperatures preserve smell the longest. But remember, other creatures and objects also have their own unique scents wafting from them, and each is specific and very distinct. (Think of each having a particular "colour.") This is the very rich world of scents and smells that a few are privy to but most are oblivious of—an animal world where smells are an unspoken form of very effective communication. The expert tracker must, therefore, not only be very careful of taking every precaution to disguise his own scent but must also develop the nose for becoming aware of the smells of the bush and how to interpret them.

> **To track successfully, your perimeter of scent must never extend beyond your perimeter of vision or perimeter of sound.**

Reawakening the Senses

Natural Tracking "Tools"

Let's list all the tracking tools and aids before discussing each one in detail. The Creator has supplied you with all the natural tools, and man has added some useful aids to assist you. Tracking involves seven "natural" tools: sight, smell, hearing, touch, taste, memory, and reason. Figure CCCH.02.04.01.

An eighth "natural" tool can best be described as "gut feel." This is usually found in very experienced trackers who are sometimes able to make sound deductions based on very little sensory sign. Let's include this as well.

Manmade Tracking Tools

A long list of aids could be drawn up, but let's concentrate on the most important and practical. The most important is a notebook and pencil. To this we could add a camera, binoculars, reference material (books, CDs, etc.), magnifying glass, tape recorder, tracking stick, and plaster of Paris (2Ca SO4.2H2O) or, as an alternative, dental stone.

Using Your Natural Tools

Let's now discuss, in detail, how to make best use of the tools we have at our disposal. The brain is, without a doubt, the most essential element. All the sensory input that is coming in via our senses is useless if it cannot be analyzed, logical conclusions drawn, and appropriate responses initiated. The brain is also the seat of knowledge and memory, both of which are essential to good tracking skills. We can store a tremendous amount of information in our brains from practical experience or by feeding in information from other sources.

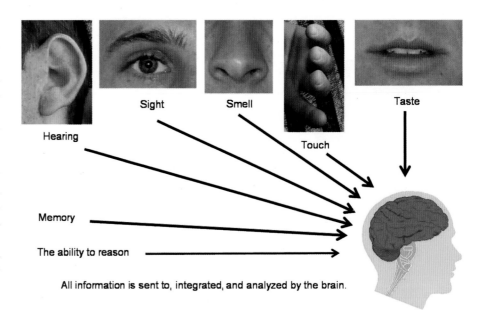

Hearing · Sight · Smell · Touch · Taste · Memory · The ability to reason

All information is sent to, integrated, and analyzed by the brain.

Figure CCCH.02.04.01: The seven natural tracking tools.

When the brain is "primed" with information, "recognition" becomes easier in practice. For example, you have looked at and studied a diagram of the spoor of a porcupine in a book on tracking. You have "primed" your brain with this knowledge. You know that there are five toes, the nails usually show, and you have a good idea of the size and shape of the spoor. You will "recognize" this track more easily the first time you see it in the natural setting than if you had no idea of what to look for in the first place. More about this later. Let's look at our five senses and how they can be put to best use.

> To be an effective tracker, you will have to teach yourself to see, smell, touch, hear, and taste all over again, as though you were in a new dimension.

One of the best techniques to help reawaken blunted senses is the following: Cover every part of your body with thick clothing, including your hands (gloves), head (balaclava), and feet (thick-soled boots or shoes). Place plugs in your ears and nostrils and get someone to blindfold you and to lead you out into the bush; then sit down somewhere. I usually perform this exercise with students in "Big Five" country where the added dimension of not knowing what might find you adds greatly to the experience. With the clothing, blindfold, nose- and earplugs, you have effectively been deprived of your senses. Sit this way for about thirty minutes. It will feel like an eternity.

Many people are totally unnerved by the exercise and will soon start lifting a corner of the blindfold to have a quick look around or remove an earplug or do something to get some sensory input. Try to avoid doing this. After half an hour remove the gloves and start to feel around you with your fingers. Feel the texture of the soil, tree bark, leaves, warmth of objects, and so on. Suddenly now, with there being less competition between your sense of touch and your other senses, your sense of touch will be greatly enhanced and you will be surprised at how much more sensitive you have become to exploring the world of touch.

After five minutes remove the nose plugs. Now you will be amazed at how aware you have become of smells, both strong and subtle—smells you were unaware of previously. After another five minutes remove the earplugs. The world of sound will suddenly come alive, and you will be flabbergasted at what you hear: tiny sounds that had escaped you, now jump out at you. The hum of insects, the sound of the breeze, your own heart beating, the call of distant birds, and so much more are now clear. Now remove all your clothing barring a pair of shorts for the men and appropriate clothing for ladies. Expose as much bare skin as is decent. Your body will feel like a huge antenna, and you will "feel" sound through small vibrations in the air and ground. You will feel subtle changes in wind direction and differences in temperature. Lastly, remove your blindfold and you will see the world through different eyes. Small details will spring to life, subtle changes in form and shape and colour and hue will now become glaringly evident. You will pick up movement more quickly.

This exercise is one of the most powerful tools to teach us to use our senses again and can be periodically repeated to refresh our senses. Figure CCCH.02.04.02.

Sight

Tracking is all about being observant and paying attention to detail without missing the obvious. Gathering visual information is probably the most important part of tracking. The bar chart (Figure CCCH.02.04.03) gives an indication

Figure CCCH.02.04.02: A student busy with the sensory deprivation exercise.

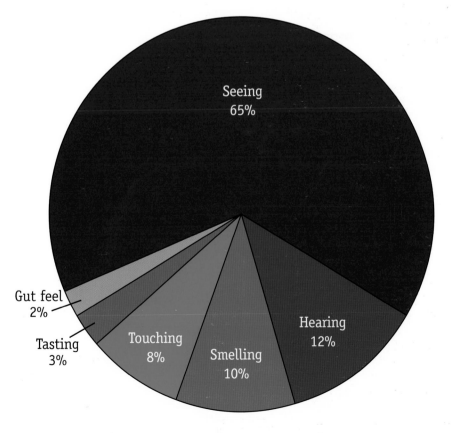

Figure CCCH.02.04.03: The extent to which we use our five senses when tracking.

of how we employ our senses, percentage-wise, when tracking. Remember, though, that one sense never operates in isolation of the rest; they must always be used in cooperation with each other.

How you see is different from what you see. Good vision and the ability to make astute observations are the hallmarks of a good tracker.

How Do You See?

The eye, the organ of sight, is evidence of the creative genius of the Almighty. Light is focused through the lens to form an inverted image on the retina. The retina is the light-sensitive portion of the eye that contains photoreceptor cells called rods and cones, which, when excited by light falling on them, send signals via nerve tracts in the retina itself and through the optic nerve to the visual cortex of the

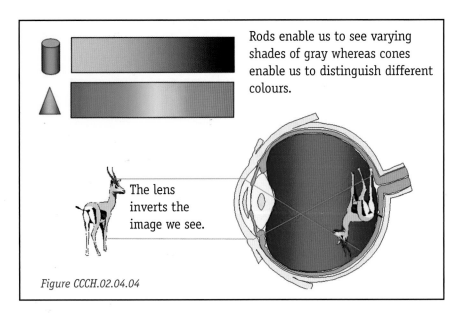

Rods enable us to see varying shades of gray whereas cones enable us to distinguish different colours.

The lens inverts the image we see.

Figure CCCH.02.04.04

brain for interpretation. Rods enable us to see shades of gray, and cones are responsible for enabling us to see colour. Figure CCCH.02.04.04.

A tracker should have 20/20 vision. It is important to be able to focus on near and far objects, have full colour vision, and be able to see in dim light. Now, this does not mean you cannot become a competent tracker if you do not have 20/20 vision. Visual abnormalities can sometimes be corrected. Having to make use of corrective aids can be a nuisance, however: Spectacles that fog up on cold days or slip off a sweaty nose and eyes that

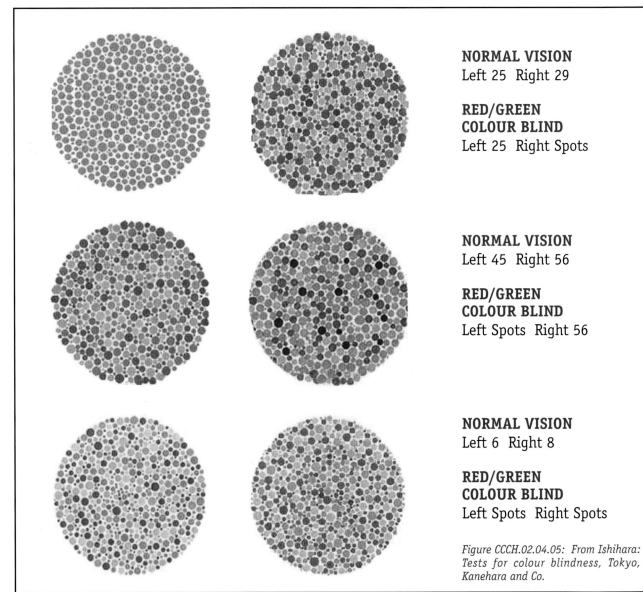

NORMAL VISION
Left 25 Right 29

RED/GREEN COLOUR BLIND
Left 25 Right Spots

NORMAL VISION
Left 45 Right 56

RED/GREEN COLOUR BLIND
Left Spots Right 56

NORMAL VISION
Left 6 Right 8

RED/GREEN COLOUR BLIND
Left Spots Right Spots

Figure CCCH.02.04.05: From Ishihara: Tests for colour blindness, Tokyo, Kanehara and Co.

Figure CCCH.02.04.06: A person with normal colour vision would see an impala as shown on the top. A red-colour-blind person would see an impala as shown at the bottom.

Figure CCCH.02.04.07: A person with normal colour vision would see a blood spoor as shown on the top. A red-colour-blind person would see the blood spoor as shown at the bottom.

become irritated caused by contact lenses under sweaty conditions are just a few of the nuisances.

Being colour blind or night blind can limit your tracking success. A tracker who is red/green colour blind will find it difficult to follow a blood spoor or distinguish a rufous (reddish) coloured animal in a green background setting. It is interesting to note that many animals are colour blind (this includes most antelope) and see only in shades of gray. This is due to a lack of cones in the retina. Are you colour blind? Look at the charts in Figure CCCH.02.04.05.

Figure CCCH.02.04.06 illustrates how a red/green colour-blind person would see an impala and Figure CCCH.02.04.07 a blood spoor.

If a person is farsighted (cannot focus up close), it is a big drawback. Poor vision can hinder the person aspiring to be an above-average tracker. As can be seen from Figure CCCH.02.04.08, a farsighted person loses much detail up close because the image is fuzzy and blurred. It is sometimes necessary to be able to see fine detail as, for example, when having to differentiate between the tracks of individuals of the same species.

From these few examples it is easy to see that poor vision can detract significantly from tracking ability. One can compensate by using optical aids but the individual with normal

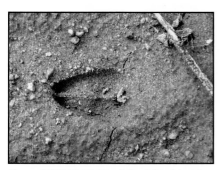 

Figure CCCH.02.04.08: A farsighted tracker will find it difficult to focus on objects close up.

vision will have a decided edge over the person with some visual abnormality.

Binocular Vision

Binocular vision allows us to determine the distance of an object from the eye. Figure CCCH.02.04.09. Animals with eyes on the sides of their heads have a very narrow field of depth perception but wide angles of peripheral vision. They cannot perceive depth close to their faces. Humans, some animals, and some birds have eyes situated on the front of the head, giving them a wide field of depth perception but a narrower width of peripheral vision. They can perceive depth close to the face. A human with only one eye or one good eye and one eye with very poor vision will find it very difficult to judge depth, making tracking difficult.

One way to help with depth perception is to move the head from side to side and up and down. This gives the brain different perspectives and enables it to pinpoint the distance to the object more effectively. Judging depth or distance accurately is very important for owls, for example. If they dived down onto a mouse and judged the distance wrongly, it could be fatal for the owl! Owls frequently move the head side to side, up and down, and even in a circular motion to get an accurate fix on depth or distance.

Some people's eyes do not become adjusted to darkness, being almost totally blind in dimly lit places. This condition is known as night blindness. It is caused by a lack of vitamin A in the diet. There is a chemical called rhodopsin found in rods that enables us to see in dim light. Vitamin A is needed to produce rhodopsin, and if vitamin A is lacking, night blindness results. This can greatly hamper the tracker who might be called on to follow sign in the dim light of early morning or the fading light of late afternoon.

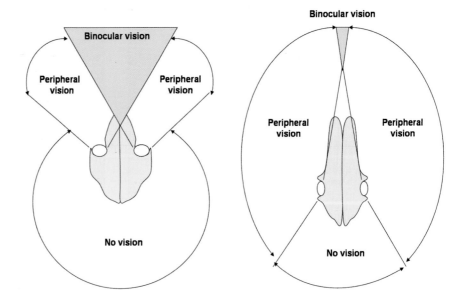

Figure CCCH.02.04.09: Binocular vision.

We have so far looked at the physiology of vision and how it affects the way we see. We are now going to look at how we look.

> **Many people look without really seeing. A good tracker notices everything.**

Some tendencies that lead to poor observation are as follows:

➤ We allow our vision to focus on the foreground.
➤ We focus on the dominant object in our field of vision.

What do you see below?

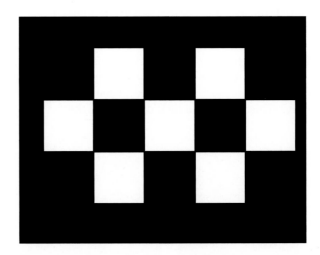

Most people will say they saw white squares. They will not mention the black squares because the eye loses this with the background. This is known as binocular rivalry and is illustrated in Figure CCCH.02.04.10 with more examples.

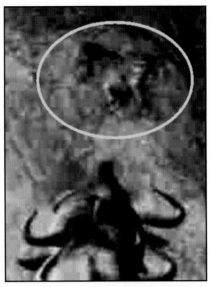

Figure CCCH.02.04.10: When you glance quickly at the main photo (top), you see the wildebeest and tend to "lose" the zebra in the background.

Law of Binocular Rivalry

When a colour or object dominates the field of vision, the eye is naturally drawn to it and tends to "lose" background or nondominant objects. It takes a conscious effort to focus on the nondominant objects. We have to train our eye to take in the whole picture. To avoid missing or losing visual information, the tracker must not "fixate" his gaze. In other words, the tracker avoids the error of allowing his focus to stay on any given point or area for a length of time by shifting his gaze continually from fore, to middle, to background and back, and from left to right, and right to left as indicated in Figure CCCH.02.04.11. The direction of visual scanning can be changed periodically to avoid visual boredom. Looking through the middle of the fore, middle, and background allows you to scan quickly and your peripheral vision is quick to notice movement and other objects.

The scanning process can take place very quickly.

An associated problem is the tendency to look at vegetation or partially transparent material (like shade cloth or netting) instead of looking through it. Often an animal will stand behind vegetation staring at you through it. If you allow your eye to "stop" at the brush, you can easily miss seeing whatever is behind it. In Figure CCCH.02.04.12, the tracker stares at the brush and not beyond it. What lies beyond the brush is a blurred image and is not "recognized." By allowing the eye to focus past the vegetation, a bushpig suddenly "stands out" and is immediately recognized.

Figure CCCH.02.04.11: Visual search pattern: 1) Scan from left to right in the foreground then move forward to the middle ground, scan left to right and move to the background and scan left to right. 2) Now reverse the process and scan from the background to foreground.

Recognition Failure

We fail to recognize an object or sign because:

➤ We are not expecting to see it.

➤ We don't know what it looks like.

➤ Our eyes are fooled by what we see, when we see it.

➤ We don't recognize what we are seeing.

Some examples to explain: Imagine someone going into the bush as a complete novice. He has never seen the parallel scratch marks left on the ground by a white rhino marking territory. The novice will walk past this sign without noticing it since he does not know what it is and is not expecting to see it. The novice, on the other hand may have seen what a nyala looks like in a photograph, but never in real life. He is likely to miss seeing a nyala standing partially obscured in its natural habitat because he is looking for the whole animal when it is only partially visible. A good tracker will often spot an animal that is well hidden by a slight flick of an ear, the shine of sunlight on a horn, or a small part of the body, for example, the rounded rump or foot. Even when we know what we are looking for, we can miss seeing it.

Blurred Images

Nature equips many wild creatures with marvelous camouflage patterns. A camouflage design works by breaking up a recognizable shape and helping the object to merge into the background. Once this happens, the eye has great difficulty reorganizing the image, and the longer you stare the more the eye becomes confused. This is due to the optical phenomenon of blurred images. If an object/ animal contrasts sharply with its background, it will stand out

Figure CCCH.02.04.12: By focusing vision on the foreground and not looking through vegetation, you can miss seeing what is behind it.

Figure CCCH.02.04.13: As an example of binocular rivalry and Ricco's law of distance vision, look at the above photographs. The camouflage pattern (left) is excellent, rendering the hunter almost invisible against the background. The eye attempts, with difficulty, to organize the image into some recognizable shape (Ricco's law of distance vision). The eye is drawn to the bold lines of the camouflage pattern (binocular rivalry) and the hunter "loses" his shape. When the pattern becomes too dense (right), the hunter takes on a shape and stands out more readily.

clearly. Disruptive camouflage patterns are very cryptic and consist of a big, bold design, a bold contrast, and good coloration. This effectively breaks up the recognizable shape. As an object moves farther away, the eye loses its ability to see in detail, and the mechanics of the eye attempts to make objects appear solid so that they can be recognized by their shape. If a camouflage pattern is too dense, it becomes ineffective especially at a distance. This is known as Ricco's law of distance vision and is illustrated together with the phenomenon of binocular rivalry in Figure CCCH.02.04.13.

Natural camouflage patterns work on the same principles just described. Do you remember the example with the wildebeest in the foreground and the zebra in the background and how easy it was to miss the zebra? One's first inclination would be to think that the bold black and white markings on a zebra would make it stand out starkly, but at a distance the pattern becomes disruptive and it becomes difficult to recognize the shape.

If the pattern of stripes on the zebra were dense, it would become more obvious and the eye would recognize the characteristic shape, especially at a distance. You must learn to look for and recognize partial images as well as whole shapes. Learn the colouration of animals and birds as it will help you to identify an animal.

One of the biggest observational errors is looking but not seeing. Our vision is our greatest tracking tool, and we should learn to make optimum use of it. Look at Figures CCCH.02.04.14 and CCCH.02.04.15 and make a note of what you see. Don't worry about making deductions yet; just make a note of what you can see.

Now look at Figures CCCH.02.04.16 and CCCH.02.04.17 for an interpretation of the sign.

As illustrated in these two photographs, there is a tremendous amount of information to be seen before deductions are made.

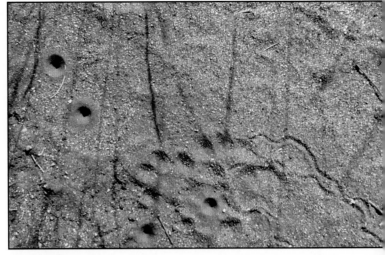

Figure CCCH.02.04.14

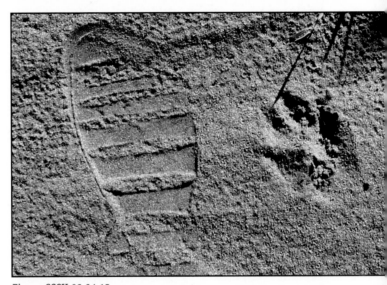

Figure CCCH.02.04.15

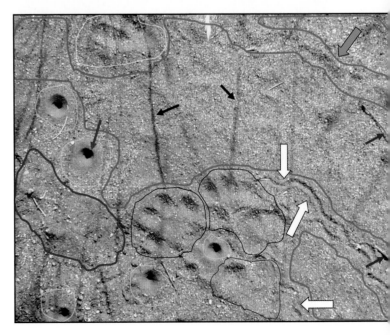

Figure CCCH.02.04.16: What can we see in this track? Five antlion pits. Long grass shadows. Clear and partial genet tracks. Recent and old antlion trails. Duiker tracks. Bits of dried grass stalks. Fine reddish clayey soil overlaid with fine white gravel. The soil is dry. There are small, relatively undisturbed patches of substrate.

Figure CCCH.02.04.17: Fresh boot print. Headed northeast. Right foot. Six transverse ribs on sole. Two visible, possibly more on heel. Person pronates (puts more weight on the inside of the foot). Piece of rib on the toe possibly missing. Clean, undisturbed areas (apart from pockmarks). Substrate smoothly compressed by ribs of boot. Green grass shoots. Long shadows. Homogenous fine sand substrate. Pockmarked by raindrops. Older, partially obliterated jackal track—looks like left front—headed northeast. Weathered by wind and rain. Ridge in sand caused by prevailing NE wind.

Failure to Look into Shady Areas

The natural camouflage of animals is enhanced when they stand in shade and dappled light. This helps to break up their outline. They often stand or rest in deep shade, and if they stand still they can be difficult to spot. This is illustrated in Figures CCCH.02.04.18 and CCCH.02.04.19. The good tracker makes a conscious effort of scanning areas of deep shadow and shade. It is sometimes necessary to stare into shady areas for a few seconds to allow the eyes to accommodate the low light.

Vision and Movement

Animals sometimes escape detection by standing absolutely still.

Our eyes are extremely quick to pick up movement even if it is in our peripheral field of vision. Stationary objects are far more difficult to spot, and the tracker must, therefore, be specifically on the lookout for animals that tend to "freeze" as a means of escaping attention.

Figure CCCH.02.04.18: A nyala ewe (left) and a kudu cow (right) resting in deep shade. The disruptive vertical white stripes on their coats, the shadows, and the patches of sunlight help them to blend into their surroundings.

Figure CCCH.02.04.19: Train your eyes to "penetrate" into deep shadow and "beyond" objects.

This freezing to avoid being spotted is a common defense mechanism in the animal kingdom, and the tracker must not be fooled by it. Remember that when tracking, the principles apply both ways. If you stand in open sunlight, if you don't use appropriate camouflage clothing, or if you fail to make use of shadow and shade, the animal will spot you more easily as well. Stationary sign takes more effort to see and recognize. The eye is drawn to movement but has to actively look for stationary sign. Visual cues are used to detect wind direction: the direction of bending grass, moving smoke, etc.

Light and Colour

What attracts our visual attention to sign? Movement does, but what about sign that is not moving? The answer to this is the following:

➤ Deviation from the normal.

➤ Differences in colour: intensity, saturation, and hue.

The tracker must have a "normal frame" of visual reference because then his attention will be drawn to any deviation from the "normal." Let us use some examples to illustrate (Figure CCCH.02.04.20).

Every single sign that a tracker becomes aware of is a deviation from a natural frame of reference. A tree pushed over is a deviation from the normal because trees normally stand upright. Claw marks on the bark of a tree are not normal because trees as a general rule do not have claw marks on them. How does the tracker acquire this frame of natural reference? This happens through exposure to natural systems (i.e., experience) and by learning (knowledge). When the tracker has a database of knowledge and experience, he will know when something is "out of place." The more proficient the tracker becomes, the more adept he will become at recognizing not only the obvious

Figure CCCH.02.04.20: A patch of undisturbed soil (top left) would be considered a normal frame of reference. The same patch of soil (top right) with beetle tracks crossing it would be a deviation from the expected normal. Dry, dead leaves on the ground (bottom left) would be considered normal. Blood drops on these leaves (bottom right) would be considered "abnormal."

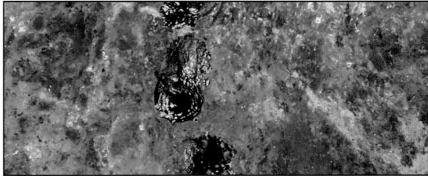

Figure CCCH.02.04.21: Here our attention is drawn to the dark red colour of venous blood in contrast to the colour of the rock substrate. Also note how the light's reflective quality of the blood changes as it begins to dry.

but also the very subtle nuances of deviations from the normal.

Recognizing the differences in light and colour and having the ability to observe these differences are two important aspects in the skill of tracking. The human eye is able to distinguish ten million shades of colour. The expert tracker is able to notice almost imperceptible variations in colour, shade, and texture. Once again let us illustrate with some examples. Figures CCCH.02.04.21 and CCCH.02.04.22.

Sometimes very subtle differences in colour are the only clues we might see. When tracking over hard, stony ground, a scuffmark might appear slightly lighter or darker depending on the substrate. A scuff will usually appear lighter on very hard or rocky ground and darker on softer ground when the sun-dried top layer of soil is removed to expose darker, more humid underlying soil.

Aerial sign such as the swath left through tall grass or dew-laden grass is often observable as a different shade of colour from surrounding vegetation. Later on you will be given practical exercises to help learn how to differentiate this. Let us now move on from sight to another important tracking tool—your hearing.

Figure CCCH.02.04.22: What draws your attention in this photograph? Pay specific attention to colour. In the area shown by the yellow line, the grass and vegetation is standing more or less upright and has slightly darker patches of colour. In the area demarcated by the blue line the grass is partially flattened and has a tinge of green showing through. The area marked in red shows a lot more green where the taller straw-coloured grass has been flattened. What does this photo show us? It tells us an antelope was bedded down for a rest. We can also get an idea of the size of the animal, which will give us a clue to the species. Do you see how colour variation gave us helpful clues?

Hearing

With respect to tracking skills for humans, hearing and smell rank closely in order of importance. Whereas we are predominantly dependent on sight, both hearing and especially smell, rank far higher in the animal world.

What sort of sounds will be of assistance to a tracker? All sounds and sometimes even the lack of sound will be of great assistance to the tracker. Just think of all the sounds in a natural environment. Weather (wind, thunder, approaching rain), water (dripping, rushing, gurgling),

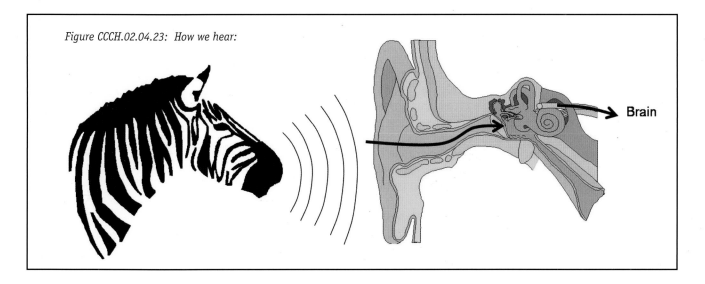

Figure CCCH.02.04.23: How we hear:

Brain

animal sounds (territorial, fighting, communicating, feeding), birds, insects, amphibians . . . there are literally thousands of natural sounds.

Once again the tracker works from a frame of reference, where the baseline is silence or expected noises. Anything other than silence will be perceived as worthy of notice. But there are times when the tracker knows that there should be sounds, but it is too quiet. This, then, will be perceived as being out of the ordinary. Before going on, let us briefly discuss how we hear.

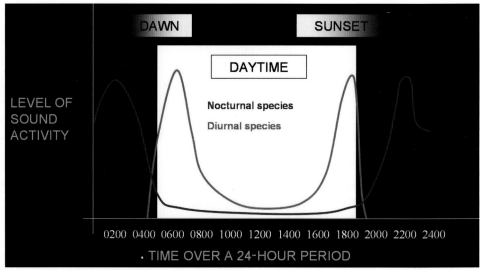

Figure CCCH.02.04.24: Sound rhythms.

How Do We Hear?

A simplified explanation is given on page 35. See Figure CCCH.02.04.23.

Sound waves are emitted by a source and are transmitted through the air at three hundred meters per second. Our ear lobes (pinnae) act to funnel the sound into the outer ear canal and onto the eardrum (tympanum). The sound waves cause the tympanum to vibrate. Small bones called the anvil (incus), hammer (malleus), and stirrup (stapes) are in contact with the eardrum, and they amplify the tiny movements of the eardrum twenty-two times and then pass the sound waves into the cochlea of the inner ear, which is the real organ of hearing. The cochlea has thousands of microscopic hairs, each tuned to a particular vibration. When sound waves are transmitted from the stirrup, it vibrates liquid in the cochlea at certain frequencies; the microscopic hairs pick these sounds up and transform them into electrical impulses, which are sent via the auditory nerve to the brain where the incoming information is analyzed.

Good hearing is a great asset to the tracker. At birth the ear can detect sound within a range of twenty to thirty thousand cycles, approximately, per second. Hearing ability declines progressively from the moment of birth. By the teenage years, the upper frequency has decreased to about twenty thousand cycles, and in the forty- to fifty-year age bracket the frequency range has declined to fifty to eighty thousand cycles per second or less. In other words, as you get older, you tend to hear less high and low frequency sounds.

The hearing ability of metropolitan people has, in general, diminished because of the loud noises we are subjected to in an urban environment. The older the tracker, the less well he will be able to hear. Obviously,

this will have a negative effect on his overall tracking ability. Sustained, high-intensity noise, such as listening to loud music—especially through earphones—can wreck hearing at a young age. If you intend on becoming a good tracker, protect your ears from high-intensity noise, which includes loud noises emanating from music, gunfire, machinery, aircraft, and so on.

We determine the direction of sound by two different mechanisms:

➤ By the time lag between the entry of sound into each ear, and

➤ By the difference between the intensities of the sound in each ear.

The implication of this is that if a person is deaf in one ear he will not be able to determine the direction from which the sound is emanating. A partially deaf person might benefit from certain tricks to facilitate optimum input from sound; a person totally deaf in one ear will not be able to use these tricks.

Listening Skills

➤ Be as quiet as you can be whilst tracking so that you can "tune in" to the sounds around you.

➤ Stop frequently to listen intently. Close your eyes whilst listening. This reduces visual sensory input and allows your brain to concentrate on the incoming auditory information.

➤ To determine the direction from which sound is coming, turn your head sideways to the perceived direction. [A totally deaf person will not be able to do this.] This increases the distance that sound has to travel to reach the farthest ear and assists the brain in processing incoming information to locate the source of the sound.

➤ Cup your ears with your hands to increase the size of the "funnel" in which sound waves can be trapped.

➤ Open your mouth slightly when listening intently. This helps to "pop" open the Eustachian tubes that are connected via the pharynx and nasal sinuses to the ear. This will enable you to hear more clearly.

➤ Learn to identify natural sounds through the use of audiotapes and by listening attentively when you are in the bush. In this way you build up a memory bank of sounds.

➤ Become familiar with the "sound rhythms" in the areas where you operate.

Sound Rhythms

Nature has daily (diurnal) and nightly (nocturnal) sounds particular to that time. Figure CCCH.02.04.24. These diurnal and nocturnal rhythms are fairly constant and predictable and can greatly assist the tracker in monitoring his environment. Of what use is this information to the tracker? He will be expecting certain sounds at specific times and not expecting them at other times. It would be unusual to hear a jackal or hyena calling in the middle of the day. However, the tracker will not consider it strange to hear them calling just after sunset or at various times during the night.

Nocturnal species of animals such as lion, hyena, jackal, and leopard and birds such as dikkops and owls are more vocal after sunset and during the nighttime hours. Diurnal species will be more vocal during the day and especially at dawn and sunset. Birds are particularly vocal at these times. During the heat of a summer's day, the level of sound drops to a minimum, except for the gray-headed bush shrike (spookvoël) whose monotonous call is very characteristic of this languid time of day. The late hours of the night are also generally very quiet. Frogs usually have a lot to say for themselves at night or just after rain; consequently, a nighttime chorus of frogs that suddenly becomes quiet is a warning to the tracker that something has disturbed them. By contrast, the sudden squawking of a crested francolin at midday will tell the tracker that something has flushed the bird.

The calls made by various bird species can be of great assistance to the tracker.

The calls of double-banded sand grouse, guinea fowl, water birds (duck, geese, waders, cormorants, etc.) can lead the tracker to water. Gray louries emit a descending *kwêêê* call to warn of predators and intruders. The frantic calls of mobbing birds can warn the tracker of the presence of a snake. The *chirring* calls

of oxpeckers can warn him of the presence of a rhino, buffalo, or other species associated with these birds.

There are many different sounds and calls that will supply the tracker with information of what is going on around him. Alarm calls such as the "bark" of a bushbuck or a kudu (a deeper tone); the chirping of vervet monkeys; the snort of a wildebeest, zebra, or impala; the trumpeting of an elephant; the growl of a lion or leopard; and birds being flushed need to be noted. Feeding, drinking, and wallowing sounds, breaking branches, and splashing all give particular information to the tracker. Animals moving, the scrunching sound of hoofs on gravel, the noise of animals' bodies brushing up against vegetation, and stones being dislodged are important pieces of information to the tracker.

Communication calls are another source of information to the studious tracker. These can be the young calling to parents, social greetings, or alarms. Some animals such as the elephant and rhino can communicate using very low-frequency sounds that fall below the human threshold for hearing.

> We discussed how we often look but do not see; we as trackers can also make the mistake of hearing but not listening. It is important that we monitor our sound environment the whole time whilst tracking. Taking in information based on sound, being aware of it, identifying and organizing it, and making logical deductions from it are all important.

If you hear a constant, repetitive sound, your brain will begin to ignore it. Be aware of this. If you find this happening, try to concentrate on some other sound (or make a soft sound) for a few seconds to break this auditory fixation.

Smell

Many of our most significant experiences and memories are associated with smell: home-baked bread, the aroma of sizzling bacon frying in a pan over an open campfire, the spine-tingling rumen smell of fresh buffalo dung, or the throat-catching stench of a decomposing carcass. The smell of damp earth with the first drops of rain or of canvas in a new safari tent, such odours can evoke powerful memories. Were it not for the odour, we may, in many instances, have forgotten the experience.

The next time you eat a meal, let part of the blessing include your lifting of the bowl to your nose and savoring the story contained within its varied and aromatic contents. The smell of the air can help you forecast weather, find food or water, avoid danger, find a particular animal, or help you track down an illusive quarry.

Observe a real man of the bush, an expert tracker. Take note of how regularly he lifts his head and with flared nostrils sniffs the air to detect any sign that lies beyond sight, sound, taste, and touch. Animals do it all the time. Smells are one of the most overlooked but one of the most useful signs available to the tracker. Bush-dwelling children routinely use scent in conjunction with their other senses to discover the world around them. In urbanized societies, children in their formative years are discouraged from bringing strange objects up to their faces to taste or smell, which has resulted in a poor memory bank of smells in urbanized man. A person who lives in a metropolitan area has learned to rely more heavily on his other senses and to depend less and less on olfactory acuity. Our investigation of the outdoors should focus on and include checking on the smells of various things. It will open up a whole new world.

How Do We Smell?

The nose has sensory receptors in the upper part of the nasal cavity that are connected to the brain by the olfactory nerve. As you breathe, air passes by these receptors, which constantly sample chemicals in the air and transmit information to the brain for analysis. Normal breathing does not cause as much stimulation as when we "sniff," which causes a larger volume of air to come into contact with the nose's chemoreceptors. If you are exposed to a particular smell for more than a few minutes, your sense of smell will become temporarily accommodated to the odour and you will cease to notice it. To break this "olfactory fixation," smell something different for a few seconds. Take some soil in your hand or crush some vegetation to get your sense of smell going again.

Table 2.2: The Seven Primary Odours

PRIMARY ODOUR	EXAMPLES
camphorlike	camphor, mothballs
ethereal	ether
floral	flowers
minty	oil of peppermint
musky	musk
pungent	vinegar, some spices
putrid	feces, rotten meat, carcasses

Different olfactory (smell) receptors in our noses recognize molecules of a certain shape. There are thought to be seven "primary odours" that we can smell (Table 2.2). Combinations of these primary odours give things their unique smell. Humans can distinguish more than ten thousand odours.

A good tracker will constantly be checking the air and objects for odours. Figures CCCH.02.04.25 and CCCH.02.04.26. The bush is filled with an incredible array of smells. Some are very unpleasant, like the stink of a carcass or the scat from lions or wild dogs. Others are a delight to the nose. A fresh marula, the peculiar smell at a river or water hole, freshly dug soil, the mixed smells of a lazy, warm afternoon can delight the senses. Some animals have a particular smell all of their own: waterbuck, civet, elephant, cheetah, impala, porcupine, and many others. Being a good "sniffer" will make you a better tracker.

Figure CCCH.02.04.25: Smelling plants (left) and checking an arrow for the smell of a gut-shot wound (right).

Smells are usually better defined and more pronounced when the air is humid. Smells last longer in cooler, moist environments.

Smelling Skills

➤ To increase the scent of something that is dry, first breathe on or through it. Odours carry better on moist air, and breath adds moisture.

➤ When trying to catch or identify a subtle scent, keep your mouth open whilst sniffing. Draw in air alternately through the nose and mouth.

Examples of smells in the bush include animal droppings, an elephant in musth, urine, vegetation, water, soil, dead animals, flowers, fire, etc. Good olfactory skills can save your life. Some examples include smelling dangerous animals that are close-by or the first whiff of smoke from a bushfire.

Touch

Skin has several kinds of sensory receptors, each of which is associated with one of the somatic senses: touch, pressure, temperature, pain, and vibration. When stimulated, these receptors send impulses to the spinal cord from where they are transmitted to the brain for analysis. Some impulses called reflexes are activated to remove a body part from a potentially harmful stimulus. The impulse goes from the receptor to the spinal cord and directly back to effect withdrawal of the body part. The impulse does not go to the brain.

How do we make use of the touch sense when tracking? Here are some examples.

Figure CCCH.02.04.26: Smelling smoke from a bushfire can give a tracker time to move to safety.

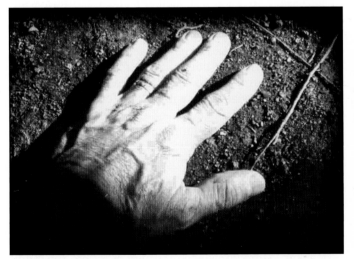 

Figure CCCH.02.04.27: Using the sense of touch to feel for residual warmth on the ground where an animal has been lying down (left) or to feel for any warmth in dung to determine how fresh it is (right).

➤ We feel a breeze on our skin or hold a wet finger up in the air to determine the direction of the wind. Probably the most important contribution touch makes to the tracking effort is in monitoring of wind direction. Without visual cues, we can be aware of wind direction by the cooling sensation it has on our skin on the windward side.

➤ We use touch to sort through material for clues.

➤ We feel the substrate to detect any warmth remaining from where an animal has been lying down. See Figure CCCH.02.04.27.

➤ We sometimes feel the temperature of dung to determine how fresh it is. See Figure CCCH.02.04.27.

➤ When stalking, the tracker is very aware of pressure on the soles of his feet as he carefully places his feet with a minimum of noise.

➤ In the dark, the tracker would become very aware of the importance of the sensation of touch if he has to find his way by feel. A good tracker is unlikely, however, to land himself in this predicament.

Taste

Taste is the sense that is least used during tracking.

How Do We Taste?

The organs responsible for taste are the taste buds located on the back, sides, and front of the tongue.

Four types of chemoreceptors identify dissolved substances in the mouth as sweet, sour, bitter, or salty. Taste buds diminish with age; consequently, older people have a diminished capacity to taste. An important aspect of taste is that there is a connection between smell and taste. When trying to determine a specific odour, it is, therefore, a good idea to open the mouth and draw air across the tongue as this enhances the ability to smell.

Taste is important to the tracker when he has to live off the land. He will make use of his sense of taste when carrying out "edibility tests" to determine if wild foods are edible or not.

Gut Feel

This is a "sense" that is difficult to define because there is nothing physical or concrete to base it on. Yet it becomes one of the most useful tracking tools when other clues are scanty. Having a gut feel for a tracking situation is based on experience. Such trackers will use a combination of knowledge of a vast range of subjects pertaining to the natural world, including premonition, understanding of behaviour patterns, and other poorly understood variables. There are no shortcuts to this learned behaviour. A gut feel is often the only reason an experienced tracker will look for an animal in a particular spot. Even though there might be an absence of physical evidence to support his hypothesis, more often than not the tracker who knows his job will be correct. This happens too frequently for it to be attributed to chance.

A beginner tracker relies almost entirely on physical evidence when following a trail. This is called systematic tracking. It is usually slow and painstaking, and the novice tracker will often lose the trail when physical clues become scarce. As the tracker's ability improves, he will start experimenting with gut feel; his tracking becomes speculative. As his experience and understanding of the natural order increases, he starts making predictions and acts on hypotheses. He then puts these to the test. In the beginning mistakes are common, but he learns from his mistakes and eventually becomes more and more adept at making accurate predictions without having to rely so heavily on physical evidence. He now uses occasional physical signs to verify predictions. Because of his gut feel, speculative tracking is faster than systematic tracking. A good imagination based on sound reasoning is necessary for systematic tracking.

Memory

It is impossible to become a proficient tracker without a good memory. All knowledge and sensory input must not only be stored but must be easily accessed from the memory. We forget fairly quickly; consequently, practice and repetition become necessary to keep our memory and its information retrieval system working optimally.

The ability to track is a function of how much time we spend doing it. If a good tracker becomes inactive for a while, he will not be in top form when he starts tracking again. If, however, he has a good databank of tracking knowledge, he will pick up form quite quickly as his memory is jogged back into action. Thus, it is necessary to keep the mind active by stimulating it on a regular basis. When walking down a street, listen for bird calls and try to identify the bird. Practice your tracking skills wherever you are—in your home, your car, and the bush. Be aware of what you are seeing, smelling, hearing, touching, and tasting. The optimal use of the senses and integrating this with knowledge of the natural order is what makes a good tracker. Store knowledge through practice, and study all available material.

TEACHING YOURSELF TO TRACK

Reasoning

Reasoning is the ability to make sense of the incoming sensory information. It is pointless making good observations if you cannot make logical conclusions and devise an appropriate course of action.

Do you remember Figure CCCH.02.04.16? We made a list of what we saw in the photograph. The list consisted of the following: five antlion pits, deep shadows in pits, long shadows cast by grass, fresh and old antlion trails, clear and partial genet tracks (front and rear), duiker tracks (right front), relatively undisturbed areas with no further signs of genet or duiker tracks, a slightly disturbed area, bits of dried grass, fine reddish clayey soils overlaid with fine gravel, and dry soil.

Now what logical conclusions can be drawn from this information? From our information we deduce the following: The ground is dry. There is very little moisture and no sign of recent rain or heavy dew (pockmarks, rivulet trails, etc.). The few grass bits are gray and dry. There is no sign of greenery. We can assume that it is autumn or winter. (This might not necessarily be true, but based on the available evidence it is a reasonable assumption.)

Let us work on this hypothesis. Genet, duiker, and antlions occur in the area. If antlions are present, then it is safe to assume that there are ants. Antlions crawl around looking for suitable areas to dig their funnel-shaped traps for about the first two hours after sunset. Some of their trails are still sharply defined, so the "picture" we see is an early morning one, probably before 8 AM.

We say this because there are long shadows from the grass and in the antlion pits. Reasoning demands that the sharpness of the fresh antlion trails will become less defined by late afternoon. Older trails can be seen in the top right hand of the picture (thirty-six-plus-hours-old). Because there are shadows, we know the sun is shining. So it is partly cloudy or clear, but not overcast.

The genet tracks were made sometime between 6 PM and 8 PM the previous evening. Why? They are superimposed on some of the antlion trails; however, an antlion pit is superimposed on the left rear track of the genet. Furthermore, there was no wind during the night; otherwise, the tracks of the animals and the antlion trails would have been obliterated.

Now why do the duiker and genet cat tracks stop? There are no further signs between the two sets of prints. The possibility is that they met at this point and ran away from each other. If they jumped back or sideways, their tracks would be out of the picture. This seems to correspond with the "picture" we have. If the duiker had arrived later (after the genet) and stopped because it had picked up the carnivore scent, then the genet track would have continued in the picture. The duiker track does appear to be displaced slightly to the right. Thus the duiker must have been at this specific place at the same time as the genet. If our assumption is correct and it is morning, the duiker was traveling in a southerly direction and the genet in a northerly direction.

The red clayey soil would indicate it is of basaltic origin. We know that clay soils have poor drainage and high water retention. They are usually shallow soils but are nutrient rich. The type of plants growing in this area will, therefore, have high nutrient requirements and relatively shallow root systems. It would be classed as sweet and is likely to be a game-rich area. There are likely to be seasonal pans in the area as the clay soils seal well. There might be very weathered granitic outcrops in the area as indicated by the weathered gravel. Now, much of what we have deduced might be speculation, but because our reasoning is based on sound logic, much of it will be true. It is amazing how much information is available when we really look. Welcome to the world of speculative tracking!

Now let's repeat the exercise with the Figure CCCH.02.04.17 that we looked at earlier. We made a list of what we saw. Boot print, pockmarked sandy soil, "damaged" jackal print, long grass shadows, green grass shoots, and ridge in sand. What conclusions can we draw from our observations?

It is early morning, for the light is bright; it is not the subdued light of afternoon. The grass shadows are long, so the time must be between 7 and 8 AM.

The sun is shining. It is partly cloudy or clear but not overcast. If it were overcast, there would be no clearly defined shadows. There was rain during the night. It rained after the jackal had been here. If the tracker knew when rain fell during the night, it would give him a good estimate of the age of the track. Assume, for example, it had rained at 9 PM; the tracker will know that the track is eleven to fourteen hours old.

Why this old? Jackals usually become active just after sunset (say from 6 PM), and we know it rained at 9 PM. It is now between 7 and 8 AM the following morning. The rain and wind eroded the jackal print, which showed the jackal traveling in a northeasterly direction. The jackal's track appears to be that of the left front foot. We deduce this from the shape. If it had been the right front foot, we should see the left front track somewhere near the top left corner of the picture.

The boot print is fresh, sharply defined, and there are no pockmarks from the rain where the ribs have made contact with the ground. There are six transverse ribs on the front sole of the boot. (This might help to differentiate it from other boot prints.) There are two visible ribs on the heel (possibly more). A portion of the toe rib could be missing. The person is standing still with the weight placed toward the toe, and the heel

THE COMPREHENSIVE GUIDE TO TRACKING SKILLS

is not showing up clearly. The person is not moving forward as there is no visible forward or backward displacement of soil. The person pronates, meaning to place more weight on the inside of the foot. The inside aspect of the boot print is deeper and more clearly defined, and there appears to be more wear on the ribs of the sole on this side. The person was headed in a northeasterly direction.

The soil is sandy and well drained. Leached, sandy soils are nutrient deficient and do not retain water well. It would be unlikely to find pans that hold water for long. Plants growing in this area will have deep root systems and will not grow optimally due to a deficit of nutrients. This area could fall within sour veld and would not be very rich in game. The rain and green grass shoots could indicate that it is spring or early summer.

Once again much of these deductions are speculative but the reasoning is sound and the hunter has a working hypothesis to go on.

	42		51	69		62		100	8
9	71	55	12	13	14	15	16	17	18
19	46	22	23	24	25	26	27	75	29
	95	54	31	87	33	34	38	76	37
39	64	41	32	90	43	91	45	59	47
81	49	50	67	52	53	48	96	56	93
58	35	60	40	61		98	63	10	65
99	86	68	66	70	28	72	36	74	20
57	44	77	78	79	80	21	83	85	73
88		82	92	84	94	11	30	97	89

Figure CCCH.02.04.28

Physical Fitness and Endurance

Hard and intensive tracking requires exhaustive concentration and physical endurance. When following a very difficult trail, the tracker can begin losing concentration within half an hour or so. Ideally trackers should work in pairs with the one doing the hard work and the other acting as support by carrying out general observations. To work optimally, they should swap tasks after every twenty minutes or so. But often the tracker does not have the luxury of a teammate and must then rely on his own physical endurance.

For this reason, if you wish to take tracking seriously, it would be of great benefit to you to have a regular training program that will keep you fit. A "physical-fitness-for-tracking" program would include lots of walking (including during the heat of the day when most other people in their right minds will be resting up in the shade with a cold drink) and a jogging program (eight to ten kilometers at a time, five days a week). And what about concentration? The tracker must stay focused on his task but must, at the same time, stay aware of what is going on around him. Practice concentrating. Here are two exercises to help you to learn to concentrate.

Concentration exercises: Make yourself a chart of ten rows by ten columns, and get someone to fill in the squares numbers 1 to 100 in random fashion. Figure CCCH.02.04.28. Take one minute and tick off as many squares as possible in the correct order, starting from number 1. Change the order of the numbers and practice this on a regular basis to increase your ability to concentrate.

Concentrate on the very centre of the target shown in Figure CCCH.02.04.29 for two minutes. Each time you feel your thoughts beginning to wander or your attention drawn away to the other objects, draw them back to concentrating on the task at hand.

How did it go? Were you easily distracted?

Condition yourself to stay focused but vigilant. Now you must correctly understand this concept of concentration and reasoning. In the field all types of input will assail our senses. We must be aware of all

Figure CCCH.02.04.29

incoming information—visual, sound, smell, etc.—but must "filter" the data so as to retain that which is relevant to the job in hand and ignore that which is not of immediate import. Focusing and concentrating does not imply being oblivious to all else. There exists a delicate balance of keeping your mind on what you are doing and screening, almost subconsciously, other incoming information so that if incoming information is related, you will give it the necessary attention.

Allow me to illustrate. You are tracking elephants in dense bush. It is nearly midday, and it is hot. Except for the call of the monotonous gray-headed bush shrike we spoke about earlier, there is little background noise. High above you hear an aircraft flying to some distant destination, but you do not stop tracking and gaze up into the sky to see if you can spot the high-flying disturbance because it is of no relevance to the task on hand. Subconsciously you "filter" it out. But now, just ahead, you hear a branch break. Now this sound has a different meaning to you, so your attention is drawn to the noise. It could be the elephant herd just ahead in the thick undergrowth. Does this illustrate the point? Do not become sidetracked by irrelevancies but be aware of incoming information that might be valid.

We will now move on to the use of manmade tools that can assist us in equipping ourselves to become proficient trackers. Remember that although we can make use of these manmade tools and they can be of great help, nothing can replace the value of practical experience.

Manmade Tools

In bygone days tracking was taught firsthand. This was (and still remains) the most effective way to teach a student. Most knowledge was passed on by word of mouth. There were very few aids to help the fledgling tracker other than to go out in the field and learn from experience. We are very fortunate that today we have wonderful tools to help us in our quest for knowledge: books, videos, films, audio tapes, CDs, etc. We should make the most of these tools, but we must recognize them for

what they are and nothing more. In the final analysis, it is the tracker's ability in the field that differentiates him from the armchair expert. Let us look at what there is available to us and how we should use these tools to best effect.

Compiling a Mental Database

We can gain a tremendous amount of knowledge from books, periodicals, scientific journals, and so on. We must try to gather as much information about the area we are going to be tracking (operating) in to "prime" ourselves so that we will be well informed, albeit theoretically, when we begin working in the area. The mental database that we can amass by reading, listening to audio tapes, looking at illustrations, videos, CDs, and DVDs can be quite considerable and will be of great benefit in the field. Let us look at some of these tools and how to put them to best use.

Notebook and Pencil

Without a doubt these are the most useful (and neglected) tools available to us when we are learning about the art and science of tracking. Later on we will make extensive use of a notebook and pencil. We should always be taking notes and making sketches (supplemented

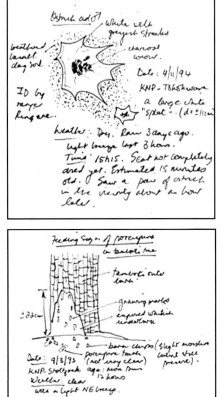
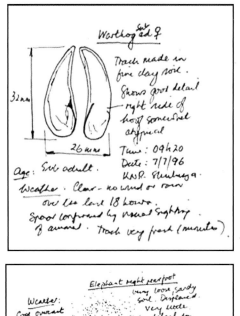
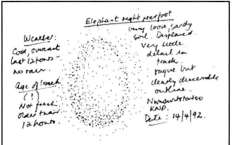

Figure CCCH.02.04.30: Extracts from a tracker's notebook.

by photographs). Do this in the field. Draw to scale or add a scale and make copious notes of everything you see. Where appropriate take accurate measurements. Figure CCCH.02.04.30.

Record the date, locality, place, time, weather conditions (past and present), type of signs, the species, age, sex, activity, type of habitats, soil types, and as many things you might consider to be useful information. Use a pencil rather than a pen as pencil notes do not smudge or blur if the notebook should become wet. Keep all your notebooks. Refer to them regularly.

Reference Material

There is a wide range of reference materials available: museum specimens, books, films, CDs, videos, and so on.

Try to read, look at, and listen to as much relevant information as possible that will assist you in your tracking skills. Hereunder follows a list of subjects you should study up on for starters.

Learn about the mammals, birds, reptiles, amphibians, fish, arachnids (spiders and scorpions), and insects that occur in your area of operation. Learn how to identify them by their physical appearance (body shape, colouring, tracks, scat), behaviour (breeding, social order, territoriality, response to danger, methods of defense), preferred habitat and feeding characteristics, distribution, calls, and so on.

Know how to identify trees, shrubs, flowers, and grasses. Know which have edible fruits, roots, leaves, etc. Know which are preferred foods by which animals. Know which are poisonous and which have medicinal uses and therapeutic applications.

Geology and soils determine plant communities and, in turn, the wildlife in a given area. Know something about the main soil types and their characteristics. How will the track of a kudu look in deep sand, in wet clay, in granite gravel, etc?

Learn something about the weather: types of clouds and what they mean, rainfall and weather patterns, and the seasonal and daily variation in temperature, humidity, precipitation, etc. A grasp of basic astronomy and navigation skills would also be of benefit.

Binoculars, Tape Recorder, Magnifying Glass, and Camera

Binoculars greatly enhance a tracker's visual capacity to scan ahead at a distance and also to enable him to look effectively into areas of deep shadow. Figures CCCH.02.04.31 and CCCH.02.04.32. If you turn

Figure CCCH.02.04.31: A binocular is a very useful tool in the field.

Figure CCCH.02.04.32: A magnifying glass is useful for seeing detail in signs and tracks and for starting a fire in a survival situation.

Figure CCCH.02.04.33: Making a plaster cast of a lion track.

the binocular around, you have a magnifying glass that enables you to look at objects in detail. A camera is an extremely useful tool for recording visual signs in detail and colour. A reference library of photos enables the tracker to refer back to material at a later stage. A tape recorder can be used to tape calls of animals, birds, frogs, etc., or to make verbal notes for later transcription.

Plaster of Paris or Dental Stone

Plaster of Paris or dental stone is very useful for making casts of animal or human tracks. See Figure CCCH.02.04.33. Dental stone sets much harder than plaster of Paris and is the better material to use. Make a form from a piece of cardboard to put around the track, taking care not to damage it. Slowly sift the plaster of Paris (or dental stone) powder into a container with water until the powder will not dissolve any more. Bump the container up and down for a few seconds to remove air bubbles. Don't mix it with a stick as this will cause the plaster of Paris/dental stone to form clumps that will entrap air bubbles and give a poor-quality cast. The consistency of the plaster or dental stone should be like thick cream. Gently poor this mixture into the track and fill the form. Allow to dry for about thirty minutes. Drying can be expedited by adding a pinch of salt to the mixture before pouring it into the form. Once well dried, remove the adhering soil with a brush and you will have a detailed cast of the track.

Tracking Stick

A tracking stick is a simple but useful device made of a pointed wooden dowel and four tightly fitting "O" rings that can be moved up or down the stick. Figures CCCH.02.04.34 to CCCH.02.04.36. When you find a set of tracks you wish to follow, go through the following steps to help you stay on track.

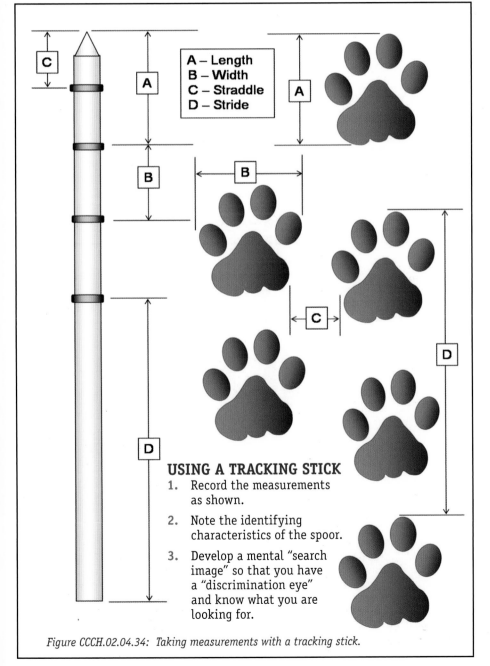

A – Length
B – Width
C – Straddle
D – Stride

USING A TRACKING STICK

1. Record the measurements as shown.

2. Note the identifying characteristics of the spoor.

3. Develop a mental "search image" so that you have a "discrimination eye" and know what you are looking for.

Figure CCCH.02.04.34: Taking measurements with a tracking stick.

Figure CCCH.02.04.35: A bow hunter making use of a tracking stick.

THE COMPREHENSIVE GUIDE TO TRACKING SKILLS

Try to find the clearest track; take the substrate into account as this can influence track details. Measure the tracks as shown and mark the dimensions on your tracking stick by sliding the "0" rings into place.

➤ The track's length is the distance from the extremity of the leading edge to the extremity of the trailing edge of the track (front to back).

➤ The track's width is the distance between the two extreme edges of the track (side to side).

➤ The length of the stride is the distance measured from the leading edge of one foot from one step to the next (of the same foot).

➤ The width of the straddle is the distance between the parallel lines of the inside edges of the track (left and right).

Track dimensions and details are unique to an individual and can be used as a fingerprint to identify individuals. With the dimensions recorded on your tracking stick and other details recorded in your memory or notebook (preferably the latter), the tracking stick can help you to identify and follow a specific animal in a group, focus on tracks you are following by pointing to them, and to check the dimensions. By sighting along the stick and traversing it in an arc, it can help you to pick up sign.

In difficult terrain, you might suddenly lose the spoor. Go back to where you last found sign. By using the lower end of the stick as the centre, describe an arc with the tracking stick, keeping an eye on the "0" ring used to mark the stride. It will then be easier to see the next bit of evidence as you will be looking in the right arc.

USING A TRACKING STICK TO HELP LOCATE SIGN

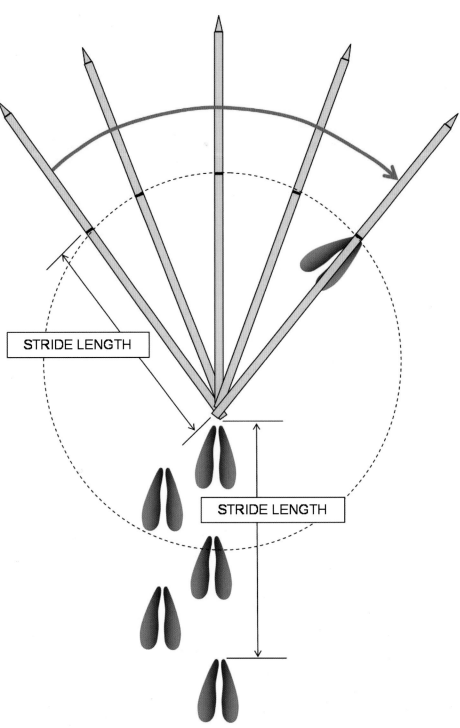

STRIDE LENGTH

STRIDE LENGTH

Figure CCCH.02.04.36: The animal you are following suddenly changes direction or you lose the spoor in difficult terrain. Use the following procedure:
1) Go back to the last clear print. 2) Place the lower end of the stick at the extremity of the leading edge of the track. 3) Describe an arc with the stick and look at the "0" ring, which marks the length of the stride. 4) The next sign should appear somewhere along this arc. Confirm that it is the right animal by checking dimensions and detail.

Learning Methodology

Tracking Practices

Stealth, the ability to move quietly and unobtrusively, is a habit you must cultivate right from the beginning of your tracking career. When following fairly old sign, speed can sometimes be more important than stealth. Moving too slowly at a stage might waste valuable time. It is likely that the animal is far ahead and will not hear your distant approach. As signs become fresher, it is wise to start moving quietly and with stealth.

➤ Stop frequently to look, listen, touch, and smell. When you are getting closer to your quarry, refrain from talking if you have a companion with you. Learn to communicate with hand signals.

➤ Look where you place your feet so that you do not step on dry leaves and twigs. Practice sound tracking technique.

➤ Use common sense; be patient and persistent.

➤ Keep signs between you and the sun, if possible.

➤ Preserve the spoor/sign; don't walk on it.

➤ Look ahead four or five meters. Don't look at your feet.

➤ Mark your route. Learn to anticipate and predict.

➤ Constantly monitor wind direction. Approach with the wind blowing in your face, diagonally toward you or across you. Move slowly and avoid sudden, big movements. Make use of shade and cover and avoid open areas. Walk hunched or crawl if necessary as you sight your quarry and approach closer. Move only when an animal is not looking your way.

Using a Tracking or "Sign" Garden

Before being able to follow and "read" signs, you must become familiar with them. One of the best ways to learn is by constructing a sign garden for yourself, keeping a notebook handy, and making detailed observations of the changes that take place over time. Construct a sign garden for yourself in the following way. See Figures CCCH.02.05.01 and CCCH.02.05.02.

Clear an area of any pre-existing sign and rake it clean. Prepare different types of substrates within the demarcated area: for example, fine clay soil, loamy soil, sandy soil, gravelly soil, grass, bare rock, and an area with natural bush. On each type of substrate, place various types of fresh signs, a patch of urine, a few drops of blood (donate your own), some finely chewed grass (yes you can chew it), feces (donated by your dog or cat), a boot track, bare footprint, a dog track (let your dog walk across the sign garden), drops of water, broken vegetation (from different types of plants), and so on. Use your imagination. The more types and variation of signs you use the better. Now what you need is time, patience, and the commitment to making careful,

Figure CCCH.02.05.01: Students working on a tracking garden study changes in sign over time.

detailed observations, sketches, and notes. From the moment signs are placed into the garden, start recording changes that take place over time and correlate these changes to prevailing weather conditions.

Pay meticulous attention to the following:

➤ Changes in colour

➤ Changes in texture

➤ Changes in smell

➤ Changes in sharpness/definition/clarity

➤ Changes in hydration (moisture content)

➤ Changes in temperature

➤ Changes in shape

➤ Changes in position (something blown from original position by the wind)

➤ Note how these changes differ on the different substrates.

➤ Note what effect heat, wind, dew, rain, humidity, shade, direct sunlight, and time has on the aging process

Make observations every minute for the first twenty minutes; then observe again at various intervals for up to thirty-six hours. This is a tedious process but one of the best learning experiences you can ever have. With practice, you eventually are able to age any sign quite accurately. Your eyes and other senses will become trained to locate, identify, and age signs that are missed by the untrained individual.

> **Environmental effects (temperature, wind, humidity) are the biggest causes of changes in signs. The substrate also has a significant effect.**

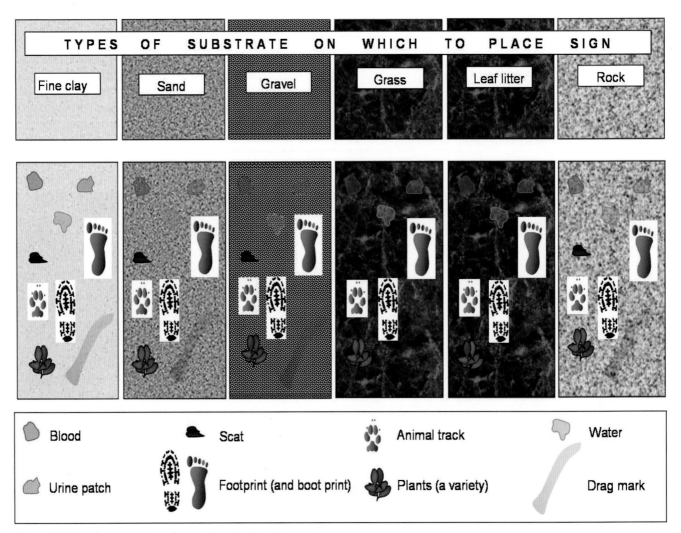

TYPES OF SUBSTRATE ON WHICH TO PLACE SIGN

Fine clay | Sand | Gravel | Grass | Leaf litter | Rock

Blood   Scat   Animal track   Water

Urine patch   Footprint (and boot print)   Plants (a variety)   Drag mark

Figure CCCH.02.05.02: Laying out a sign (tracking) garden.

TYPE OF SIGN (clay substrate)	CHANGE AFTER 1 MINUTE	CHANGE AFTER 5 MINUTES	CHANGE AFTER 10 MINUTES	CHANGE AFTER 20 MINUTES	CHANGE AFTER 30 MINUTES
BOOT PRINT	Edges sharp and clearly defined; slight moisture squeezed out of soil into track	No detectable change	Moisture drying out but track still sharply defined	Track dried out; still sharply defined	No further detectable change
URINE PATCH	Soil wet and more darkly coloured than surroundings; urine frothy; puddle; strong odour	Frothy bubbles disappearing, only a few left; still visibly wet but puddle has seeped into soil; can still smell the urine	No more froth or bubbles; patch still wet; colour still different from surroundings; smell still present	Starting to dry around the edges; colour beginning to fade; urine smell weaker but still detectable	Drying further; starting to take on the colour of the surrounding soil; faint smell detectable
BLOOD	Highly visible; bright red (arterial); still very liquid; does not soak into the soil; slight "iron" smell	Sticky to the touch and starting to coagulate; more dull in colour	Still highly visible but has clotted into droplets on top of soil; serum is expressed when compressed	Dry; no further serum expressed when compressed; colour still visible but becoming duller	Shrinkage visible and colour darkening
WEATHER CONDITIONS	Warm—about 27 degrees; no wind; $1/8$ cloud cover; low humidity	No change	No change	No change	Light northwesterly wind; $2/8$ cloud cover; slightly cooler

Table 2.3: Example from a sign (tracking) garden logbook—note how the prevailing weather conditions are recorded with each observation.

Water, for example, is absorbed into sandy soil, whereas it lies on bare rock. The temperature of clay soil in the shade is much cooler than a bare rock exposed to bright sunlight, and so on. Signs can also be damaged or changed by water falling onto them, animals trampling them, and vehicles driving over them. What you will now do is carefully record the changes you see taking place over time. Prepare a logbook to record your observations. An example of one appears in Table 2.3.

Practical Field Exercises

Sense of Smell: Tracking with Your Nose
Begin training your nose to smell. Start with these exercises.

➤ Smell flowers, leaves, fruits, and a variety of vegetation. Note how the smells can change in relation to temperature, humidity, age of the sign, and time of day.

➤ Lift your plate of food each time you eat and savor the aroma. Try to identify the contents before opening your eyes to see what is on offer.

➤ Note how the smell of your underarm changes when you are fearful or angry, as opposed to when you are physically exerting yourself.

➤ Dig into the ground and smell a variety of soils. Try to account for what may be causing the differences in smell.

➤ Note how the smell of your own scat changes with your diet and general health.

➤ Smell your pets and other animals you can come into contact with: dogs, cats, horses, cows, pigs.

➤ Collect scat samples of wild animals and learn to identify them by smell. You will be amazed how, with a little practice, you can learn to identify different animal groups and even species by the smell of their scat.

➤ Be aware, daily, of your sense of smell and consciously try to identify what you are smelling.

Figure CCCH.02.05.03: A carcass provides a good source of smell for scent tracking.

Sense of Smell: Field Exercise

Find some object that has a good "pong" to it, like old meat, fish, or a carcass. We use a dead dwarf mongoose in Figure CCCH.02.05.03. If you prefer, it can also be something pleasant, like your wife's best perfume.

Take the object itself or a rag saturated with some test liquid into the veld and have someone place it out for you about a hundred meters away. Make sure the source of the smell is upwind of you so that the scent can be carried on the wind toward you. There should be at least a moderate breeze blowing to assist you in your learning phase. The procedure for this exercise is illustrated on page 51. When you pick up a scent, analyze it to determine its origin. Is it alive or dead? If dead, for how long? Is it plant or animal? Is it smoke from a bushfire or the smoke from a campfire? (Yes, they can smell different.) Make rapid, short, canine-type sniffs or repeated deep inhalations to test the air; this will dull your olfactory senses. Take sporadic, long, slow sniffs to give the sensory receptors time to analyze the subtleties of the scent.

What often works well is to catch the scent as you breathe normally. Because smell and taste are connected, it works well to keep the mouth slightly open whilst smelling and alternately breathing through your nose and mouth. There are some smells you can almost "taste." If you need to keep "contact" with a scent trail, take in just enough air to catch the scent.

Begin at a point and walk at a right angle to the wind until you pick up the first hint of smell. Continue until you lose the scent. You have now established the boundary width of the scent trail. Now turn and walk into the wind, occasionally veering to the left and right to establish the boundaries. When you start losing the scent at a boundary, turn and walk in the opposite direction. The trail will narrow down until you reach the source. Figure CCCH.02.05.04.

The distance to the source can be modified by a number of factors: wind (as shown in Figure CCCH.02.05.05), vegetation, rocks, or landforms in or near the path of the scent; all can spread, narrow, or diffuse the scent. You will never develop the nose of a dog (it probably would not look good on your face anyway!), but you will gain a life-enriching olfactory aptitude and a unique skill that will stand you in good stead as a tracker.

Let's now turn to a few listening exercises.

Listening Exercises

Cultivate the habit of hearing what is going on around you. Even in a domestic/urban setting, we can train our ears to hear and to be aware of what we are hearing. Practice these exercises.

Establish Rhythms

In whatever environment you live in, whether it be a city, a farm, or in the wilds, try to establish the sound rhythms of your environment. Yes, they will be very different. A city is never quiet, yet there are lulls in the noise. Dogs bark more at certain times and traffic is noisier at peak hours and quieter in the early hours of the morning. On a farm, roosters crow at dawn and the tractor starts up ready for the day's work, sound activity seems to drop off during the heat of the day, and nights are usually very quiet.

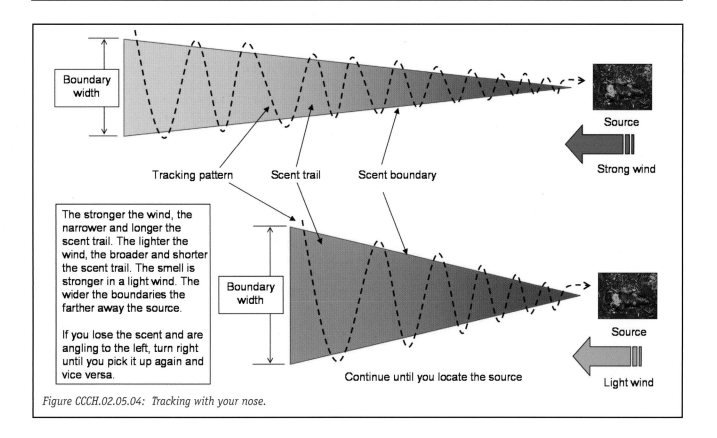

Boundary width

Tracking pattern   Scent trail   Scent boundary

Source

Strong wind

The stronger the wind, the narrower and longer the scent trail. The lighter the wind, the broader and shorter the scent trail. The smell is stronger in a light wind. The wider the boundaries the farther away the source.

If you lose the scent and are angling to the left, turn right until you pick it up again and vice versa.

Boundary width

Source

Continue until you locate the source

Light wind

Figure CCCH.02.05.04: Tracking with your nose.

Sounds in the wild are generally different yet also follow a distinct pattern. Train yourself to become aware of these rhythms. When you get out into the wilds, you will then be trained to establish and tune in to these rhythms.

Identify Sounds

Make a point of identifying sounds. Right at this moment, where you are sitting, what sounds can you hear? Try to identify their source and their meaning. Get hold of some audio or video tapes of bird, animal, insect, and frog calls and learn to identify them. Pay special attention to those that occur in the areas you intend frequenting.

Try to find out when the animal is most vocal. Is it in the morning or at night? Is it more vocal during the breeding

season? What different sounds does a particular animal make? How do I differentiate between the warning snort and rutting sounds of an impala? This is a whole new and exciting world for you to investigate. As you become more proficient in learning to identify sounds, your tracking ability will be significantly enhanced.

When learning to identify the calls and sounds of wild creatures, it is beneficial to see a picture or video

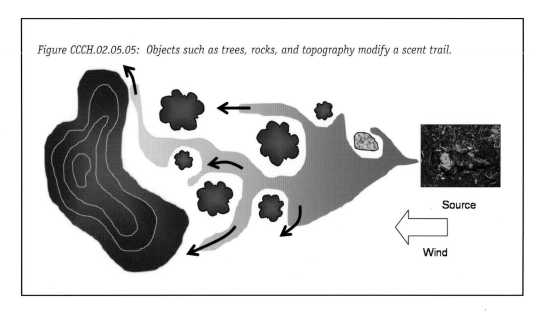

Figure CCCH.02.05.05: Objects such as trees, rocks, and topography modify a scent trail.

Source

Wind

of the animal; the brain can then make an association between the visual and sound information.

The Best Way to Learn

Get out into the wilds and start listening. Listen to sounds and try to identify them and what their significance is. Taking a tape recorder will help. The tape will provide a record of background sounds that you can listen to over and over again to pick up anything you might have missed the first time around. It will also allow you to record a specific sound/call for later identification.

Learn to Mimic

Try to learn to mimic sounds and calls. This will help you to remember them and can be very useful in the field. For example, a guinea fowl makes a very contented call when it is relaxed and undisturbed. Animals know this sound. By mimicking this sound, you can sometimes calm animals down when they become nervous or restless.

By now you will be aware of the requirements and how to prepare yourself to become a tracker. We've gone over the need for good senses, acute observation, alertness, an analytical mind, an understanding of nature, intuition, a good memory, physical fitness, patience, perseverance, and a creative imagination. Now let's put this information into practice.

After having prepared ourselves by learning to use our senses properly, we can now get started with practical field exercises. The key to becoming proficient is practice, practice, and more practice. There are no shortcuts. Apart from the tracker's own ability, the ease or difficulty of tracking depends on other factors as well. The type of ground, weather conditions, and vegetation will determine the level of skill required to recognize, interpret, and follow sign. The best and easiest way to learn is to be taught by an experienced tracker who would be able to point out all the signs and subtle nuances until you become proficient enough to recognize and correctly interpret them yourself. Teaching yourself is possible but more time-consuming; it requires concerted effort and dedication. It is ultimately more rewarding and exciting if you make the discoveries yourself.

Phase 1

Track Yourself on Easy Tracking Ground

1. Find suitable, very easy terrain, such as bare sandy or clay soil.
2. Mark a starting point and randomly walk across the terrain not paying any particular attention to where

you are walking. If it is open ground and safe, you can even do this with your eyes closed.

3. Stop after thirty meters or so. Circle back to your starting point. Now try to follow your own tracks. Pay attention to every sign you can detect. Take your notebook along to record your observations. Try to follow your tracks to where you stopped. In this phase, you concentrate on recognition and interpretation and are not concerned about speed and momentum. Repeat this exercise until you can do it well. Do not worry at this stage about speed.

Now repeat this exercise, but move onto progressively more difficult terrain. Once again the objective at this stage is not speed but seeing and recognizing sign. Also make notes of sounds, smells, textures, and taste. Take specific note of how different the same type of sign can look on different substrates. The same track on hard clay can look completely different on loose sand for example. Blood on rock will look different to blood on sand.

Phase 2

Build on Speed and Momentum

Repeat the previous exercises. In phase one you concentrated on spoor recognition. In phase two you have become more familiar with sign recognition. Now you begin to concentrate on aspects previously neglected, namely looking ahead, speed, and momentum. At first you will probably miss a lot of signs, but with time and practice you will begin to spot signs more regularly. Begin on easy terrain and gradually work toward more difficult types.

Phase 3:

Track Someone Else

Now things are going to get a bit more difficult. The object of the exercise is to develop an ability to anticipate and predict an unknown trail. Now that you have developed an aptitude to follow your own sign, let someone else lay a trail for you. Go through the same exercises in different types of terrain. Once you can do this with regular success, start trying to follow the trail by anticipating and predicting the person's movements. Look at the terrain ahead. Try to imagine the most likely route the person would have taken, and look for signs well ahead while ignoring those in between. You can save a lot of time by predicting correctly and taking shortcuts. If you know the area well and you have a good idea as to where the person might be headed, you could go directly to this point and see if you can pick up the trail from there. Search areas that have likely access or exit routes (e.g., a saddle over a ridge) and likely places where you might find clear sign (e.g., game paths, around water holes, etc.). If you lose the trail, return to where you last saw definite sign and start again.

Phase 4

The Real Test: Tracking Animals

If a human being does not know he is being followed, it is relatively easy to anticipate and predict his movements. It is more difficult to follow an animal if you do not know it well. Learn about wild creatures in the area where you intend tracking. Study their habits and behaviour patterns. Which habitats do they prefer, what food do they prefer? When and how often do they drink? How do they advertise territory? What do their tracks and dung look like? What sort of feeding sign do they leave behind, and so on?

Once you are familiar with the above, go out into the field and start getting some practice. It can be a good idea to start with your own domestic pets and farm animals (dogs, cats, cattle, sheep, and horses). If you live near some wild areas, you can now start tracking wild creatures. If you would like to get an idea of what animals occur in an area, you can set up "track traps."

To set up a track trap do the following:

1. Find a spot that you anticipate will be quite active with animal movement and with a substrate that will register tracks in detail.

2. Clear the area of debris. Rake or sweep it to remove all previous sign.

3. Bait the area with a variety of foods to attract animals and birds.

4. Check the area in the morning. Record and identify tracks of nocturnal species. Sweep the area clean and visit it again in the late afternoon to check for sign and track of diurnal (day) species that have visited the site.

The final stage is to track wild animals in their natural habitat, using the same principles as described. Begin in easy tracking areas and progress to more difficult areas. Eventually, as you get to know the different species, you will be able to predict and anticipate their movements with consistent regularity.

Practicing Blood Trailing

It is important as a tracker to understand something about blood and the blood clotting process because it will help you to interpret blood sign. Figure CCCH.02.05.06 illustrates the blood clotting process. Also refer to chapter 6 on Blood Trailing.

Blood is the body's transport system. It transports respiratory gasses (oxygen and carbon dioxide), food, antibodies to fight infection, and waste products.

Transporting oxygen to the tissues of the body is one of its most vital functions. Blood picks up fresh oxygen in the alveoli of the lungs and transports it as oxyhemoglobin to the body tissues. The blood being pumped out of the aorta and through the arteries is highly oxygenated and bright red in colour. At the tissue level, blood gives off oxygen and takes up carbon dioxide that is transported in the veins back to the lungs, via the heart. It is exhaled from the lungs. Because venous blood is low in oxygen content, it is darker than arterial blood. Lung blood is bright red with a pinkish hue and is often frothy or bubbly in appearance.

Several mechanisms help to prevent blood loss from ruptured vessels: The severity of blood loss is determined by the body's capacity to control blood loss. The amount and type of blood loss can inform the tracker about the type of wound and the effect it is having on the animal/person.

➤ Severe blood loss leads to a decrease in blood pressure, which reduces the flow of blood from the damaged area.

➤ Damaged blood vessels constrict and, thereby, decrease blood loss.

➤ The most important mechanism, however, is the closing of blood vessels at the site of the injury by a plug consisting of coagulated protein and blood cells. Such a plug, or clot, is important in the complete arrest of bleeding from minor injuries, but if major blood vessels have been ruptured a clot will not suffice.

To be effective, a clotting mechanism must act rapidly, and yet, the animal must be assured that blood does not clot within the vascular system. Blood must, therefore, have the inherent ability to clot and the clotting mechanism should be ready to be turned on when needed; on the other hand it must not be set into motion inadvertently as this, in itself, could be fatal (intravascular clotting).

A blood clot consists of the protein fibrin, an insoluble fibrous protein that is formed from fibrinogen, a soluble protein present in normal plasma. An enzyme called thrombin catalyzes the transformation of fibrinogen to fibrin, and the reason that blood does not clot within the circulatory system is that thrombin is absent from the circulating blood. Its precursor, prothrombin, is, however, present in circulating plasma. Clotting is normally initiated when blood comes into contact with damaged tissues. When a blood vessel is cut, thromboplastin is released from the vessel wall; this initiates the clotting process. If the cut is ragged and made by a fairly blunt object, more thromboplastin is released. The stronger

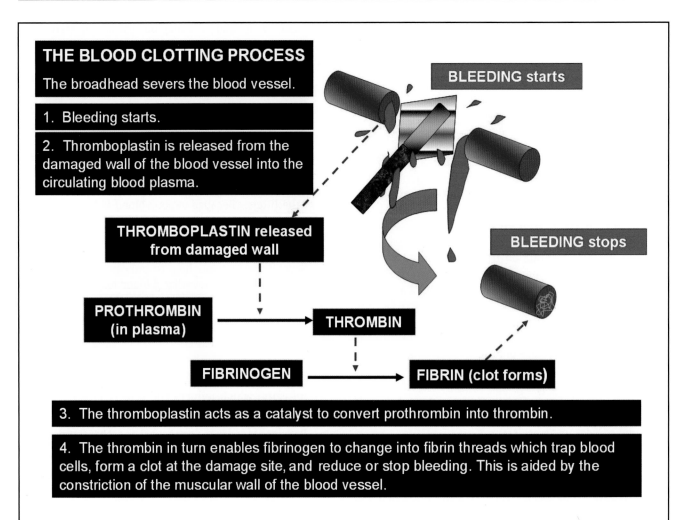

THE BLOOD CLOTTING PROCESS
The broadhead severs the blood vessel.

BLEEDING starts

1. Bleeding starts.

2. Thromboplastin is released from the damaged wall of the blood vessel into the circulating blood plasma.

THROMBOPLASTIN released from damaged wall

BLEEDING stops

PROTHROMBIN (in plasma) → THROMBIN

FIBRINOGEN → FIBRIN (clot forms)

3. The thromboplastin acts as a catalyst to convert prothrombin into thrombin.

4. The thrombin in turn enables fibrinogen to change into fibrin threads which trap blood cells, form a clot at the damage site, and reduce or stop bleeding. This is aided by the constriction of the muscular wall of the blood vessel.

Figure CCCH.02.05.06: The blood clotting process.

constriction of the vessel wall from a ragged cut will stop the bleeding sooner than if the vessel wall was cut with a sharp object (such as a sharp knife or broadhead). A clean cut causes the blood vessels to constrict less vigorously and bleeding is prolonged.

What is necessary to initiate coagulation is the formation of thrombin from prothrombin. This is the final step in a complex sequence of biochemical events. When blood vessels are damaged, a series of enzymatic steps is generated in which the enzyme formed in the first step serves as a catalyst or activator for the next step and so on. This series of steps forms an "enzyme cascade" that ends with the formation of a clot in which the soluble fibrinogen is changed into the insoluble fibrin.

As long as the animal is bleeding it will leave a blood trail to follow.

Tracking Wounded Animals for Hunting

When an animal is shot, the tracking process begins the moment a shot is fired, whether it be from a bow or firearm.

At the shot (when hunting with bow and arrow): The first few seconds after the shot are usually a jumble of events. You have a fleeting impression of your arrow flying toward your target, with the animal exploding away and running out of sight (unless the brain or spine has been hit). Did you miss? Was it a good shot or was the animal just running away at the sound of your bow or your arrow landing somewhere near it? Getting an arrow into a vital area is only part of a successful hunt, for after hitting the target, the bow hunter faces a considerably more difficult task, which is tracking and recovering the animal. The main thing to do is to have a strategy worked out before you need to use it. The following guidelines will facilitate the task.

1. As you release your arrow, try to register where it hits. The watermelon "plunk" of an arrow hitting the rib cage or the liquid "crack" of a broadhead smacking bone is unmistakable. Arrows hitting rocks, branches, or the ground make entirely

different sounds. Follow the flight of your fletching as it will often indicate where the shot impacts.

2. As your shot lands, make a mental note of exactly where the animal was standing when you released. Don't be vague. It must be an exact spot. Pick an object like a rock or a tuft of grass, something that you can locate after the animal has run off so that you know where the animal was standing. It is there that you must look for the first signs.

3. As the animal runs off, watch it for as long as you can so that you have a mental note of the last place you saw it. Also listen carefully to the sound of running because this may be heard long after you have lost visual sighting. This may also aid you in recovering your quarry.

4. Take careful note of the animal's reaction as the arrow impacts and it runs off:

     › A spinal or brain shot will drop the animal in its tracks.

    › Missed shots will cause the animal to run off at the sound of the string and the arrow landing close-by. After initial fright, some animals, like zebra for example, will sometimes return or stop to try to locate what gave them a fright and might, if you are lucky, present you with a chance for a second shot.

An animal hit with a good chest shot will race away at great speed after jumping or bounding high in the air as it takes off. It will then set off running low to the ground. It will hold its tail clamped down hard against its rump and corkscrewing. Sometimes it will run into obstacles.

If it runs off with back arched high, the chances are it is gut-shot. That means you are going to have a long, hard trailing job to locate it.

A lightly wounded animal will probably have its tail held high or in the normal down position as it leaves the scene; it will have a more upright run than for a heart/lung shot animal and will leap high over obstacles as it runs off.

Does the animal stagger or run off trailing a leg? If so you may have hit it in the rump, low down on the shoulder, or legs. Once again it must be stressed that shot placement is critical. Be prepared to pass up shots you are not sure of.

5. The next thing to do is to . . . wait! For at least thirty minutes before you move to the spot where the animal was standing before you shot it. This wait is very important. Some animals will run off for a short way before they stop and rest or look for cover. If you approach too soon, they will run off a long way and make recovery extremely difficult.

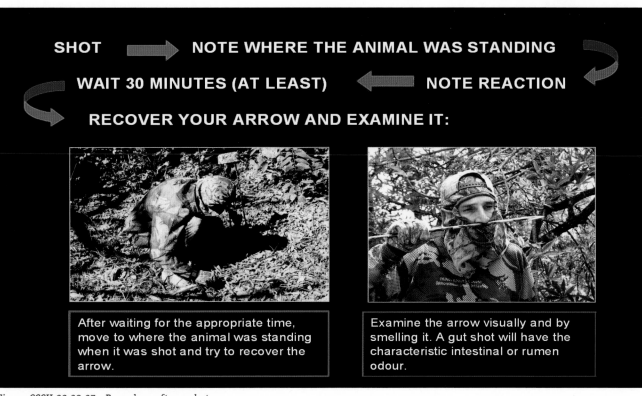

SHOT ➡ **NOTE WHERE THE ANIMAL WAS STANDING**

WAIT 30 MINUTES (AT LEAST) ⬅ **NOTE REACTION**

RECOVER YOUR ARROW AND EXAMINE IT:

After waiting for the appropriate time, move to where the animal was standing when it was shot and try to recover the arrow.

Examine the arrow visually and by smelling it. A gut shot will have the characteristic intestinal or rumen odour.

Figure CCCH.02.08.07: Procedure after a shot.

There are a few exceptions to this general rule:

➤ If you have actually seen the animal go down and expire.

➤ It begins to or was raining at the time of the shot. All spoor and sign will be obliterated if there is moderate to heavy precipitation.

➤ If an animal is shot just before dark, consider postponing follow-up until first light. If you decide to follow-up in the dark, make sure you are not contravening any hunting laws.

6. Now, assuming the animal has run out of sight, and you can no longer smell or hear it, you can recover your arrow (if it is not in the animal) and examine it for clues. Interpreting these clues is important information for the follow-up. Figures CCCH.02.05.07 to CCCH.02.05.09 illustrate how to "read your arrow."

Figure CCCH.02.05.09: "Reading" an arrow can provide the tracker/hunter with useful information.

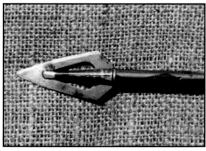

Arrow is covered with dark red blood. Blood with a low oxygen content is found in veins. Could indicate a liver, spleen, or kidney hit. Chances of finding your animal will depend on what organs or major veins have been hit. A long and difficult tracking session can be expected. Wait at least one hour before initiating follow-up.

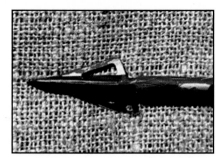

A gut-shot animal. Note greenish fluid and rumen contents on broadhead and shaft. A gut-shot animal will be indicated by greenish, brownish, or yellowish fluid and a strong "gut" smell. Possible organs that have been hit are rumen (in ruminatis), stomach, (non-ruminants), or intestines. Very difficult to find a gut-shot animal. Wait up to six hours before follow-up.

Blood or other physiological material on fletches indicates a complete pass through. Finding your animal will depend on where the arrow passed through and the type of sign on the arrow.

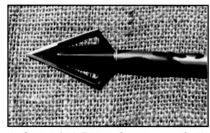

A clean miss! Better than a wound. No contact has been made with the animal and no injury inflicted.

A nick. Just a trace of blood on one side of the arrow. Skin and superficial muscles hit. No major organs. This is a minor injury and you will not recover the animal. A cursory follow-up to make sure would do no harm.

Figure CCCH.02.05.08: A broken shaft can indicate the depth of penetration. The type of sign will also give you a clue as to the possibility of finding the animal.

Arrow is covered with bright red frothy blood. This indicates that either heart, lungs, or major artery has been hit. Highly oxygenated blood from arteries is bright red in colour. Chances of finding your animal are good. Wait 30 minutes before initiating follow-up. Note white hairs on shaft which can also give an indication of where the animal was hit.

TEACHING YOURSELF TO TRACK

Figure CCCH.02.05.20: Following-up on a wounded animal.

Keep an arrow ready for a follow-up shot.

Keep an eye open for sign.

On the ground

and higher up

Mark your back trail

Examine your arrow and then wait!

1. Mark the place where the animal was standing when it was hit.

2. As you follow sign, mark the trail with some easily seen biodegradable material like toilet paper. This will enable you to backtrack should you lose the spoor or become lost. Looking back at it will also give you an indication of the flight path's direction.

3. As an ethical hunter, you have an obligation to find the animal you have shot. Be patient, walk silently, and keep your bow and arrow (or rifle) handy should the animal need to be dispatched.

4. It is likely that the animal will move to thick cover or water.

5. Remember that a fatally wounded animal can bleed internally and leave a poor blood trail.

6. If the blood spoor dries up, you must search the area in ever expanding circles as you cast about for additional clues.

After the Shot (Firearm)

The difference between a bow and a firearm is that the bullet cannot be seen in flight and it will be more difficult to identify the point of impact. A bullet will also not generally be found where the animal was shot. A bullet also hits with a more solid "crack" sound. A badly placed bullet would also be more likely to break a leg, which the animal might drag as it runs off. Apart from these observations, the procedure is very much the same as with a bow.

When following up on wounded dangerous game, always exercise extreme caution and ensure that you have adequate backup.

Using a tracking box

A tracking box is an extremely helpful aid, especially when it comes to learning about pressure releases. The sandbox will become your tracking "university." It is readily accessible, usable in all weather, and a source of limitless information.

A tracking box is a wooden box about 3 meters long, 1 meter wide and at least 150mm deep, filled with finely textured damp river or beach sand which is lightly compacted. Different tracks are registered in the sand which captures fine detail—tracks of someone standing, walking, jogging, running, swerving to one side, coming to an abrupt stop, carrying a heavy load, suddenly changing direction, and so on. The tracks can be studied to see what effect different actions have on the track. Many of the tracks in chapter 5 on gaits and pressure releases were recorded in a tracking box.

Construct a sandbox as illustrated in Figure CCCH.02.05.11 and fill it with clean beach or play sand. This is the ideal medium and the best one on which to learn how to track. Later, as you learn to identify the major pressure releases correctly, you can move on to more difficult and challenging substrates.

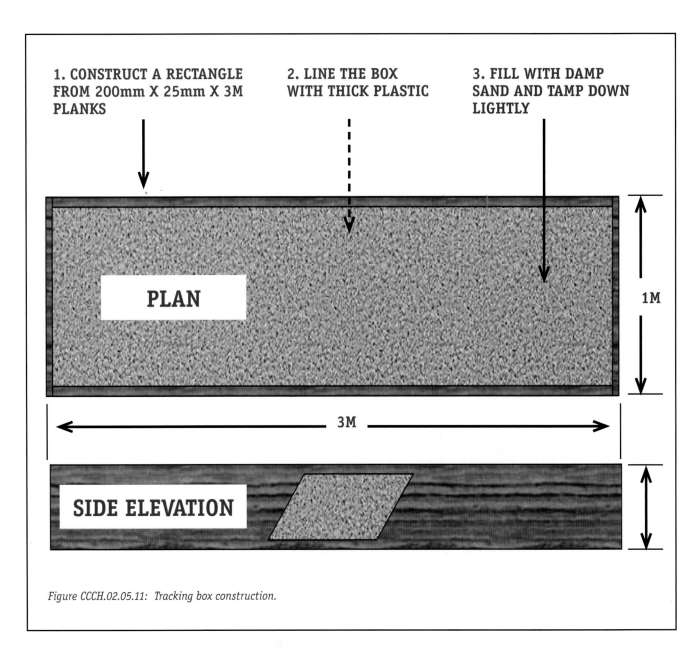

1. CONSTRUCT A RECTANGLE FROM 200mm X 25mm X 3M PLANKS

2. LINE THE BOX WITH THICK PLASTIC

3. FILL WITH DAMP SAND AND TAMP DOWN LIGHTLY

PLAN

1M

3M

SIDE ELEVATION

Figure CCCH.02.05.11: Tracking box construction.

Substrate Character

Sign can be registered on a variety of substrates such as vegetation, rock, soil, and manmade objects. The nature of the substrate will determine the clarity and detail of the sign and will play a significant role, together with environmental and other criteria, in the longevity of the sign. If the tracker understands the nature of the substrate, he will better understand the nature of the sign recorded: what it will look like and how it will "age" with time.

We must now expand our knowledge of substrate types and explain how sign will look on different substrate and how it will change with time on different substrates. We will begin by looking at variations in soil types and soil structure. This will give us a better understanding between sign and different soil types.

Soils

Soils can be very different from each other. These differences are reflected primarily by variations in texture, arrangement, structure, and colour. All of these characteristics will influence how signs are recorded on the soil. Whether the sign will hold fine detail or not, how long it will last, the depth to which it will be registered, and so on are all important variables for tracking.

Before we look at these characteristics of soils let us look how soils are "arranged" in the natural environment. The "arrangement" is called a soil profile. See Figures CCCH.02.06.01 and CCCH.02.06.02. Soils are arranged in layers called horizons. There are five primary horizons: O, A, B, C, and R.

The O horizon is the thin surface layer, formed above the mineral layer and composed of fresh or partly decomposed organic material of plant and animal origin. This, as well as the upper part of the underlying A horizon, is the region of the soil where life is most abundant. It is subject to the greatest changes in soil temperatures and moisture conditions, and it contains the most organic carbon. The photos on page 60 show examples of O horizons.

The organic or O horizon can be removed by trampling, overgrazing, or erosion. The underlying A horizon is then exposed as shown in Figure CCCH.02.06.03. The O horizon is the first layer of minerals. It is characterized by an organic matter accumulation that develops near or at the surface and consists largely of resistant minerals such as quartz, sand, or silt. The different horizons are sometimes all present and there are all variations in between. If horizons O, A, B, and C are missing, for example, then bedrock (the R horizon) is exposed. Sign will look different when registered on the different horizons. Most of the sign that we see on the ground is registered in either the O or A horizon.

B horizon, which lies directly under A, generally has a concentration of iron and aluminum compounds, clay, and humus. The B horizon is usually firmer and may have a granular, blocky, or prismatic structure. It may be absent in some

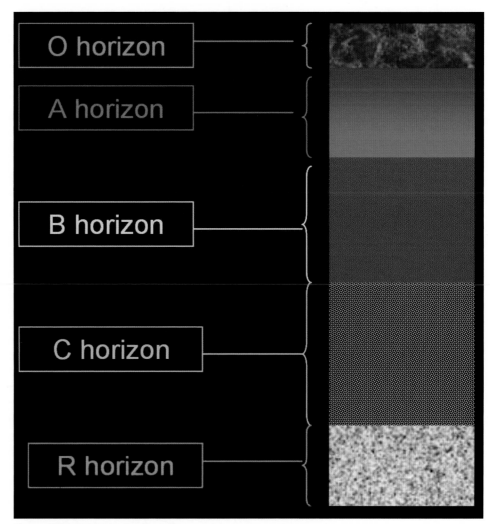

O horizon

A horizon

B horizon

C horizon

R horizon

Figure CCCH.02.06.01: A soil profile.

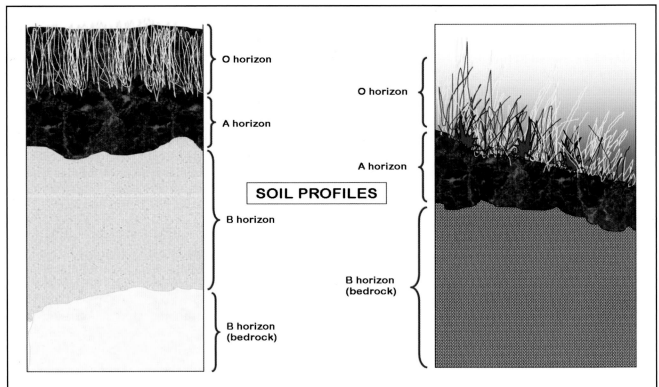

SOIL PROFILES

Figure CCCH.02.06.02: Some examples of soil profiles. Notice that the one on the left has no C horizon and the one on the right no B or C horizon.

Figure CCCH.02.06.03: The organic O horizon is absent, exposing the underlying A horizon.

soils. The C horizon is material weathered from the original material from which the soil was formed. As stated above, the R horizon is underlying bedrock. The structure, density, and moisture content are generally different in the different layers, and sign will, therefore, register and look different on the different layers. I'm repeating this because it's important to recognize this fact.

Let us get back to the soil morphology. One of the variations we find between soils is texture. The proportion of the different sizes of soil particles determines the texture of a soil. Particles are classified on the basis of size into gravel, sand, silt, and clay. Gravel consists of particles larger than 2.0mm. Sand ranges from .05 to 2.0mm, is easily seen, and feels gritty. Silt consists of particles from .002 to .05mm in diameter, which can scarcely be seen by the naked eye, and it looks and feels like flour to the touch. Clay particles are too fine to be seen even under an ordinary microscope. It is the clay that controls the most important properties of soils such as plasticity, adhesion, and moisture retention. Most soils are a mixture of these particles. Based on the proportions of the various particles contained in them, soils can be grouped into four texture classes: coarse, medium, moderately fine, and fine.

Coarse-textured soils are loose, consist mainly of sand and gravel, and hold particles together when moist. They hold only small amounts of water and dry out quickly.

Medium-textured soils are a mixture of sand, silt, and clay high enough in fine particles to hold water.

Moderately fine-textured soils are fairly high in clay, moderately sticky, plastic when wet, and may form a crust on the surface when drying out.

Finely textured soils contain more than 40 percent clay, are very sticky, plastic, and when wet hold considerable water and may drain poorly.

A soil's texture can vary in a soil profile. Surface horizons tend to be more coarsely textured than the B horizon since the clay particles may have been leached down from the surface and deposited deeper in the soil. It should be obvious now that with such different properties tracks and sign will look different and have different histories on different soil textures.

Soil Structure

Soil particles are held together in clusters or shapes of various sizes, called aggregates or peds. The arrangements of these aggregates are called soil structure. Soil aggregates may be defined as granular, crumblike, platelike, blocky, subangular blocky, prismatic, and columnar. Structureless soil can be either single grained (such as in loose sand) or massive (large clods or peds). Soil aggregates tend to become larger with increasing depth. A soil's structure is also influenced by texture, the plants growing in it, and other soil organisms.

> The structure, texture, and moisture content of the soil determines how sign will be fixed/registered and what it will look like on soil substrate. Together with weather and mechanical influences, these variables also play a role in how long sign will last.

For example, a track will have little detail in very coarse and dry soil. Conversely, a fine clay soil will register the minute details of a track. Although it will record excellent detail, a fine clay soil will deteriorate rapidly in windy conditions because the particles are very small and easily moved by even the lightest wind. Although a track in sandy soil will have less detail, it will, however, last longer than in fine, dry clay soil because the individual grains are larger and heavier and less easily blown about by light wind.

Figure CCCH.02.06.04: If you were following the tracks of an animal or human across this landscape, the visual appearance of the tracks and the history of the tracks will change because of the changes in soil profiles and substrate properties. The proficient tracker must be able to follow and read sign over all types of substrate, and this includes solid rock.

Sign—even of the same type—will change across a landscape because soil profiles change. See Figure CCCH.02.06.04.

Another factor to be taken into account is the degree of compaction. The exact same track on the exact same substrate will look different if the degree of compaction of the substrate is different. We will use this fact to modify our sandbox, which has much more to teach us. Look at the example in Figure CCCH.02.06.05.

Substrate Response

All tracking mediums respond in essence in the same way. That is to say that for any force applied to a substrate, the substrate responds with an equal and opposite force (for every action there is an equal and opposite reaction). The result which is dependent on the properties of the tracking medium might not look the same when comparing different substrates but the response to the force acting on the medium is essentially the same. The characteristics of a track should be present in any type of tracking surface but will be easier or harder to see depending on the properties of the substrate.

Pressure releases are the peculiar patterns formed in a track in response to forces applied to the substrate. They are present everywhere in the sand of your tracking box, in forest litter (leaves and material collecting under the trees), on gravel, and even, according to some tracking experts, on solid rock. Pressure releases also remain readable even when severely weathered. Wind and weather work to erase signs and the more subtle components are fragile but remain for far longer than most people realize.

The serious tracker has to become a dedicated student of soils and substrates. He has to experiment with them until there is an understanding of how they react to different types of signs and variables. To help us gain a better understanding, we now modify our tracking box as shown in Figure CCCH.02.06.06.

The three compartments in the tracking box shown in Figure CCCH.02.06.06 are representative of most tracking mediums irrespective of adhesive qualities, composition, or any other property. There are many

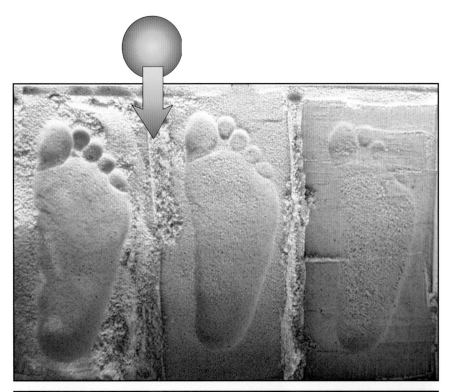

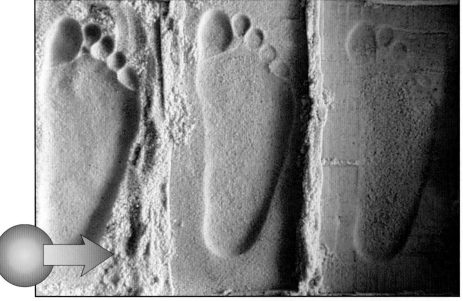

Figure CCCH.02.06.05 shows the same set of tracks with lighting from different angles to enhance clarity; it also demonstrates the effect of soil compaction on track definition. The same substrate (sand) was compacted harder from left to right. The same person stood with the same foot in each section. The difference is obvious and the conclusions clear: When the substrate is harder, much track information is lost, harder to see, and requires more careful investigation.

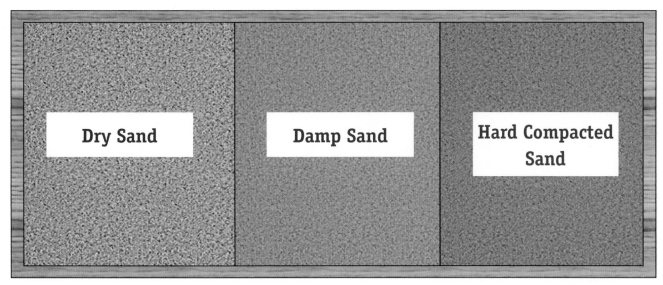

Figure CCCH.02.06.06: Modified sand box.

ways in which soil responds; the "behaviour" of the soil can be grouped into categories to help us have a better understanding of what is happening. We will now discuss these categories.

Density

Soil density refers to the degree of particle compaction that, for convenience sake, is classed as low, moderate, or high. Low-density soils have a lot of "give" and will deform easily. An example is dry, loose sand. Hard-compacted soil such as one would find on a well-worn foot or game path would resist deformation and have far less "give." The pressure releases, although present in both, will look different. The harder the substrate (generally speaking), the more subtle will be the pressure releases. Figure CCCH.02.06.07.

Moisture Content

The "plasticity" and "stickiness" of soils are dependent on two major factors: the clay and moisture content. Different soils have different water-retention ability. Sandy soils have poor moisture retention and dry out quickly, whereas clay soils that have been wet will retain moisture for long periods.

> **The water content of soils will greatly influence the soil's ability to register sign characteristics in detail.**

Too much water, for example sloppy mud or waterlogged sand, will result in very little information being retained. Once a foot is withdrawn, the track collapses in on itself. See Figure CCCH.02.06.08. On the other end of the spectrum, much detail is also lost in very dry substrates such as deep, dry

Figure CCCH.02.06.07: The illustrations above show two extremes of density from the loose sand of a riverbed to a tar road. The pressure releases, although present in both substrates, will be more difficult to see in the elephant tracks crossing the tar road.

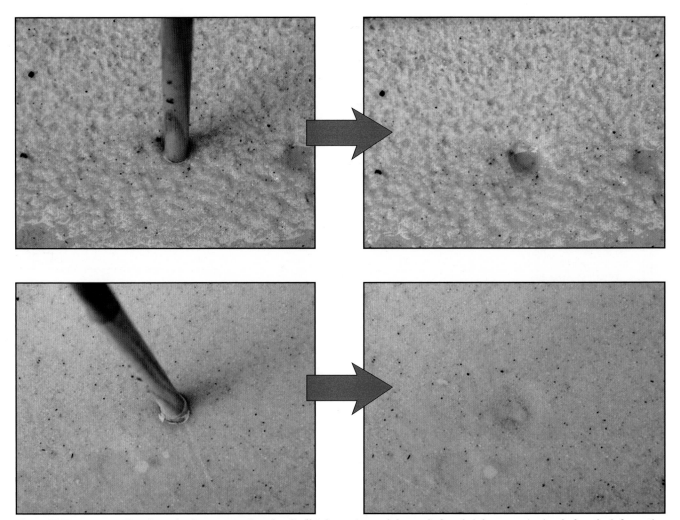

Figure CCCH.02.06.08: Waterlogged substrates retain only a little information and then only for a brief moment in time before the information is lost. In the top photo the cavity left by the withdrawn stick is filled almost immediately with water, but it still retains the shape for a few minutes. In the lower photo where the substrate is even more waterlogged, the hole left by the withdrawn stick collapses in on itself almost immediately and the sign disappears within a few seconds.

sand. The aging of a track is also closely correlated to the moisture content of the substrate. The tracker must, therefore, experiment with different substrates having different moisture contents to see what the sign looks like in each and how the sign looks as the substrate dries out. Photos in Figure CCCH.02.06.09 show sign registered in different substrates of differing moisture content.

Adhesive Qualities or Stickiness

The adhesive qualities of a soil will not only determine how particles stick together but will have a significant influence on how pressure releases build. The adhesive property of the soil is determined, by and large, by the water and clay content of the soil. While tracking, you should test the adhesive quality of the soil. Take it in your hand and squeeze your fist tight to compress the soil. Open your hand and examine what has happened. If the ball falls apart easily, the soil has relatively low

adhesive quality. If it fissures or falls apart under its own weight, it has medium adhesion, and if it retains the shape that your fist compressed it into, it has high adhesive qualities. The photos in Figure CCCH.02.06.10 show the tracker testing for soil adhesion.

As soil dries out, its adhesive properties diminish. Pressure releases start to fall apart if the soil itself does not have strong adhesive properties. Soils that have high adhesive properties (such as clays) will retain the pressure release formations long after the soil itself has dried out. Soils with poor adhesive properties (sand for example) will fall apart, together with the pressure release signs, as soon as it becomes dry.

Integrity of Composition

This refers to the purity of the medium. If you have clean sand with no impurities, its quality of content could be said to be 100 percent homogenous. If you took

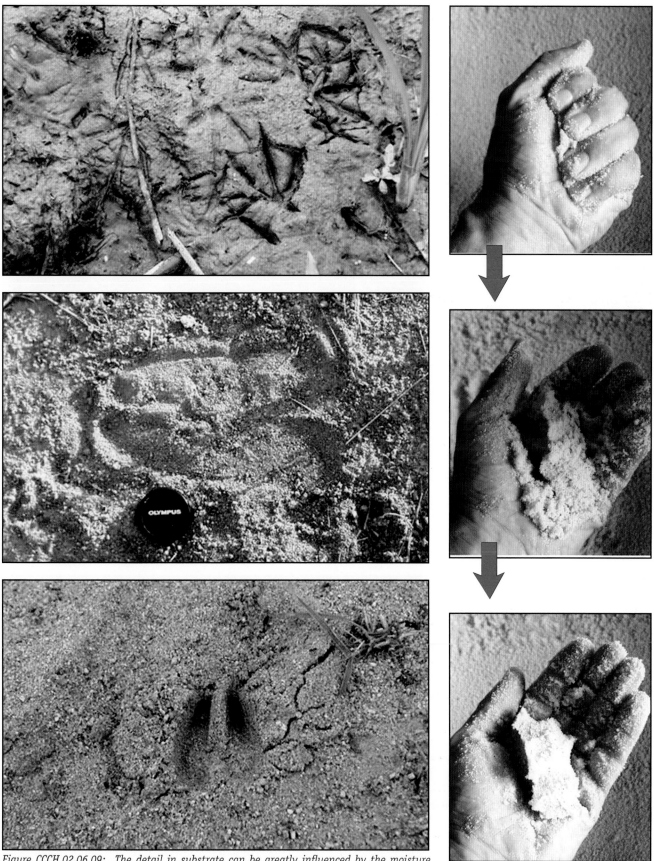

Figure CCCH.02.06.09: The detail in substrate can be greatly influenced by the moisture content of the soil. Detail is usually preserved for longer in substrates with relatively high moisture content. Waterlogged substrates, however, quickly lose detail.

Figure CCCH.02.06.10: Testing for soil adhesive properties.

sand and gravel and old vegetation and small rocks and bits of rubbish (plastic, paper etc.) and mixed it all together, you would have something on the opposite end of the scale, a heterogeneous mixture of many impurities. The greater the purity of the substrate, the less distorted the pressure releases will be. When examining pressure releases and making correct deductions, the tracker must take into account distortions induced by impurities in the substrate. Once again dedicated experimentation is required to learn the effects of substrate impurities. See Figure CCCH.02.06.11.

Pressure Response

This property determines how any given substrate will react to pressure. Is it unyielding or spongy. Does its elastic qualities cause it to spring back after pressure is removed? The response to pressure is directly proportional to the amount of debris mixed in with the soil.

Substrate "Memory"

Some substrates have "memory," which means that it will attempt to return the substrate back to its

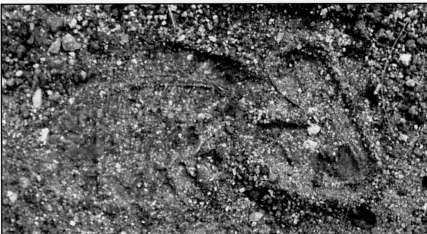

Figure CCCH.02.06.11: In the figure above, the substrate on the top is homogenous, causing fewer "landscape-induced distortions" in the pressure releases. On the bottom is a substrate with impurities (sand, gravel, small stones); this substrate causes pressure release distortions that the tracker must be able to identify and filter out.

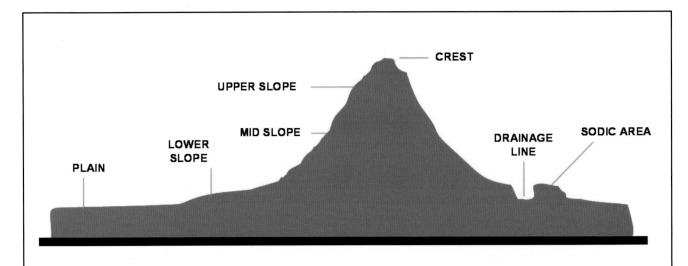

Figure CCCH.02.06.12: Not only the position on the landscape profile but also the direction the slope faces will have an effect on the track and the aging of the track. In southern Africa, northern slopes are warmer and drier, so signs will desiccate more quickly on them. This means that soils of the same type will react differently, depending on their location in the landscape.

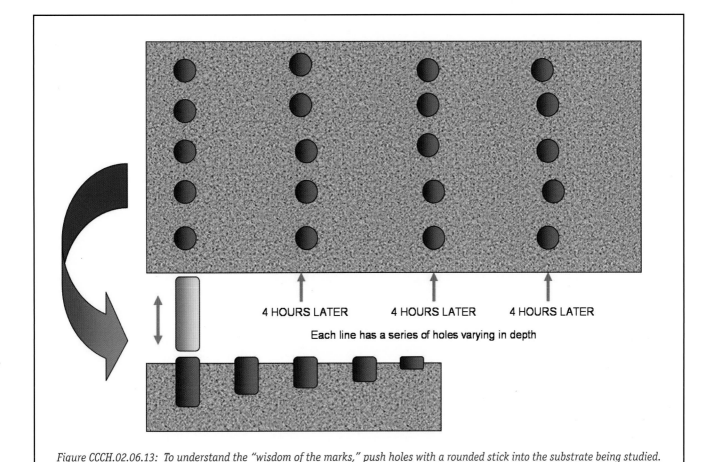

4 HOURS LATER   4 HOURS LATER   4 HOURS LATER

Each line has a series of holes varying in depth

Figure CCCH.02.06.13: To understand the "wisdom of the marks," push holes with a rounded stick into the substrate being studied. The holes must vary in depth from about 25mm to about 6mm. Repeat every 4 hours.

original state. Think of grass, for example. Standing on it bends or distorts it. As soon as the force is removed (the foot lifted for example), the grass will attempt to "spring back" to its original position. Understanding the capacity for memory of the different substrates can assist the tracker in determining the age of the sign.

Retention Capacity or "Memory Span"

The lifespan of a particular pressure release under a variety of weather conditions is known as its retention capacity. To study this requires frequent returns to a specific set of pressure releases. It is important to monitor what happens to this specific set of pressure releases and then to correlate this set to past weather events. This is where a "tracking garden" is a valuable tool.

Position in the Landscape

Tracking substrates differ significantly from one locale to another as was shown in an earlier illustration. The landscape can be divided up into different parts. A track will register differently and age differently depending on its position in the landscape profile. See Figure CCCH.02.06.12.

Building Capacity

The ability of a soil to build a pressure release of certain height, width, and thickness is a function of that specific type of soil. Different building capacities can produce considerable differences in pressure releases produced by the same movement. Building capacities are influenced by many variables, including mixed substrates. These cause landscape distortions and make the pressure release look different to what it would look like in a homogenous medium. The experienced tracker is able to "filter out" these distortions to see the real picture.

Aging Characteristics

The properties of any given substrate will have a significant influence on how pressure releases break down during the aging process. The best way to learn the aging characteristics of any given substrate is by meticulous, experimental observation. A method called by the Apache Indians the "wisdom of the marks" is one of the best ways to learn to interpret the aging characteristics of substrates. See Figure CCCH.02.06.13.

When the initial five marks have been made in the substrate, the tracker observes closely what they look

like when they are fresh. He must record what he sees because some changes are so subtle that they are difficult to describe in words. Four hours later he returns and makes a second set of marks. He now notes the changes that have taken place in the first set of marks and correlates this to weather events (rain, wind, humidity, temperature, etc.) over the past four hours. This process is repeated over a forty-eight-hour period.

Each time the tracker will compare the previous sets of marks to the new ones. The volume of information that can be learned through this process is enormous. The tracker can vary the experiment by making the marks at more frequent intervals (say every hour). The learning potential is limited only by the ingenuity and dedication of the student. Once you have experimented in your tracking box, go to the field for some real-life exercises.

Locate some animal tracks and then visit them every hour, every few hours, or over a few days to observe the changes taking place. Correlate these to the changes in the weather. Each time you return to the track, make your own mark next to the track so you can compare a new mark with the aging track. You can see the dramatic effects in Figure CCCH.02.06.14. Note how the observations are closely tied to the weather.

Figure CCCH.02.06.14: First row registered at 12:00 PM. Substrate damp. Weather sunny, partly cloudy, warm, humid. Second row registered at 3:00 PM. Substrate dry. Weather overcast, cooler but still warm. Light SW breeze. Third row registered at 7:00 PM. Light, intermittent drizzle began at 5:30 PM. Weather overcast and cool. Substrate wet. Heavy rain during the night erased all sign and waterlogged substrate would not register sign. Experiment with different substrates and under different weather conditions. Certain consistent patterns will emerge that will help the tracker to draw accurate conclusions from field observations.

The Qualities of a Good Tracker

The ability to track is a decided advantage to anyone who is exposed to the outdoor environment. Skilled tracking could almost be regarded as the pinnacle of bushcraft. Although most people can learn to track, certain qualities will quickly separate a mediocre tracker from a good one. As I said previously, these qualities include good eyesight, memory, sense of smell, hearing, ability to focus, fitness, patience, persistence, common sense, and knowledge of the bush.

Conclusions

The skill of tracking is like a detective game. You should try to gather all the clues possible. The more clues gathered and correctly interpreted, the more accurate your prediction will be. Avoid the pitfall of making rash conclusions on the basis of a single piece of evidence, for too often you will be wrong.

You need to start thinking like an animal. At the risk of sounding anthropomorphic, the more you think like an animal the more successful you will be at tracking. Figure CCCH.02.08.01. Think about it for a moment. What dominates an animal's thought

Figure CCCH.02.08.01: A tracker must learn to think like an animal.

Figure CCCH.02.08.02: Don't look for sign only on the ground; also search higher up.

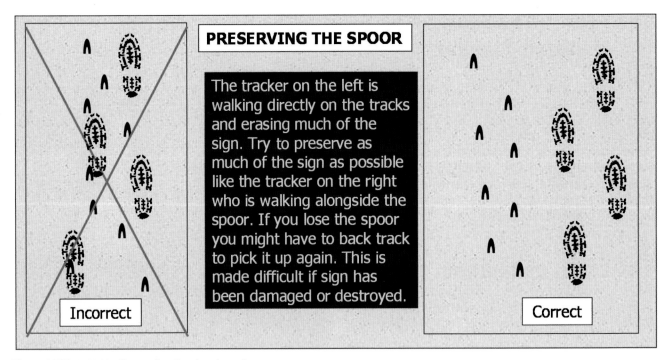

PRESERVING THE SPOOR

The tracker on the left is walking directly on the tracks and erasing much of the sign. Try to preserve as much of the sign as possible like the tracker on the right who is walking alongside the spoor. If you lose the spoor you might have to back track to pick it up again. This is made difficult if sign has been damaged or destroyed.

Incorrect

Correct

Figure CCCH.02.08.03: Preserving the sign (spoor).

processes? These include its stomach (food and water), its hormones (reproductive drive), and its survival (flight from danger, shelter from inclement weather, etc.). Once you know the natural history of the animals being hunted, the easier it is to think like them and to anticipate behaviour. Correct interpretation of sign as you track is more important than speed.

Use all your senses to search for relevant signs. Monitor what is going on in the bush around you. Look for specific signs of the animal you are following but also analyze other incoming data. Remember that signs are not confined to just spoor on the ground; there are many types of signs. See Figure CCCH.02.08.02. Often signs are evident at higher levels and are referred to as "aerial signs."

It's necessary to identify signs and mark your starting point. Make a mental note or sketch of the specific tracks you are going to follow, noting the identifying characteristics of the spoor. Is there a chipped hoof? What is the pattern of cracks under the hoof? Does the animal walk in a peculiar way, and so on. Develop a mental image for your search. Mark the route you are following with some highly visible biodegradable material

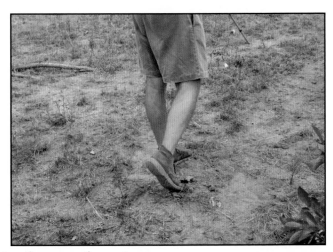

Figure CCCH.02.08.04: Note how the tracker is walking next to and not on the game path so as to preserve spoor.

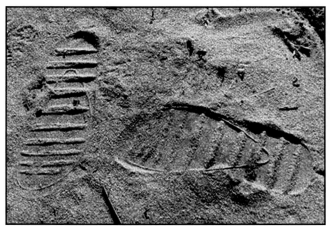
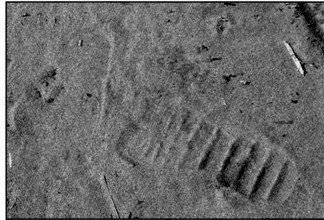

Figure CCCH.02.08.05: Note the difference in the tracks at 8:00 AM (left) and at 2:00 PM (right). When the sun is low, the deep shadows make the spoor far more visible.

If following an animal over difficult terrain or to differentiate one set of tracks from another (of the same species), make use of a tracking stick. Once the track information has been recorded on the tracking stick, it's a simple and quick procedure to check the tracks you are following.

When tracking, take great care not to destroy or obliterate the signs, for you might have to backtrack. Figures CCCH.02.08.03 and CCCH.02.08.04. Don't walk on spoor; walk alongside it. Don't allow more than a maximum of two trackers on the spoor at any given time. A crowd (more than two!) will destroy the signs.

Following spoor is much more difficult on overcast days. There is no sun to cast shadows that brings tracks into sharp relief and makes them more visible. Tracking is easier when the sun is low in the sky, so tracking is best in the morning and afternoon. With the sun at its zenith, spoor definition is lost because little or no shadows are cast by the depressions made in the substrate. See Figure CCCH.02.08.05.

The best way to track is to keep the spoor between yourself and the sun. Shadows cast by the sun will give the spoor a highly visible, three-dimensional effect and make it easier to follow. Figure CCCH.02.08.06.

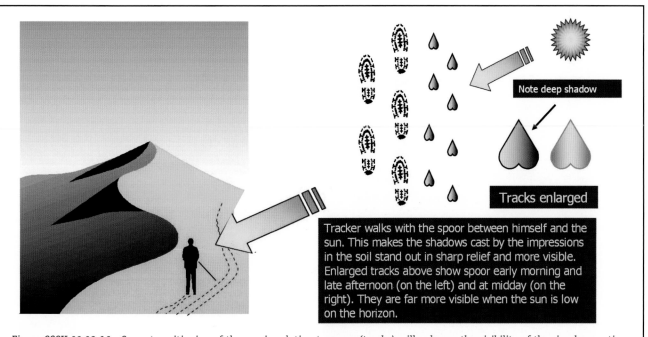

Note deep shadow

Tracks enlarged

Tracker walks with the spoor between himself and the sun. This makes the shadows cast by the impressions in the soil stand out in sharp relief and more visible. Enlarged tracks above show spoor early morning and late afternoon (on the left) and at midday (on the right). They are far more visible when the sun is low on the horizon.

Figure CCCH.02.08.06: Correct positioning of the sun in relation to spoor (tracks) will enhance the visibility of the sign by creating deeper shadows.

Never track looking down at your feet when tracking. It is slow and can be dangerous if you are following up on a wounded animal or operating in areas where dangerous game is present. Look four to six meters ahead of you for sign. Figures CCCH.02.08.07 and CCCH.02.08.08. This is a much quicker way of tracking and also allows your visual field to range farther ahead so that you will pick up sign or movement in time for you to take appropriate action

The behaviour and activities of animals, insects, and birds can be of inestimable value to the tracker, which is why a thorough knowledge of the bush is mandatory for a tracker. Broken spider webs can indicate that an

Figure CCCH.02.08.08: Note that the tracker is staring well ahead and using his tracking stick to help him concentrate.

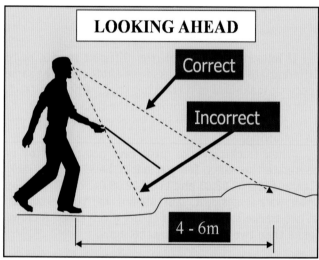

Figure CCCH.02.08.07: Look ahead of you and not down at your feet when tracking.

Figure CCCH.02.08.09: An intact spider web (left) is an indication that nothing has passed that way recently, whereas a broken spider web (right) or one being repaired could indicate recent passage.

Figure CCCH.02.08.10: Repair of a termite run can indicate the recent passage of an animal.

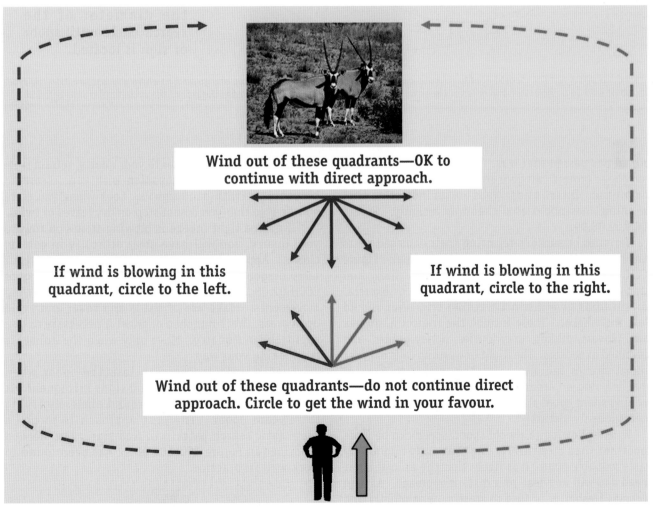

Figure CCCH.02.08.11: Using the wind to your advantage.

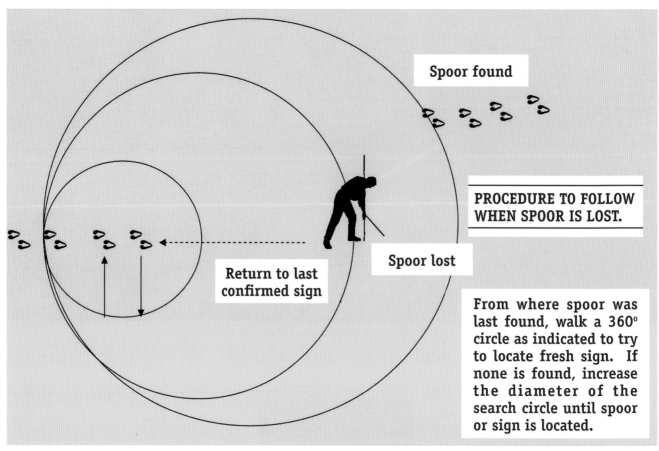

Spoor found

PROCEDURE TO FOLLOW WHEN SPOOR IS LOST.

Spoor lost

Return to last confirmed sign

From where spoor was last found, walk a 360° circle as indicated to try to locate fresh sign. If none is found, increase the diameter of the search circle until spoor or sign is located.

Figure CCCH.02.08.12: The method used to relocate lost sign: 1) Spoor or sign lost. 2) Stop and go back to where you last saw sign. 3) From that point walk in a circle; exit and enter at the same point. 4) If no sign is found, increase the size of the circle until a sign is found.

animal has passed that way. The height of the broken web above ground can give an indication of the size of the animal. Intact spider webs are an indication that an animal has not passed that way recently. Figure CCCH.02.08.09.

Termites or antlions repairing their damaged nests can indicate the recent passage of an animal. Figure CCCH.02.08.10. Flies, mopane bees, butterflies, and dung beetles are good indicators of urine or excreta. Certain birds give distinct warning cries that should alert the tracker. These include the francolin, guinea fowl, plovers, dikkop, gray louries, honey guides, and red-billed oxpeckers. The flight or warning calls of other animal species can also assist the tracker to monitor what is going on around him. Birds or frogs suddenly keeping silent could also be interpreted as them having been suddenly disturbed.

When following fairly old spoor, speed can be more important than stealth. Moving cautiously might only waste valuable time. It is likely that the animal is far ahead and will not hear your distant approach. As sign becomes fresher, it is wise to start moving quietly and with stealth. Stop frequently to look, listen, and smell.

When you are getting closer to your quarry, refrain from talking if you have a companion with you. Learn to communicate with hand signals. Look where you place your feet so that you do not step on dry leaves or twigs.

If even a light breeze is blowing from you toward your quarry, you will have great difficulty in getting closer. Approach with the wind blowing into your face, diagonally toward you, or, across you. Figure CCCH.02.08.11. Move slowly and avoid sudden, big movements. Make use of shade and cover and avoid open areas. Walk hunched or crawl if necessary as you approach your quarry. Move only when the animal is not looking your way.

Even a good tracker can lose the spoor when conditions become difficult and signs infrequent. It is then pointless to wander around aimlessly trying to relocate spoor. The best approach is to use a systematic search pattern to find sign. The method described in Figure CCCH.02.08.12 has been found to work well in practice.

CHAPTER 3

UNDERSTANDING WILDLIFE BEHAVIOUR

The Key to Tracking Wild Animals

The key to successful animal tracking is not only being able to identify features of the species—what their tracks and scat look like, what their calls sound like, and what they smell like—but also to understand the behaviour patterns that are characteristic of the species. Tracking is more than just simple identification of a sign. It is the ability to reliably interpret sign and predict from it what an animal is going to do. This is where understanding an animal's behaviour comes in; it is of inestimable value. It is what sets the good tracker apart from the mediocre tracker.

An animal's "hierarchy of need" could be summed up as eating and drinking, looking for a comfortable environment (e.g., resting in shade during the heat of the day), interacting socially, procreating and avoiding danger. The study of animal behaviour is called ethology. A tracker should know the feeding and watering habits of animals, be acquainted with their breeding patterns, understand their habitat preferences, home range sizes, and their responses to human presence, perceived danger, and so on.

Animals do some things instinctively, and some types of behaviour are learned. A tracker can learn a tremendous amount about animal behaviour by reading wildlife magazines, watching nature programs, and studying relevant textbooks. The best way, however, is through practical observation in the field. Make notes of your observations and keep these for future reference.

Observing animals going about their day-to-day activities is exciting. It is an experience of unfolding wonder as you begin to see the order and pattern in the lives of animals. As your understanding increases, you begin to predict, with greater and greater consistency, what an animal is going to do; this gives you the edge that is needed to track successfully.

Animals express curiosity, submission, anger, and caring. The tracker will need to know when an animal is bluffing, what the animal looks like when it wants to avoid a threat, how it advertises, and how it manifests displacement behaviour. How does each species mate, feed, rest, drink, and so on? Correctly interpreting animal behaviour will help the tracker for the following reasons:

➤ It will help you avoid danger when encountering potentially dangerous animals.

➤ You will know where to look for the animals.

➤ You will know how to approach close enough to animals if they have to be shot, darted, or observed.

➤ Recognizing abnormal behaviour will help the tracker realize there is something wrong: The animal is injured, sick, etc., which in turn helps the tracker to know how to proceed.

Stop and observe any animal without it being aware of you, and you will find that it is eating or searching for food, resting, scanning its surroundings to detect enemies or friends, or interacting socially, aggressively, or sexually with others of its kind. Herbivores have to spend a good half to two-thirds of their time eating and digesting. Carnivores, because of the high-energy protein in their diet, can afford to be far more laid back, so they spend much of their time sleeping or resting.

Social and reproductive activities occupy about 10 percent of an animal's time. Sociable species, especially those that live in herds, family groups, or harems such as baboon, suricates, and elephant, interact more frequently than unsociable species (e.g., black rhino and leopard). Primates are the most active socially and sexually. Many of the hoofed mammals such as impala, zebra, and wildebeest have active social interactions.

Young animals are often extremely entertaining to watch as they seem to have more time and more inclination to play and interact than the adults. Social interactions between females are usually more subtle. Males (in most species), being preoccupied with rank and reproductive status, interact more frequently and more aggressively than females. The opposite is found in some species where the female adopts the more dominant role. A good example of this is found in hyena.

To understand the behaviour of animals, you must not only be able to identify the different species but also the sexes and age groups. This is because certain behavioural traits are specific to age and sex classes. There are often similarities in the behaviour of certain wild animals to the domestic species. Buffalo behaviour is in many respects similar to domestic cattle, zebras to horses, domestic dogs to jackals, and house cats to wild cats. Let us now look at the types of behaviour we might observe and how we can interpret their actions.

Early morning or late afternoon is the peak activity times for most animals. The transition from light to dark and dark to light triggers all sorts of reactions. Nocturnal species are still active as the diurnal species leave their night refuges and resting areas to begin foraging. As night falls the reverse takes place. Crepuscular animals are most active at dawn and dusk.

During the heat of the day, activity is at low ebb for many animals. They seek out shade and rest to prevent overheating and water loss. Lions and other nocturnal carnivores usually sleep. Midday is a time, however, when other animals such as baboons, many herbivores, mongooses, vervets, and diurnal carnivores such as cheetah are very active. Many animals drink during the heat of day whereas others such as white rhinos will prefer to drink at sunset. Nocturnal species such as white-tailed mongooses, aardvarks, porcupines, civets, bushbabies, and aardwolfs will rarely be seen during daylight hours.

Feeding and Drinking

Animals can be grouped into species that have similar feeding and drinking habits. Table 3.1 summarizes and gives examples of the types of feeding behaviour of animals.

When the tracker understands the feeding and drinking behaviour (Figure CCCH.03.02.01) of a particular species, it narrows down the places to look to find it. The animal's diet is also reflected in the colour and consistency of its scat. The tracker needs also to be aware of feeding signs and to know which animal was responsible for which sign.

Animals can also be grouped into species that have similar drinking habits. Knowledge of the water requirements of different species will enable the tracker to predict when to find animals at water holes or other drinking points. Table 3.2 summarizes and gives examples of the types of drinking behaviour of animals.

Of the carnivores, lions, leopards, hyenas, wild cats, servals, genets, polecats, weasels, and white-tailed mongooses are mostly active and hunt for food from dusk till dawn; they are nocturnal. Diurnal carnivores

UNDERSTANDING WILDLIFE BEHAVIOUR

Figure CCCH.03.02.01: Animals have preferred drinking times.

Table 3.1: Feeding Behaviour

FEEDING BEHAVIOUR	DIET CONTENT	EXAMPLES
OMNIVORE	Both meat and plant material.	Baboon, jackal, vervet, civet, dwarf mongoose, banded mongoose, bushpig, hedgehog, bushbaby, bat-eared fox
CARNIVORE	Meat; some catch their own food, others scavenge off kills.	Lion, leopard, cheetah, wild dog, hyena, serval, caracal, African wild cat, genet, striped polecat, striped weasel, honey badger, white-tailed mongoose, slender mongoose, raptors (eagles, hawks, falcons), vultures
FRUCTIVORE	Fruits and berries	Certain bats, many bird species
SEED EATERS	Seeds of grasses and flowers	Many bird species
INSECTIVORE	Insects	Many bird species, certain bats, aardvark, pangolin, aardwolf
HERBIVORE	Grass(grazers) Leaves, fruits, flowers, and twigs (browsers)	Hippo, buffalo, white rhino, wildebeest, zebra, buffalo, oribi, reedbuck, waterbuck, roan, sable, tsessebe, red hartebeest, Lichtenstein hartebeest, hare
	Mixed (both graze and browse)	Black rhino, kudu, klipspringer, hyrax, giraffe, steenbok, Sharpe grysbok, suni, bushbuck, nyala, impala, elephant, warthog, duiker, porcupine, cane rats

hunt for food during the day; these include cheetahs, wild dogs, slender mongooses, dwarf mongooses, and banded mongooses. Honey badgers may hunt for food during the day or night.

Most herbivores feed mainly during daylight hours—early morning and late afternoon—but can also feed to a lesser extent at night. Hippos leave the water after sunset to graze and return before dawn; they may also graze on cool, overcast days. Porcupines, hares, and cane rats feed mainly at night. The aardvark, aardwolf, and pangolin roam around at night and feed mainly on termites.

Omnivorous animals that look for food and feed during the day include baboons, vervets, dwarf mongooses, and banded mongoose, whilst civets, hedgehogs, bushbabies, jackals, bat-eared foxes, and bushpigs feed mainly at night.

Insectivorous and fruit eating bats begin feeding just after sunset and return to roost before dawn.

Unusual Feeding Behaviour

Unusual feeding behaviour may sometimes be observed. This includes chewing bones and eating soil or feces. Unusual diets are usually an indication that an animal is lacking in trace elements such as iron, selenium, phosphorous, or calcium, which is often available in soils, bone, or feces.

Water Requirements

Animals that have to drink water on a daily basis are said to be water dependent; those species that can get enough moisture from their diet are said to be independent of surface water. See Table 3.2. Animals that are not dependent on water will drink when water is available.

Most animals prefer drinking during the day; some will drink day or night; and a few only at night. Table 3.3 summarizes preferred drinking times of some species.

Table 3.2 Water Requirements

WATER DEPENDENT	INDEPENDENT OF WATER
Blesbok, bontebok, zebra, bushbuck, bushpig, Lichtenstein hartebeest, red hartebeest, hippo, impala, lechwe, mountain reedbuck, reedbuck, white rhino, roan, sable, tsessebe, waterbuck, blue and black wildebeest	Duikers, Damara dik-dik, eland, gemsbok, giraffe, gray rhebok, Cape grysbok, klipspringer, nyala, oribi, springbok, steenbok, suni, warthog

Table 3.3: Preferred Drinking Times

PREFER DRINKING DURING THE DAY	PREFER DRINKING DURING THE NIGHT	DRINK DAY & NIGHT
Blesbok, bontebok, zebra, duiker, bushbuck, bushpig, giraffe, Lichtenstein hartebeest, red hartebeest, hippo, impala, lechwe, mountain reedbuck, reedbuck, white rhino, roan, sable, springbok, tsessebe, waterbuck, blue and black wildebeest	Hyena, jackal	Buffalo, eland, elephant, gemsbok, kudu, black rhino, warthog, nyala

UNDERSTANDING WILDLIFE BEHAVIOUR

Habitat Preference

Animals tend to prefer so are more likely to be found in certain habitats. Grazers will spend most of their time in grassland, browsers in bushveld, and those preferring dense undergrowth will frequent riverine habitat. Table 3.4 summarizes habitat preferences of some African game species.

Table 3.4: Habitat Preferences

SPECIES	HABITAT PREFERENCE
Aardvark	Tree and grass savanna where termite mounds are present
Baboon	Woodland with rocky hills; will feed in open country
Blesbok	High veld grasslands
Bontebok	Coastal plains, *fynbos*
Buffalo	Open savanna, tall grass, shade
Bushbuck	Riverine thickets, dense bush, near water
Bushpig	Open savanna, shrub, and grassland to dense forest, tall grass, and reeds
Caracal	Tree and bush savanna where water is available
Cheetah	Open woodlands or plains; avoids dense forest
Civet	Varied: grassland, savanna, bushveld, broken country with rocky hills
Duiker: common	Thickets, savanna, and woodlands; shade and cover
Eland	Varied: mesic to open arid savannas
Elephant	Varied: savannas, forest, and occasionally deserts
Gemsbok	Open arid savannas to shrub grassland
Giraffe	Arid to mesic savannas
Hartebeest: red	Arid grasslands and open savannas
Hyena: brown	Dry tree and bush savanna; arid grasslands and coastal dunes
Hyena: spotted	Varied: grassland, savanna, bushveld
Impala	Open savannas and acacia veld
Klipspringer	Cliffs, mountains and rocky hills
Kudu	Open to dense savannas; broken and rocky terrain
Leopard	Varied: grassland, savanna, bushveld, and riverine habitat
Lion	Varied: grassland, savanna, bushveld
Mountain reedbuck	Arid, grass-covered stony slopes; rocky hills and lower slopes of high mountains
Nyala	Dense shrubs to thickets; riverine vegetation; forests and flood plains

SPECIES	HABITAT PREFERENCE
Oribi	Open areas with slopes; flood plains, *vleis*, short grassland, and scattered patches of tall grassland
Pangolin	Woodland and open sandy ground
Porcupine	Very adaptable; all types of habitat
Reedbuck common	Tall grasslands or reeds
Rhebok: gray	Stony hills; high mountain slopes and plateaus with shrub and grass cover
Rhino black	Open to dense savannas
Rhino white	Flat savannas with short grasslands
Roan	Open savannas; medium to tall grasslands, *vleis*, and scattered low shrubs
Sable	Open savannas with scattered low shrubs bordering *vleis*; medium to tall sweet grasslands
Serval	Well-watered broken country with long grass *vleis*, reedbeds, or thick underbrush; will move into open country when hunting
Sitatunga	Semiaquatic, dense papyrus
Springbok	Arid, open, and short grasslands; Karoo veld
Steenbok	Open savannas and grasslands with scattered tall grass clumps and low shrubs
Tsessebe	Grasses, shade and water in areas with few stones
Warthog	Open savannas, grassland, *vleis*, and flood plains with short grass
Waterbuck	Open savannas, *vleis*, flood plains, and grasslands
Wild dog	Open savanna, woodland, and grassland savanna
Wildebeest black	Open plains, particularly high veld grasslands
Wildebeest blue	Open savannas with trees and shrubs; shade
Zebra: Burchell	Tree, bush, and grassland savanna
Zebra: Cape Mountain	Coastal plains, *fynbos*

Grouping Behaviour

Antelope and Bovids

Solitary and Territorial

Both sexes become territorial as adults. Young of both sexes disperse as subadults, face equal risks, and survive in approximately equal numbers, giving rise to an equal adult-sex ratio. Examples are dik-dik, klipspringer, duiker, and other dwarf antelopes.

Sociable Territorial

Adult males are territorial. Females and young share the same home range and associate in female herds. Female offspring remain in the herd. Territorial males evict male offspring at adolescence. Dominant males are territorial. Higher male mortality leads to a higher female to male adult-sex ratio. Examples in this group include the impala, springbok, wildebeest, roan, sable, gemsbok, waterbuck, rhebok, and most other social antelope species.

Solitary and Nonterritorial

Home ranges overlap to a large extent but each adult has a small exclusive core area. The largest social unit is the female with her dependent calf. Example: only bushbuck.

Sociable and Nonterritorial

Females with a shared home range associate in herds. Males compete directly for mating opportunities. A dominance hierarchy is based on size and seniority. Subadult and adult males associate in loose bachelor herds, but mature males tend to become more solitary with age. Examples in this group include the kudu, nyala, eland, buffalo, and giraffe.

Hippo Family (Hippopotamidae)

In the water, hippos tolerate close contact. At night all except mothers and independent offspring disperse. The water component of the home range is partitioned into mating territories by dominant bulls who will tolerate the presence of young adult or subadult males as long as they do not become competition. If this occurs they will be evicted and will form small bachelor herds or live alone in marginal habitat. Cows and calves associate in nurseries which guard young against crocodiles and intruding bulls. There does not appear to be an association between cows but cows and calves remain together until the calves are almost fully grown.

Pig Family (Suiformes suidae)

The basic unit is a sow with a litter of piglets. Two different grouping and mating systems exist. The first is a male harem system. One or more females and their offspring are led and guarded by a dominant boar. Immature and unsuccessful adult males live alone or in small bachelor herds. The bushpig is an example of this type. The second type of system is a segregated society. Sounders contain one or more females and the young. Males are solitary or associate in small bachelor groups. Warthogs live in a segregated society.

Rhino Family (Rhinocerotidae)

The white rhino is semisocial. Males are territorial but quite tolerant of other bulls. The black rhino is generally considered territorial but might form small groups under certain circumstances. It would appear that rhinos tend to be solitary and territorial at low densities* in closed habitats and may be more sociable at high densities in open habitats. *(Density is the number of animals occupying a given area.)

Zebra (Equidae)

All equids are sociable; they are nomadic or migratory. Two systems occur: In the territorial system, the males compete for land. The dominant male is tolerant of other males in its territory. Females and bachelors form mixed herds between territories and during migrations. The Grevy zebra is an example of this type. In a harem or family system, the males compete for females. Males in this system are very possessive and protective over females and offspring. Herds of zebra are composed of distinct family units and bachelor herds. Burchell and mountain zebra represent this second type of system.

Zebra communicate primarily by sight, then by scent, and lastly by sound, although all three are important. Facial expressions and body posture are equally important.

Hyrax (Hyracoidea)

Adult males are territorial. Colonies are composed of a harem of several related females and their offspring under the watchful eye of a dominant male.

Elephant (Proboscidae)

Social and Mating System

An elephant will be part of a matriarchal clan society; the basic units consist of a mother with her dependent offspring and grown daughters with their offspring. Males live separately, alone, or in bachelor herds. Being nonterritorial, mating success depends on the size and fighting ability of the male. Large bulls, therefore, are the most successful breeders.

Cow Herds

When the herds get too big, they will split but stay in proximity; these are referred to as bond groups. They communicate through infrasound. Different bond groups may share a home range and belong to the same clan. The home range can vary greatly in size depending on resource availability. The matriarch is responsible for the herd's well-being; it is she who determines direction, walking pace, rest times, and so on. When in danger, the herd will cluster around the matriarch for protection; they will place the calves in the middle. Should the matriarch be killed or mortally injured, the herd will mill about her and attempt to help. As she grows old or weak, she will be replaced by the next largest cow.

Bull Elephants

Males leave a breeding herd at twelve years or older, depending on the onset of adolescent behaviour and the intolerance of the cows with young calves. These males will then wander alone or will join with other bulls to form bachelor herds. As bulls grow older, they wander less and become more sedentary. They will often have one or two young bulls, sometimes referred to as askaris, for company.

Elephants feed for about sixteen hours a day and rest for the remainder. They will drink and bathe daily if water is available. Bulls drink approximately two hundred liters of water a day.

Primates

Prosimians (Bushbabies)

The basic unit consists of a mother with offspring of assorted ages. These primates occupy a permanent home range/territory. Males disperse in adolescence; the fittest ones have territories through the ranges of several female groups. Related females and young sleep together in day nests and are sometimes joined by the resident male, but adults all forage independently. Territorial males may tolerate subordinate adult males in their territories, whereas ranges of rival males overlap only slightly.

Monkeys, Apes (Vervets, Samangoes, Baboon)

➤ Vervets
  〉 The basic unit is a family group of females and young that share and jointly defend a traditional home range. A number of attached males jointly defend the females and their land against males from other territories, while also competing with one another for social and reproductive dominance. There is a rank order of families within the troop.

➤ Samango monkeys
  〉 A troop of related females occupy a permanent home range or territory with a resident dominant male.

➤ Baboons
  〉 A baboon troop is one of the most complex, subtle societies in the animal kingdom. Social relations are influenced by gender, by standing in the dominance hierarchy, by male/male and female/female alliances, and by emigration and immigration. This complex society is all made possible by a highly developed communication system. Internally, baboon troops consist of males and females all competing for status; externally, troops compete with other troops for resources. In either situation, baboons must protect themselves from predators. Different troops avoid one another unless competing for a scarce resource.

A family group of females and offspring is the core of a baboon troop. Females spend their entire lives in the natal troop and home range unless the troop grows too large or if it outgrows its resources. Should that happen, the troop will subdivide. The female rank order is family based, strict, and stable. Daughters inherit their mother's rank.

Aardvark and Pangolin

These are usually found singly; they come together only to mate.

CARNIVORES

Table 3.5 gives the social groupings of some carnivores.

SPECIES	SOCIAL GROUPING
Aardvark	Singly
Aardwolf	Pairs
Caracal	Singly or in pairs
Cheetah	Singly, pairs, and family groups
Civet	Solitary or in pairs
Honey badger	Male and female live as permanently mated pair
Hyena: brown	Single, pairs, or pair with young
Hyena: spotted	Family groups (clans); sizable clans separate rank orders; females dominate; alpha males sire most offspring
Jackal	Pair with young of year and yearling offspring
Leopard	Singly or in pairs; male and female associate only while mating; both sexes territorial; male territory includes two or more female territories
Lion	Singly, bachelor groups, or prides (4–25)
Mongoose: slender	Singly or in pairs; male and female associate only while mating; both sexes territorial; male territory includes two or more female territories
Mongoose: banded	Family groups of up to 30
Mongoose: dwarf	Dominant pair monopolizes reproduction; family groups
Serval	Singly or in pairs; male and female associate only while mating; both sexes territorial; male territory includes two or more female territories
Wild dog	Family groups; dominant pair monopolizes breeding

Figure CCCH.03.05.01: A pair of mating elephants.

Breeding Behaviour

Breeding Seasons

Some animals are seasonal breeders and others breed year-round. Table 3.6 gives a summary of breeding times for some African game species. Antelopes sometimes become reckless during the breeding season in that they are so busy with mating and courting that they tend to become less vigilant for danger. Species like lions, elephants, and leopards can become very aggressive during mating and should be avoided if possible. See Figure CCCH.03.05.01. Having knowledge of breeding characteristics can assist the tracker in knowing when young will arrive. Correctly interpreting breeding behaviour will give the tracker an understanding of which species become dangerous when breeding; thus, he'll know which ones to avoid.

UNDERSTANDING WILDLIFE BEHAVIOUR

Table 3.6

SPECIES	BREEDING SEASON	GESTATION (DAYS)	LAMBING SEASON	PEAK
Blesbok	March–May	210–240	Nov–Jan	Nov–Dec
Bontebok	Jan–Apr	235–254	Aug–Nov	Sept–Oct
Buffalo	March–May	330–346	Oct–Apr	Jan–Feb
Bushbuck	Year round	180–200	Year round	Oct–Nov
Bushpig	Year round	110–120	Oct–Feb	–
Cheetah	Year round	90–95	Year round	–
Duiker	Year round	195	Year round	Sept–Oct
Eland	Year round	271–279	Year round	Aug–Nov
Elephant	Nov–Apr	660	Sept–May	Jan–March
Gemsbok	Year round	261–275	Year round	Aug–Sept
Giraffe	Year round	450–457	Year round	March–July
Grysbok, Cape	Year round	191–210	Year round	Apr–May
Grysbok, Sharpe	Year round	191–210	Year round	Sept–Nov
Hartebeest, red	Feb–Apr	240	Sept–Feb	Sept–Feb
Hippopotamus	Year round	225–257	Year round	Oct–March
Hyena, spotted	Year round	110	Year round	–
Impala	Apr–June	194–200	Oct–Jan	Dec–Jan
Klipspringer	Year round	210–215	Year round	Dec–Jan
Kudu	June–July	260–280	Dec–May	Jan–Feb
Leopard	Year round	100	Year round	–
Lion	Year round	110	Year round	–
Nyala	Year round	220–230	Year round	Aug–Dec
Oribi	May–June	200–210	Nov–Jan	Oct–Dec
Reedbuck, common	Year round	225–240	Year round	Dec–May
Reedbuck, mountain	Year round	236–251	Year round	Oct–Dec
Rhebok, gray	Year round	241–261	Year round	Nov–Jan
Rhino, black	Year round	450	Year round	June–July
Rhino, white	Year round	480	Year round	March–Apr
Roan	Year round	279–290	Year round	–
Sable	May–July	224–240	Jan–March	Feb–Apr
Springbok	Year round	165–180	Year round	Aug–Jan
Steenbok	Year round	160–180	Year round	Oct–March
Tsessebe	Jan–Apr	235–245	Sept–Dec	Oct–Nov
Warthog	May–July	160–175	Oct–Dec	Nov–Dec
Waterbuck	Year round	270–280	Year round	Feb–March
Wildebeest, black	March–Apr	250–260	Nov–Jan	Nov–Jan
Wildebeest, blue	March–May	250–260	Nov–Jan	Nov–Jan
Zebra, Burchell	Year round	360–390	Year round	Oct–March
Zebra, Cape	Year round	364–365	Year round	Nov–March

Care of Young

Parental care refers to the attention given to, the providing for, and the rearing and protecting of the young. In many species parental care involves a close relationship between the adult mother and the young, with the adult father playing an insignificant or no role after mating with the female. This is the case with most antelope species and leopards. In other species the young are well cared for and protected by all members of the group. This is especially true of the primates. In other social animals, the adult males well help, to a lesser or greater extent, to defend the young from aggressors as is the case with the buffalo and zebra, for example. Elephants are especially devoted to the care of their young.

Parental behaviour can manifest itself in a number of ways, including providing food for the young, grooming, defending, teaching them to hunt, providing physical contact, and discipline. In herd animals, the young often congregate into nurseries that are looked after by a few adult females (for example, impala) or are entrusted to the care of subadult or subordinate individuals (e.g., baboon).

Typical infantile behaviour is sometimes observed in the young with tantrums (hyena and baboon), begging, and play. Some animals are highly protective of their young and will become very aggressive if they are threatened. The species that deserve mention are elephants, hippos, leopards, lions, buffaloes, and baboons. The tracker should exercise caution when approaching these species when there are young animals present.

Aggressive Behaviour

Aggression is shown either to assert dominance, to protect a territory, to guard a food source, or to defend itself when it feels threatened. For a field guide operating on foot, any sort of aggressive behaviour should be identified during its early stages so that the guide can take appropriate action to avoid or defuse a potentially dangerous situation. Sometimes aggression is preceded by subtle changes in behaviour that should be recognized in time. A good example of this is when an elephant that has been contentedly feeding suddenly "freezes" and becomes very attentive when its suspicion is aroused. Aggression can take a number of forms:

Dominance Displays

These are assertions of superiority without an immediate threat of attack. These are intended to intimidate and occur in all sociable species. Dominance may be displayed by erect posture, a broadside stance, a confrontational head-to-head posture (more threatening than side on), a supplanting and displacing walk toward a subordinate (universal), or a slow, stiff approach that includes high stepping and prancing. See Figure CCCH.03.07.01.

Offensive Threat Displays

These are actions that demonstrate the intent and readiness to attack. It is important that the tracker be able to recognize these instantly, especially in the more dangerous species such as elephant, rhino, leopard, lion, buffalo, and hippo. Behaviour that demonstrates readiness to attack can include the following (appropriate to the species): kneeling position (two combatants facing off); medial, low, high, or angled horn threat; staring, sideswiping, or a feinting attack; rushing, charging, or chasing; marching in pursuit; and cavorting.

Zebras will kick from the rear and bear their teeth. In carnivores, offensive threat displays include growling, snarling, baring of teeth, and a fixed stare. The eyes will be wide, the ears pricked or flattened, the position of the body flattened (usually just prior to charging), and the tail erect or lashing from side to side.

Elephants will adopt an erect posture, shake their heads, slap their ears against the side of their heads, trumpet, and carry out a warning charge with ears fanned out. If it's a serious charge, the ears will be flat against the head and the trunk will be tucked up under the chest.

Buffaloes will approach with their head up and their nose in the air; their posture will be alert and their tails arched. Hippos open their mouths wide and roar. Black rhinos will utter puffing shrieks, approach with their heads up, tails curled, upper lips raised, and ears flat. White rhinos will utter gruff squeals or snorts, their heads will go up and then down, they will swing their heads from side to side, and their tails will be raised.

Defensive Threat Display

These are acts associated with self-defense and are carried out in response to aggressive threats. These can be observed as head low postures (antelope, buffalo, and rhino), symbolic biting, pushing with snout, and neck winding (bushbuck, nyala), low body posture, or rolling onto back (carnivores).

Submissive Behaviour

A behaviour elicited in response to dominance, threats, or sexual harassment functions to appease the aggressor. If submissive behaviour fails, an attack or some form of discipline or punishment is likely to follow. Submissive behaviour can be demonstrated in many ways.

Displacement Behaviour

This involves the acting out of everyday maintenance activities in tense situations; these are generally performed to defuse potential conflict. Displacement behaviour can also be neutral. It occurs universally and can take the following forms:

➤ **Displacement Grooming**
  › Usually carried out to placate or curry favour with the more dominant individual. The type of grooming will be characteristic of the particular species.

➤ **Displacement Grazing**
  › This can be a neutral type of behaviour with two individuals showing mutual consent or tolerance, i.e., no aggressive or confrontational tendencies and where neither is threatening nor submissive.

Figure CCCH.03.07.01: A dominant nyala bull displays in front of a rival.

➤ **Fly shooing or Sideswiping**
  › The same movement to chase away flies or other bothersome insects is also used as an aggressive display. The head is swung abruptly toward the shoulder or flank. This is often seen in sables, roans, and elands.

➤ **Displacement Alarm**
  › This is alarm given in the absence of danger in an effort to divert attention of a potential aggressor away from a subordinate individual.

Social Behaviour

Sociable behaviour can be defined as any act that tends to improve or enhance individual bonding. It can take the following forms:

➤ **Meeting and Greeting**
  › This is a fairly universal form of behaviour and involves friendly social interaction beginning with nasal contact and sniffing; this also serves as a means of identification.

➤ **Social Grooming**
  › This behaviour occurs when two animals take turns to groom one another (uncommon in antelope but common in primates). It can take

the form of scraping the other animal with its lower incisors, licking, nibbling, or rubbing the preorbital glands on the partner.

Self-Advertising Behaviour and Territoriality

Self-advertising behaviour is any action that calls attention to the presence, social status, and/or mood of the individual. These actions are distinct from, but often combined with, aggression and mating. This behaviour usually takes place to elevate or maintain social standing or breeding dominance and is usually directed toward animals of their own species. This type of behaviour can be demonstrated by:

➤ Standing or lying in a conspicuous location (e.g., wildebeest bull on a mound); this is typically off to one side and apart from the herd.

➤ Body posture or actions include scuff marking on the ground, herding and chasing, cavorting, head nodding, kneeling, neck rubbing, stotting, tail flourishing, and so on.

➤ Vocalizing includes roaring, growling, snorting, and grunting.

➤ Stamping.

➤ Scent marking can involve marking an area with urine, feces (middens), or other body secretions from special glands; it can involve thrashing vegetation with horns to indicate an aggressive mood that is not necessarily directed toward any specific individual (antelope) or rolling in smelly substances. Animals will daub or rub their glandular secretions on objects, ground, self, or other individuals in the group/clan. Defecating or urinating on middens is often emphasized by pawing and doubles as a visual display and is made conspicuous by posture and/or associated actions. Territorial males along boundaries and at spots regularly frequented perform this action.

➤ Self-adornment is a rather comical form of self-advertising in which the individual coats its horns, face, and shoulders with mud or vegetation. The latter is usually picked up whilst thrashing vegetation. (This is a type of behaviour seen most commonly in antelopes such as kudus, wildebeests, and elands.)

Predator and Danger Avoidance

This behavioural response occurs when an animal feels threatened by what it perceives to be a potential predator or something out of the ordinary. The type of responses will depend on the animal's perception of the threat level; they might range from curiosity (trying to determine what the threat is) to flight and even attack. It is important for the tracker to be able to read this type of behaviour as it can warn of the presence of predators or other humans in the vicinity. It must also be well understood that an animal's first choice when threatened is to run away. If an obvious escape route is available, it will usually take this course of action. If it feels hemmed in, however, or you are standing in the way of its escape route (e.g., a hippo path leading back to water), it can then quite easily go into attack mode. Responses to predators or dangers elicit the following behaviour patterns:

➤ Alert posture and intent staring at the source of disturbance (universal).

➤ Strutting, style trotting, bounding, running, stampeding.

➤ Lying down flat. This occurs especially with young animals that will flatten themselves in cover.

➤ Standing dead still ("freezing").

➤ Using defense systems. For example, a porcupine will erect its quills, polecats will spray foul-smelling substances, etc.

➤ Skulking (hiding in dense cover).

➤ Forming a defense perimeter. Good examples of this are buffaloes and elephants that shield their young when danger threatens. Rhinos will form a star defense pattern with their rumps close together and their horns facing outward.

➤ Mobbing. Baboons will collectively mob an intruder or predator that threatens the troop. This sort of behaviour can be very intimidating even to the boldest of predators.

➤ Vocalizing. Giving vocal warning is almost universal. Some primates, such as vervets for example, have specific warning calls for different types of danger.

➤ Stamping (antelope).

➤ Escaping into or submerging beneath water. A response found in hippos, crocodiles, leguans, otters, and water-associated antelopes.

➤ Kicking. A defense mechanism used by equids (zebras) and giraffes.

➤ Responding to warnings by birds or other animals.

➤ Charging or attacking when provocation exceeds a certain threshold.

Play Behaviour

This type of behaviour varies with the group. Play is sometimes just for fun, but it mostly serves the purpose of helping to establish a pecking order of hierarchy within the group. During play, the stronger and more assertive individuals become recognized amongst their peers, and in this way begin to establish themselves as dominant individuals. In contrast to this, the weaker and more timid individuals are ranked on a lower order of the system. In predators, play serves the very important role of not only helping to establish hierarchy but it is also the mechanism whereby the young are taught such hunting skills as stalking, pouncing, and other effective techniques.

Danger Signals

Because a tracker might be called upon to track dangerous game or work in areas where dangerous animals occur, it is important to be able to identify signs of aggression in different species. See table below.

BUFFALO

- Tall erect posture
- Tossing the head
- Nose held high—animal peering down its nose at you
- Snorting and/or pawing the ground
- Approaching at a walk—staring
- ⭐ Approaching at a trot or run—head held up, staring at you
- ⭐ Full-on charge

ELEPHANT

- Trunk held aloft—sniffing the air
- Erect "tall" posture
- Staring
- Ears fanned out
- Trumpeting or making a noise
- Throwing objects or kicking up dust
- Approaching at a fast walk
- ⭐ Running toward you; ears folded back; trunk tucked up under body; silent.
- ⭐ Full-on charge

HIPPO

- Silent, fixed stare
- Gaping—opening mouth wide
- Swimming closer—submerged or partially visible
- Lunging rush in water, snorting
- ⭐ Exiting water toward you
- ⭐ Trotting closer when on land
- ⭐ Full-on charge—running toward you, mouth gaping

LEOPARD

- Leopards mating
- Finding or hearing young cubs
- Fixed stare—not running off
- Flattening itself—tail flashing
- Ears flattening—snarling and growling
- ⭐ Full-on charge—low to the ground

  If you are confronted by an aggressive leopard—back off slowly, and as far as possible, *avoid* direct eye contact.

LION

- Signs of young
- Lions mating
- Tall erect posture; approaching at a trot
- ⭐ Crouching, snarling, growling, tail flashing
- ⭐ Body held low; rushing in snarling; full-on charge

RHINO

- Mother with young—especially white rhino
- Staring at you; ear pricked; head held high
- Snorting and pawing the ground
- Approaching at a trot with gaze fixed on you
- ⭐ Approaching at a run
- ⭐ Full-on charge

- USE CAUTION
- DANGER
- ⭐ EXTREME DANGER

CHAPTER 4

IDENTIFICATION OF MAMMAL TRACKS AND SIGN

Identification of Mammal Tracks

In this section we will learn how to identify and interpret tracks and other mammal signs. By tracks we mean the marks left on the ground by an animal's hoofs, paws, or feet.

Track Identification

How can you identify a track as belonging to a specific species? Identifying a track requires some prior knowledge of anatomical characteristics. This can be acquired from any good zoology textbook. First, examine the track carefully. Second, a sound knowledge of an animal's habitat and food preferences and social groupings will provide additional clues. Third, knowing something about peak times of activity will further help to narrow down the possibilities. Fourth, you should be acquainted with the species of animals that occur in the area. Fifth, look at the track for details. Sixth, look for supporting evidence to confirm your hypothesis.

Remember that the detail of the track will depend on the surface (substrate), the speed at which the animal was moving, and the age of the track. Often only a partial track will show up because it has been eroded by wind, been scuffed by a passing animal, or the substrate did not lend itself to recording the total print.

Being able to identify an animal from a partial print separates the expert tracker from the novice. This ability is usually based on the functional characteristics of the spoor. The following steps will help you to identify a track:

➤ Try to find the clearest track and take the substrate into account as this can influence track details.

➤ Determine the group to which the track belongs. Is it a bird, an animal with a hoof, a paw, or a foot?

➤ Is the animal on its own or in a group?

➤ Look at the details of the track. How many toes are there? Are there claws? Is the hoof cloven or not? Are dewclaws present?

➤ What species of this group is likely to occur in the habitat in which the track is found?

➤ Measure the length and width of the track as well as stride length and straddle width.

➤ Is there some preferential food source or cover to which the species would be attracted?

➤ Is there some indication of when the tracks were made?

➤ Is there some other sign that would lend support to what you think made the track? Look for signs like territorial marking, droppings (scat), feeding, etc.

Measurement of Tracks

It is important to standardize how to record track information. The length and breadth of the track as well as the stride length and straddle width are measured as follows:

➤ Track length is the distance from the extremity of the leading edge to the extremity of the trailing edge of the track from front to back.

➤ Track width is the distance between the two extreme edges of the track from side to side.

➤ Stride length is the distance measured (at trailing edge of one foot) from one step to the next (of the same foot).

➤ Straddle width is the distance between a line joining the inside edges of the feet on the same side and the opposite side.

These measurements can be recorded on a tracking stick or in a notebook. See Figure CCCH.04.01.01.

Mammals

Feet have functional adaptations specific for locomotion; they can also be used as weapons (e.g., a leopard's claws) or tools (e.g., the heavy claws of an aardvark used for digging). The tracks of animals that rely on speed will have a small contact patch with the ground. The paws of predators have soft pads that enable them to stalk quietly. The feet of predators, depending on the species, are equipped with either sharp claws to grab

Figure CCCH.04.01.01: Measuring tracks.

and hold prey (e.g., lions, genets, caracals), or with blunt claws for traction (e.g., hyenas and cheetahs).

Feet may also be adapted to suit environmental conditions. For soft, muddy substrates, the feet must have a large contact area to prevent the animal from sinking into the mud (e.g., lechwe and sitatunga antelope). For aquatic habitats, feet are sometimes adapted by having webs between the toes to enable the animal to swim (e.g., spotted-necked otter and sitatunga). On soft, sandy soils, feet can be adapted either by having a large surface area (e.g., hippo and elephant), or by having sharp pointed hoofs that enable the hoof to dig deep into the soil to obtain a good purchase. On hard or rocky surfaces, small hoofs can find small indentations for swift and agile movement (e.g., klipspringer).

IDENTIFICATION OF MAMMAL TRACKS AND SIGN

Animals adapted to an arboreal environment are equipped with either sharp claws to dig into bark (e.g., tree squirrels, genets, leopards) or with opposable toes for gripping onto branches (e.g., vervets, baboons, and bushbabies). Heavier animals generally have larger feet to support their larger mass. The shape of the feet can, however, also be determined by the animal's body structure, with robust, sturdily built animals having broader feet and rounded toes and slender animals having narrow feet and narrow toes. A good example of this would be the comparison of a spotted hyena and a black-backed jackal. This same observation can be made in hoofed ungulates. A good example would be to compare the tracks of a giraffe to a kudu.

Differences in track characteristics can also sometimes be observed within a species. These variations make it possible for an experienced tracker to differentiate between sexes, ages, body masses, and sizes. With a few exceptions (e.g., spotted hyena and some of the smaller antelopes), the tracks of male animals are usually bigger than those of females. The forefeet are generally broader than the hind feet because most animals carry more mass in the forequarters. Association may also determine sex. In gregarious species such as impala, for example, the track of a solitary individual can be assumed to be an adult male. In animals with hoofs, younger animals have sharply defined hoofs whereas older individuals may have chipped and more rounded edges to the hoofs.

The depth of imprints on similar substrates can indicate the relative size (body mass) of individuals of the same species. The depth of imprint is also a function of the pressure exerted due to acceleration. A walking animal will leave a shallower imprint than one jumping or running. Apart from species characteristics, random differences may be found from individual to individual. In larger species such as rhino and elephant, track characteristics may be so unique that individual animals may be recognized. The shape of feet may also be altered by habitat. On hard, rocky substrates, the hoofs of ungulates may become chipped and blunted whereas in deep, sandy soils, hoofs may grow abnormally long. These observations can also apply to animals with claws.

The shape of the track will also depend on the type of substrate. On a very soft substrate, the hoofs of antelopes may splay and the track may appear larger than on firmer ground. On very hard ground, only the tips or edges of the hoofs may show. Tracks lose their definition in soft, loose sand and can be more difficult to identify. The dimensions of a track will also be dictated by the substrate, and the type of activity will also influence the shape of the track. The foot may slip and leave an elongated impression. Twisting or dragging can obliterate features of the track, and the speed of movement will influence its shape. Despite variations caused by the variables mentioned, the feet of animals leave very distinct imprints on suitable substrates.

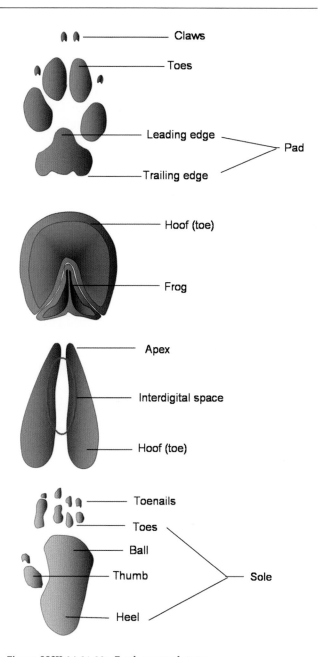

Figure CCCH.04.01.02: Track nomenclature.

Fore and hind feet may superimpose so that the toe of one foot may be confused with that of another. The condition of an animal may be determined from its tracks (e.g., shorter stride, wider straddle, stumbling, etc). Tracks will also indicate the gait of an animal (walking, running, stotting, etc.) and other activities, such as scent marking, fighting, digging for food, etc.

We will now deal with each group and give attention to specifics, especially where these are very different from the general shape of the group. Before doing this, let's first familiarize ourselves with the names of parts of a track so that we know what we are referring to. See Figure CCCH.04.01.02.

Paws with Claws

This is quite a large group and comprises species that have four or five toes with claws. See Figure CCCH.04.01.03. The size of the tracks can help to identify the species; groupings are shown in Table 4.1. Don't include claws in the measurement of length because these might vary according to substrate, be worn down by use, or grow abnormally long. Most species show only four toes in the track. There are a few that register five toes in the spoor.

Table 4.1: Species Registering Paws with Claws in the Track

LENGTH	SPECIES OF TRACK
15–20mm	Rats, mice, and dwarf mongooses
20–25mm	Slender mongooses, banded mongooses, and striped polecats
30–40mm	Cape foxes and bat-eared foxes
40–52mm	African civets and side-striped jackals
50–60mm	Black-backed jackals and aardwolfs
70–85mm	Wild dogs and cheetahs
86–96mm	Brown and spotted hyenas
50mm (front) 80mm (rear)	Porcupines
54mm (front) 82mm (rear)	Honey badgers

There are other distinguishing features that can help to narrow down which animal has left a particular spoor. The trailing or posterior edge of the main pad of the cheetah, mongoose, civet, aardwolf, and black-backed jackal has three lobes, whereas there are only two lobes on the hyena and side-striped jackal. The latter two are easily differentiated from each other on the basis of size.

Paws without Claws

This group includes the lion, leopard, serval, caracal, genets, and African wild cat. They all have the typical shape depicted in Figure CCCH.04.01.04: no claws visible, four toes visible front and rear, and three lobes on the trailing edge of the main pad. By virtue of size, the lion and leopard are easily identified. On the other hand, serval and caracal could be confused. Caracal tracks are rounder and slightly bigger. The smallest of this group is the genet, which are slightly smaller than the African wild cat. The size of the tracks can help to identify the species and can be grouped into size as shown in Table 4.2.

Table 4.2: Size of Tracks of Certain Species

LENGTH OF TRACK	SPECIES
30–40mm	African wildcats and genets
40–50mm	Servals
50–60mm	Caracals
85–95mm	Leopards
120–130mm	Lions

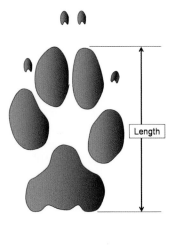

Figure CCCH.04.01.03: This typical track of a paw with claw shows where to measure the track's length. The example on the right is from a side-striped jackal.

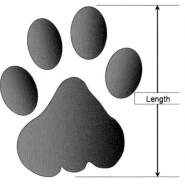

Figure CCCH.04.01.04: A typical track of a paw without claws shows where to measure the track's length. The track on the right is that of a leopard.

IDENTIFICATION OF MAMMAL TRACKS AND SIGN

Cloven Hoofs (Even Toes)

A typical example of a cloven hoof is illustrated in Figure CCCH.04.01.05. There will be variations according to size, locality, social groupings, etc. Animals with the typical even-toed, cloven-hoof shape include all the antelopes, bovids, and wild pigs. Those that differ from the typical are the warthogs, bushpigs, elands, giraffes, buffaloes, and klipspringers. The key areas to examine are the apex of the track, the outer margins of the track, and the interdigital space. These are shown in Figure CCCH.04.01.06. The size of the tracks can help identify the species; groupings according to size are shown in Table 4.5.

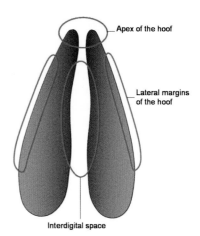

Figure CCCH.04.01.06: This shows the critical areas to examine in order to identify a cloven-hoof track.

Table 4.5: Species Registering Cloven Hoofs in the Track

LENGTH OF TRACK	SPECIES
Less than 35mm	Duiker, suni, grysbok
Less than 35mm oval shaped	Klipspringer
35–42mm	Oribi, steenbok
40–50mm	Gray rhebok, impala, warthog
50–60mm	Mountain reedbuck, reedbuck, bushbuck, nyala, springbok, and bushpig
60–70mm	Kudu, blesbok
80–90mm	Waterbuck, tsessebe
90–100mm	Red hartebeest, black wildebeest, blue wildebeest, eland
100–110mm	Gemsbok
110–120mm	Sable, roan, buffalo
180mm	Giraffe

Noncloven Hoofs

The only representatives of this group are the zebra, horse, and donkey. See Figure CCCH.04.01.07. Horse tracks are very similar in appearance to those of zebra; the difference is they have a more rounded appearance and are bigger. The frog* in the tracks of this group might not register on very hard substrate. Track lengths are shown in Table 4.4. (*The frog is the triangular shaped portion of the hoof–see figure below.)

Table 4.4: Species Registering Noncloven Hoofs

LENGTH OF TRACK	SPECIES
80–90mm	Burchell zebra
90–95mm	Donkey
100mm	Cape mountain zebra
100mm	Horse

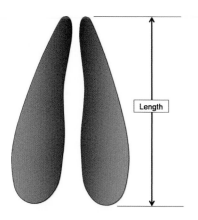

Figure CCCH.04.01.05: This typical cloven-hoof track shows where to measure the track's length. The example on the right is from an impala.

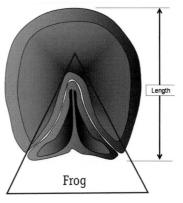

Figure CCCH.04.01.07: This typical noncloven hoof shows where to measure the track's length. The example on the right is from a zebra.

Three Toes Visible

Two species, the springhare and aardvark (antbear), are found in this group, and the tracks are so distinctive that it is unlikely to confuse the two. See Figure CCCH.04.01.08 and Table 4.5. The tracks of the springhare will show only the three toes when running but will include the elongated pad of the hind foot when sitting. The small, reduced forefeet do not leave a track. The antbear has four toes on the front foot and five on the rear, but only three toes show up in a track. The toes and claw impressions are big.

Table 4.5: Species Registering Three Toes in the Track

LENGTH OF TRACK	SPECIES
41–52mm (front) 100–105mm (rear)	Springhare
90–100mm (front) 90–100mm (rear)	Aardvark

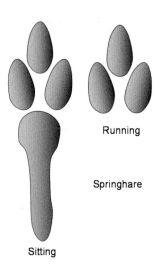

Running

Springhare

Sitting

Figure CCCH.04.01.08: This typical three-toe track is from a springhare.

Hands and Feet

The species found in this group include Cape clawless otter, vervet monkey, rock hyrax, bushbabies, and baboon. Figure CCCH.04.01.09 and Table 4.6. The features that distinguish the different species are as follows: Vervet monkeys and baboons both have five digits visible on hands and feet. The big toes stick out at an angle of 45 degrees. An adult baboon (80mm in front and 138mm in the rear) is significantly larger than that of the vervet monkey. Another difference between the two is the tail drag of the monkey. The baboon's tail does not reach to the ground whilst walking and will not reflect in the track.

Bushbabies also have five digits on their hands and feet, but the big toe sticks out at a right angle. The thumb is very pronounced. The track is also smaller than either that of the baboon or vervet. Rock hyraxes have four digits on the hand and three on each foot; the toes and fingers are short and stubby. The Cape clawless otter has five digits on both front and rear feet. The fingers are not webbed as in the case of spotted-necked otters.

Table 4.6: Species Registering Hands/Feet in the Track

LENGTH OF FRONT TRACK (mm)	LENGTH OF REAR TRACK (mm)	SPECIES
50	30	Bushbaby
60	75	Vervet
80	138	Baboon
105	110	Cape clawless otter
30	50	Hyrax

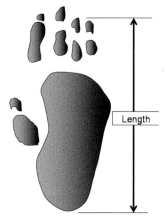

Length

Figure CCCH.04.01.09: The hands and feet show where to measure the track's length. The example on the right is from a baboon.

Other Big Animals

Animals whose tracks do not fall into the above categories are the hippo, elephant, and rhino. Their tracks are very distinctive and are not easily misidentified. Hippos have a four-toed track. Their tracks are often found on well-used paths that lead to or from water. An elephant's front foot is round, whereas the rear foot narrows toward the apex and can be used to determine the direction of travel. The pattern on the tracks of elephants and rhinos is very distinctive, much like the fingerprint of a human. Elephants have four toes on the front foot and three on the rear foot. White and black rhinos have three toes in their tracks. The track of the black rhino is slightly smaller than that of the white rhino; it also lacks the distinctive indentation on the posterior margin of the track. See Table 4.7 and Figures CCCH.04.01.10 through CCCH.04.01.12.

Table 4.7: Specifications for Hippo/Elephant/Rhino

LENGTH OF FRONT TRACK (mm)	LENGTH OF REAR TRACK (mm)	SPECIES
500	550	Elephant
230–250	230–250	Hippo
250	250	White rhino
200	200	Black rhino

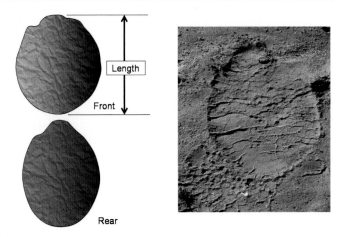

Figure CCCH.04.01.11: Elephant tracks.

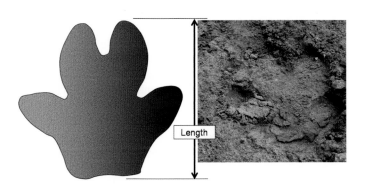

Figure CCCH.04.01.10: Hippo tracks.

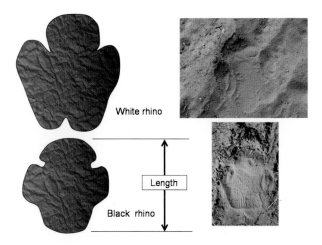

Figure CCCH.04.01.12: Tracks of white rhino (top) and black rhino (bottom).

Track Distortion

We can identify tracks through a process of elimination by asking ourselves eight questions:

➤ Question 1: What is the overall track configuration?

➤ Question 2: What is the size of the track?

➤ Question 3: What is the overall shape?

➤ Question 4: How many toes register in the track?

➤ Question 5: What is the shape of the heel pad?

➤ Question 6: Could this animal occur here, and is the habitat right?

➤ Question 7: Is the animal alone or in a group, and was the track made during the day or night?

➤ Question 8: Are there other signs that might confirm my identification?

In practice, not all tracking conditions are easy, and as you progress to more advanced levels, you will find that some conditions make it very difficult to follow a track, especially when signs are not clearly visible. Tracking under ideal conditions include good light, clear skies, and shadows cast by the sun. It's also ideal to be tracking in the early morning or late afternoon when signs show up best, when the weather is favourable, when there is a lot of sign, when the sign is clearly registered on good substrate, and when the wind is in your favour. And then there are the human variables that can help or hinder when tracking. Tracking is best when the hunters you are leading are cooperative and when you are fresh. It is also ideal when the animal you are tracking is unaware of the fact that it is being followed and when there is sufficient cover to conceal your approach.

With each change for the worse in one of the abovementioned conditions, tracking becomes progressively more difficult. You might have to track an animal toward the middle of the day when the sun is high in the sky and spoor visibility becomes less well defined. Perhaps rain has partially obliterated sign, or there is an impending storm with the possibility of high wind and rain. You might have a hunter client who is noisy and uncooperative. Sign might be scarce or registered on a substrate that does not record detail well. You might be tired, making it difficult to concentrate. As stated in the previous chapter, there are many variables that can add difficulty to tracking, definition of the spoor being one.

The ease of recognition of tracks depends on their clarity and their "completeness." A complete track shows all its component parts and is easier to identify on ideal substrate (slightly compacted, damp, fine sand), but becomes progressively harder to identify on more difficult substrate and when the track is distorted or obscured by superimposed signs. See Figures CCCH.04.02.01 and CCCH.04.02.02.

Let us concentrate for the moment on tracks or spoor. When an animal stands on the ground, its weight leaves an imprint of the underside (sole) of the foot, hoof, or paw on the underlying substrate. The substrate determines the amount of information that can be transferred. Ideal substrate is usually defined as fine river or beach sand that is lightly compacted and slightly damp. This captures and retains a lot of information. Other substrates will capture and retain far less information, good examples being coarse gravel or rock. On less than ideal substrate, only partial tracks may register.

Tracks may be distorted as they are being registered. There are a number of ways this can happen. An animal may slip, slide, come to a sudden stop, be fearful, indecisive, turn, or pivot as the track is being registered; this will leave a distorted impression of the spoor. As the speed of forward motion increases, the track detail will also change. Let us look at some track distortions and how they are caused. We will make use of an ideal tracking substrate and use the nomenclature as described by Brown in his excellent book *The Art and Science of Tracking* (Berkley Books, 1999). See Figures CCCH.04.02.03 to CCCH.04.02.21.

Changes in the speed of forward motion or slight changes in direction also cause track distortions. The three you should be aware of for now are shown in Figures CCCH.04.02.22 to CCCH.04.02.24.

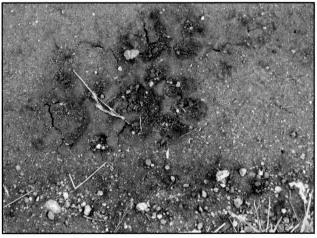

Figure CCCH.04.02.01: Past weather conditions (wind and rain) have removed a lot of information from this lion track and made it less visible.

Figure CCCH.04.02.02: Information loss caused by superimposition of tracks by other tracks. In this photograph an emerald spotted wood dove has walked across the track of a hyena (left), and the track of an impala has all but been obliterated by some other animal walking over. Only the tips of the hoofs are still clearly visible (right)

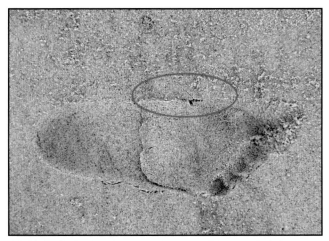

Figure CCCH.04.02.03: A crest. This is an inward or outward curving ridge that could have (but not always) a wavelike lip. These can be formed when the maker of the track turns sharply to one side.

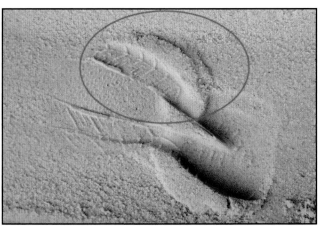

Figure CCCH.04.02.04: A mound. A prominent hill either inside or outside of the track is caused by twists and turns.

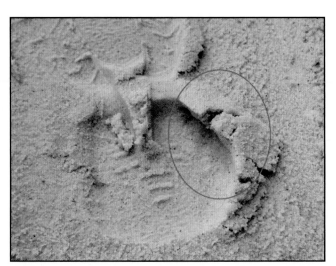

Figure CCCH.04.02.05: A cave. A large recess on the inside wall of a print indicates extreme inward and downward pressure. A cave can result from a sudden stop or leap to one side. In dry substrates with low adhesive qualities, a cave can be filled in so quickly on removal of pressure (cave-in) that a "cave" is often not observable.

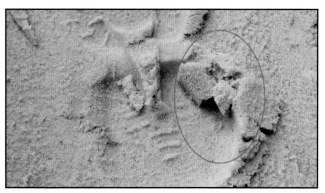

Figure CCCH.04.02.06: A cave-in is a pile of rubble left by the collapse of a cave, ridge, or crest after the supporting foot, hoof, or paw is removed. It can also be an indication of a violent impact such as a kick or a dramatic turn.

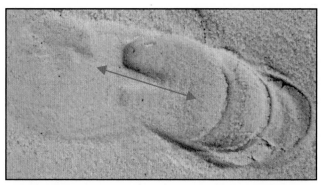

Figure CCCH.04.02.07: A stutter is the lengthening and deepening of the track caused by a rapid and repeated forward movement of the foot. It can indicate hesitation, loss of balance, or indecision.

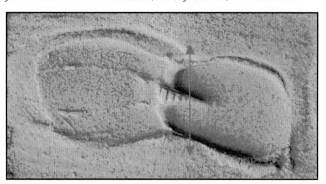

Figure CCCH.04.02.08: A wobble is a deepening and widening of the track caused by a repeated sideways movement of the foot. It can indicate excitement, fear, or extreme anxiety.

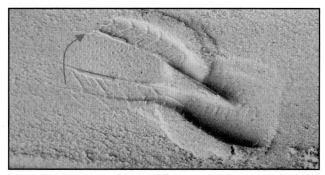

Figure CCCH.04.02.09: A twist indicates a rotation or twist between 0 degree and 45 degrees that leaves a smooth arc in the substrate.

Figure CCCH.04.02.10: A pivot indicates a turn between 45 degrees and 90 degrees, and is usually indicated by a smooth arc and a mound.

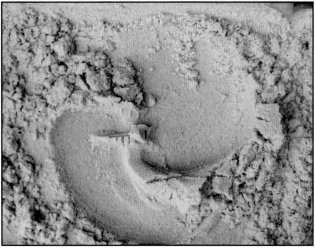

Figure CCCH.04.02.11: A spiral is a turn between 90 degrees and 360 degrees and is generally accompanied by considerable mounding, crevassing, and crumbling.

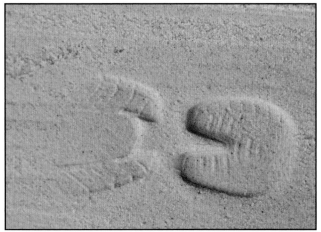

Figure CCCH.04.02.12: A pitch is a lengthwise angle of the track relative to the ground. An even pitch is horizontal. A forward pitch happens when the toe is deeper than the heel. A backward pitch occurs when the heel is deeper than the toe. A pitch shows the overall weight distribution when the track was registered.

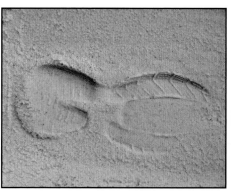

Figure CCCH.04.02.13: A roll is a lateral (side to side) angle of the track relative to the ground. If the track is level on the lateral plan, there is no roll. A right roll occurs when the track is inclined to the right. A left roll is a track inclined to the left. It can indicate anything from loss of balance, to a gentle turn, to a sideways fall.

Figure CCCH.04.02.14: An overhang is a cliff sloping more than 90 degrees inward. This very commonly occurs with sharp-pointed hoofs. It can indicate a sudden stop or when an animal has pushed off in the opposite direction. Overhangs collapse almost as soon as pressure is removed in dry substrates with low adhesive qualities; they are difficult to observe "after the fact."

Figure CCCH.04.02.15: A slope is an angle sloping off at less than 90 degrees. It usually occurs at the toe or heel and indicates where the foot went in and out. When on the side, it indicates a lean, sidestep, sharp turn, or someone who walks on the outside of the feet (likely bowlegged as opposed to knock-kneed). A slope is far less pronounced on some substrates.

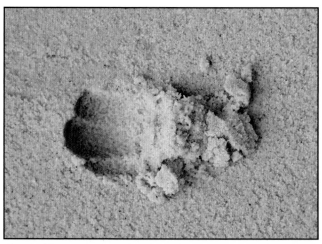

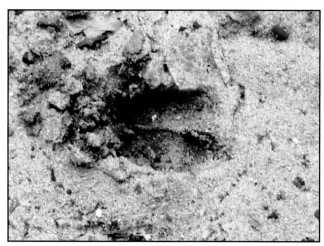

Figure CCCH.04.02.16: A shovel is soil scooped up and deposited in a pile just outside the track. It can indicate boredom or frustration if the animal is standing on the spot; it can indicate an animal digging or stumbling.

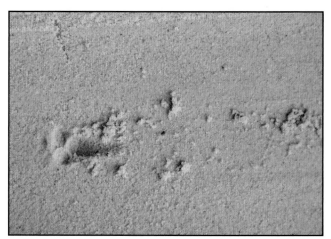

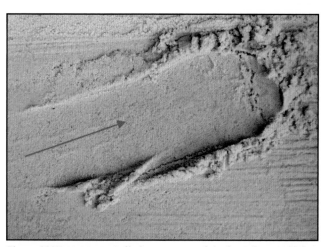

Figure CCCH.04.02.17: A plume is soil scattered in a line. If found beyond the track, it usually indicates a fast gait in the direction of the plume. If found behind the track, it indicates quick acceleration. If found in an arc around the track, it shows a sudden pivot or whirl.

Figure CCCH.04.02.19: A slip is a gouge mark in the soil caused by an unintentional skid. The claws that are usually retracted in certain animals might be evident in a slip. The next track either shows a fall or a recovery.

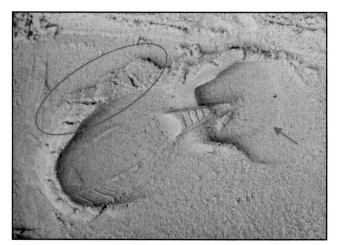

Figure CCCH.04.02.18: A slide is a gouge mark in the soil caused by an intentional skid. The claws that are usually retracted in certain animals might be evident in a slide. It is often accompanied by mounding.

Figure CCCH.04.02.20: A gouge is a drag mark at the front or back of the track; it can indicate fatigue, injury, high speed, foot protrusions, or heavy weight.

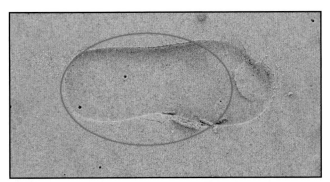

Figure CCCH.04.02.21: *A flat is the relatively featureless part of the track used as the baseline against which other features in the track are measured and compared. With the exception of a small disc in the toe area, most of this track is flat.*

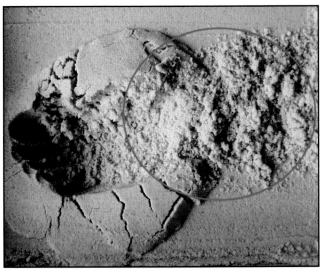

Figure CCCH.04.02.24: *An explosion is soil thrown out of the track by a sudden force. It can be caused by sudden acceleration, jumping away, a very sharp turn, or a slip.*

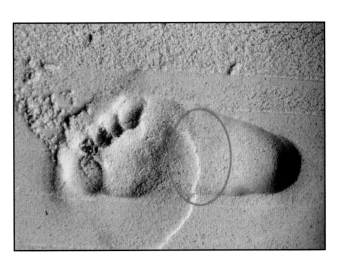

Figure CCCH.04.02.22: *A disc is a relatively large round or ovoid clump of soil that is fractured off a wave because of increased pressure and intensity. Indicates a fast "push off."*

You must remember that irrespective of what caused the track—a lion, human, buffalo, or whatever—the substrate reacts in the same way. That is why it is possible to learn from human tracks made in a "tracking box."

The competent tracker should be able to identify partial tracks or tracks that have been distorted. He should also be able to interpret the track and describe what the animal was doing when the track was registered. Some further examples are shown in Figures CCCH.04.02.25 to CCCH.04.02.32.

Figure CCCH.04.02.23: *A dish shows increased speed with greater pressure and intensity. A dish causes a disc-shaped plate to break off from a wave and locate in the latter half of the track. Discs and dishes are not always obvious in fine, dry substrates with low adhesive qualities.*

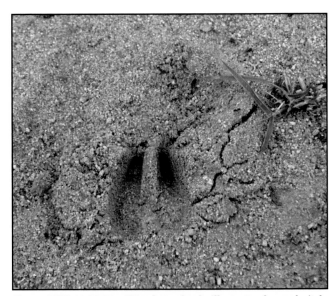

Figure CCCH.04.02.25: *This photo clearly illustrates forward pitch. The impala was standing, but the toes are deeper than the heel. This indicates that its weight is displaced forward and shows that the animal's head was down when the track was registered.*

Figure CCCH.04.02.28: *This shows an explosion, a sign that a warthog took sudden flight away from perceived danger.*

Figure CCCH.04.02.26: *A slip made by a kudu (top) and zebra (bottom). The correct shape of the track is often registered at the end of the slip.*

Figure CCCH.04.02.27: *A gouge in the track of a Natal francolin indicates a fast forward motion.*

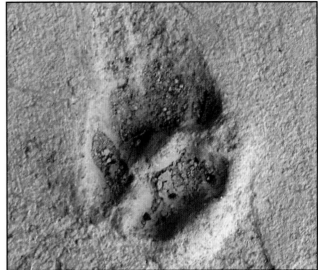

Figure CCCH.04.02.29: *Above is a normal genet track; a slip forward is on the bottom.*

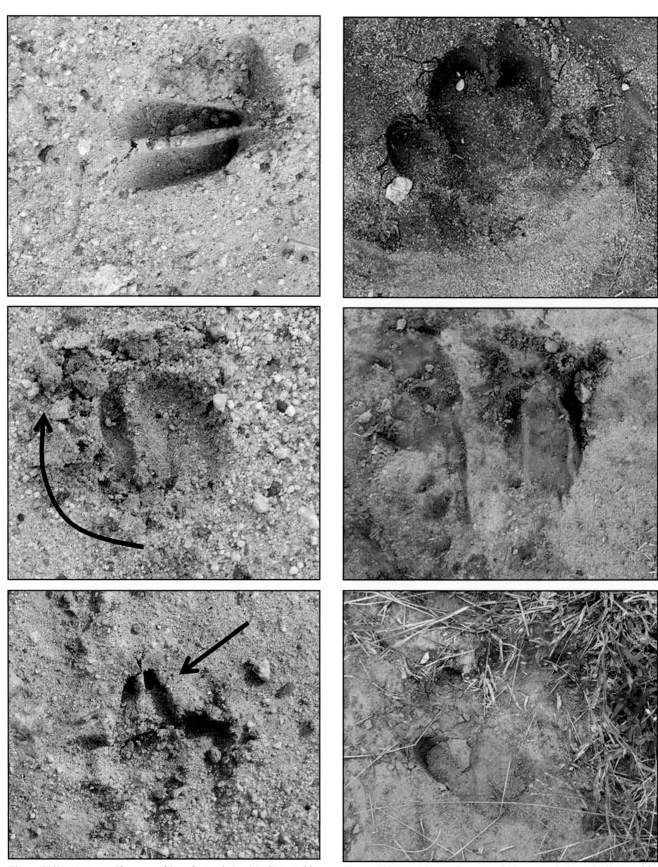

Figure CCCH.04.02.30: The normal impala track (top) is distorted by swiveling in the direction shown (centre); the partial track on the bottom shows only the apex of the track (black arrow).

Figure CCCH.04.02.31: The normal hippo track (top) is distorted by a slip (centre); the partial track shows only three toes (bottom) with a shoe track superimposed on it.

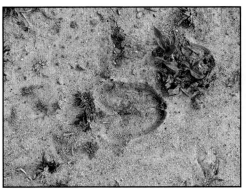
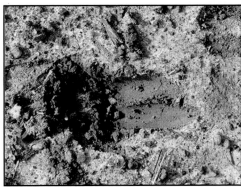
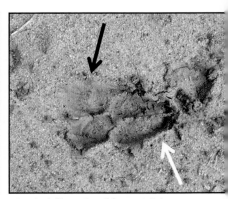

Figure CCCH.04.02.32: The normal wildebeest track above left is distorted by a slip (centre); there is a mechanical distortion (above right) where an impala track (white arrow) is superimposed on the wildebeest track (black arrow), leaving only a partial track.

We have classified mammal tracks into broad categories, and this helps us to identify them in the field if they are clear and not distorted. When tracks are poorly registered on unsuitable substrate or have been distorted in some way, correctly identifying and following them increases in difficulty. When that happens, we must pay closer attention to the track's detail. There are characteristics peculiar to each species that can assist the tracker in identifying them. These key features include physical dimensions, gait patterns, and defining shapes within the classified groups.

Partial or Distorted Track Identification

Some tracks are unique and are easy to identify even when distorted or only partially visible. An elephant or hippo track is a good example. See Figure CCCH.04.03.01. The tracks of a rhino are the only ones that could possibly be confused with those of a hippo. The difference is that rhinos have three toes and hippos four.

In a partial or distorted hippo track, it is relatively easy to differentiate it from a rhino track. A bisecting line drawn from the base will pass between the toes in the track of a hippo but through the middle toe in the track of a rhino. See Figure CCCH.04.03.02. Because of its large size, shape, and peculiar tread pattern, an elephant's track even when only partially registered or distorted is difficult to confuse with any other track. See Figure CCCH.04.03.03.

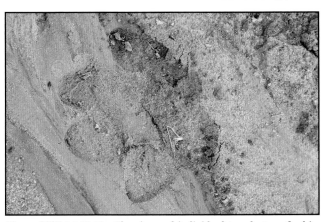

Figure CCCH.04.03.01: The size and individual toe shapes of a hippo (left) make the tracks easy to identify, even if they are distorted like those shown on the right.

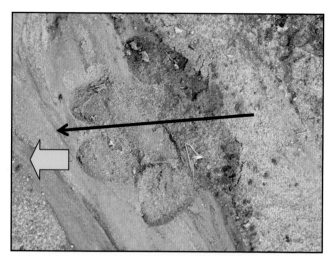

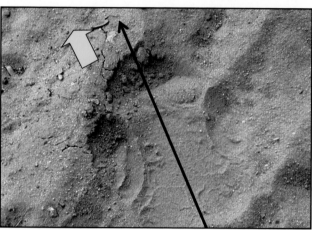

Figure CCCH.04.03.02: It is easy to differentiate, even in partial or distorted tracks, between rhino and hippo tracks once a line is drawn through the centre of the toes in the track.

Paws registering claws, and paws not registering claws can be more difficult to identify when deformed or only partially registered. There are, however, finer details that can help the tracker to identify partial or deformed tracks. The three areas of interest are the claws (presence or absence of them), the anterior margin of the pad (one or two lobes), and the posterior margin of the pad (two or three lobes). See Figure CCCH.04.03.04.

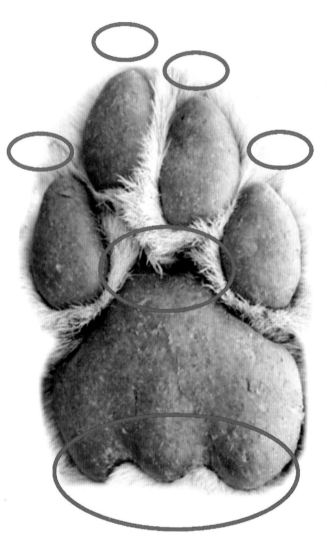

Figure CCCH.04.03.04: In partial or deformed tracks, the three areas indicated above can supply the information we need to make a correct identification.

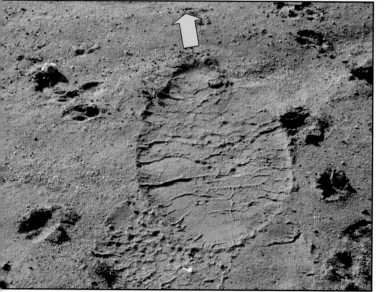

Figure CCCH.04.03.03: The size, shape, and tread pattern make it difficult to mistake an elephant track for anything else.

The posterior margin of the footpad makes it possible to separate certain species from each other. Some species register two lobes in the posterior margin of the footpad and others three. See Table 4.8 and Figure CCCH.04.03.05.

Table 4.8

SPECIES WITH THREE CLEARLY DISTINGUISHABLE LOBES ON THE POSTERIOR MARGIN OF THE FOOT PAD	SPECIES WITH TWO CLEARLY DISTINGUISHABLE LOBES ON THE POSTERIOR MARGIN OF THE FOOT PAD
Mongoose species, bat-eared fox, African wild cat, genet, serval, caracal, black-backed jackal, aardwolf, civet, leopard, lion	Brown hyena, spotted hyena, wild dog

Species showing three lobes can again be grouped into two categories—those registering claws in the tracks and those not registering claws in the tracks. See Table 4.9 and Figure CCCH.04.03.06.

Table 4.9

THREE LOBES IN POSTERIOR MARGIN; REGISTERING CLAWS IN TRACKS	THREE LOBES IN POSTERIOR MARGIN; NOT REGISTERING CLAWS IN TRACKS
Mongoose species, bat-eared fox, black-backed jackal, aardwolf, wild dog, cheetah	African wild cat, serval, genet, caracal, leopard, lion

When we look at the anterior margin of the pad, we see that some species have a single lobe and some a double lobe. See Table 4.10 and Figure CCCH.04.03.07.

Table 4.10

ONE LOBE ANTERIOR IN MARGIN; REGISTERING CLAWS IN TRACKS	ONE LOBE ANTERIOR IN MARGIN; NOT REGISTERING CLAWS IN TRACKS
Bat-eared fox, black-backed jackal, aardwolf, spotted and brown hyena, wild dog	Lion (sometimes)
TWO LOBES ANTERIOR IN MARGIN; REGISTERING CLAWS IN TRACKS	**TWO LOBES ANTERIOR IN MARGIN; NOT REGISTERING CLAWS IN TRACKS**
Mongoose species, striped polecat, civet, cheetah	Leopard, caracal, serval, African wild cat, genet, lion (sometimes)

Figure CCCH.04.03.05: The lion (top and centre) registers three lobes on the posterior margin; the spotted hyena (bottom) registers two lobes.

Figure CCCH.04.03.06: On the left a leopard track shows the two lobed anterior margin and the three lobed posterior margin of the pad. The track on the right is partially erased in the toe area. We cannot see claw marks, but when we look at the anterior margin (one lobe) and the posterior margin (two lobes) we know that the only animal that fits this description together with its length of 95mm is a spotted hyena.

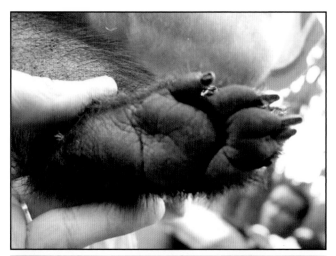

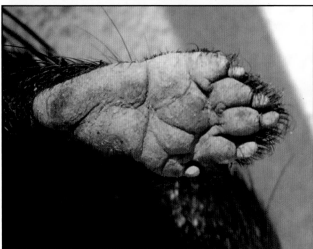
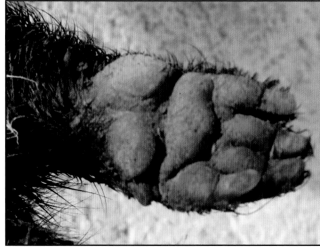

Figure CCCH.04.03.07: The track of the porcupine's rear foot (top left and bottom left) has three intermediate and two proximal pads. The front foot of a porcupine is shown on the bottom right. The track of the honey badger (top right) has a fused intermediate pad and a single proximal pad. Porcupine quills also leave scratch marks on the ground, which aids in identification and tracking.

Other species falling in these two groups, such as the porcupine and the honey badger, have very distinctive tracks, which are difficult to mistake. See Figure CCCH.04.03.07.

In summary, when identifying tracks of species with paws registering claws in the tracks and those with paws not registering claws in the tracks, the anterior and posterior margins of the pad and the size of the track can help us identify the species. This is true even when there is only a partial track or if the track is deformed.

The deformed or partial tracks of hoofed ungulates are probably the hardest to identify because their general shape and dimensions are very similar in many species. Shape, size, and association can help the tracker narrow down options. The areas of interest where differences occur are shown in Figure CCCH.04.03.08.

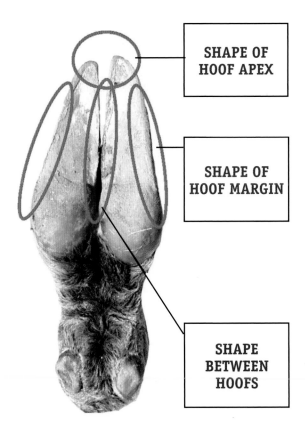

Figure CCCH.04.03.08: *In partial or deformed tracks, the three areas indicated above can supply the information we need to make a correct identification of a cloven-hoofed animal.*

Let us first examine the apex of the hoofs. Some species have a rounded apex, others have a slightly rounded apex, and some have a pointed apex. See Table 4.11 and Figure CCCH.04.03.09 for examples.

If the tracker finds tracks of different species with a similar apex, he will then have to resort to checking their size, shape, hoof margin, and association to assist in identification.

The shape of the margins of the hoof can be described as rounded, slightly rounded, or straight. See Table 4.12. The interdigital gap or the space between the hoofs can also be diagnostic in identifying similar species.

Table 4.11

CLOVEN HOOFS WITH ROUNDED APEX
Buffalo, giraffe, klipspringer
CLOVEN HOOFS WITH SLIGHTLY ROUNDED APEX
Warthog, bushpig, duiker, kudu, nyala, waterbuck, blesbok, tsessebe, red hartebeest, sable, roan, gemsbok, black wildebeest, blue wildebeest, eland
CLOVEN HOOFS WITH SHARP APEX
Suni, grysbok, steenbok, mountain reedbuck, gray rhebok, oribi, impala, common reedbuck

Table 4.12

CLOVEN HOOFS WITH ROUNDED MARGINS
Buffalo, eland, klipspringer
CLOVEN HOOFS WITH SLIGHTLY ROUNDED MARGINS
Warthog, bushpig, duiker, suni, bushbuck, kudu, nyala, waterbuck, giraffe, gemsbok, roan, sable
CLOVEN HOOFS WITH STRAIGHT MARGINS
Grysbok, steenbok, mountain reedbuck, gray rhebok, oribi, impala, common reedbuck, blue and black wildebeest

In summary, when identifying tracks from species of cloven-hoofed animals, the length of the track, the shape of the apex of the track, and the interdigital gap can help us identify the species when there is only a partial track or if the track is deformed. Association can also help. Was the animal on its own or in a herd? Was it in the right type of habitat?

Knowing what species occur in an area can also help with identification. As an example it is easy to identify and track partial or deformed tracks registered by noncloven species in the Kruger National Park because there is only one species representing this group, the Burchell zebra. The only other animals that might somehow get into the park and cause some initial confusion would be horses and donkeys. Donkeys have smaller tracks than those of zebras, while horses have bigger and more rounded tracks. See Figure CCCH.04.03.10.

Figure CCCH.04.03.09: Examples of the apex of hoofs. Top row: rounded apex of a buffalo (left and centre) and of a giraffe (right). Middle row: slightly rounded apex of a kudu (left), blue wildebeest (centre), and warthog (right). Bottom row: pointed apex of the common reedbuck (left) and impala (centre and right).

Figure CCCH.04.03.10: Zebra hoof (left) and track (centre). Partial or distorted tracks of zebras are easy to identify and follow and can be differentiated from horse tracks (right), which are bigger and rounder in shape.

The tracks of aardvarks and pangolins are very distinctive and should not be confused with other species, even if they are distorted or only partially registered. The pangolin has five toes in front and rear but only three toes show up in the front track. A tail drag is also often seen in the tracks of an aardvark and sometimes in those of the pangolin as well. See Figures CCCH.04.03.11 and CCCH.04.03.12. The animals are also, almost invariably, "loners."

Species registering hands and feet are vervet monkeys, otters, baboons, bushbabies, and hyraxes. A bushbaby's tracks are small and they have a massively

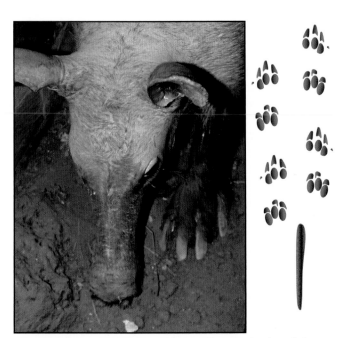

Figure CCCH.04.03.11: These tracks are of an aardvark and show a front foot, rear foot, and a tail drag.

Figure CCCH.04.03.12: These tracks of a pangolin show front foot claw marks, rear foot, and tail drag.

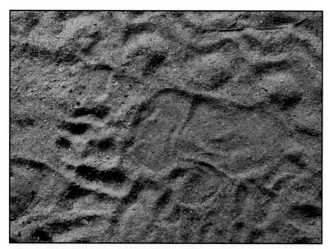

Figure CCCH.04.03.13: On the left is a track of a baboon's foot, and on the right is the track of a baboon's hand.

Figure CCCH.04.03.14: These vervet tracks show both hand and foot (left) and a tail drag mark (right).

developed thumb. Vervet tracks are in turn smaller than those of an adult baboon. See Figure CCCH.04.03.13. Another distinguishing feature of vervet spoor is a tail drag, which is absent in baboon tracks. See Figure CCCH.04.03.14.

A partial spoor means that some of the track has been erased, deformed, or has not registered clearly. If the tracker knows what the typical or normal track looks like, he will know to look for some of its distinguishing characteristics when trying to identify a partial track. Let's look at a lion, baboon, and buffalo track for example. See Figures CCCH.04.03.15 to CCCH.04.03.20.

The distinguishing features mentioned above are what make a lion's track a lion track. An adult lion track by virtue of its size cannot be confused with similar tracks of another species (e.g., a leopard). If the tracks were made by a subadult lion, the three lobed posterior margin of the pad and absence of nails would set it apart, for example, from a hyena.

Let us partially erase some of the above track. See Figure CCCH.04.03.16.

About two and a half toes have been erased in Figure CCCH.04.03.16 in the left-hand track, but we can still recognize the track as that belonging to a lion due to its size. We see the track registers paws without claws, and the trailing edge of the pad shows three lobes. Figure CCCH.04.03.16 in the right-hand track still has enough information in the size of the track and the three lobes on the rear end of the pad to inform us that it was made by an adult lion.

We will now repeat the exercise with a baboon track. See Figure CCCH.04.03.17.

Let us partially erase some of the baboon track. See Figure CCCH.04.03.18.

Although a large portion of the track in Figure CCCH.04.03.18 has been erased and only a partial track remains, there is still enough information to identify it as that of a baboon. Look at the size of the track, the thumb sticking out at a 45-degree angle, the long foot pad, and the two toes. These diagnostic features make a partial track of a baboon recognizable. As our last example, we will use a buffalo track. See Figure CCCH.04.03.19.

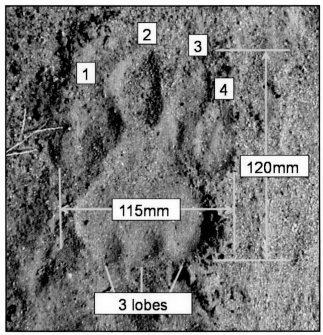

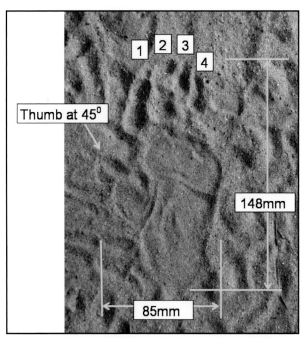

Figure CCCH.04.03.15: Distinguishing features of a "normal" lion track: 1) It is a paw track that does not generally register claw marks. 2) It is a large track (adult measures 120–130mm in length and about 110–120mm in width.) 3) There are four toes and a pad. 4) The toes are more oval in shape than round. 5) The posterior margin of the pad has three lobes.

Figure CCCH.04.03.17: Distinguishing features of a "normal" baboon track: 1) We know by looking at the track that it is grouped under "hands and feet." This immediately narrows down the options to one of six possibilities—vervet, Samango monkey, bushbaby, or one of two otter species. 2) Its size will immediately set it apart from other possibilities—138mm in length and 80–90mm in width. 3) There are four toes and a thumb; all show nails. The pad is elongated. The thumb stands out at an angle of about 45 degrees (75 degrees in the hand).

Figure CCCH.04.03.16: Partially erased lion tracks.

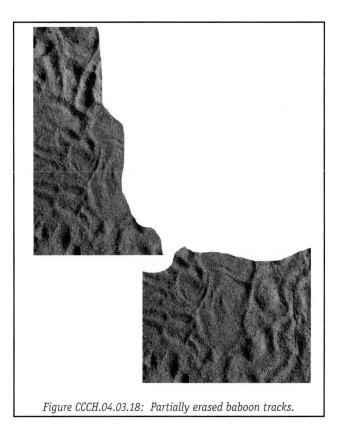

Figure CCCH.04.03.18: Partially erased baboon tracks.

Let us partially erase some of the buffalo track. See Figure CCCH.04.03.20.

In the partial buffalo tracks shown in Figure CCCH.04.03.20, the size of the track, the overall rounded appearance, the rounded apex, and the rounded margins make it possible to identify it as a buffalo track and to differentiate it from similar tracks, such as eland and gemsbok. Track identification can also be based on circumstantial evidence such as scat, smell, herd association, feeding sign, species distribution, etc.

The responsibility rests with the tracker to take the trouble to look at each type of track and to study it carefully. He needs to learn to identify the distinguishing features of any animal's track. This includes the overall shape, size, the shape of the apex of hoofs in cloven-hoofed species, the shape of hoof margins, the shape and number of toes in species with toes and pads, the gaps between toes, etc. This takes time and effort.

This is a useful exercise. You and a friend should go out into the bush; one will walk ahead of the other. The idea is to erase easily identifiable spoor partially so that the other person will then have to identify it. See Figure CCCH.04.03.21. Continued practice will eventually make it easy to identify partial tracks.

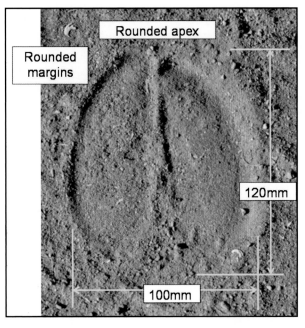

Figure CCCH.04.03.19: *Distinguishing features of a "normal" buffalo track: 1) It is a track belonging to the group of cloven hoofs. 2) It is a large track with dimensions of 110–130mm in length and 100–110m in width. 3) The apex is rounded. 4) The lateral (side) margins (edges) of the track are rounded. 5) The track is more rounded than that of the eland and gemsbok.*

Figure CCCH.04.03.21: *Working together in a team, one person walks ahead and partially erases a track. The second person then is called up and must try to identify the partially erased track. Above is an impala track, which is partially erased on the bottom.*

Figure CCCH.04.03.20: *Partially erased buffalo tracks.*

IDENTIFICATION OF MAMMAL TRACKS AND SIGN

How to Tell Which Track Is That of a Canine, Feline, or Hyena

Introduction

Identifying tracks can be confusing if you are not systematic. The correct method works initially on a process of elimination and ends up by leaving you with a few options. Then you must be able to distinguish one track from another by specific criteria. Remember that we work on some generalizations, and there might be variations from the norm. How does one tell the difference between a track made by a feline and one made by a canine?

Scientific Classification

Before we look at specific tracks let us first clarify what animals are represented by felines and canines.

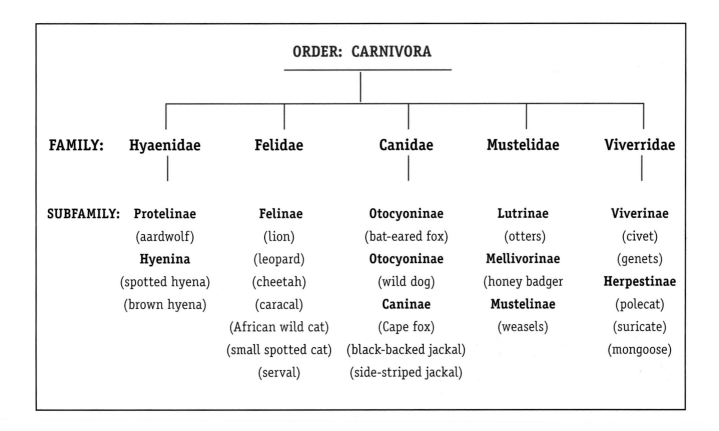

African mammals belonging to the subfamily of the felidae include the lion, leopard, cheetah, caracal, African wild cat, small spotted cat, and serval. Representatives of the canidae include the bat-eared fox, wild dog, Cape fox, black-backed jackal, and side-striped jackal. The canidae are commonly referred to as the "dog family" and the felidae as the "cat family." Note that the aardwolf and the spotted and brown hyenas, although they look "doglike," do not fall under the canidae group but into a subfamily all of their own, the hyaenidae. For the purposes of this book, we will focus our attention on the hyaenidae, felidae, and canidae.

General Distinguishing Features of the Canidae and Hyaenidae

The similarities between the two species include four toes and claws on each foot. See Figures CCCH.04.04.01 to CCCH.04.04.03. Claws might not register in a track if the animal lives in a very rocky area where the claws are worn down. Claws are not usually observed in the felids. The fifth claw, or dewclaw, does not show on the track because it is too high up on the foot. Other similarities are the single lobe on the leading edge of the heel pad and the two-lobe register on the trailing edge of the heel pad. (Although some individuals have three lobes, the

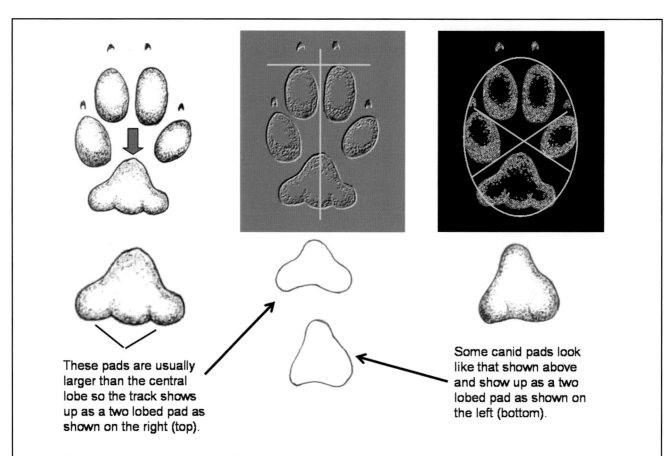

These pads are usually larger than the central lobe so the track shows up as a two lobed pad as shown on the right (top).

Some canid pads look like that shown above and show up as a two lobed pad as shown on the left (bottom).

Figure CCCH.04.04.01 shows the distinctive features of canidae tracks. Front and rear tracks register four toes and four claws each. The trailing edge of the heel pad can have two or three lobes but usually only two pads show up on the track. The leading edge of the heel pad usually has only a single lobe. The front toes are aligned side by side or very close to it. The general shape of the track is an elongated oval and is symmetrical around a central axis. An "X" can be drawn along the ridge between the heel pad and the outer toes. The front track is generally larger than that of the rear. The rear track is more oval in shape.

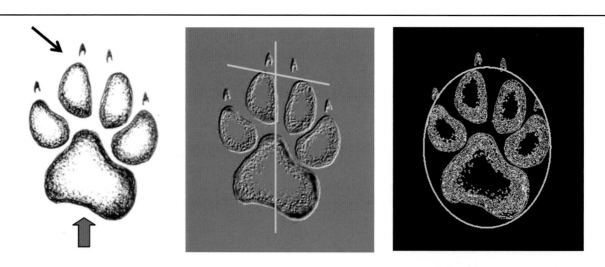

Figure CCCH.04.04.02 shows the distinctive features of hyena tracks. There are four toes in front and rear and four claws on each. The trailing edge of the heel pad has two lobes, and the leading edge has a single lobe. The overall shape is rounder than canids but more oval than felids. The front toes are not aligned. The toe that is farther forward will indicate if it is a left or right foot. The above example shows a right foot. The front track is larger than the rear. The track is asymmetrical around a central axis. An "X" cannot be drawn along the ridge between the heel pad and the outer toes.

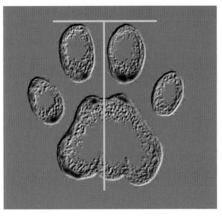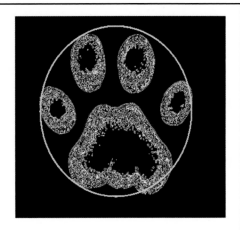

Figure CCCH.04.04.03 shows the distinctive features of felidae tracks. Notice the register of four toes in front and rear. Claws do not normally show up when walking (with the exception of the cheetah) but may be visible when the foot is splayed when running or pouncing. The heel pad has three distinct lobes along the trailing edge that register in the track as three lobes. The leading edge of the heel pad has two lobes. The overall shape of the track is much rounder than either canidae or hyaenidae.

central lobe is reduced in size and does not register in the track.) These features of the heel pad make them distinguishable from felidae. In both subfamilies, the front track is generally larger than the rear track.

There are several differences between tracks of the hyaenidae and those of the canidae. One such difference in the tracks is the canids have symmetry around a central axis whereas the members of the hyena family do not. The front toes are aligned in canids but are "skewed" in the hyaenidae. The overall shape of the tracks of the canids is an elongated oval whereas it is rounder in hyena. An "X" can be drawn along the ridge between the heel pad and outer toes in the canids but not in the hyena group. Species within these groups can generally be identified by the size and shape of the track, individual toe shape, and claw lengths.

General Distinguishing Features of the Felidae

All felidae register four toes on each of the front and rear tracks. See Figure CCCH.04.04.03. Claws do not normally show in the tracks because they are retracted into sheaths. When a felid runs, the toes tend to splay and the claws extend, which might then register in the track. Claws might also be seen as a felid pounces. Once again the paws splay and claw marks might register on the substrate. Claw marks are also seen when one of the cat species scratches sand over scat or dead prey or when sharpening claws on tree trunks or climbing trees.

The cheetah, one animal within this group, will register claws irrespective of its gait. The overall shape of the track

is much rounder than that of either the canids or hyaenidae. Two other distinguishing features of the cheetah are its two lobes on the leading edge of the heel pad and the three lobes on the trailing edge of the heel pad.

The symmetry about the central axis of the felidae can vary within and between species. The front tracks are generally larger than the rear. The alignment of the front toes can vary between and within the species. The tracks of species within the group can be identified by virtue of size and pad shape.

The alignment of the felidae's front toes can vary, as can the symmetry about a central axis. An "X" can be drawn along the ridge between the heel pad and the outer toes in the African wild cat and the front foot of caracal but not in lion, leopard, cheetah, and serval. The front track is usually larger than the rear.

Summary

The characteristics that can be used to differentiate between felids, canids, and hyaenidae are:

➤ The presence or absence of claws (with cheetah an exception)

➤ The one or two lobes on the leading edge of the heel pad

➤ The two or three lobes on the trailing edge of the heel pad

➤ The overall shape of the track: elongated oval for canidae, oval for hyaenidae, or roundish for felidae

Scat Identification

Animal droppings or dung, more correctly referred to as scat sign, are one of the most useful indicators of animals present, their locality, numbers, activities, nutritional status, feeding preferences, and state of health.

Feeding Behaviour

The diet of any particular animal will be reflected in the final product of digestion—its feces or scat. How do we classify feeding behaviour? Let's take a look.

➤ Carnivores eat meat

➤ Herbivores eat plant material

➤ Insectivores eat insects

➤ Fructivores eat fruit

➤ Omnivores eat both plants and animals

Carnivores

Carnivores eat relatively small quantities of food containing large amounts of protein. They have simple and relatively short digestive tracts because they eat a very concentrated food source.

Figure CCCH.04.05.01: The size, colour, texture, content, and shape of scat are very diagnostic.

They defecate relatively small quantities of digested material. The end products of their main diet will include digested animal proteins, hair, teeth, feathers, quills, bone fragments, and fats. The scat of large carnivores may also contain undigested hoofs or horn material (keratin). Carnivores sometimes eat grass and plant material as a purgative. This passes through the intestinal tract undigested, as carnivores do not have the micro bacteria that herbivores do to break down the cellulose of the plant materials. It is, therefore, not unusual to find quite a lot of grass in the scat of lions, members of the dog family, leopards, and other carnivores. The scat of carnivores such as otters will contain significant quantities of fish scales and bones, crab parts, and other invertebrate remains. Scavengers such as vultures can also be grouped under carnivores.

Herbivores

The main dietary component of herbivores is plant material. Herbivores have a digestive system specially adapted to digesting complex starches with the aid of cellulolytic bacteria. These bacteria occur in the fore-stomach (rumen) of ruminants or in the enlarged hindgut (caecum) of animals such as zebras. They break down cellulose into simple sugars, which can then be utilized by the animal. Because herbivores do not ingest a concentrated food source, they have to take in relatively large amounts of food; therefore, they defecate more frequently and in greater quantities than carnivores. Herbivores can be subdivided into grazers (grass eating), browsers (feed off leaves, small twigs, bark, and herbaceous plants), and mixed feeders. Gnawers (such as porcupine and other rodents) will feed on roots, stems, bark, underground bulbs, tubers, and rhizomes.

The scat of herbivores consists of the digested products of plant material and can contain grass, seeds, leaf fragments, fibrous strands of bark material, twigs, etc. The content of the scat will depend upon the dietary preferences of the species in question.

Omnivores

Omnivores have a mixed diet consisting of both animal and plant products. Examples of omnivores include primates, jackals, and civets. The scat analysis of an omnivore will contain elements of both plant and animal origin.

Insectivores

As the name implies, the diet of these species consists mainly of insects. The scat, therefore, contains a lot of chitinous remains, which make up the exoskeleton of insects. Two examples of animals that are insectivores are bats and aardvarks, with the latter feeding almost exclusively on termites. Many birds feed predominantly on insects. Amphibians and some reptiles also eat insects and relatives of insects (centipedes, millipedes, spiders, etc.)

Fructivores

These species feed almost exclusively on fruit. Some examples are fruit-eating bats and many bird species. There are many herbivores and omnivores that will also feed on fruit. The scat of fructivores is usually fairly liquid, often contains seeds of the fruit, and are coloured according to the fruit making up the main part of the diet.

Criteria for Identifying Scat

The following criteria should be taken into account when trying to identify a scat sample:

➤ Shape
➤ Colour
➤ Consistency
➤ Diet content
➤ Odour
➤ Size
➤ Quantity
➤ Position

Shape

The shapes of droppings are one of the most common features used to identify the animal. The shape is very useful for narrowing down options, but in some cases the shape alone is not enough and additional information will be required to make a positive identification.

The type of digestive tract determines the shape of the scat. The shape will also be influenced by the diet and subsequent content of the scat. See Figure CCCH.04.05.01. The higher the liquid-to-solid-material ratio, the less shape it will have. Often after the first rains and green flush of the early growing season, the scat of herbivores can become very liquid as a result of the high moisture content of new grass. The shape can also be determined by the animal's physiological condition and its state of health. The scat of an animal under stress will be far more fluid than normal, and certain disease states can cause watery diarrhea.

The shape can also be influenced by the height from which the scat falls. The dung of elephants often breaks because it falls from a greater distance to earth. Other animals sometimes break up their dung with their tails (hippos) or hind feet (black and white rhinos).

Larger Cylindrical Pellets and Elongated Spherical Pellets with a "Nipple"

Examples of animals that have scat with this shape are most antelopes and giraffes. See Table 4.13 and Figure CCCH.04.05.02 for an example.

Table 4.13: Large, Cylindrical Pellets/Elongated Pellets with One End Narrow

SPECIES	LENGTH OF SCAT (mm)
Blesbok	15
Bontebok	15
Bushbuck	13–14
Duiker, common	11
Eland	25
Gemsbok	14–20
Giraffe	30
Grysbok, Sharpe	10
Hartebeest, red	16–18
Impala	12–14
Klipspringer	10–11
Kudu	16–18
Mountain, reedbuck	12–13
Nyala	16–18
Oribi	10–12
Reedbuck, common	14
Rhebok, gray	12–13
Roan	20–22
Sable	20–22
Springbok	12–14
Steenbok	7–10
Tsessebe	16–18
Waterbuck	20
Wildebeest, black	18
Wildebeest, blue	20

The moisture content in the food can influence the pellet's shape. When food has a high percentage of moisture, the scat tends to lose its characteristic shape and becomes more fluid. When food is dry, the shape of the scat is more consistent. Wildebeest scat has the tendency for the individual pellets to clump together.

Figure CCCH.04.05.02: Larger cylindrical pellets and elongated spherical pellets with a "nipple." A typical example (nyala) is shown above.

Figure CCCH.04.05.03 shows irregular-shape or -form scat. The example shown above is from a baboon.

Steenboks have the habit of burying or scratching sand over their droppings. Territorial species such as impalas deposit their pellets in piles referred to as middens or latrines.

Irregular Shape or Form

Examples of animals that have scat with this shape include the baboon, monkey, bushpig, aardvark, tortoise, worm, toad, and Cape clawless otter. See Table 4.14 and Figure CCCH.04.05.03 for a typical example. This type of scat has a fairly sloppy consistency with no predictable shape.

Table 4.14: Animals with Irregular Shape/Form Scat

SPECIES	SCAT DIMENSION (mm)
Aardvark	Variable
Baboon	Variable
Bushpig	80 (diameter)
Cape clawless otter	22–30 (diameter)
Toad	Variable
Tortoise	20–100 (length)

Large Barrel Shape or Elongated Cylinder

Examples of animals that have scat with this shape include the hippo, elephant, and white and black rhino. See Table 4.15 and Figure CCCH.04.05.04 for a typical example.

Elephants deposit their dung at random but one might find large accumulations at favourite feeding and drinking sites. The colour when fresh may be greenish to yellowish, depending on the diet, and it becomes darker with age. The length of individual droppings is about 200mm. The content of the dung consists of coarse plant fibres, bark, leaves, seeds, and undigested fruits. Elephants may deposit as much as 100 kilos of dung in 24 hours. Elephant droppings may be soft if the animal is under stress or if it has had a high intake of water.

Table 4.15: Animals with Barrel/Elongated Cylinder Shape Scat

SPECIES	LENGTH OF SCAT (mm)
Elephant	200
Hippo	100
White rhino	200
Black rhino	200

Black and white rhinos deposit dung randomly and also make use of middens. After defecating, both species kick their dung deposits vigorously with their hind legs, often leaving parallel scrape marks on the ground. Fresh droppings are a dark olive green when fresh. Old dung from a black rhino is generally lighter. It is relatively

Figure CCCH.04.05.04 shows barrel- or elongated-cylinder-shape scat. The example shown above is from an elephant.

Figure CCCH.04.05.05 shows scat with a kidney shape. Above is an example of zebra dung.

easy to differentiate between black and white rhino dung. The dung of the black rhino is far coarser and contains a lot of fibre, twigs (cut mostly at a 45-degree angle), and undigested leaf material (they are browsers). It is darker in colour than the dung of the white rhino. White rhinos are grazers; their dung consists mostly of finely digested grass material. Droppings are about 200mm in length.

Hippo droppings average about 100mm in length and can be found scattered throughout their grazing areas often "splashed" or deposited up against bushes. As the animal defecates, the short, strong tail swishes back and forth breaking up the dung.

Kidney Shape

Examples of animals that have scat with this shape include the zebra, warthog, horse, and donkey. See Table 4.16 and Figure CCCH.04.05.05 for a typical example.

Table 4.16: Animals with Kidney-shape Scat

SPECIES	LENGTH OF SCAT (mm)
Zebra species	50
Warthog	40–45

The scat of the zebra and warthog family is a kidney shape. Zebras are grazers and their dung is made up of finely digested grass. Zebra dung will often develop a crack across

the centre (not so with warthog). Between 10–30 pellets can be deposited at any one time. When fresh, they are olive green to light brown, becoming almost black with age. Zebra and warthog deposit their dung at random and do not make use of middens or latrines. Warthogs feed both on grass and forbs. When dry their dung is pleasantly aromatic.

Cord, Sausage Shape, Pointed at One End, and Generally Unsegmented

Examples of animals that have scat with this shape include the wild dog, civet, genet, mongoose, porcupine, hedgehog, and spotted-necked otter. See Table 4.17 and Figure CCCH.04.05.06 for a typical example.

Table 4.17: Animals with Cord/Sausage-Shape Scat, Pointed at One End

SPECIES	DIAMETER OF SCAT (mm)
Bat-eared fox	18
Black-backed jackal	18–20
Civet	55–60
Small spotted genet	15
Banded mongoose	12–16
Dwarf mongoose	8
Water mongoose	20
Porcupine	15–17
Wild dog	30

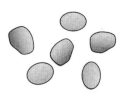

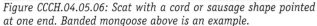

Figure CCCH.04.05.06: Scat with a cord or sausage shape pointed at one end. Banded mongoose above is an example.

Figure CCCH.04.05.07 shows lozenge-shape pellets. The example above is scat from a scrub hare.

Droppings leave the anus with the pointed end last. Some species deposit droppings at latrine sites (dwarf mongooses, genets, and civets) whereas others will defecate at random. Civet middens/latrines are referred to as civetries. Because of their omnivorous diet, their droppings can contain the remains of plants, fruit, small mammals, and insects.

They are particularly fond of eating millipedes, especially during the wet summer months, and their droppings are then full of millipede segments. The droppings of the dog family vary in size and content. The droppings of a wild dog are dark in colour and are sometimes eaten by black-backed jackals and hyenas. The scat of a black-backed jackal sometimes has a slightly segmented appearance. Porcupine scat usually contains bark fibres and has a dome or cigar shape.

Lozenge-Shape Pellets

Examples of animals that have scat with this shape include rabbits, hares, and hyraxes (dassies). See Figure CCCH.04.05.07. These pellets are usually found in small clusters (rabbits and hares) or large clusters (hyraxes). Individual pellets are spherical to slightly oblong, firm, and slightly flattened. The diameter is 10–15mm. The colour of hare pellets is fairly light and those of a hyrax darker. Depending on the type of diet, hyrax scat can form sausages composed of aggregates of pellets. When dry and

powdered, the lozenge-shape scat makes good tinder for starting fires.

Segmented Sausage or Cord and Tapered at One End

Examples of animals that have scat with this shape include the lion, leopard, hyena, serval, aardwolf, caracal cheetah, and African wild cat. The scat from a brown hyena is usually found in latrine accumulations. Of the cats, only the African wild cat makes use of latrines; the other cats defecate at random sites. Some cat species may make attempts to bury their droppings by scratching sand over it. Hyena droppings whiten with age due to its high calcium content (from eating bones). Lion scat usually loses its characteristic shape after the lion has ingested a meal with a lot of blood. Scat in this group usually contains hair and bone fragments because all the representatives are carnivorous. See Figure CCCH.04.05.08. The diameter "d" of some of the species with segmented sausage-shape scat and pointed at one end is shown in Table 4.18.

The diameter will vary according to the animal's diet, fluid intake, and health. The content of scat in this group can consist of digested proteins, hair, bones, claws, feathers, hoofs, and a small amount of vegetable matter such as grass. Aardwolf droppings contain a large amount of soil and termite remains.

Figure CCCH.04.05.08 shows a sausage-shape scat segmented at one end. The example shown above is that of a caracal.

Figure CCCH.04.05.09 shows a liquid splat. The example shown above is that of a hadeda ibis.

Liquid Consistency or a "Splat"

Examples of animals that have scat with this shape include birds, hyraxes, fruit bats, and animals with diarrhea. See Figure CCCH.04.05.09. Scat described as liquid are also designated as a "splat."

Table 4.18: Animals with Segmented Sausage/Cord Shape Scat, Pointed at One End

SPECIES	DIAMETER OF SCAT (mm)
Aardwolf	20–25
African wild cat	12–15
Caracal	15–20
Cheetah	25–35
Hyena	40–50
Leopard	20–30
Lion	40–45

Figure CCCH.04.05.10 shows a sausage-shape scat that is pointed at both ends and has a hardish white cap. The example above is from an agama.

Scat with a Sausage Shape, Pointed at Both Ends, and a Hardish White Cap

Examples of animals that have scat with this shape include snakes and lizards. The white cap on the end is uric acid. See Figure CCCH.04.05.10.

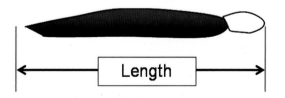

Length

Figure CCCH.04.05.11 shows sausage-shape scat with a partial white coating. The example is from a francolin.

Sausage Shape with a Partial White Coating

Examples of animals that have scat with this shape include the francolin, guinea fowl, bustard, pigeon, duck, geese, and other waterfowl. The white cap on the end is uric acid. See Figure CCCH.04.05.11. Some species defecate at random whilst accumulations will sometimes be found at favourite nesting sites, roosts (guinea fowl), feeding sites, or advertising sites such as on top of termite mounds.

Small Cylindrical Pellets

Examples of animals that have scat with this shape include rodents (squirrels, rats, and mice) and insectivorous bats. See Figure CCCH.04.05.12. Accumulations are often found at the entrance to rodent nests or burrows and in caves frequented by bats. Bat droppings are referred to as guano.

Flattened Pellets, with and without Grooves

Examples of animals that have scat with this shape include springhares, cane rats, and vlei rats. See Figure CCCH.04.05.13.

Figure CCCH.04.05.12 shows small cylindrical pellets. The example is scat from tree squirrels.

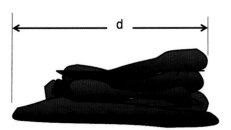

Figure CCCH.04.05.13 shows scat that is flattened pellets, with or without grooves.

Figure CCCH.04.05.14 shows cow pat or layered pancake. The example above is scat from a buffalo.

Cow Pat or Layered Pancake

Examples of animals that have scat with this shape include cows, buffaloes, or animals with diarrhea. See Figure CCCH.04.05.14.

➤ **Colour**

The colour of dung is influenced largely by:

› Its origin, which can be plant or animal or mixed

› Its moisture content

› Its age

› Its condition

As a generalization, the dung of herbivores, which can vary from a light tan (e.g., hares), light olive green, olive green to a brownish green, usually darkens with age. Carnivore scat, because of the blood content, is usually very dark brown to almost black when fresh; it generally becomes darker with age.

There are some exceptions, especially in carnivores that have a high intake of bone tissue, hair, and invertebrates, such as crabs and mussels. The colour of crocodile, hyena, and otter dung, therefore, becomes much lighter with age. Because of the high calcium and phosphate content of their diet, the scat of hyena becomes almost chalky white after a while. White scat can also be caused by fungus growing on it. The colour of dung in animals or birds feeding on fruit can often take on the colour of the fruit. The more moisture in the scat, the lighter it tends to be. Watery diarrhea, caused pathogenically, can vary in colour from bright, yellowish green all the way through to dark, bloody stools.

In the early spring when grazing animals have a change in diet from coarse, dry grass to fresh, succulent, new growth, the droppings sometimes change from well-defined pellets to a sloppy, lighter and less well-defined shape. When very fresh, dung has a high moisture content and is shiny, becoming duller as it begins to dry out.

➤ **Consistency or Texture**

Consistency refers to the "solidity" of the feces and ranges from liquid to hard. The consistency will depend on the animal's moisture content, type of diet, and condition. Dry diet produces hard scat. Wet diet produces soft or even runny feces. The consistency of dung is more solid in plant-eating species and softer in carnivorous species. The relative ratio of browsing to grazing also influences moisture content, and hence scat texture. Grazing of grasses and shrubs will produce softer scat. Carnivore diets with a greater content of hair and bone will produce harder scat. The amount of fluid intake will make the dung softer. If an animal has been without water for a time, the feces will be harder (constipation)

than if there has been a recent water intake. Some mammals will try to obtain nutrients from natural salt licks, and their scat can be sandy or contain rock-hard pieces of dried clay. The scat of pangolins, aardwolfs, and aardvarks contain quite a bit of sand. The consistency of scat can be seasonal, with it being generally harder in the dry months and softer in the wet months. Most birds have a watery scat.

➤ **Odour**

Diet content enables the tracker to isolate the group and even species according to their feeding behaviours. The odour of herbivore scat is not disagreeable and is, in some instances, quite aromatic, "herby," and pleasant. The smell of carnivore scat is usually strong and unpleasant and results from the breakdown of animal protein. The consistency and odour of omnivore scat can be variable, depending on the diet. The scat of insectivorous bats, known as guano, is very strong and pungent. See Table 4.19.

Table 4.19: Scat Odour

ANIMAL	ODOUR OF SCAT
Herbivores	Not unpleasant; aromatic, "herblike" smell
Carnivores	Strong and very unpleasant, lingering odour due to breakdown of protein
Omnivores	Variable according to diet but generally quite strong and unpleasant due to the breakdown of protein
Insectivores	Variable; slightly unpleasant to pungent
Fructivores and seed eaters	Variable; slightly unpleasant to pungent

➤ **Diet and Scat Content**

The diet of the animal will determine the contents of the scat. This is illustrated in Table 4.20.

➤ **Position**

The position of dung can also be a useful indicator to the tracker. Firstly in terms of locality. You will find the most scat of any particular species in their preferred habitat. Hyrax and klipspringer droppings will be found mostly on rocky outcrops, bushpig and bushbuck scat in riverine vegetation, hippo dung on well worn paths leading to and from water, etc. Some species, such as dwarf mongoose for example, practice sanitation by defecating outside their burrow or by

Table 4.20: Scat Content and Colour

FEEDING TYPE	EXAMPLES	MAIN DIET	SCAT CONTENT
Herbivores			
Grazer	Zebra, hippo, wildebeest, sable, roan, hartebeest, white rhino, buffalo, gemsbok, reedbuck, waterbuck, mountain reedbuck, gray rhebok, blesbok, bontebok, springhare, and tsessebe	Grass	Digested grass remains with incidental leaves; colour lime green to greenish brown
Browser	Kudu, black rhino, giraffe, eland, bushbuck, nyala, suni, dik-dik, klipspringer, duiker, warthog, bushpig, oribi	Leaves, twigs, fruit, and forbs	Leaves, bark, stems, twigs, roots, and fruit remains; colour lime green to greenish brown
Mixed feeder	Impala, elephant, Sharpe grysbok, springbok, dassie	Food of grazers and browsers	Digested grass and browse materials; colour lime green to greenish brown
Gnawers and nibblers	Porcupines, rat, and mice	Graze and browse bark, roots, and tubers	Digested grass, browse, fruits and bark; colour dark olive to dark brown
Carnivores	Lion, leopard, cheetah, serval, genet, honey badger, caracal, otters, mongoose, suricates, and raptors such as eagles, hawks, kites, and vultures	Meat (high protein	Digested protein, hair, bone fragments, feathers, hoofs, and occasionally plant material; colour brown to tar black
Omnivores	Jackals, civet, baboon, vervets, and humans	Plant and animal foods	Variable combinations of digested plant and animal material; colour variable
Insectivores	Bats, birds, antbears, and pangolin	Insects	Digested insect material: wings, legs, chitinous exoskeleton; colour light to dark brown
Fructivores and seed eaters	Bats, rodents, and many birds; seeds	Fruits and seeds	Colour depends on fruit

scat disposal. Another example is by burying scat (as is seen in some cat species) or scratching sand over them as in steenbok.

When the male of the species urinates and defecates at the same time, there will be a distance between the urine and scat patches. They will be superimposed in female scat. This is obvious because of differences in their anatomy. The position of dung relative to urine deposits can give an indication of sex of the animal. See Figure CCCH.04.05.15.

➤ **Size**

The size of scat generally (but not always) corresponds to the size of the animal. Notable exceptions are giraffe and civet cats. The relatively small, individual pellet size of giraffe scat is somewhat incongruous when compared to the size of an adult giraffe. In contrast to this, the sausage-shape scat of civet cats appear very large in comparison to the size of this animal. The diameter of scat is generally determined by the size of the anus, but this can be variable.

➤ **Quantity**

The quantity of dung will depend on the size of the animal, its level of food intake, and its behavioural patterns. Herbivores have a much greater bulk of fecal mass when compared to carnivores. An animal that has not eaten for a while will obviously have a lower volume of fecal mass than one that has eaten well and regularly. The visible amount of feces will also be influenced by the behaviour of the species in question. Young animals obviously pass smaller volumes and size of scat.

Territorial species will often demarcate territory by depositing scat at specific sites, referred to as middens. Nonterritorial species and territorial species not in times of rut will deposit scat randomly, which will be less obvious to the observer.

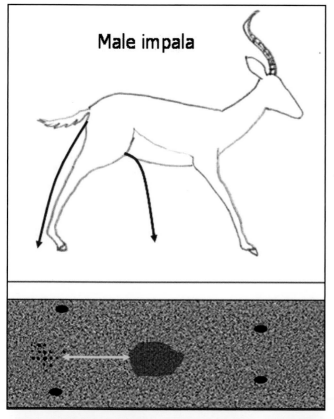

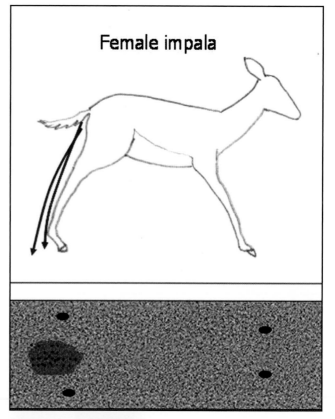

Figure CCCH.04.05.15: Due to differences in anatomy, the relative position of dung and urine can indicate the sex of the animal. This example below of an impala scat/urine deposit shows the sex to be female.

Estimating Age from Fluid Signs

Fluids originating from an animal's feeding or drinking habits can provide valuable clues as to the time elapsed since the sign was registered. Cud, water, urine, blood, and the moisture remaining in scat are useful indicators of the age of sign. See Figures CCCH.04.05.16 to CCCH.04.05.19.

Fresh Splat

<1 Minute

3 Minutes

5 Minutes

5 Minutes

90 Minutes

7 Minutes

Figure CCCH.04.05.16: Urinating is a normal body function performed every day by animals. Urine deposits change with time, so learning how to interpret these changes allows the tracker to estimate the age of the sign. Look above left to see how urine sign changes over time. Fresh urine is frothy. This foamy component usually disappears within five to six minutes. Urine takes on a fine crystalline appearance as it dries out. The crystals are made up of sodium chloride and urea.

Figure CCCH.04.05.18: Animals often drip water from their muzzles after drinking. The rate at which the water dries up is a function of temperature, wind, and humidity. Understanding how these variables influence the rate of drying enables the tracker to accurately predict the age of the sign. Note how the splash reduces in diameter with time. The heat of the substrate (the rock), wind, humidity, and solar heat will determine the rate of drying.

<1 Minute

5 Minutes

10 Minutes

30 Minutes

60 Minutes

90 Minutes

3 Hours

5 Hours

Figure CCCH.04.05.17: Sometimes herbivores drop food from their mouths. Look how the cud ages with time in the series of photographs, starting from fresh out of the mouth to five hours later. Note the changes in colour, the decreasing moisture content, and the way the cud shrinks in diameter.

| 2 Minutes | 5 Minutes | 15 Minutes |
| 60 Minutes | 120 Minutes | 24 Hours |

Figure CCCH.04.05.19: When blood is exposed to air, it starts to coagulate very quickly. This is a natural process that helps to prevent blood loss. By knowing how to relate the appearance of blood to its age, the tracker can formulate a good idea of when the animal passed that way. Depending on the species, blood coagulates within four to eleven minutes. Note the change of the leaves over the period of time recorded.

Collecting Scat Samples

It is a good idea to make a collection of scat samples for identification purposes. You must remember however that diseases and parasites can be picked up through the handling of scat so it is a wise precaution always to wear gloves when doing so or using forceps/tweezers or a plastic bag over your hand when picking up scat samples. See Figure CCCH.04.05.20.

To preserve scat samples, prick the scat with a needle to aerate it (Figure CCCH.04.05.20) and place it in a warm dry spot to dry out thoroughly. Once dried, it does not give off much of a smell. The smell of dried herbivore dung can be quite aromatic and "herby." Once the dung is dry, it can be sealed by spraying it with a clear lacquer.

Samples can be kept in screw-top glass jars or plastic bags with a sealable opening. Always remember to include details of the specimen such as species, sex, age (if known), colour, odour when fresh, location, weather conditions, and so on.

Figure CCCH.04.05.20: It is always a good idea to wear gloves (right) when collecting scat samples. Handling scat without gloves (left) can result in you picking up a disease or parasite.

CHAPTER 5

GAIT PATTERNS AND PRESSURE RELEASES

Gait Patterns

Atracker should be able to identify and interpret gait patterns. What is meant by gait? Gait is an animal's coordinated pattern of movement. The relationship between prints shows the type and speed of movement and is also a useful indicator to determine the animal's physical status. A good, clear track sequence over a long distance is rarely found in certain types of habitat; thus, interpretation of gait pattern often has to be attempted on partial evidence. Gait terms are used very indiscriminately and without adequate definition and can lead to much confusion. The term "running," for example, is too general and inaccurate, especially in quadrupeds (four-leg animals). Transitions between gaits are very difficult to describe.

The principle gait patterns are walking, trotting, galloping, and jumping. This classification is also inadequate to describe the range of motions animals are capable of producing. Let us look at the principle gait patterns and discuss the ranges of motion within these main groups.

Track patterns can generally be divided into symmetrical (walk and trot) and asymmetrical (gallop and jump) types. Symmetrical gaits are those where the interval between tracks are evenly spaced and are symmetrical between left and right sides. In asymmetrical gaits, the spacing between tracks is uneven and the patterns differ from left to right sides. As a point of reference, all gait patterns in quadrupeds start with the right front foot.

Walking

All terrestrial animals and many birds walk, if not frequently then occasionally. In some animals, walking is not the gait of preference; hares, for example, either hop or run. When walking, each foot moves independently; at no time during a walk are all four feet off the ground. Walking can be subdivided into:

➤ A normal crawl (slow walk) is when three or even four feet may be on the ground at one time.

➤ An amble (fast walk) has a maximum of two feet on the ground at any one time.

Walking is slow but energy efficient. The tracks left by a walking animal show two parallel rows of evenly spaced prints that alternate. During the cycle, the right front (RF) and left rear (LR) legs work together and the left front (LF) and right rear (RR) work together. These are termed diagonal walkers; a giraffe is an exception. The stride is short and the straddle wide. Direct register (when the rear foot imprints directly on

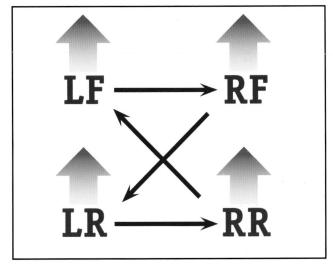

Figure CCCH.05.01.01: The foot sequence when walking is the right front (RF) followed by the left rear (LR) followed by the right rear (RR) and the left front (LF).

top of the front foot) occurs when an animal is moving stealthily, such as when a jackal or leopard is stalking prey. Mostly, the rear foot will slightly overstep the front foot. See Figures CCCH.05.01.01 and CCCH.05.01.02.

Trotting

Trotting is a faster type of locomotion that is energy efficient relative to the speed attained by the animal. Many species such as zebra, jackal, tsessebe, and eland can trot for extended periods of time and cover long distances. In trotting, diagonal feet move simultaneously. The right front (RF) and left rear (LR) and left front (LF) and right rear (RR) work together. As each diagonal pair of legs leaves the ground, there is a brief interval during which all four feet are off the ground. The trail left behind by a trotting animal shows two parallel rows of alternating, evenly spaced prints. The straddle is narrower and the stride longer than in walking. During a trot the hind foot will register in front of the forefoot. The overstep and interval (distance) between the pairs of prints increases with increasing speed. Some members of the dog family occasionally trot with the bodies held at an angle to the direction of travel. The result is that all front prints show on one side and the hind prints on the opposite side of the trail. See Figure CCCH.05.01.03.

Galloping

The fastest gait, the gallop, leaves an asymmetrical track pattern. The gallop requires a large amount of energy and is usually

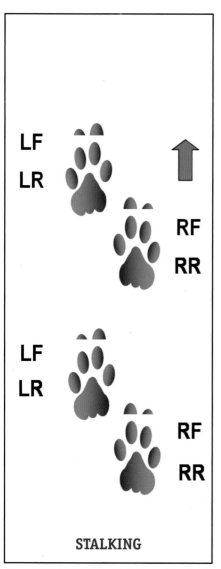

STALKING

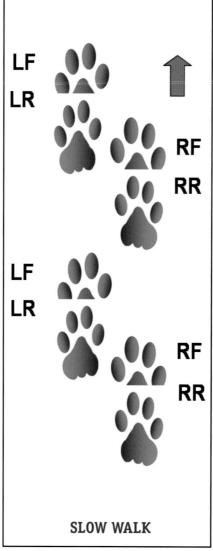

SLOW WALK

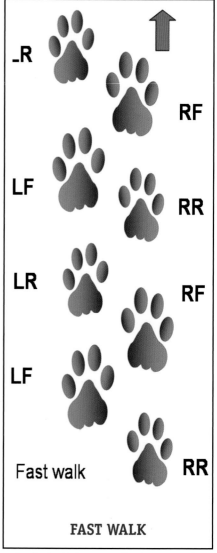

FAST WALK

Figure CCCH.05.01.02: Walking gaits. During stalking, the rear tracks superimpose almost completely (and often completely) on the front tracks. The animal moves very slowly and deliberately. During a slow walk, the rear tracks partially superimpose on the front tracks. When walking fast or ambling, the stride is lengthened and the tracks are separated.

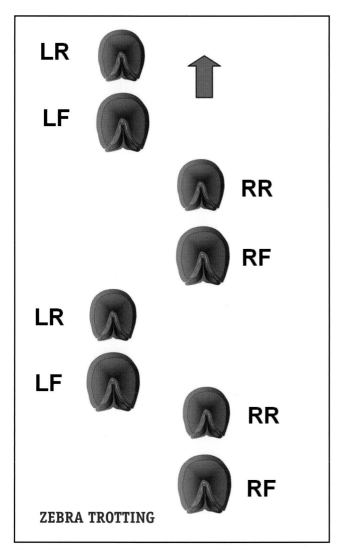 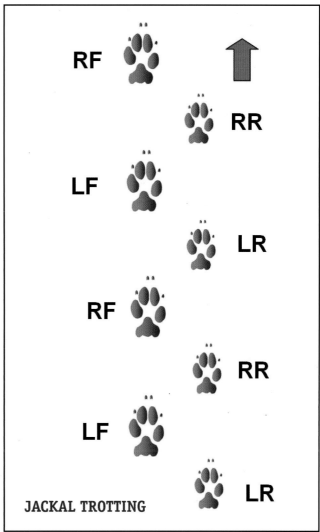

Figure CCCH.05.01.03: When a zebra trots, the hind foot oversteps the front foot. The front and rear feet alternate on each side of the direction of travel. When a jackal trots, the hind feet are registered on one side and the front feet on the other side in the direction of travel.

of short duration. The diagnostic feature of the gallop is an airborne phase when the animal takes off from the forelegs. Gallops with only one airborne phase are referred to as a canter or a lope. Loping or cantering is generally more efficient than trotting. During fast gallops, there might be a secondary airborne phase when the animal takes off from the hind feet. The straddle is greatly reduced during the gallop with prints lying nearly on a line in the direction of travel. Gallops are classified into two types, rotatory and transverse (cross), depending on which hind foot strikes the ground first. Mammals may use either

pattern but the transverse gallop is commonly used in zebras, buffaloes, lions, leopards, and smaller cats. Rotatory gallop is more common in antelopes, wild dogs, and hyenas. During the gallop, the overstep of the hind feet increases with increasing speed until both hind feet register ahead of the forefeet. See Figure CCCH.05.01.04.

Jumping

The jump requires great physical effort and energy. Although similar to the gallop, it is slower. The diagnostic feature of the jump is an airborne period when the animal

takes off from the hind feet or from all four feet. Examples would be a kudu clearing a fence (taking off from the hind feet) and a springbok "stotting" (taking off on all four feet). Landing takes place on the forelegs. The forelegs then briefly leave the ground before the hind legs land laterally and to the front of the forelegs. The characteristic gait of hares, rabbits, and some rodents—referred to as hoppers—is a jump referred to as a "bound." See Figure CCCH.05.01.05.

When speed increases, the stride lengthens and the straddle width decreases. This is illustrated in Figure CCCH.05.01.06.

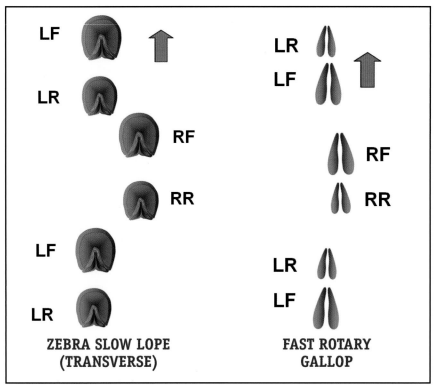

ZEBRA SLOW LOPE (TRANSVERSE)

FAST ROTARY GALLOP

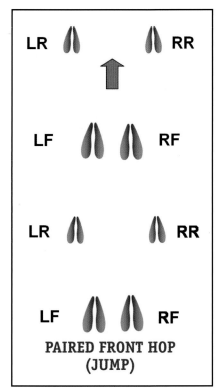

PAIRED FRONT HOP (JUMP)

Figure CCCH.05.01.04: During the gallop, the overstep of the hind feet increases with increasing speed until both hind feet register ahead of the forefeet. Note also how the straddle width decreases with increasing speed. The example is of a zebra (left) and an antelope (right).

Figure CCCH.05.01.05: Note how the front legs register between the hind legs on this jump.

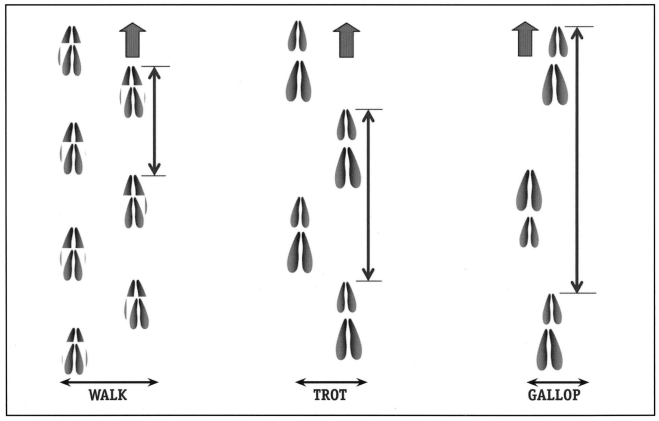

WALK

TROT

GALLOP

Figure CCCH.05.01.06: Note the effect of speed on stride length and straddle width. Note how straddle width (red) decreases and the stride length (blue) increases with an increase in speed.

Interpreting Gait Patterns

Since most animals have the ability to use almost any gait, the gait pattern registered on the substrate can reflect a lot of information with regards to the activity of the animal. The speed of travel may be determined by comparing the dimensions of the stride and straddle. See Figure CCCH.05.01.06. An animal that is not in any particular hurry will take its time and walk, perhaps whilst grazing or browsing. If an animal is intent on covering distance but is not in any particular hurry and wishes to conserve energy, it will utilize a trot or a lope. A good example of this would be a jackal out foraging for food. An animal in a hurry will gallop for short distances and a startled animal will jump. A carnivore may begin its stalk with a slow, painstaking walk and end it with a galloping rush and a final jump onto the prey.

Changes in the pattern of the gait represent changes in the animal's attitude, behaviour, or level of excitement. This may be reflected by a sudden speeding up at the sight of perceived danger (such as a predator, usually in a direction away from the danger) or a slowing down to rest. Sudden changes in direction are always worth investigating as they can reflect either a major change in attitude or physical condition.

Figure CCCH.05.02.01 illustrates the following gait patterns: 1) A normal walking pattern. 2) A weaving and irregular pattern of direction; irregular stride and straddle; animal sick or injured. 3) Irregular gait pattern; inconsistent straddle and stride; animal weak, has stumbled, fallen, and struggled to its feet again.

Hurt or Wounded

When a hurt or wounded animal begins to weaken, the following gait patterns might become evident:

➤ The gait pattern will reflect a slowing of pace. After running away from the source of disturbance or injury, the animal will slow from a gallop to a trot to a walk.

➤ The gait pattern will become irregular with no distinct pattern.

➤ The gait will indicate a stumble or fall and struggling to get back up again.

➤ The straddle width will increase as the animal splays its legs to steady itself.

➤ The stride will become progressively shorter.

➤ The direction of travel will begin to weave from side to side.

➤ A broken leg can be indicated by a drag mark and possible absence of a track from the injured leg.

Some of these gait patterns are illustrated in Figures CCCH.05.02.01 and CCCH.05.02.02.

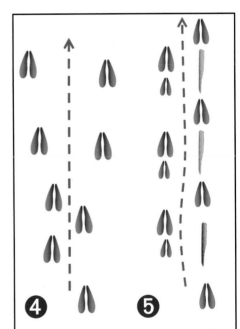

Figure CCCH.05.02.02: Animal becoming weak and spreading its legs to support itself. 4) Straddle width increasing and becoming shorter. 5) The animal's right leg is injured and dragging.

Pressure Releases

Introduction to Pressure Releases

In the previous section we looked at interpreting animal movement and behaviour through gait patterns. A tracker will often be presented with the challenge of tracking on ground that is not conducive to registering whole sets of sequential tracks and will have to make deductions from, perhaps, only a single track. Yet it is possible to do this by using information in the track referred to as "pressure releases." Correctly understanding and interpreting pressure releases can help the tracker to deduce the following:

➤ Accurately determining the speed of an animal, whether it is hesitating or stopping

➤ Secondary efforts required to maintain forward motion

➤ Accurately determining directional changes (to within one or two degrees)

➤ Determining from the track which way an animal or person is looking

➤ Major shifts in body position

Usually animals and humans are in contact with the earth through our hands and feet and sometimes with our bodies. The point of contact is the ground or some other surface like the floor of a building. The "ground" is made up of soil particles derived from the breakdown of parent rock and organic material, which we refer to as vegetation. Soil has different properties related to, amongst other things, its particle size. Coarsely grained soil we call gravel or sand, whereas soil composed of tiny particles we loosely refer to as clays. Vegetation can be living (grass, plants, etc.) or dead; if it's in various stages of decomposition it is described as detritus or litter. In both cases, soil and vegetation in

whatever form are physical entities that obey laws of the physical world. Because soils and vegetation are subject to physical forces, they therefore behave and respond in a predictable pattern.

When the sidewalls of a track (imprint in the soil) are subjected to pressure of an ever-increasing magnitude, they, as will be demonstrated, react or respond, in a logical, sequential, and predictable pattern. These patterns of response have been termed by Brown in his studies on tracking as "pressure releases." This refers to the reaction that takes place in the soil or other substrate when a force (pressure) has been applied to it and then removed (released). Hence the term "pressure releases."

> Understanding pressure releases and how to interpret them ushers in a whole new dimension for a tracker. It is well worth the effort and dedication to explore this "new discovery" of ancient bush lore.

Understanding pressure releases involves a grasp of some basic principles of physics. Firstly, every particle of matter is attracted by the force of gravity. So any object that has mass will experience a force acting downward toward the earth. The body of an animal or human is made up of different parts: head, arms, legs, stomach, tongue, etc. Each one of these parts has mass but the body must function as a whole and must be kept in balance or else we would fall unless counter balanced by some opposing force.

The point of intersection of all the parts of mass is called the centre of gravity (CG). Another way of saying this is that the "weight" of an object or body always passes through the CG. A force whose line of action lies to one side or the other of

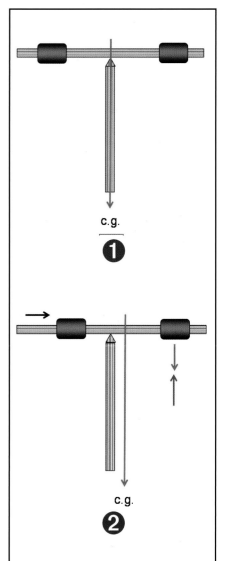

Figure CCCH.05.03.01: In 1 the system is in equilibrium and balanced with the resultant force F of the mass of each individual part passing through and coinciding with the centre of gravity (CG). Consider now what happens in 2 if one of the objects is moved to the right. Mass distribution is altered and the system will be unbalanced with the CG shifted to the right. This will make the system want to move or rotate downward in a clockwise direction as indicated by the red arrow, and will do so unless countered by some force acting in the opposite direction (blue arrow). This is what is happening the whole time with our bodies as we move. As mass distribution is constantly changed and CG shifts, the reaction force that enables us to maintain balance (or lack thereof) will register as "pressure maps" on the soles of the feet.

the CG will change both translational and rotational motion of the body on which it acts. Translational motion is movement in a straight line.

We will look at some examples to see what this has to do with practical tracking. The fact is that "foot maps" tell us what the body is doing and how it is compensating to shifts in the centre of gravity and changes in mass distribution. Let's begin

with a few simple illustrations. See Figure CCCH.05.03.01.

What happens when a person picks up a heavy suitcase or when a lion drags a zebra carcass? The centre of gravity (CG) moves as weight is redistributed. This is done to maintain balance and will be reflected in the pressure maps of the feet. See Figure CCCH.05.03.02.

Just as these large movements are reflected in pressure responses, so are delicate movements. Our bodies must be held in a continual state of balance; otherwise, we will fall. Every movement, even the smallest one, will cause a shift in equilibrium and must be compensated for. Virtually all compensation to maintain balance is transmitted through our feet in contact with the ground, so every movement of the body should in some way reflect or be registered in the track. This makes logical sense, but few people realize how sensitive the dynamics are. Look at the experiments on the next few pages and try them for yourself.

It is best to conduct these experiments barefoot on a cool, bare floor for best results. We will start with some gross movements and then move on to small movements.

Begin by standing upright, feet together, arms at your sides, and head upright and well balanced. Keep your eyes closed so that you can concentrate. We will refer to this as the starting position. Bending at the waist, look down at the floor and pay very careful attention to what you feel in your feet. As you bend forward and tilt your head down, your centre of gravity changes, and unless you compensate for this shift you will fall forward. What prevents you from overbalancing? A reaction somewhere in your feet works opposite to the forces bringing about the imbalance; this reaction-response brings equilibrium. See Figure CCCH.05.03.03.

Let's try some slight movements. Adopt the starting position. Lift your right arm and touch your right ear, then move your hand to the top of your head, then touch the tip of your nose. Lower your arm back to your side. Pay careful attention to what you are feeling on the soles of your feet. You will have been aware that for each small movement of the arm, your feet compensated for this change, however small, in your centre of gravity. See Figure CCCH.05.03.04.

Right foot | Left foot

Foot pressure index

Very high
High
Moderate
Light
Low

c.g

Figure CCCH.05.03.02: As the heavy suitcase is lifted, the centre of gravity and weight distribution shifts. Note how the shoulder bearing the weight drops lower. To maintain balance, the person pushes down harder on the right foot and this results in greater pressure on the sole of the right foot. On a soft substrate (such as sand), this would result in a deeper track on the right.

Now let's make an even smaller movement. Adopt the starting position. Once again, concentrate hard on what you are feeling in your feet. Turn your head all the way to the left and then to the right; look up and then down (tilting only the neck, not the body). Once again, you will be aware of a rolling motion in your feet that will be compensating for the shifts in the centre of gravity and restoring dynamic equilibrium. See Figure CCCH.05.03.05.

Amazing and as unlikely as it may seem, even actions like sticking your tongue out, taking a deep breath, or even swallowing cause a shift in centre of gravity and will register in the tracks. Each of these actions will provoke a compensating response.

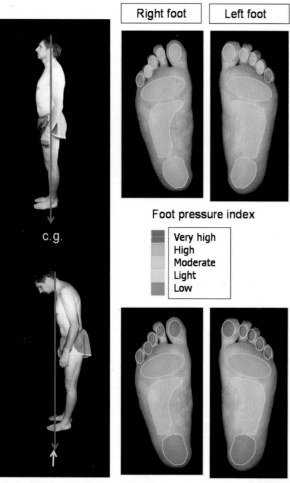

Figure CCCH.05.03.03: Remember from your science days at school that for every action there must be an equal and opposite reaction? As you bent forward, you would have been aware of your feet flexing forward and the balls of your feet pressurize in compensation. Thus, as the feet record both action and reaction, it registers in the track.

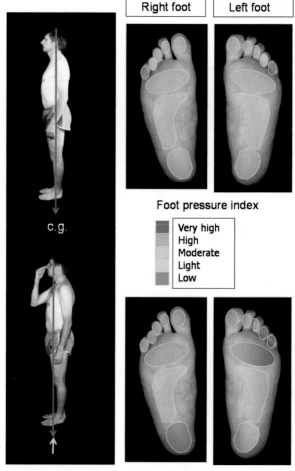

Figure CCCH.05.03.04: Even slight movements like lifting your arm to touch your nose or the top of your head will be reflected and recorded in pressure maps.

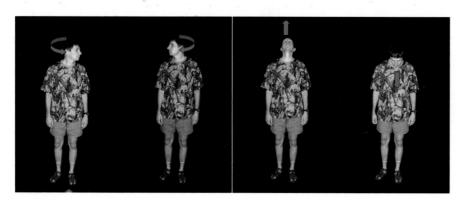

Figure CCCH.05.03.05: Slight movements of the head in looking to the left or the right or up and down shifts the weight (mass) of the head. This shifts the centre of gravity and will be compensated for in the feet. Again, even for these minor movements, the pressure responses will record the event.

Directional Pressure Releases (Turning or Rotating)

Tom Brown, whom I've mentioned several times, developed an excellent system to describe pressure releases; we will, therefore, with a few exceptions, stick to his terminology as it is most practical and useful, and it would be foolish to "reinvent the wheel."

"The message (voice) in a track begins to be registered when the foot applies pressure to the ground, bending and shaping the ground to the rhythm of the body's movements and thoughts, creating ridges, fissures, valleys, and all manner of features with each feature becoming a visible expression of the reaction of the body and mind of its maker. Its fluid movements are not fully born until the pressure is released and the track settles into its full reality. It is then that the track is fully born." (This was slightly modified from Tom Brown.) The dramatic and startling implications of this quote are that thoughts, emotions, and physiological well-being are registered in the track and are "readable"! This is quite different from what we've been discussing earlier concerning large and slight human and animal movements.

Emotions affect the way we walk and will be registered in our tracks. See Figure CCCH.05.03.06.

Levels of tiredness will register in tracks. See Figure CCCH.05.03.07.

Expert trackers can tell from a track not only what animal (or human) made it, but they can also give the sex, age, speed at which it was traveling, its condition (hungry, thirsty, healthy, sick, or injured), the way it was looking, and even what it was thinking!

"Pressure-release systems are so intricate and defining that you can know more about an animal than you ever believed possible . . .tracks will never again be lifeless depressions on the ground."
(Tom Brown)

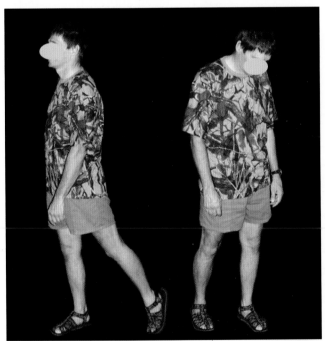

Figure CCCH.05.03.06: The person on the right is feeling sad and depressed. Note how the head hangs, shoulders slump, arms hang, and feet drag. The stride of the sad, depressed person will be shorter than those of the happy person. The straddle width will also be wider when the person is downcast. The person on the left is happy. Note how the head is held up high, shoulders are back, arms are swinging, and the feet are lifted high. It is clear from these examples that posture is affected by emotion and that the centre of gravity shifts with different emotions; any shift will be registered in the tracks.

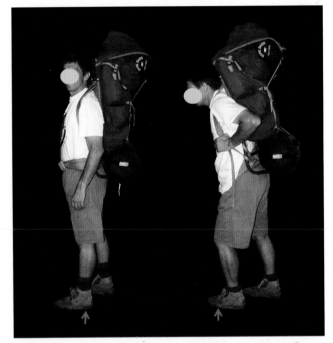

Figure CCCH.05.03.07: The person on the left has just started out on a hike and is well fed, well hydrated, fresh, and full of energy. The stride will be longer, the straddle width narrower, and the weight more evenly distributed. Once again much could be learned from the tracks of this hiker. As he tires, he will slump farther forward and his stride will shorten. He will continually shift his pack that is causing him discomfort. He will not look around as much as he did when he was fresh. All this information and much more will be evident in his tracks. Notice too how the reaction pressure from the foot moves from the arch to the ball of the foot as the hiker tires.

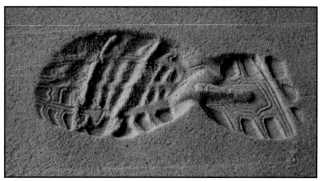

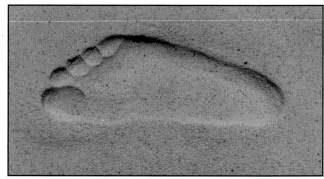

Figure CCCH.05.03.08 shows a stamp or a dead track. There is only downward pressure and no movement in any other direction in this track.

A track is a wealth of information, frozen in time and space, waiting to be deciphered and interpreted. Brown describes the pressure releases in a track as a map made up of features that are equivalent to large-scale landscapes but in miniature form. And so we have crests, ridges, cliffs, caves, plates, and so on. Different movements, reactions, physiological states, and emotions are responsible for causing different pressure releases, and Brown estimates there are more than six thousand pressure releases. Each one is a code for a specific reaction and is registered on the ground as a decipherable message—for those who are able to interpret it.

There are essentially two categories of pressure releases: the major and minor Pressure Releases. Brown states that there are more than fifteen hundred major pressure releases and over forty-six hundred minor pressure releases! It is well beyond the scope of this book to even begin to explore all these pressure releases—an understanding of them is well beyond my knowhow. I have taken a lot of trouble to try to duplicate many of the pressure releases described by Brown, and I must admit that I have only been successful in duplicating and interpreting some of the major pressure releases; consequently, we will confine ourselves in this book to looking at the "easier" pressure releases that would be of practical use to a tracker. I highly recommended that you get hold of Tom Brown's books if you want to go into a more detailed study of pressure releases.

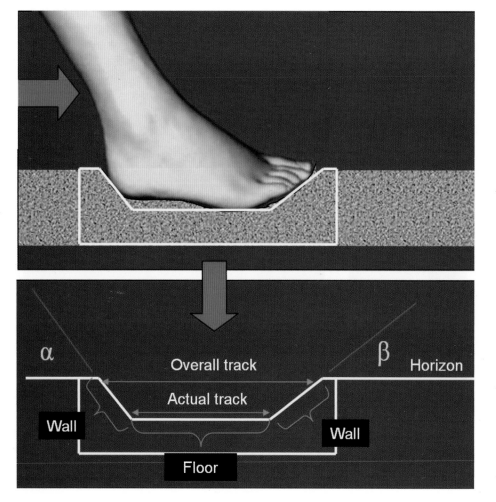

Overall track

Actual track

α   β   Horizon

Wall   Wall

Floor

Figure CCCH.05.03.09: Normally tracks are not made with a stamp. This illustration shows a cross section of a track the way it is actually made. When moving forward, the foot enters or strikes the ground at an angle (œ), registers, spreads as weight is applied, and then exits at an angle (ß). The track therefore has sloping walls at the heel and toe. Notice that because of the sloping walls, there is a difference between the overall and actual track dimensions.

GAIT PATTERNS AND PRESSURE RELEASES

I was very impressed with the ease by which it was possible to duplicate major pressure releases in a sandbox or on the fine sand of a beach, as illustrated in Brown's book. I believe my photographs show that an understanding of them can be of great help to a tracker. As discussed in an earlier chapter, a sandbox is the ideal tracking medium and the best one on which to learn. Construct and fill it with clean beach or play sand. As you learn to identify the major pressure releases correctly, you can move on to more difficult and challenging substrates; the pressure releases will still be there but will just be more difficult to see. The sandbox is readily accessible, usable in all weathers, and a source of limitless information—it must become your tracking "university."

Remember to keep the sand slightly damp and smooth it with a wide board. Tamp it down slightly. Weather conditions, soil properties, and a host of other factors determine the ultimate and final shape of the pressure releases, but the principles that bring them about remain identical. The best illustrations and, therefore, the best conditions from which to learn about pressure releases are on damp sand. Brown refers to this as "zero soil or zero earth." We will use his terminology. It is important to remember that the depth of the sand must be at least 150mm. If it is less than this, there is not enough buffer, and secondary pressure releases will be affected. We will now start to learn some basic pressure releases and interpret what they practically mean.

The first pressure releases we will look at are those that are static, where the subject is stationary. When

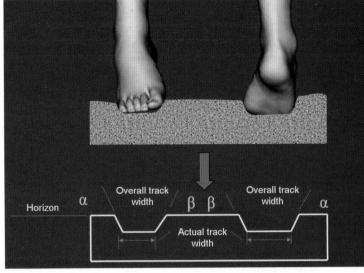

Figure CCCH.05.03.10: Viewed from the heel or toe, the same thing happens. The foot enters, spreads, registers, and is withdrawn, also leaving sloping sides from this aspect. The angles of the sloping sides are shown as angles α and ß. Notice, too, that because of the slope, there is an overall track width and an actual or true track width.

a track is made on the ground, it "registers" or leaves an impression/imprint. See Figure CCCH.05.03.08. This indentation has "walls," and a study of the walls will help determine if the animal or person has changed direction in any way, shifted his body weight, had a loss of balance, turned his head, has stopped, or is slowing.

The first example is referred to as a stamp and is illustrated in Figure CCCH.05.03.08. When a stamp is registered, weight has been applied with the foot and the foot carefully removed without disturbing the track in any way. Other than applying downward pressure, there has been no movement in any direction. Brown refers to this as a "dead track."

It is important to become familiar with the terminology of pressure releases; otherwise; as you will see it can become quite confusing. Refer to Figure CCCH.05.03.11.

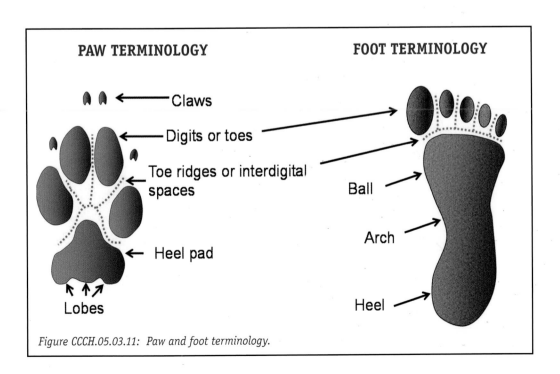

Figure CCCH.05.03.11: Paw and foot terminology.

Primary Pressure Releases Indicating Turning or Rotating

As the foot is turned or rotated, an increasing amount of pressure is applied to the sidewalls of the track. This causes it to progressively deform as more pressure is applied. The changes that come about due to rotation or turning follow a given sequence. By studying even a single track, it is possible to determine changes in direction accurately. The sequence of pressure releases for changes in direction are shown in Figure CCCH.05.03.12 and begin with a stamp (dead track) then goes to the cliff, ridge, peak, crest, crest-crumble, cave, cave-in, plate, plate-fissure, plate-crumble, and explosion . . . in that order.

Linear motion pressure releases are indicators of changes in forward movement.

Now we will investigate pressure releases that Brown tells us can give an accurate indication of how fast an animal or human is moving, when they are increasing or decreasing speed, pausing, or stopping. This can

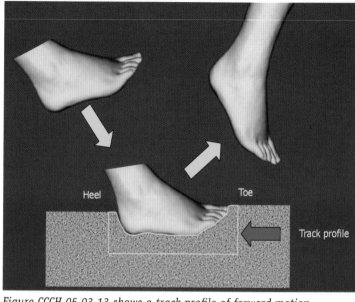

Figure CCCH.05.03.13 shows a track profile of forward motion.

PRESSURE RELEASE PROFILES INDICATING CHANGE OF DIRECTION

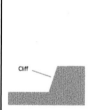 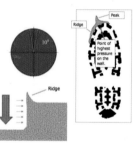 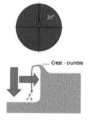 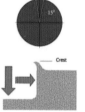 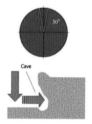 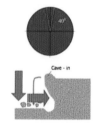

1. The cliff: No pressure on wall.

2. The ridge and peak: A slight turn of 10 degrees will raise a ridge. A peak will be formed at the highest point of pressure on the ridge.

3. The crest: A turn of 15 degrees will cause a crest to form.

4. The crest-crumble: A turn of 20 degrees will cause the crest to break and fall into the track.

5. The cave: Indicates a 30-degree turn. The foot pivots and moves into the wall to form a cave.

6. The cave-in: This will occur at a change in direction of 40 degrees or more.

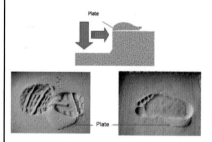 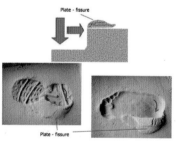 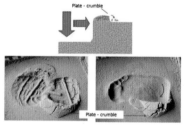

7. The plate: The wall buckles under pressure and splits far back, forming a plate. Occurs with drastic turns or stops.

8. The plate-fissure: A dramatic turn increasing pressure will cause the plate to fissure.

9. The plate crumble: With increasing pressure and intensity, fissures widen and deepen and the plate begins to fall part.

10. Explosion: Extreme force explodes the wall in the direction of force.

Figure CCCH.05.03.12: The pressure forces exerted on the sidewalls of the track bring about the changes in rotating or turning pressure releases. The more drastic the turn, the greater will be the effect on the track.

GAIT PATTERNS AND PRESSURE RELEASES

SEQUENCE OF NINE PRESSURE RELEASE PROFILES FOR LINEAR MOTION WITH INCREASING SPEED

1. The wave: Indicates a slow ambling walk. The heel forces up a small mound ahead of it.

2. The double wave: Indicates a purposeful walk. Pressure on the existing wave creates a smaller secondary wave.

3. The disc: A small disc fractures off at the front of the wave and rides up it. Indicates a fast walk.

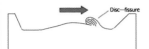

4. The disc fissure: Pressure builds in the disc, causing small cracks or fissures to appear. A slow jog in humans or a trot in animals.

5. The disc crumble: Increasing pressure causes the disc to crumble. Indicates a jog in humans or a fast trot in animals.

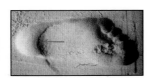

6. The dish: The entire wave shears off and moves backward to create a large disc now referred to as a dish. Indicates a fast jog in humans or a bound in animals.

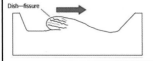

7. The dish fissure: Pressure builds, causing the dish to crack or fissure. Indicates a slow run, lope, or canter in animals.

8. The dish crumble: The dish now falls apart under the pressure, indicating a fast run in humans and a gallop in animals.

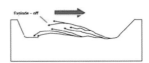

9. The explode off: At sprint intensity the forces are too great for the available surface area. The track blows out and scatters soil particles beyond the heel. Indicates a sprint or a sudden take off.

Figure CCCH.05.03.14: Linear pressure releases indicate changes in the speed of forward motion.

also be determined from the gait of an animal, but it is seldom that one has the luxury of finding a whole sequence of tracks on a suitable substrate. This is where understanding pressure releases becomes a valuable tool. It is said that the speed of motion can be accurately determined from a single track. Let us see if this is so.

The diagrams and photographs in this section are a cross section of the track with the heel on the left and the toes exiting on the right. The human foot will be used to illustrate the examples. The profiles we will be looking at to illustrate forward motion will be those of a human foot entering with the heel on the left and pushing off with the toes on the right. See Figure CCCH.05.03.13.

The sequence for pressure releases indicates a change in forward motion and is shown in Figure CCCH.05.03.14. Changes in direction follow a sequence also: the wave, double wave, disc, disc-fissure, disc-crumble, dish, dish-fissure, dish-crumble, and explode-off.

Well so far, so good, we have been able to duplicate the pressure releases for forward motion with relative ease in our ideal substrate. It is impressive to see how accurate the pressure releases are in indicating the magnitude of directional change or the change in linear speed. I will now explain how to go about deciding when a disc becomes a dish.

Up until now we have been discussing the maintenance of forward motion. This will leave behind a uniform sequence of tracks that indicate continuity in speed and motion. You will, therefore, have a series of tracks showing consistent disc–fissures if you are maintaining the speed of a slow jog, for example. If you should increase your pace to that of a slow run, you might expect to suddenly see the pressure release profile change to that of a dish–fissure. Not so. Before you get to that point, you will have to go through an acceleration phase with an increase in pressure and

Figure CCCH.05.03.15: The lope or canter of this blue wildebeest will be evident in the track as dish-fissures.

Figure CCCH.05.03.16: The dish-crumble pressure and explode-offs may be evident in this galloping red hartebeest.

intensity to get you to the required speed. So you will more likely have something like: disc–fissure, disc–fissure, dish, dish, dish–crumble, dish–fissure, dish–fissure . . . Test this on the beach if you have access to one. You will be impressed with the results. The dish, and disc–crumble are acceleration steps to bring you up to the desired speed; once having been reached it is then maintained as dish–fissure pressure releases.

Having now an understanding of what is involved in changing and maintaining the speed of forward motion, we can turn our attention to drawing a distinction between a disc and a dish. The line that divides a disc from a dish is very definitive for footprints, hoofs, and paws. The distinction between a disc and a dish in human prints is shown in Figure CCCH.05.03.18. Brown states that it makes no difference if footwear is being worn, for these will show up through shoes or boots.

To find the dividing line for paws, work as follows: Imagine a line connecting the trailing edge

Figure CCCH.05.03.17: On top, the scattered soil lying far beyond the track itself indicates a sudden jumping away or a sprint by an impala. The soil is granular and sandy. Below, a warthog has sprinted off to the right when it became aware of my presence. Note the scattered soil beyond the track. The substrate is clay soil.

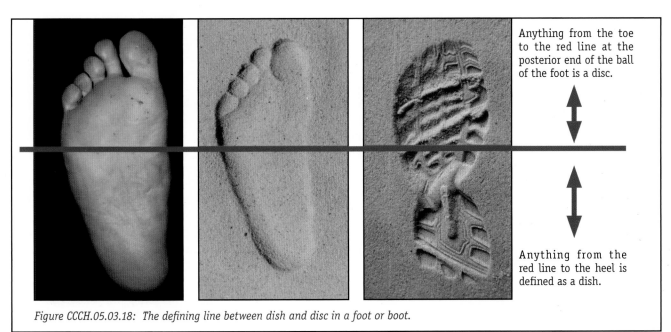

Anything from the toe to the red line at the posterior end of the ball of the foot is a disc.

Anything from the red line to the heel is defined as a dish.

Figure CCCH.05.03.18: The defining line between dish and disc in a foot or boot.

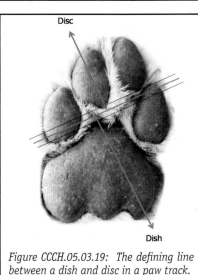

Disc

Dish

Figure CCCH.05.03.19: The defining line between a dish and disc in a paw track.

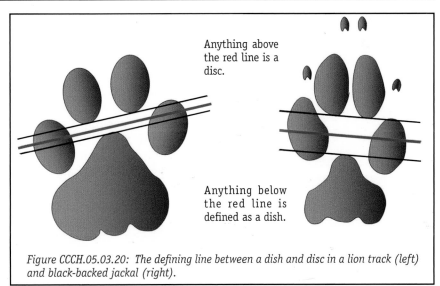

Anything above the red line is a disc.

Anything below the red line is defined as a dish.

Figure CCCH.05.03.20: The defining line between a dish and disc in a lion track (left) and black-backed jackal (right).

of the middle two digits (toes) and a line, parallel to this and just touching the leading edge of the heel pad. Bisect the distance between these two lines, and it will give you the position of the dividing line. See Figures CCCH.05.03.19 and CCCH.05.03.20.

The distinction between a disc and a dish in a hoof print is shown in Figure CCCH.05.03.21. Simply divide the track in two equal halves. The bisecting line will define the changeover point between disc and dish.

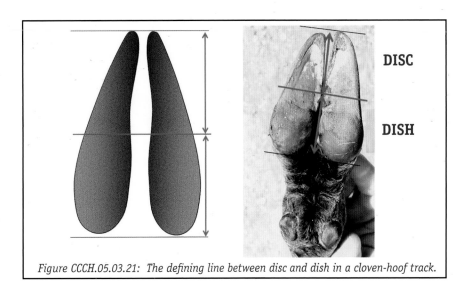

DISC

DISH

Figure CCCH.05.03.21: The defining line between disc and dish in a cloven-hoof track.

Head Position and Pitch

From what we have learned so far, we see that we can accurately determine changes in direction and in forward motion. Now we ask ourselves the question: "Is it possible to determine from a track which way the animal was looking when the track was registered?" See Figure CCCH.05.03.22.

Let's begin by looking at head roll. This is the position of the head on the vertical plane—in other words looking up, down, and including all the intermediate positions as well. See Figure CCCH.05.03.23.

Let us deduce from Figure CCCH.05.03.23 how this information will be recorded in the tracks. The pressure releases you will now see do not have anything to do with building up of anything but have to do exclusively with pressure and track depth. When an animal's head is held in a neutral position, the track depth will be equal at the toes and at the heel. A neutral position is generally the most comfortable and the one usually adopted by an animal when it is walking.

In the head-down position (whether feeding, drinking, grooming, or looking at something on the ground), the forward displacement of body mass will cause a difference in track depth between the toes and heel. This is referred to as positive pitch and will result in the depth of the track being appreciably deeper at the

Figure CCCH.05.03.23: In the photographs we have the two extremes: head all the way up (the impala browsing) or all the way down (the warthog grazing).

Figure CCCH.05.03.22: In the photograph with the buffaloes, the head of one is down and grazing, the other bull's head is lifted and is staring toward the photographer. The impala is looking to its left. Could we determine these facts by examining the tracks? Yes, it is possible for, once again, weight distribution changes as our heads move from side to side and up and down.

Figure CCCH.05.03.24: The track of a grazing animal with its head down will be evident when comparing the depth of the track at the toe and heel. In this photograph the impala's head is down and it is scratching itself. This would leave an interesting track, for only three feet will register. More weight will be transferred to the right front and right rear foot to maintain balance. A head-down position is referred to as positive pitch.

Cross-section through a track

Heel   Toe

GAIT PATTERNS AND PRESSURE RELEASES

toes than at the heel. See Figure CCCH.05.03.24.

When the head is held in a neutral position, which is the one most comfortable for the animal and usually adopted when walking, the depth of the track is the same from heel to toe. The floor of the track is level on the horizontal plane. See Figures CCCH.05.03.25 and CCCH.05.03.26.

The head-up position (negative pitch) can be adopted when an animal is lifting its head to sniff the breeze, looking intently at something that has caught its attention, adopting an upright aggressive pose, or feeding. See Figure CCCH.05.03.27. The animal's body mass is displaced to the rear, with the result that greater pressure in the heel area will cause the track to be deeper than at the toe end of the track.

From your knowledge of the relationship between head pitch and track, you should be able to determine the position of an animal's head from a single track. See Figure CCCH.05.03.29.

Cross-section through a track

Heel   Toe

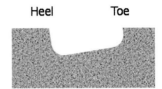

Cross-section through a track

Heel   Toe

Figure CCCH.05.03.25: The elephant and baboon are walking with their heads in neutral pitch.

Figure CCCH.05.03.27: Head-up or negative-pitch position.

Figure CCCH.05.03.26: These photos show a zebra with its head held at a neutral pitch (above right) and the tracks of a giraffe (top left) and a buffalo (bottom left) that indicate their heads are being held in a neutral position.

Looking up	Neutral position	Looking down

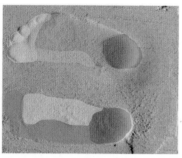 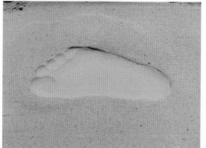 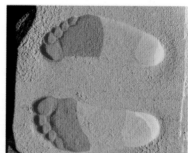

In this example the person is looking up with weight on the right foot. The heels are deeper than either for the neutral or head-down position and the toes shallower. The track is tilted backward in the horizontal plane.

With the head held in the neutral position, weight is evenly distributed with pressure on the toes and heel being more or less equal. The track is level in the horizontal plane.

Pressure is from very high (red) to low (green)

With the head down, mass is displaced forward and the toes dig in because of increased downward pressure. Toes are deeper than for either of the other two positions and the track tilts forward in the horizontal plane.

Figure CCCH.05.03.28 illustrates pressure maps on the soles of the feet of a person with his head held at positive, neutral, and negative pitch. These three images make the effect of head position on the track easily comparable.

Figure CCCH.05.03.29: In this photograph there are two zebras with their heads down, one zebra with its head up, and a giraffe walking in the background with its head held in a neutral position. From your knowledge of pressure releases, you should be able to read this from a single track of each animal.

Head Position and Turns

Now we can move on to how to determine exactly in which direction an animal was looking when the track was registered. These pressure releases are referred to as head turns and are independent of head pitch. Again these pressure releases, as for those of head pitch, only have to do with track depth and have nothing to do with building up of pressure releases.

Head turns are part of an animal's natural surveillance routine as it monitors its surroundings for potential prey, food, or danger. Whereas we looked for the pressure releases for head-pitch only on the longitudinal axis of the track, we now include the side-to-side or lateral axis to determine the position of the head. See Figure CCCH.05.03.30.

These measurements of head pitch and direction are fairly crude in comparison to the pressure releases we have studied so far for direction and motion in a straight line. They must suffice for now, however.

Make extensive use of your sandbox and easy tracking mediums to master the linear, turning, and head position pressure releases. This is where you will learn a tremendous amount. I tried duplicating the pressure releases studied thus far on more complex substrates and then found how much more difficult it is to see and interpret them when compared to the ideal tracking medium of the sandbox. Even when one knows where to look, it is not always easy to find the pressure release you know should be there. This happens because

➤ The changes are more subtle.

➤ Some of the changes taking place happen quickly and do not leave

Figure CCCH.05.03.30: Head turns will also register in the track.

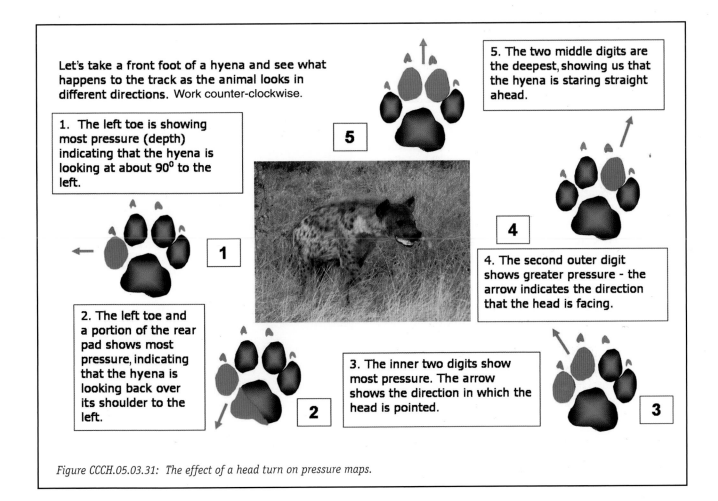

Let's take a front foot of a hyena and see what happens to the track as the animal looks in different directions. Work counter-clockwise.

1. The left toe is showing most pressure (depth) indicating that the hyena is looking at about 90° to the left.

2. The left toe and a portion of the rear pad shows most pressure, indicating that the hyena is looking back over its shoulder to the left.

3. The inner two digits show most pressure. The arrow shows the direction in which the head is pointed.

4. The second outer digit shows greater pressure - the arrow indicates the direction that the head is facing.

5. The two middle digits are the deepest, showing us that the hyena is staring straight ahead.

Figure CCCH.05.03.31: The effect of a head turn on pressure maps.

behind the results one sees in ideal substrates. For example, fissures and caves are very transient in dry substrates with low cohesive properties. The fissures and caves fill in the moment pressure is released and leave little trace.

You have now been introduced to the fundamentals of pressure releases. Where to look for them, how to identify them, and how to interpret their meaning. Once having been made aware of these signs, it becomes self-evident that there is a wealth of information hidden in a track. Not only physical information can be garnered from the imprint of a foot, hoof, or paw registered on the substrate, but also physiological conditions and, as impossible as it may seem, even thought processes!

From the characteristics of the track caused by pressure of the foot against the substrate and the reaction of the substrate to that pressure, it is possible to determine, from a single track:

➤ the direction of travel

➤ the speed of travel

➤ the direction and pitch of the head when the track was registered

There are many more difficult and complex pressure releases to learn, but they are beyond the scope of this book. The reader is urged to read Tom Brown's books for more information on the fascinating subject of pressure releases.

Tracking Shorthand

Brown also came up with a "shorthand" to describe a track and the effects it had on a substrate. This defines a "universal" tracker language that enables a tracker to "read" the information in an illustration or tracking sketch without being physically on the ground. It is a wonderful way to relay information or to keep personal tracking notes. I have made a few changes to Brown's system to simplify it but have not deviated from it significantly. Accompanying each shorthand symbol, I have taken photographs to show you what each symbol represents so that you will know what the track looks like on the ground.

Also take note that I have done this on an ideal substrate; the track characteristics and pressure releases will look different on different substrates. You will have to experiment with different substrates to see what they look like and how they differ from the ideal. Brown states that the pressure releases are visible on all substrates (even rock?) if you know what to look for and where to look. To be honest, we found it very difficult and often impossible on difficult substrates to see the pressure releases or their effects that Brown says are visible to the practiced eye. This is, perhaps, a reflection of how "unpracticed" our

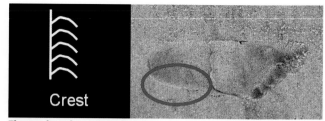

Crest

The track maker turns sharply to one side, causing a ridge to form which may have a wave-like lip.

Crest-crumble

A large lateral force is applied to the crest, causing it to break up.

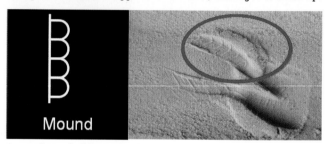

Mound

A prominent build-up of soil on either the inside or outside of the track, caused by an abrupt twist or turn.

Figure CCCH.05.03.32 illustrates tracking shorthand for crest, crest crumble, and mound.

Cave

Can be caused by a sudden leap to one side or an abrupt stop. In soils of low cohesive qualities, removal of pressure may result in immediate collapse of the cave, often making it difficult to observe.

Cave-in

When a cave, ridge, or crest collapses when the supporting foot is removed, it leaves a pile of soil. A cave may be caused by a kick, abrupt turn, or severe impact.

Figure CCCH.05.03.33 illustrates tracking shorthand for cave and cave-in.

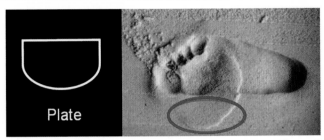

Plate

Caused by increased pressure or abrupt stops or turns. The wall buckles under pressure, forming a layer which radiates outward.

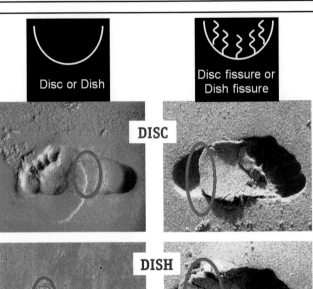

Plate crumble

Plate fissure

The plate begins to break up as the degree of turn increases and pressure builds up. Plate fissures do not register well in soils with low-cohesive properties.

With increased pressure and intensity, the fissures widen and break up in a mosaic-like pattern. Plate crumbles may be very difficult to observe in soils with low-cohesive properties.

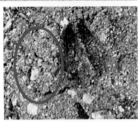

Figure CCCH.05.03.34 illustrates tracking shorthand for plate, plate fissure, and plate crumble.

Disc or Dish

Disc fissure or Dish fissure

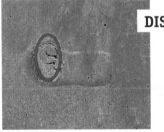

DISC

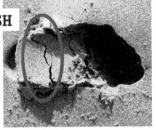

DISH

Disc-crumble or Dish-crumble

Explosion

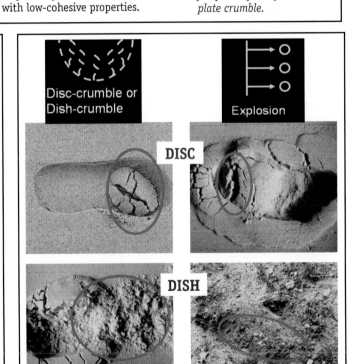

DISC

DISH

Disc: a round or ovoid clump of soil that detaches from a wave as a result of increased pressure and intensity and is indicative of a fast "push-off."
Dish: as speed increases, the pressure and intensity causes a plate, shaped like a disc, to break away from a wave and is found in the rear half of the track.
Disc and dishes are not always obvious in soils with low cohesive properties.

With an increase in speed, both discs and dishes will eventually fissure.
A disc fissure will be indicative of a slow jog in humans and a lope in animal tracks.
Disc and dish fissures are not always obvious in soils with low cohesive properties.

Figure CCCH.05.03.35 illustrates tracking shorthand for disc, dish, disc fissure, and dish fissure.

A disc crumble or dish crumble indicates a harder "pushing off" effort with greater intensity and pressure. A disc crumble is indicative of a jog in humans and of a galloping animal. These pressure releases are difficult to observe in substrate with low cohesive qualities.

High pressure casued by a sharp turn, sudden acceleration, slip, or jumping away can cause soil to be thrown out of the track. On the bottom a sudden takeoff by a warthog results in an explosion of soil particles that are thrown out of and beyond the track.

Figure CCCH.05.03.36 illustrates tracking shorthand for disc crumble, dish crumble, and explosion.

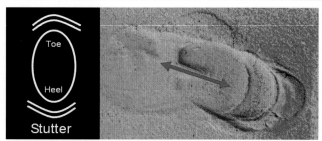

Stutter

A lengthening and deepening of the track caused by rapid and repetitive forward movement of the foot. Can indicate hesitation.

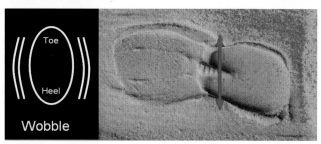

Wobble

A widening and deepening of the track caused by repetitive sideways movement of the foot. Can indicate excitement, fear, or anxiety.

Figure CCCH.05.03.37 illustrates tracking shorthand for stutter and wobble.

Pitch

Pitch is the lengthwise angle of the track relative to the ground and shows the overall weight distribution of the track. An even pitch is horizontal. In a forward pitch the toe is deeper than the heel and a backward pitch is indicated by the heel deeper than the toe. Above right, forward pitch in an impala track.

Roll

Roll is the lateral angle of the track relative to the ground. No roll—track inclined to the right. Left roll—track inclined to the left. Can indicate a loss of balance, gentle turn, or a fall.

Figure CCCH.05.03.39 illustrates tracking shorthand for pitch and roll.

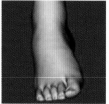

Twist

Indicates a twist or rotation of between 0–45 degrees, creating a smooth arc in the substrate.

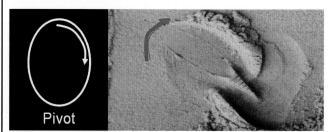

Pivot

Indicates a twist or rotation of between 45–90 degrees, creating a smooth arc and mound in the substrate.

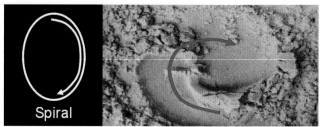

Spiral

Indicates a twist or rotation of between 90–360 degrees, with considerable mounding, crevassing, and crumbling in the substrate.

Figure CCCH.05.03.38 illustrates tracking shorthand for twist, pivot, and spiral.

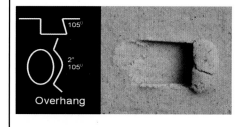

Overhang

This is a cliff with an overhang sloping more than 90 degrees inward. Common with sharp, pointed hoofs. Can be indicative of a sudden stop or when an animal has pushed off in the opposite direction. Overhangs collapse almost as soon as pressure is removed in soils with low cohesive properties and are difficult to observe "after the fact".

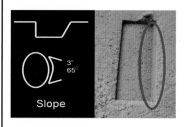

Slope

An overhang sloping less than 90 degrees. Occurs at the toe or heel where the foot has gone in or been withdrawn. Indicates a lean, sidestep, or someone that supinates (bowlegged) when on the side of the track. A slope is less pronounced in soils with low cohesive properties.

Figure CCCH.05.03.40 illustrates tracking shorthand for overhang and slope.

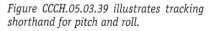

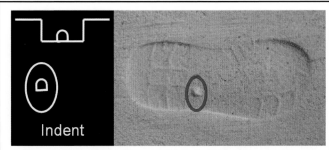

Indent

A protrusion in the track caused by an indentation in the foot, hoof, or paw. Could indicate a possible injury.

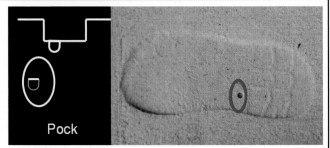

Pock

An indentation in the track caused by a protrusion in the foot, hoof, or paw. Could indicate an embedded object or growth. Both indentations are far less evident on hard substrates and in soils which are dry and have low cohesive qualities.

Figure CCCH.05.03.41 illustrates tracking shorthand for indent and pock.

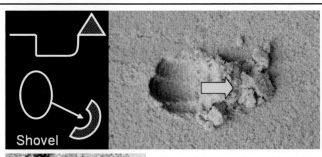

Shovel

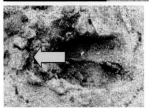

When soil is scooped up and deposited just outside the track, it can indicate boredom or frustration if the person or animal is standing on the same spot. It can also indicate an animal digging or a stumble. The bushbuck track on right shows a shovel.

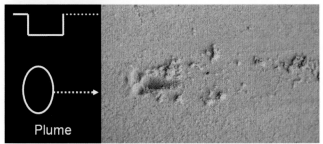

Plume

When soil is scattered in a line beyond the track, it indicates a fast gait in the direction of the plume and fast acceleration if it is behind the track. If the plume is in an arc near the track, it shows a sudden pivot or whirl.

Figure CCCH.05.03.42 illustrates tracking for shovel and plume.

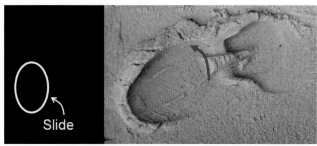

Slide

A gouge mark in the soil caused by an intentional skid. Often accompanied by mounding. In animals with retractable claws, the claw marks may be evident.

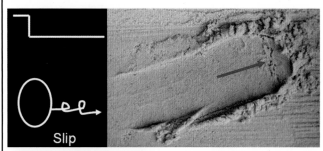

Slip

A gouge mark in the soil caused by an unintentional skid. The next track shows either a recovery or a fall. In animals with retractable claws, the claw marks may be evident. Above right shows the slip of a kudu at a water hole.

Figure CCCH.05.03.43 illustrates tracking shorthand for slide and slip.

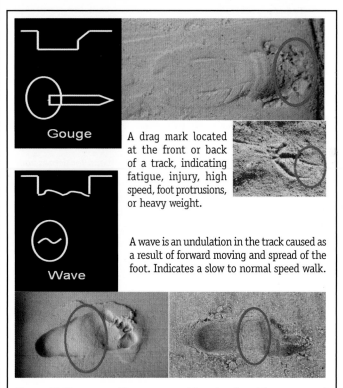

Gouge

A drag mark located at the front or back of a track, indicating fatigue, injury, high speed, foot protrusions, or heavy weight.

Wave

A wave is an undulation in the track caused as a result of forward moving and spread of the foot. Indicates a slow to normal speed walk.

Figure CCCH.05.03.44 illustrates tracking shorthand for gouge and wave.

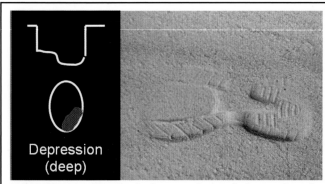

Depression
(deep)

Depressions are areas in the bottom of a track deeper than the average depth, which indicate weight distribution.

Depression
(shallow)

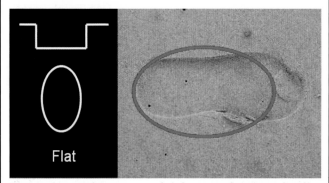

Flat

Features in a track are measured and compared against a baseline of flat and featureless parts of the track. With the exception of a small disc in the toe area, most of this track is flat.

Figure CCCH.05.03.45 illustrates tracking shorthand for depressions and flat.

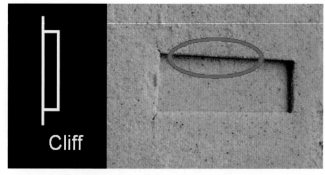

Cliff

Occurs at the sides of the feet, indicating an animal traveling in a straight line. A cliff is a vertical edge where the soil is pressed downward at a right angle.

Ridge

A ridge is caused by pressure to one side, as, for example, when turning. A turn causes a sharp edge to be lifted above the surrounding soil level and can occur between the toes or between the hoofs of cloven-footed animals.

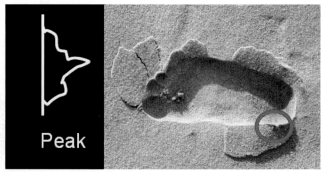

Peak

The highest point on a ridge indicating the location of greatest pressure and the line of greatest force.

Figure CCCH.05.03.46 illustrates tracking shorthand for cliff, ridge, and peak.

GAIT PATTERNS AND PRESSURE RELEASES

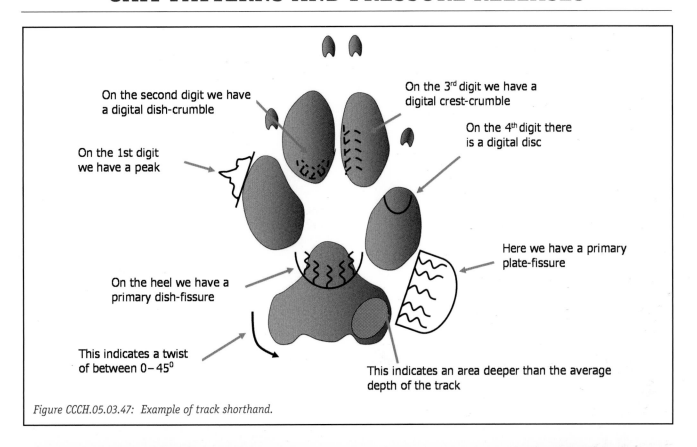

On the second digit we have a digital dish-crumble

On the 3rd digit we have a digital crest-crumble

On the 1st digit we have a peak

On the 4th digit there is a digital disc

On the heel we have a primary dish-fissure

Here we have a primary plate-fissure

This indicates a twist of between 0–45⁰

This indicates an area deeper than the average depth of the track

Figure CCCH.05.03.47: Example of track shorthand.

The final sketch of pressure release information would look like that shown below. Remember, we are not recording other information at this stage such as track patterns—that is something different—we are looking at and recording pressure release data.

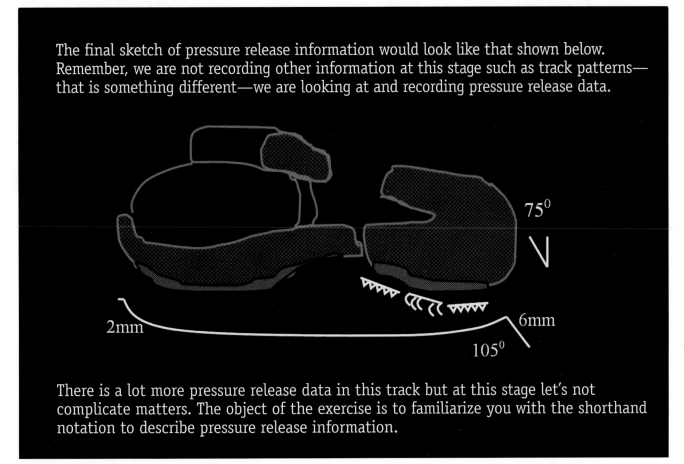

There is a lot more pressure release data in this track but at this stage let's not complicate matters. The object of the exercise is to familiarize you with the shorthand notation to describe pressure release information.

Figure CCCH.05.03.49: Recording track information.

Figure CCCH.05.03.48: Recording track information.

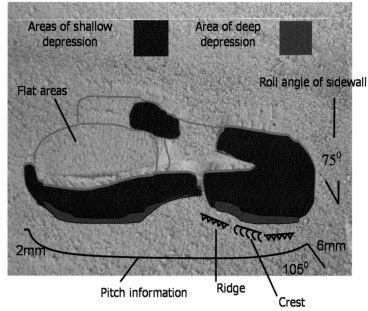

Areas of shallow depression

Area of deep depression

Flat areas

Roll angle of sidewall

75°

2mm

6mm

105°

Pitch information

Ridge

Crest

Figure CCCH.05.03.50: Recording track information on an impala.

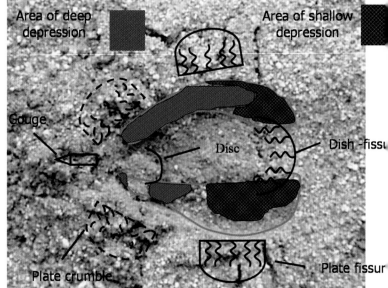

Area of deep depression

Area of shallow depression

Gouge

Disc

Dish-fissu

Plate crumble

Plate fissur

powers of observation are and how much we still have to learn. See Figures CCCH.05.03.32 to CCCH.05.03.46.

Without trying at this point to make an overall interpretation of what the track is telling us, Figure CCCH.05.03.47 illustrates how we can use the shorthand symbols to describe what we see in a track.

Two more practical examples of how shorthand notation can be used to record track information are illustrated in Figures CCCH.05.03.48 and CCCH.05.03.49.

This is where we will stop with the more complex pressure releases. There is still much to learn: how digital pressure releases can make each part of a track (e.g., a toe) function independently and have its own pressure releases and how heel or lobular pressure releases can give us insights into the inner workings of an animal's body, mind, and emotions.

The final sketch of pressure-release information on the impala would look like that shown below. Once again there is a lot more information in the track that we have not indicated in this sketch—to avoid cluttering make an additional diagram if you wish to include additional information.

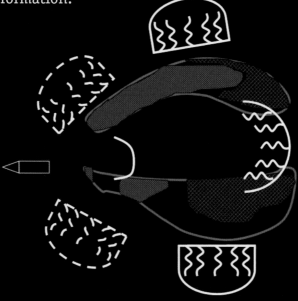

Once we understand that the digit, like a whole track, behaves in the same way, it is easy to grasp the fact that each digit can have its own pressure releases.

Figure CCCH.05.03.51: Recording track information on an impala.

Figure CCCH.05.03.52: Indicator pressure releases are like individual fingerprints. If we enlarge some parts of this lioness's pad (left front foot), we will clearly be able to see some features that will enable us to identify the tracks as belonging to this specific individual. The size, shape, and dimensions of the track are also important diagnostic identification features. The features circled in yellow are unique only to this lioness and none other.

Indicator Pressure Releases

Depending on the substrate, indicator pressure releases can best be described as a fingerprint. There will be certain physical structures in a track that will be peculiar to the specific individual, like an old scar or a chip out of a hoof for example. These characteristics will indicate a particular individual. Sometimes the indicator pressure releases might be very small. Even if, for example, the tracker is following ten people all wearing the same type and size of boot, there will still be certain indicator pressure releases defining each boot print. We will look at some lion tracks and point out some features that will create indicator pressure releases. See Figure CCCH.05.03.52.

Looking at the right front foot of the same lioness in Figure CCCH.05.03.53, we see more distinguishing features like the two fissures ringed in yellow. By careful examination, we will soon find many features that will register as indicator pressure releases and enable us to identify individuals with accuracy. Footwear also has distinct features other than the basic shape, size, and tread pattern. Note carefully the wear pattern of the tread, which will also give you an indication of how the person walks. Does the person walk with his toe in or toe out; does he supinate (walk on the outer edge of the foot) or pronate (walk on the inner side of the foot, etc.)? When we have identified indicator pressure releases, we can then proceed to foot mapping. Indicator pressure releases will always be present in the track and have nothing to do with the momentum and function of the human or animal.

Foot Mapping

Foot mappings are schematic diagrams that record not only the size and shape of a track but also the specific features. By keeping

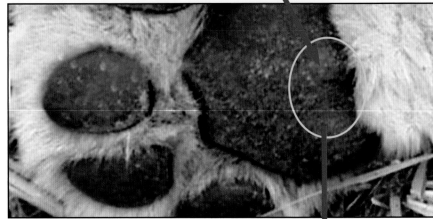

records of foot maps, you will be able to locate an animal at a later time by referring to its record so you don't have to rely on your memory. There are a number of options when constructing a foot map.

1. Take a photograph of an actual foot or track, blow it up to normal size for larger tracks, and enlarge smaller tracks to a scale. Construct a grid as shown on the following pages over the photo so that distinguishing features can be mapped using the grid system.

2. Make a tracing or accurate full-size drawing of the track and construct a grid over the drawing. Features that will leave indicator pressure releases can also be drawn onto the diagram. See Figures CCCH.05.03.59 and CCCH.05.03.60.

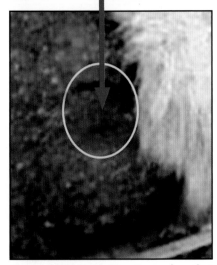

Figure CCCH.05.03.53: Remember that indentations or raised features in foot/paw will register the opposite in the track. Fissures will show up as small raised ridges. Raised features will show up in the track as indentations.

GAIT PATTERNS AND PRESSURE RELEASES

Foot maps can be very useful for identifying animals for conservation purposes, in law enforcement and criminal cases, and for military purposes when tracking insurgents. Once again, we will use the system developed by Brown. See Figures CCCH.05.03.54 to CCCH.05.03.58.

Begin by drawing in a vertical axis (VA) to bisect the track bilaterally in half.

Now measure the length of the print from the tip of the longest toe to the farthest point of the heel pad; bisect this with a horizontal axis (HA).

You now have four quadrants: QI, QII, QIII, and QIV. Use Roman numerals so that we don't mix up quadrant numbers with other identifying numbers.

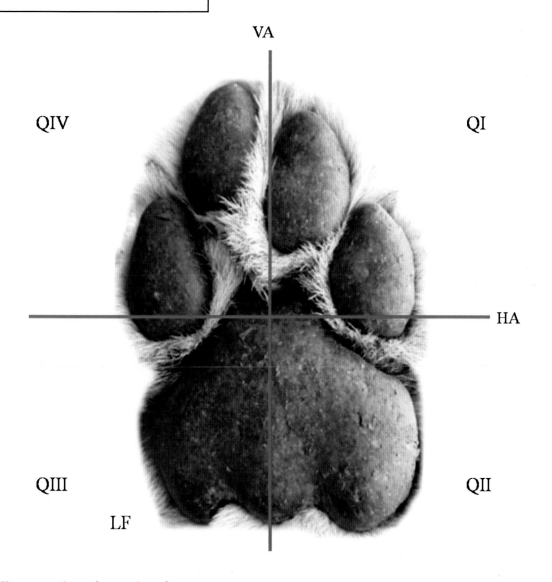

Figure CCCH.05.03.54: Step 1 for mapping a foot.

Figure CCCH.05.03.55: Step 2 for mapping a foot.

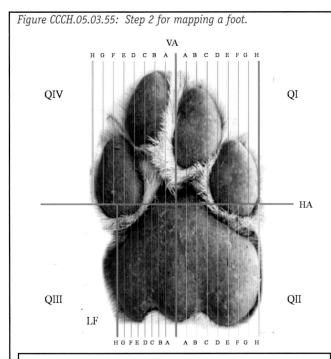

Once the horizontal and vertical axis have been located, we must now grid the track. Tracks are not always symmetrical, so when we draw in vertical grid lines we do so individually for each quadrant as follows: Measure the distance from the VA to a line passing through the outer edge of the track in that particular quadrant and divide it into eight equal parts labeled with the letters A to H as shown. Each quadrant is measured independently of the other.

Figure CCCH.05.03.56: Step 3 for mapping a foot.

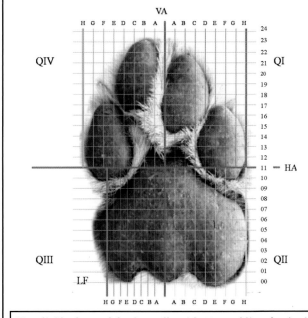

Now divide the track horizontally with 24 equal lines beginning at the farthest edge of the heel pad and ending at the toe. You can use up to 40 horizontal divisions, but this tends to clutter the diagram. Because of differences in track symmetry, the different quadrants can have different looking grid patterns. This is especially obvious in asymmetrical tracks, as will be illustrated farther on. Now we can record specific information using this grid system. Let us look at two distinguishing features of the tracks as ringed in the diagram.

Figure CCCH.05.03.57: Step 4 for mapping a foot.

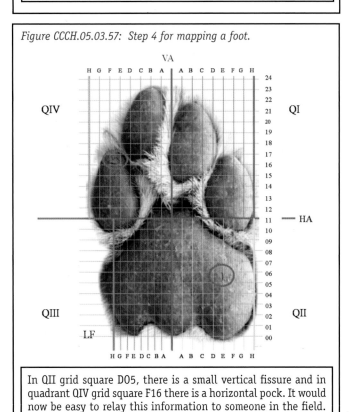

In QII grid square D05, there is a small vertical fissure and in quadrant QIV grid square F16 there is a horizontal pock. It would now be easy to relay this information to someone in the field. It is accurate and will identify a specific individual.

Figure CCCH.05.03.56: Step 5 for mapping a foot.

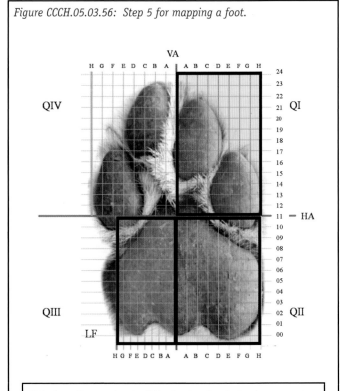

Note how the quadrants differ in size due to track asymmetry.

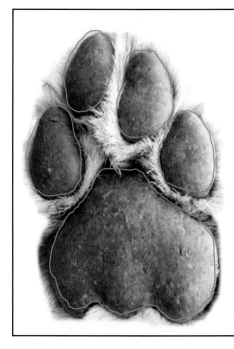

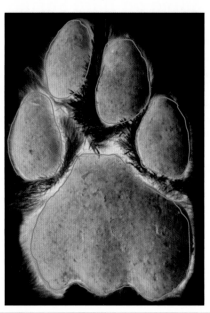

Make a tracing of the photograph (left) or of the actual track (right).

Figure CCCH.05.03.59: Make a tracing of the photograph or actual track.

Figure CCCH.05.03.60: Foot map completed.

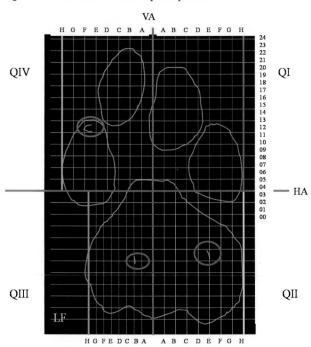

This is what a drawing of the foot map would look like when the three features are noted; these will leave very characteristic indicator pressure releases. If I wished to relay information about this track, it would look something like this:

LF/QIID05QIIIB05QIVF16

The person receiving the information will now know to look for indicator pressure releases on the left foot in quadrant II grid square D05, quadrant III grid square B05, and quadrant IV grid square F16.

Note that grid squares are given in the same way as one would indicate grid squares on a topographical map. The lines intersecting in the left-hand corner of the square being used to designate the square. Note how the grids in the quadrants can differ in size in asymmetrical tracks. See Figure CCCH.05.03.61.

Tracking is a skill that you can teach yourself anywhere and at any time. What it does require is a passion to learn and an acute sense of observation. Here are some things you can do:

➤ Watch how people walk in their homes, along the street, in the wilds. Watch how they place their feet, how their stride length varies with terrain, and how walking characteristics change with mood. A person who is sad or dejected has a very different gait from someone who is excited or scared. Someone in good health walks differently from someone who is ill or injured. Look at the tracks people leave and study them; then correlate your findings to moods and states of health. Watch how people and animals walk, stand, sit, work, and how they leave signs of their passing. Note how their posture changes with mood, emotion, illness, and hunger. Household pets are readily available subjects.

➤ Look at the patterns of wear on people's shoes. Do they wear on the inside margin, indicating that their feet bend inward when they walk (pronation) or do they walk on the outside of their feet (supinate)? See Figure CCCH.05.03.62.

➤ Examine the paws of your pets to observe the detail and the patterns of wear on their feet. See Figure CCCH.05.03.63.

Reading on Hard Surfaces

Our natural inclination is to do things that are easy and avoid doing things that are difficult. When a person learns to track, he spends most of his time on easy tracking substrates. While this is not wrong, we must not neglect studying more difficult surfaces as well. Tracks and pressure releases are present on hard surfaces; they are just a lot more subtle and difficult to see, especially by an untrained eye.

There are two fundamental rules to remember when tracking on hard surfaces:

1. Always keep the track between yourself and the source of light.

2. Look at the tracking surface from an extreme angle. A sign can virtually disappear when viewed from angles approaching the vertical, yet can suddenly stand out when viewed from a shallow angle. Figure

CCCH.05.03.64 shows how some tracks can be seen on hard surfaces when viewed from the correct angle.

To view tracks at extreme angles, you might often have to resort to the technique of "side heading." This means viewing a track with the side of your head flat on the ground.

What causes tracks/footprints/fingerprints to be visible on a hard surface? Dust and grit compressions, fatty or oily deposits, and moisture gradients all play a role in making a track visible.

Figure CCCH.05.03.62: Good tracking practice is to examine footwear to see how and where it is worn down. The pattern of wear can tell you a lot about how the person walks and what type of tracks they will leave behind.

QIV   QI

QIII   QII

Figure CCCH.05.03.61: Grids in the quadrants can differ in size in asymmetrical tracks (some of the grid lines have been omitted for clarity).

Figure CCCH.05.03.63: Your pets make good and convenient subjects for study.

GAIT PATTERNS AND PRESSURE RELEASES

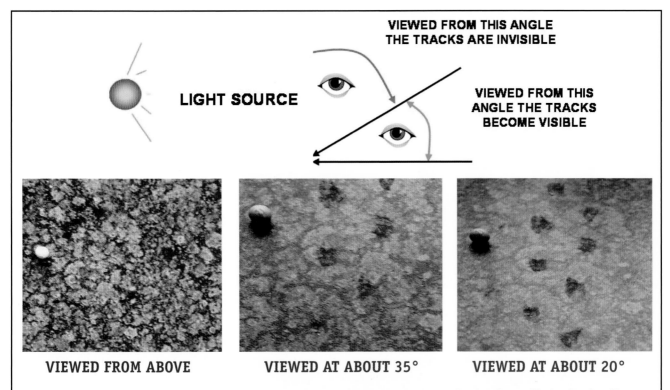

VIEWED FROM ABOVE   VIEWED AT ABOUT 35°   VIEWED AT ABOUT 20°

Figure CCCH.05.03.64: In the photo sequence above, it becomes clear how hidden tracks on a hard surface suddenly "flare" and become visible when viewed from a low angle. Another interesting feature about looking at tracks on hard surfaces is if the overall surface is dull, tracks will appear shiny. If the overall surface is shiny, tracks will appear dull.

Almost everything is coated with a fine layer of dust. Even a well-swept room will gather a layer of dust on the floor and other surfaces within an hour or two. In the outdoors there is an abundance of dust that covers everything. If an animal or person walks across a hard surface that has a layer of dust, the dust particles are compressed, and the compressed area has different light-reflecting qualities. These will show up when viewed from the correct angle and with the light source in the right place. If feet, paws, or hoofs are damp or wet, they pick up soil or dust, which can be deposited on a hard surface and leave a clear track. Figure CCCH.05.03.65.

Figure CCCH.05.03.65: The hyena tracks (left) and elephant tracks (right) have been registered on the hard substrate of a tarred road because of moisture. When walking across wet ground, the hyena and elephant picked up damp soil on the soles of their feet. This was then transferred to the hard, smooth surface of the road. It is clear from these and foregoing illustrations that signs can be very evident on hard surfaces. Contrasting colours between signs and substrates will also make a sign more visible (as this example shows). If the hyena and elephant had walked across exposed rock with a colour similar to the surrounding soils, the tracks would have been less visible but definitely still present.

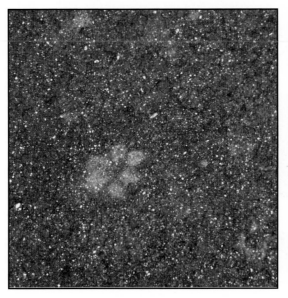

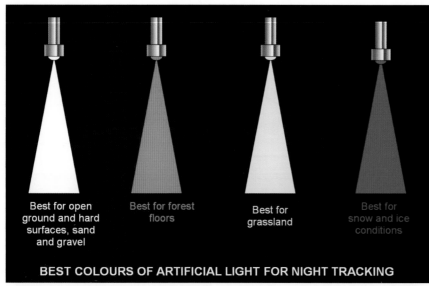

Figure CCCH.05.03.66: The colour of the light source can be adapted and certain colours work better under certain conditions; the purpose of working with a light source is to throw the sign into sharp relief with a minimum of washout.

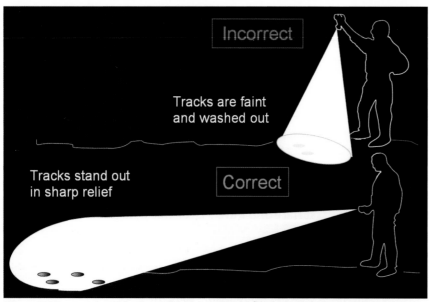

Figure CCCH.05.03.67: This shows the angle of light incidence for night tracking.

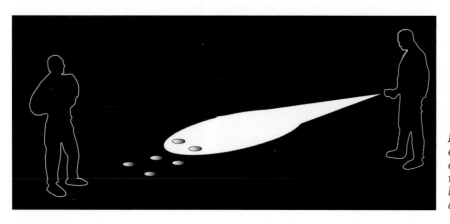

Night Tracking

It is possible to track at night but under most circumstances you must provide some light source—for example, a flashlight or spotlight. It is possible to track on a bright moonlight night, but an additional light source is always advisable. The colour of the light source can be adapted, and certain colours work better under certain conditions. Find the right light adaptation in order to throw the sign into sharp relief with a minimum of washout. This is illustrated in Figure CCCH.05.03.66. One can buy interchangeable colour filters with quality flashlights.

When tracking at night, hold the flashlight low and close to the ground so that the incident light is at a very shallow angle. In this way much more detail will be seen in the tracks because they will show deeper shadows. Do not direct the flashlight beam straight down in front of you as this will cause washout and poor track definition. Direct the light rays a few meters ahead of you.

When tracking at night using an artificial light source, keep the angle of the light source very shallow so that the rays shine well ahead and not close to the feet at a steep angle of incidence. See Figure CCCH.05.03.67.

We know from what we have already learned that the best way to see a track is for the track to be between us and the light source. The best way, therefore, for us to see tracks at night is for someone to shine a light toward us. This is ideal but not always possible. This is illustrated in Figure CCCH.05.03.68.

Figure CCCH.05.03.68: You will have to experiment with light angles to get the best effect. Too much light, and the tracks become washed out and difficult to see. Too little light, and they are in deep shadow and just as difficult to see.

CHAPTER 6

BLOOD TRAILING

Blood Sign

The one skill that all trackers should become proficient at is following a blood trail. An injury may come from fighting, an accident, or from being shot. When an arrow or bullet enters an animal or human, blood will be lost from the entry wound as well as the exit wound if there is one. The amount and type of blood that is lost will depend on the following factors:

1. The size of the wound channel
2. Whether the wound channel stays open or closes off
3. The organs and tissues damaged by the projectile

Size of the Wound Channel

The type of broadhead or bullet used will determine the size of the wound channel. Three-blade broadheads create a bigger wound channel than do two-blade broadheads and leave a better blood trail. In the case of broadheads, the cutting width of the blade will dictate the width of the wound channel.

With bullets, the width of the wound channel will be influenced by the expansion properties designed into the bullet. Solids create an entry wound slightly bigger than the diameter of the bullet. If only soft tissue is encountered on the way through, the exit wound will be about the same size as (or slightly bigger) than the entry wound. If "softs" are used, the entry wound will be slightly larger than the bullet's diameter. The exit wound will be up to two-and-a-half times the diameter of the bullet because it mushrooms on the way through. A solid can also cause a larger exit wound than the entry wound if bone is hit on the way through.

The amount of blood lost will depend on the path of the projectile through the person or animal and the number of blood-rich organs (heart, lung, spleen, kidneys, and liver) or blood vessels it damages along this path.

Figures CCCH.06.02.01 to CCCH.06.02.05 illustrate wound profiles caused by different projectiles.

Wound Channel Opening

The volume of blood lost will be influenced by whether the wound channel stays open or closes. If there is a large entry wound and/or a large exit wound and if blood-rich organs or blood vessels were hit, there will generally be a good blood trail to follow. See Figures CCCH.06.03.01 and CCCH.06.03.02. An animal hit in the heart and/or lungs will often bleed through the nose and mouth and leave a blood trail from these orifices. See Figure CCCH.06.03.03. A small entry wound with no exit wound can result in a scant blood trail or no blood trail at all (Figure CCCH.06.03.04).

A wound can close up in two ways. Some animals have a fairly mobile and flexible skin (such as waterbuck) that can move across the wound channel and seal it off. If this happens, the amount of blood lost will be drastically reduced or stopped altogether even though the animal continues to bleed internally. This should always be borne in mind if a blood trail stops or becomes reduced to tiny and infrequent droplets. It does not necessarily imply that the animal has stopped bleeding.

The second way in which a wound channel can be sealed off is through the intrinsic clotting mechanism of the body. When tissue is damaged, clotting factors are released. These combine with clotting components

WOUND PROFILE OF A SOLID (OR FMJ) BULLET

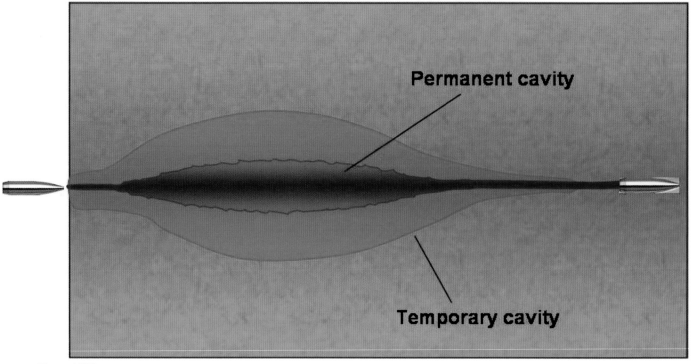

Figure CCCH.06.02.01

WOUND PROFILE OF AN EXPANDING SOFTPOINT BULLET

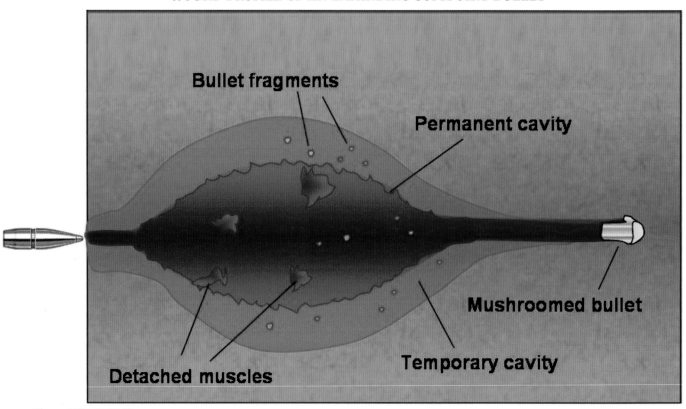

Figure CCCH.06.02.02

BLOOD TRAILING

WOUND PROFILE OF A FIXED BLADE BROADHEAD

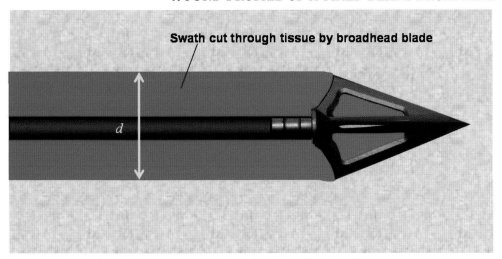

Swath cut through tissue by broadhead blade

d

The wound channel will be along the trajectory path of each blade (seen from behind)

Figure CCCH.06.02.03: Wound channel caused by a fixed blade broadhead.

WOUND PROFILE OF AN OPEN-ON-IMPACT (MECHANICAL) BROADHEAD

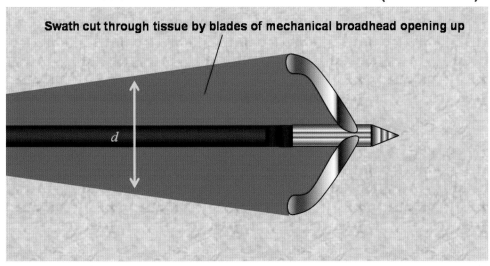

Swath cut through tissue by blades of mechanical broadhead opening up

d

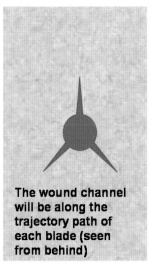

The wound channel will be along the trajectory path of each blade (seen from behind)

Figure CCCH.06.02.04: Wound channel caused by an "open-on-impact" (mechanical) broadhead.

WOUND PROFILE OF SHALLOW CRATERING WOUND

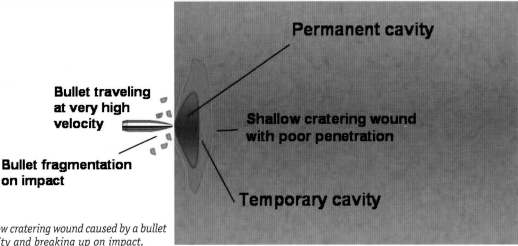

Permanent cavity

Bullet traveling at very high velocity

Bullet fragmentation on impact

Shallow cratering wound with poor penetration

Temporary cavity

Figure CCCH.06.02.05: Shallow cratering wound caused by a bullet traveling at very high velocity and breaking up on impact.

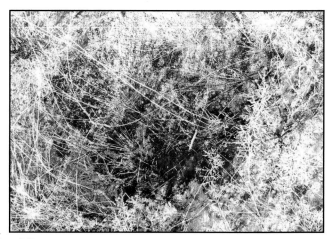

Figure CCCH.06.03.01: A large exit wound will leave a good blood trail to follow.

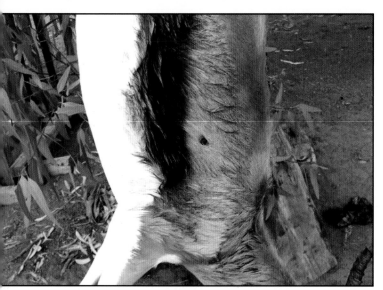

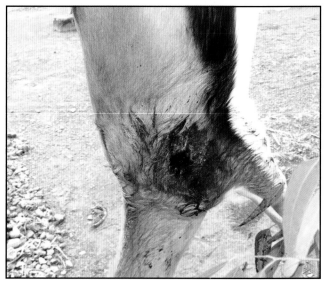

Figure CCCH.06.03.02: A small entry wound (left) and a large exit wound (right).

Figure CCCH.06.03.03: An animal hit in the lungs will often also bleed through the nose and mouth, leaving a trail of frothy pink or bright red blood that is easy to follow.

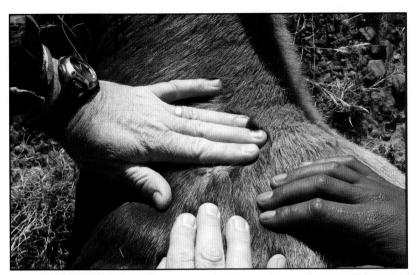

Figure CCCH.06.03.04: A small entry wound with no exit wound can result in a scant blood trail.

in the blood to form a dense matrix of fibrin threads that trap cells and coagulate to form what is known as a blood clot. Because of the geometric configuration of the blades (60-degree angle to each other), wounds made by three-blade broadheads tend to keep a wound channel open more effectively than does a two-blade configuration where blades are at a 180-degree angle to each other. A two-blade broadhead with bleeder blades also create a wound channel that tends to stay open more easily. See Figure CCCH.06.03.05.

Organ and Tissue Damage— Types of Bleeding

The most important factor influencing the type and quantity of blood lost is which organs and tissues have been damaged by the bullet or broadhead on their way through the body. There are three types of bleeding that can occur. These can occur individually or simultaneously.

Arterial bleeding happens when an artery has been hit. The arteries of the body carry oxygenated blood pumped from the heart to various organs and tissues. Because of the high oxygen content of arterial blood, it is bright red. In the case of arterial blood from the lungs, it is not only bright red but also frothy. All organs are supplied with arteries, so a bullet or broadhead can sever an artery in numerous places of the body.

Hunters normally place their shots at a specific point where large blood vessels, including arteries and veins, come together. The area of choice is generally the heart/lung area because it is richly supplied with large blood vessels. Large arteries in this area include the coronary arteries of the heart, the aorta exiting the

Figure CCCH.06.03.05: Three-blade broadheads (bottom) or two-blade broadheads with bleeder blades tend to keep a wound open (top).

Figure CCCH.06.04.01: With arterial bleeding there will be copious volumes of bright red blood (bottom). If a lung or lung artery has been damaged, the blood will be frothy and bubble (top).

Figure CCCH.06.04.02: With venous bleeding the blood is dark red (low-oxygen and high carbon-dioxide content) and may vary in volume from tiny drops to pools.

top of the heart, and the pulmonary veins (which are actually arteries) carrying freshly oxygenated blood back to the heart. Arteries are thick walled and pump blood at high pressure; consequently, an arterial blood trail is characterized by blood sprays because the blood is being forced out under high pressure. With an arterial wound, the hunter will find large quantities of bright red blood. See Figure CCCH.06.04.01.

Venous bleeding happens when a vein has been hit. Veins are blood vessels that carry deoxygenated blood back to the heart. The pulmonary artery (which is actually a vein) pumps oxygen-deficient blood from the heart to the lungs. (It is by definition called an artery because it is pumping blood away from the heart.) Large veins in the heart/lung area include the superior vena cava (blood returning to the heart from the head and shoulders), the inferior vena cava (blood returning to the heart from the lower parts of the body), and the pulmonary artery.

Veins supply all organs and tissues of the body and carry deoxygenated blood and waste products back to the heart. Again, placement of a broadhead or bullet is important. An excellent place to aim is the heart/lung area because there are at least five or six major blood vessels coming together in a fairly well-defined area. The organs of the heart and lungs are vital to life and are also found in this area. The heart's main function is to pump blood; if it is damaged, the pump shuts down. The lungs are responsible for removing carbon dioxide from blood and charging it with oxygen. If the lungs are hit, they collapse and the blood cannot be oxygenated. This soon leads to hypoxia (low blood-oxygen levels) and unconsciousness.

Veins are thin walled and are not under high pressure. Blood from a damaged vein does, therefore, not spray out; it runs out. A venous blood wound is characterized by a trail where a smaller quantity of blood drips out; the blood is dark red. See Figure CCCH.06.04.02.

Capillary bleeding occurs when a capillary has been hit. Capillaries are tiny blood vessels that wend their way between individual tissue cells. Capillary bleeding is more commonly seen as blood oozing out. A good example most of us will be familiar with is the yellowish fluid (plasma) that oozes out of a grass burn. Loss of blood from capillaries is only significant in serious burns that cover extensive parts of the body; it is not significant with wounds resulting from bullets or broadheads.

An animal will die after losing approximately 30 percent of its blood volume. Because large volumes of blood are quickly lost from a damaged artery, we can expect that animals will not run far before collapsing and expiring. When an animal is bleeding from its veins, the time it takes to expire depends on where it was hit. Some large veins such as the superior and inferior vena cava and hepatic portal vein will lose blood fairly quickly and animals are likely to collapse before going too far.

Smaller veins will lose blood slowly and can even close up. The blood trail can stop after a while and it will require a lot more time and effort to locate such an animal.

Interpreting Blood Sign

We will now look at how to determine the age of blood sign and the direction of travel from blood drops. As soon as tissue is damaged, the blood clotting process begins. It is a very complicated process and the time taken for blood to clot varies from species to species.

To be effective, a clotting mechanism must act rapidly, and yet, the animal must be assured that blood does not clot within the vascular system. Blood must, therefore, have the inherent ability to clot and the clotting mechanism should be ready to be turned on when needed; on the other hand, it must not be set into motion inadvertently because this, in itself, could be fatal (intravascular clotting).

Clotting is normally initiated when blood comes into contact with damaged tissues. When a blood vessel is cut, thromboplastin is released from the vessel wall. When this happens, it initiates the clotting process. If the cut is ragged and made by a fairly blunt object (like a blunt broadhead), more thromboplastin is released, and there is stronger constriction of the vessel wall. This will stop the bleeding sooner than if the vessel wall was cut with a sharp object (such as a sharp broadhead). A clean cut causes the blood vessels to constrict less vigorously and bleeding is prolonged.

The degree to which blood has clotted can give the tracker an indication of how long ago the wounded animal passed that way. If the blood is still liquid, it is an indication that it is very fresh. If it is sticky to the touch and makes strings when something sharp passes through it, we know that it is a few minutes old. Clotted blood indicates that the sign is older. Because the clotting time of blood varies with the species, the age of the blood trail will also depend on the species of animal from which the blood originated.

Blood also tends to darken with age. Drops of blood that have dried will also develop minute cracks.

Table 6.1 and 6.2 gives an indication of how to determine the age of blood sign.

Direction of Blood Sign

The shape of a blood droplet can provide an indication of the direction in which the animal was traveling and its speed. If the animal stands still or lies down, blood will pool on the spot, especially if bleeding is profuse. See Figure CCCH.06.05.01. If bleeding is slight, blood will make a shape as shown in Figure CCCH.06.05.02 (a) when it drops to the ground.

If the animal is moving, the shape of the droplet will spread in the direction of travel as shown in Figure CCCH.06.05.02 (b). If the animal is in the act of turning as blood drops from it, the elongated tip of the drop will turn in the direction the animal turned. See Figures CCCH.06.05.02 (c) and CCCH.06.05.02 (d). Also see Figure CCCH.06.05.03.

Speed of Travel

The distance between drops can give an indication of just how fast the animal is moving. This is illustrated in Figure CCCH.06.05.04.

Table 6.1: Average Clotting Time for Some Species

ANIMAL GROUP	AVERAGE TIME IN MINUTES
Horse family (e.g., zebra)	11.5
Dog family (e.g., jackal, hyena)	2.5
Pig family (e.g., warthog, bushpig)	3.5
Antelope family (e.g., impala, kudu, duiker)	2.5

Table 6.2: Approximate Age of Blood Sign

ANIMAL GROUP	BLOOD STILL LIQUID	BLOOD STICKY BUT NOT YET CLOTTED	CLOTTED
Horse family	Blood sign < 7 minutes old	Blood sign > 7 $\leq$ 11.5 minutes old	Blood sign $\geq$ 11.5 minutes old
Dog family	Blood sign < 1.5 minutes old	Blood sign > 1.5 $\leq$ 2.5 minutes old	Blood sign $\geq$ 2.5 minutes old
Pig family	Blood sign < 2 minutes old	Blood sign > 2 $\leq$ 3.5 minutes old	Blood sign $\geq$ 3.5 minutes old
Antelope family	Blood sign < 1.5 minutes old	Blood sign > 1.5 $\leq$ 2.5 minutes old	Blood sign $\geq$ 2.5 minutes old

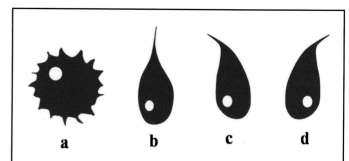

Figure 06.05.02: Indications of direction of travel from blood drops include the (a) animal standing still; (b) the animal moving straight ahead; (c) the animal moving to the left; and (d) the animal moving to the right.

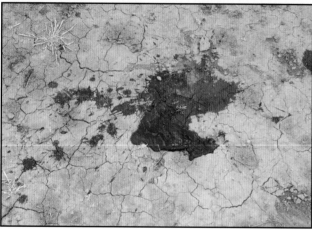

Figure CCCH.06.05.01: Blood will pool if an animal stands still or lies down.

Figure CCCH.06.05.04 shows (a) the animal standing on the spot; (b) walking slowly; (c) trotting; and (d) running.

Figure CCCH.06.05.03: The arrows indicate the direction of travel of a wounded antelope.

CHAPTER 7

TRACKING SPECIFIC ANIMALS

Animals can be tracked just for fun but mostly they are tracked for specific and practical purposes. Rangers need to locate and find specific animals to monitor their whereabouts and well-being or shoot them if they are a problem. Hunters need to locate their quarry and to be able to get within range for a shot or to track wounded animals. Researchers have to track animals to dart them or follow them after they have been darted. Professional bush guides are paid to find animals and take paying guests up close enough to observe the animal. Tracking animals can vary from being fairly easy to extremely difficult. Following the signs left by a rhino that has had a good recent mud wallow is pretty straightforward, but following a skittish leopard on the other end of the spectrum can be very difficult, indeed.

The ultimate thrill in tracking is what I would call tracking to completion as opposed to general tracking. General tracking is just scouting around on the lookout for sign and identifying the sign. This can be very rewarding, and you can learn a great deal this way. But the real challenge is to take the spoor of an animal and eventually track it to the point where you find the feet (or hoofs) still in the tracks. That brings a sense of huge satisfaction and accomplishment.

Tracking an animal from old sign with the idea of actually finding the individual is usually a waste of time and a source of frustration. If you want to have some chance of success, then look for fresh sign. Fresh scat is always a good starting point as it is relatively easy to estimate the age of the dung accurately and to know if it will be worth your while following the tracks or not.

It would be impossible to describe every sign for every type of animal, but I will do so for the Big Five as well as hippo and some of the more popular nondangerous-game species.

Tracking the Big Seven

Tracking Elephants

You may one day have the privilege of tracking an elephant, which is both exciting and relatively easy. It can be extremely frustrating to track an animal such as a lion, for example, that does not leave much sign; elephants are definitely easier to track. Although elephants have the ability to move almost silently through the bush, their size makes it very difficult for them not to leave traces of their passing. Their feeding, drinking, wallowing, and social behaviour also betray their presence, and even their characteristic odour is a dead giveaway.

Of course, one of the main reasons that it is exciting to track elephants is that they are potentially very dangerous animals. Don't be surprised when the sign gets fresh to feel a pulse throbbing palpably in your neck and your heart thudding almost audibly against your rib cage. Let's have a look at the types of sign you will be looking for when tracking an elephant.

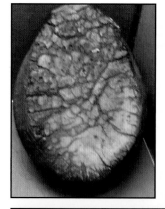

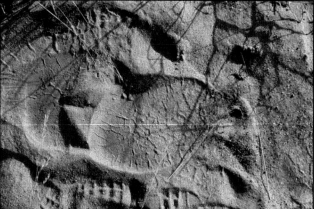

Figure CCCH.07.01.02: Examples of elephant tracks.

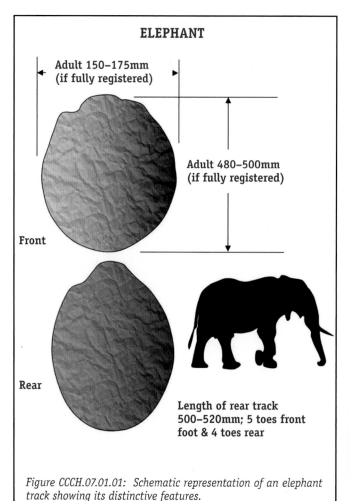

ELEPHANT

Adult 150–175mm
(if fully registered)

Adult 480–500mm
(if fully registered)

Front

Rear

Length of rear track
500–520mm; 5 toes front
foot & 4 toes rear

Figure CCCH.07.01.01: Schematic representation of an elephant track showing its distinctive features.

Figure CCCH.07.01.03: Elephant tracks crossing a tarred road.

Tracks

Elephants have huge feet. The bones of the lower leg rest on large cartilage cushions that enable the elephant to walk softly and silently. Elephants leave behind very distinctive tracks as they wend their way through the bush, and by virtue of not only their size but also their shape they are unmistakable. The tracks of the forefeet are more rounded, whereas the rear tracks are oval with a distinct apex on the leading edge, which clearly indicates the direction of travel. See Figures CCCH.07.01.01 to CCCH.07.01.03. The circumference of the front track can give you a fairly good indication of the shoulder height of the animal. The forefeet have five toes and the hind feet four, which are difficult to distinguish in a track. The length of the front tracks is about 500mm and the rear tracks about 550mm. If you measure the circumference and multiply this measurement by 2.5, you will have a pretty accurate idea of how tall the elephant stands at the shoulder.

Like rhinos and hippos, elephants have the soles of their feet crisscrossed with small fissures. The pattern of these fissures are unique to each individual, much the same as fingerprints are to humans; consequently, individuals can be identified by tread patterns. Elephant tracks will show up on all types of soils: clay, sand, rock, and can even register on a tar road as dust or mud

footprints. See Figure CCCH.07.01.02. A single set of large elephant tracks usually indicates a lone bull. Breeding herds will be evidenced by many tracks including those of adults, subadults, and young. Exercise great caution when following a breeding herd of elephants, for cows are very protective toward their young and will not hesitate to attack an intruder. Partial elephant tracks are also easy to identify by virtue of their shape and characteristic fissures and cannot be easily confused with other animals.

Scat (Droppings) and Feeding

Elephants feed for up to eighteen hours a day and can be described as destructive feeders. They will pull up grass by the roots, break branches to browse or to get at fruit, strip bark, and dig up tubers. They leave behind

Figure CCCH.07.01.05: Signs of feeding elephants are conspicuous.

Figure CCCH.07.01.04: Bark stripping.

Figure CCCH.07.01.06: Elephant scat.

very obvious signs of feeding. See Figures CCCH.07.01.04 and CCCH.07.01.05.

Adults consume between 180 to 270 kilos of fodder per day. It is obvious that large quantities of scat must be passed each day. As the animals move over long distances to feed, scat is one of the most obvious signs you'll find. See Figure CCCH.07.01.06. The shape is that of large elongated cylinders, each about 14 cm in length and 12-14 cm in diameter. When fresh, the colour is a dark, olive green that becomes very dark brown with age. Fresh dung is covered with a layer of mucus that evaporates within half an hour on a hot day. It is coarse and consists of the remains of digested grass, twigs, leaves, bark, fruit (especially marula during February to March), and tubers; it has a strong but not unpleasant odour. As elephants age and their last pair of molars begin wearing down, their dung becomes more fibrous because the food cannot be chewed and ground down as effectively as when they had their earlier sets of teeth. Elephants do not mark territories with dung, so it is deposited randomly.

Elephant Paths

Elephants can be described as "movers and shakers," and their ability to cover vast distances across Africa is well documented. They are partial to traveling well-known routes, so, over the centuries, their well-compacted "elephant highways" crisscrossing the length and breadth of their favourite haunts in Africa have become permanent roads.

Wallowing and Bathing

Elephants not only enjoy bathing and wallowing, it is a necessary exercise to help them control their body temperature. They thoroughly enjoy their times in water and mud wallows, and the surrounding area will be mud spattered and splashed with water. Their great weight and large feet will leave deep impressions in the mud. See Figures CCCH.07.01.07 and CCCH.07.01.08.

Digging

Elephants will use their heels to dig for underground roots and tubers (Figure CCCH.07.01.09); they will excavate large holes using their feet and trunks in dry riverbeds in search for water (Figure CCCH.07.01.10).

Figure CCCH.07.01.07: Signs of elephants wallowing and rubbing mud onto trees.

Figure CCCH.07.01.08: Elephants love bathing and will leave signs where they exit the water.

Vocalizing

You will hear elephants vocalizing if they are close-by. Elephants are very vocal creatures and will trumpet, squeal, and bellow, and these sounds carry far in the quiet of the bush.

Infrasound

What might sound like and are often referred to as "belly rumbles" are, in fact, the upper harmonics of a range of communication sounds made by elephants. They are known as infrasound. This is an additional sign that the tracker will listen for.

Smell

Elephants have a distinctive body odour that, if the wind is in the trackers' favour, can be detected by a good tracker for quite a distance. Another strong smell emitted by elephant is a watery secretion from the temporal gland, known as musth. Under conditions of stress, copious amounts of fluid pour down the side of the face. In bulls this is often accompanied by strong-smelling urine that dribbles down the elephant's back legs. Both the mush and urine are strong odours and can be detected from a distance. See Figure CCCH.07.01.11.

While tracking elephants is an adventure, beware when you finally track down one of these giants. You might be in for some nasty surprises!

Figure CCCH.07.01.10: Digging for water.

Figure CCCH.07.01.09: Digging for underground food.

Figure CCCH.07.01.11: An elephant with musth being secreted from the temporal gland.

Tracking Lions

Tracking lions is an exciting and a potentially hazardous pursuit. It is not to be undertaken lightly. Lions can be very difficult animals to track in bushveld or savanna where there is good ground cover. Unlike the sharp hoofs of cloven animals that leave a distinct print on harder surfaces and even on grassy substrates, the soft paws of a lion leaves indistinct impressions on hard ground and grass. Lions can also be very evasive and stealthy if they are aware they are being followed, and they will slink off into dense cover leaving not much sign behind. Let's have a look at the different signs that will betray the presence of a lion.

Tracks

Lion tracks are classified as paws without claws. This might sound confusing because lions do have claws but under normal circumstances the claws are in a retracted position and do not show up in the track. When a lion is sprinting after prey, braking, taking evasive action, or trying to avoid slipping, then the claws may well be evident in the track.

What is distinctive about lion tracks and how can you recognize them? See Figures CCCH.07.01.12 and CCCH.07.01.13.

The distinguishing features of a lion's track include the following: show paws but no claws, register four

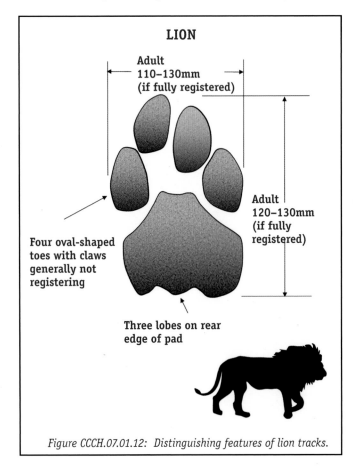

LION

Adult
110–130mm
(if fully registered)

Adult
120–130mm
(if fully registered)

Four oval-shaped toes with claws generally not registering

Three lobes on rear edge of pad

Figure CCCH.07.01.12: Distinguishing features of lion tracks.

Figure CCCH.07.01.13: Lion paws.

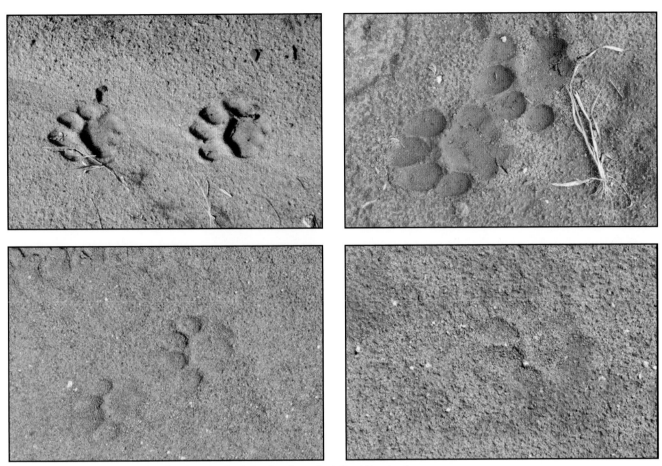

Figure CCCH.07.01.14: Examples showing clearly defined and poorly defined lion tracks.

toes, have a pad with three lobes on the trailing edge and one at the leading edge. On hard ground and on grass substrates, lion tracks may be very difficult to see. When you are tracking over hard substrate, getting your head down low to the ground to observe the track at a very shallow angle may help you see indistinct tracks more clearly. When walking on a grass substrate, grass will be slightly flattened and will show up as a slightly different colour. When walking through long grass, lions may leave a visible swath.

The tracks of younger lions may be confused with that of a large leopard. The leopard track, however, is rounder and will generally be solitary whereas the track of a young lion is most likely to be found in the company of others. A young lion will have a track comparative in size to that of a spotted hyena. The two are easy to tell apart, however. The hyena track has a pad with a trailing edge that has two large asymmetrical lobes; it will also show claws in the track.

Scat

The shape, smell, and consistency of an animal's scat are determined by its diet. The diet of lions may include anything from termites to elephants. Lion are essentially carnivores and feed mainly on meat, but they often eat

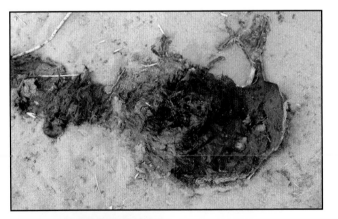

Figure CCCH.07.01.15: The colour and consistency of lion scat will depend largely on when a meal was eaten and the volume of food ingested.

Figure CCCH.07.01.16: The remains of a buffalo killed by a lion.

Figure CCCH.07.01.18: Hangers-on around a lion kill—vultures, marabou storks, and jackals.

grass, most probably as a form of roughage to aid digestion and consistent bowel movement. Sometimes a lion will vomit a clump of chewed grass. The contents of lion scat is most likely to contain digested protein (blood, muscle tissue, etc.) and will be visible as a dark, tarry, sticky, and very smelly matrix. In the scat can be embedded horns, chewed bones, hoofs, hair, scales, grass, or other matter that has not been digested. The consistency will depend on what they have eaten and when. Usually after a heavy meal the scat will be semiliquid, very dark brown to almost black, may be scattered instead of deposited on one spot, and will have a strong, unpleasant smell. Scat may also be shaped like segmented sausage or a cord that tapers at one end. See Figure CCCH.07.01.15.

Vocalizations

Lions can be extremely stealthy and quiet when they choose to but are at times quite vocal. Lions roar most frequently from dusk till dawn. They also communicate with grunts, growls, and plaintive mewing; between a

Figure CCCH.07.01.17: This zebra shows the canine puncture marks of a lion on its throat.

mother and her cubs you can hear *umf* sounds. If you hear these latter sounds, exercise extreme caution. Stumbling across a lioness with young cubs can lead to hazardous consequences. Roaring can be heard for a few kilometers, growling up to a few hundred meters, and the soft communication between a mother and her cubs is heard at close range.

Kills

Carcasses (Figures CCCH.07.01.16 and CCCH.07.01.17) and the associated hangers-on around kills can betray the presence of lions. Vultures, marabou storks, and other scavengers (hyenas, jackals, etc.) are always first on site at a kill. See Figure CCCH.07.01.18. If you see vultures descending from the skies to a focal point or sitting in large numbers in trees and low bushes, be very careful, for it could indicate a lion or other predator kill in the vicinity.

Lions are frequently quite vocal at a kill. This is especially true if the kill is recent and the lions are feeding—and even more so if there are animals, such as hyenas, competing for "a slice of the cake." Lions generally kill by strangling or suffocating their prey.

Puncture wounds around the throat or muzzle of prey, inflicted by large canines, are typical of lion kills. Exercise caution when approaching lions on a kill. Their response to your presence might vary from aggression (if the kill is fresh and they have just begun feeding) to flight (if they have eaten well) . . . and anything in between. When lions have fed well, they become extremely lazy, so be careful of stumbling across sleeping lions in the vicinity of a kill. This is especially true in dense bush.

Smell or Odour

Experienced rangers, hunters, guides, and trackers can detect the odour peculiar to lions from quite long range. The distance the tracker is able to pick up the smell depends on environmental factors such as humidity, ambient temperature, wind strength, and direction.

Scrapes, Scuffs, and Claw Marks

When lions urinate and defecate, they sometimes scratch backward with their hind feet and leave scuff marks on the ground. Marks may also be evident on tree trunks where they sharpen their claws.

It is always dangerous to generalize, especially when it comes to animals that can be potentially life-threatening, so keep this axiom in mind when reading the following observations.

1. Healthy adult lions (without cubs) will run off when they see you approaching in the daytime. This might not apply after dark. Be careful of an animal/animals that do not run off and express an interest in you. See Figure CCCH.07.01.19.

2. The behaviour of lions changes dramatically at night. They become much bolder and more aggressive.

3. Well-fed lions are more likely to run off as opposed to hungry lions.

4. Lionesses with cubs are dangerous; they have a strong maternal instinct to protect their young. Don't approach a lioness with cubs. If you see or hear sounds of a lioness with cubs, it would be wise to leave the area.

5. Injured or cornered lions are likely to act aggressively.

Figure CCCH.07.01.19: Lions that do not run off when approached are potentially life-threatening.

Tracking White Rhinos

It helps to know something about the behaviour, physiology, and habits of the white rhino in order to track it. We know that the animal is a grazer, that it frequents open to light bushy habitat, that it is water dependent, that it enjoys wallowing, and that it can occur singly or in small groups. Based on these facts, what signs will white rhinos leave behind to indicate their presence in an area?

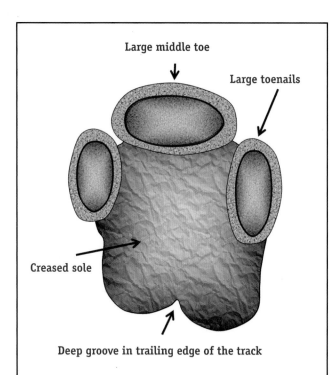

Large middle toe

Large toenails

Creased sole

Deep groove in trailing edge of the track

Figure CCCH.07.01.20: Schematic representation of a white rhino track showing its distinctive features.

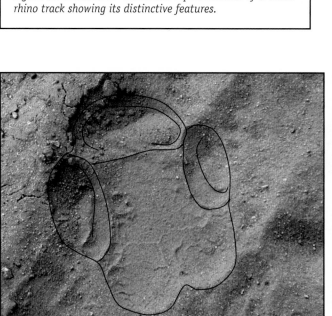

Figure CCCH.07.01.21: Examples of white rhino tracks.

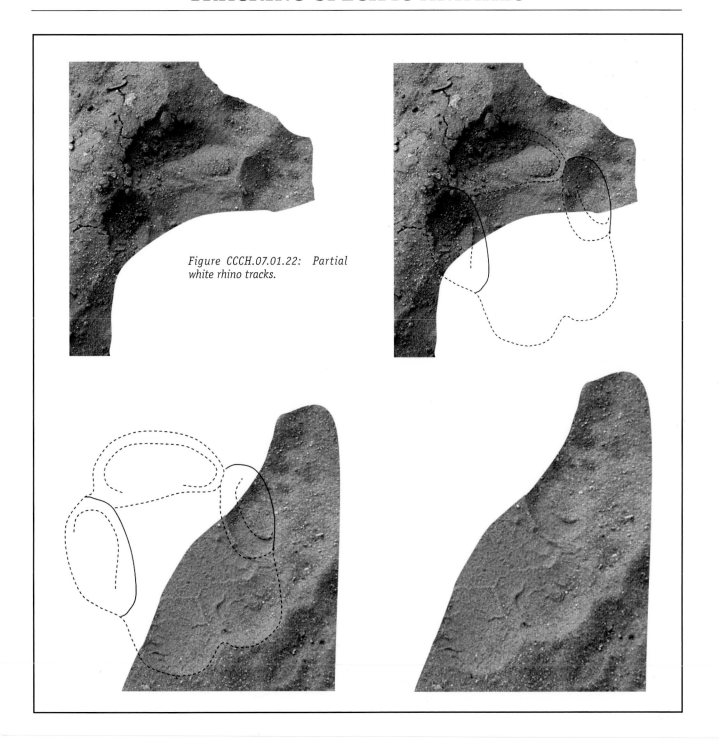

Figure CCCH.07.01.22: Partial white rhino tracks.

White Rhino Tracks

What makes white rhino tracks distinctive? Animals can be divided into three groups based on their foot posture. These are plantigrade, digitigrade, and unguligrade. The rhino belongs to the group referred to as unguligrades. This group consists of ungulate animals that stand on one, two, three, or four toes; it is divided into two subgroups, namely the Perissodactyla and Artiodactyla. Perissodactyla represents odd-toed ungulates and includes the rhino, which walks on three

toes, and the zebra, which walks on a single toe (hoof). Artiodactyla represents those that walk on two toes such as antelopes and buffaloes, and those that walk on four toes, such as hippos.

So some of the distinctive features of white rhino tracks are that they have three distinct toes with the middle larger than the other two. Each toe on a white rhino has an enlarged nail. The underside of the foot is very creased, much like that of an elephant, and the pattern is different in each animal, much like a fingerprint for a human. The rear or trailing edge of the track has a distinct indentation that is far less pronounced in black rhino. See Figures CCCH.07.01.20 and CCCH.07.01.21. The approximate dimensions of an adult track are 280mm long and 270mm wide for the front track and 280mm long and 250mm wide for the somewhat narrower rear track. The tracks of white rhinos are bigger than those of black rhinos and have a squarer as opposed to a more oval shape of the black rhino.

Being aware of the peculiar features of a rhino track makes it possible to identify even a partial track.

Look at Figures CCCH.07.01.21 and CCCH.07.01.22. Even though parts of the track have been obliterated, the three toes, the size of the track, the creased sole, and the "w"-shape indentation on the trailing edge identify the track as that belonging to a white rhino. It cannot be mistaken with that of an elephant track: The shape is different, elephants do not walk on three toes, and an elephant track does not have the indentation. The only animal it might be confused with is the black rhino, but the "w" indentation, size, and shape of the track will prevent any confusion.

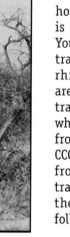

Rhino cows with calves have distinctive behaviour, and their tracks reflect this. If you find tracks of a rhino cow with a calf, how do you decide whether it is from a white or black rhino? You will be able to identify the tracks as belonging to a white rhino if the mother's tracks are superimposed on the calf's tracks. The reason is a young white rhino will generally run in front of the mother. See Figure CCCH.07.01.24. If the tracks were from a black rhino, the calf's tracks will be superimposed on the mother's because the calf follows the mother.

Scat (Droppings)

White rhino scat consists of large barrel shapes that are deposited randomly or, as often as is the case, in heaps called middens. Rhino bulls mark territorial boundaries by using these middens. Dung beetles, francolin, and hornbills are often found associated with the middens. See Figures CCCH.07.01.25 and CCCH.07.01.26. Because white rhinos are grazers, their dung consists of undigested grass. (Black rhinos are browsers that eat small branches, twigs, and leaves, so their scat differs from that of the white rhino.) A white rhino's dung is dark brownish olive when fresh and brownish black as it ages.

White rhinos are partial to grazing around the basal circumference of large termite mounds where the grasses are

Figure CCCH.07.01.24: White rhino young run ahead of the mother.

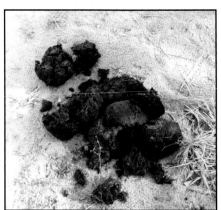

Figure CCCH.07.01.25: Old scat from a white rhino (top left) and fresh scat (bottom left). Above is a rhino midden.

usually more palatable and sweeter because of the nutrient rich soils provided by termite activity. Grass in areas around termite mounds will have the appearance of having been mown. This is the result of the broad, flat muzzle of the white rhino grazing the grass all the way to the ground.

L = 170–190mm

W = 160–180mm

Figure CCCH.07.01.26: Rhino scat that shows chewed grass and no twigs or branches.

Figure CCCH.07.01.27: White rhino scrapes.

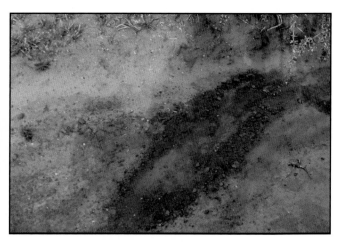

Scrapes

When a white rhino urinates, it will kick its hind feet rearward. A tracker will often find two parallel scrapes on the ground; he should associate these scrapes with the toilet habits of the white rhino. See Figure CCCH.07.01.27.

Figure CCCH.07.01.28: Clearly defined rhino paths, above and right.

Figure CCCH.07.01.29: These mud signs show a wallow (top), mud dropped on the ground (lower left), and mud scraped onto vegetation (lower right).

Figure CCCH.07.01.30. They sometimes frequently return to favourite rubbing posts, which eventually become very smooth.

The height at which mud is rubbed off against a tree can give a clue as to which animal left the sign. Warthogs rub low down, buffaloes and rhinos rub higher around the same height, and elephant rubs are the highest up on a tree.

Vocalization

Another clue to the presence of white rhinos are the sounds they make. Rhinos are quite vocal animals and will puff, grunt, snort, and squeal when communicating. When bulls fight, they emit roars that have been mistaken for lions.

Figure CCCH.07.01.30: Rubbing against a tree to remove mud.

Game paths

When rhinos walk along the perimeters of their boundaries—often from midden to midden—they create well-defined paths. If the animals are still active in the area, it would be one of the most obvious places to search for fresh tracks. See Figure CCCH.07.01.28.

Wallowing

Rhinos are addicted to wallowing, especially during hot weather, because it helps to cool themselves and to rid themselves of external parasites. Not only will they leave telltale signs of their large bodies and tracks in the mud, but they will also drop little pieces of mud and scrape mud off onto foliage as they head back into the bush. See Figure CCCH.07.01.29. As the mud hardens onto their bodies into a crustlike layer, they will rub this off onto tree trunks or stumps. See

Tracking Black Rhinos

If you are an adrenaline junkie, if you like looking for trouble, and if you have your life-insurance premiums well paid up, you might consider tracking black rhinos. Tracking these, if you are not very careful, just might land you into more than you had bargained for.

Black rhinos are aggressive animals. If you get close enough or are detected by them, the probability of being charged is high. Unlike white rhinos that will generally only charge once, black rhinos can charge repeatedly if the initial or subsequent charge is not turned. No figures are available, but black rhinos have, without doubt, accounted for the deaths of many people in Africa. Injuries sustained from being gored by a two-and-a-half-ton angry pachyderm are often fatal.

Because black rhinos are a critically endangered species, it is not legal to hunt them. The only people that track black rhinos are rangers who are tasked to monitor their movements and establish their whereabouts. Qualified field guides do this as part of ongoing, proactive, antipoaching operations. Nevertheless, all who venture out into the bush should

be aware of the signs left by black rhinos, if nothing else other than to avoid them.

Black rhinos betray their presence in a number of ways. When tracking them, it's best to be "totally aware" of your environment. We must look, listen, feel, and smell for black rhinos if we find ourselves in their territory. We should also have some knowledge of their habits and behaviour.

Let's begin with using our eyes. We should know what a black rhino looks like. The preferred habitat of the black rhino is dense bush, so often you might get nothing more than a glimpse of part of the animal. That first glimpse should be the first warning of its presence. Look for a flicking ear, a rounded portion of rump, a hint of horn.

You should also know the differences between black and white rhinos. Figures CCCH.07.01.31 and CCCH.07.01.32 show the main differences. The white rhino has a square lip that is used for cropping grass short and the black rhino has a pointed hooked lip used for stripping leaves off branches. White rhinos have a distinct hump above the shoulders; this hump is not as

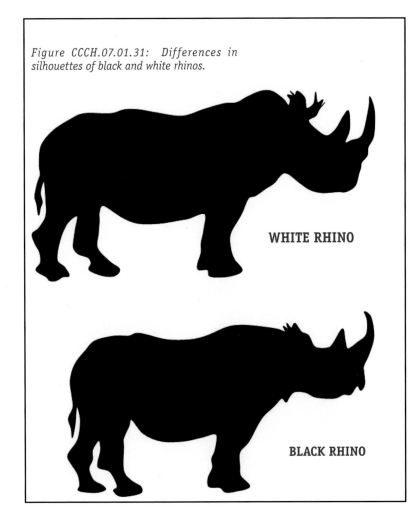

Figure CCCH.07.01.31: Differences in silhouettes of black and white rhinos.

WHITE RHINO

BLACK RHINO

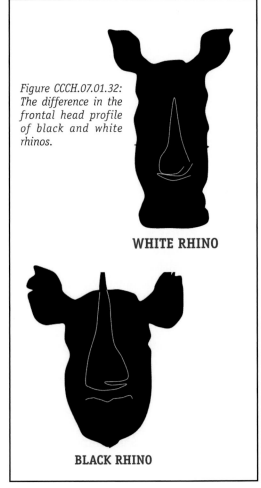

Figure CCCH.07.01.32: The difference in the frontal head profile of black and white rhinos.

WHITE RHINO

BLACK RHINO

evident in black rhinos. White rhinos are bigger and have a more rectangular-shape head when seen from the front; black rhinos have a more oval shape to their heads. We will be using our eyes to identify some of the visual signs left behind by black rhinos; these include the following:

Tracks

Black rhino tracks are large. There are only three other species with tracks as large: white rhino, elephant, and hippo. The tracks of these three species are easy to differentiate. Elephant tracks are larger (adults), oval, or round in shape, and the toes are not readily distinguishable. Hippos will show four toes in the track.

The only track that might confuse a learner/tracker would be that of a white rhino. It is, however, easy to distinguish between the two. Black rhino tracks show three distinct toes, a mosaic pattern of creases, and a continuous trailing edge. See Figure CCCH.07.01.33. White rhino tracks are larger, and the trailing edge of the track has a distinct indentation that is not as obvious in a black rhino. The overall shape of the black rhino track is rounder, while the white rhino has a squarer track. See Figures CCCH.07.01.34 to CCCH.07.01.36. White rhinos tend to be more gregarious, so there will often be tracks

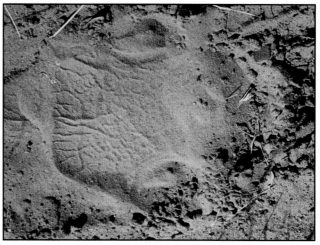

Figure CCCH.07.01.34: A typical black rhino track.

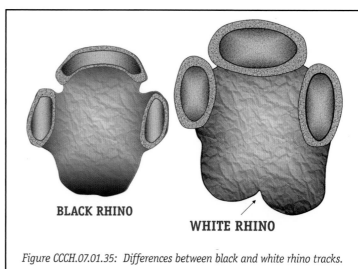

BLACK RHINO WHITE RHINO

Figure CCCH.07.01.35: Differences between black and white rhino tracks.

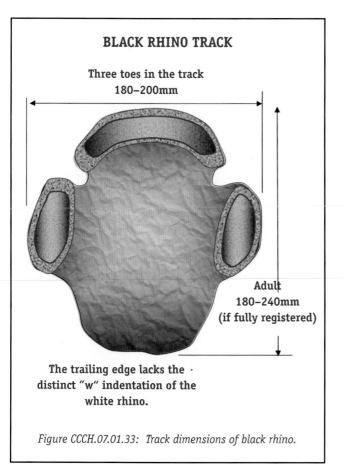

BLACK RHINO TRACK

**Three toes in the track
180–200mm**

**Adult
180–240mm
(if fully registered)**

The trailing edge lacks the · distinct "w" indentation of the white rhino.

Figure CCCH.07.01.33: Track dimensions of black rhino.

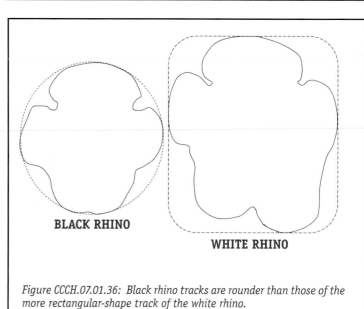

BLACK RHINO

WHITE RHINO

Figure CCCH.07.01.36: Black rhino tracks are rounder than those of the more rectangular-shape track of the white rhino.

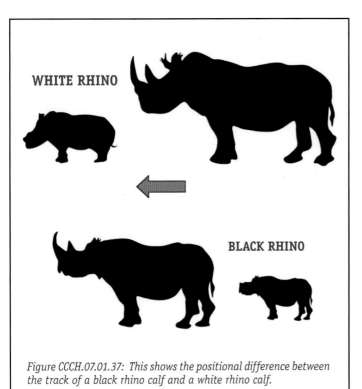

of a group of animals together; the black rhino often leads a solitary existence, so it would be unusual with this race to find tracks of a group of animals together. Finally, the tracks are found in different types of habitat: the white rhino in more open grassland habitat and the black rhino in thick bush. Their home ranges may, however, overlap.

Scat

Black rhinos are browsers and consume leaves, twigs, and small branches, which are bitten off at an angle

Figure CCCH.07.01.37: This shows the positional difference between the track of a black rhino calf and a white rhino calf.

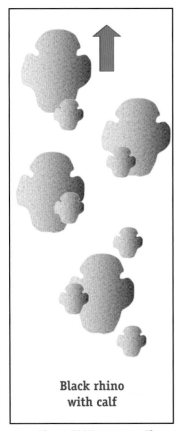
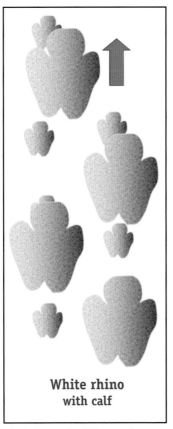

Black rhino with calf

White rhino with calf

Figure CCCH.07.01.38: These tracks indicate the difference between the cows and young of black rhinos and those of white rhinos.

Figure CCCH.07.01.39: Black rhino middens and scat.

of 35 to 45 degrees. The scat is therefore coarse. See Figures CCCH.07.01.39 and CCCH.07.01.40. While it is often deposited in piles called middens, dung may also be deposited at random. The colour of fresh scat, which looks like round to elongated large cylinders, is olive green with yellowish mottling. It becomes darker with age, turning dark brown.

Scrapes

When defecating, black rhinos kick back with their hind legs, leaving parallel scrape marks on the ground. See Figure CCCH.07.01.41. They will often spray urine backward at the same time. When fresh the urine has quite a strong odour. White rhinos do the same, but it is easy to distinguish between the two because of the scat content that is kicked up.

Figure CCCH.07.01.41: A black rhino scrape.

Figure CCCH.07.01.40: Scat content.

Figure CCCH.07.01.42: A favourite stump rubbed smooth by black rhino.

Rubs

Rhinos (black and white) enjoy scratching themselves against convenient rocks or old tree stumps. This eventually leads to the rock or stump becoming smooth and polished. See Figure CCCH.07.01.42.

Feeding and Drinking Signs

When in suitable habitat for the black rhino, the observant tracker will see bitten and nibbled off twigs and branches. Black rhinos will drink regularly if water is available and will usually frequent water holes at night. The substrate around watering points is a good place to scout for tracks. If you catch a glimpse of a rhino feeding in thick cover, the white rhino's head will be held low down to the ground (it will be grazing) whereas that of the black rhino will be held aloft (as it is browsing).

Wallows

Black rhinos love wallowing in mud to cool themselves off in the heat and to provide some relief from irritating ectoparasites. It is relatively easy to follow them after they have been for a wallow as they will drop bits of mud and will wipe off mud onto vegetation as they head off into the bush.

Sound

Black rhinos emit a range of sounds that include squealing, puffing, and snorting. This usually occurs when there is some sort of challenge or confrontation between individuals or when they are charging. The young and mothers communicate with a plaintive but subdued squeal that is different from that emitted when angry. Oxpeckers, which feed off the ectoparasites found on rhinos, will warn a tracker of the presence of a rhino by making high-pitched calls as they are flushed up or descend down onto the backs of the huge pachyderms. Keep a good lookout for these birds; they just might save your hide. Dung beetles will be attracted to fresh scat deposits, so the sound of the noisy flight of these insects is also a clue to the possible presence of a rhino.

Smell

Black rhinos have a smell similar to their dung; it is not unpleasant but rather "herby". When they kick up scat, it sticks to their feet, and that is where the smell comes from.

Times of Activity

Black rhinos are most active at night and will rest in dense cover during the day. It is easier to bump into them unexpectedly if they are not "up and about," so make sure your senses are on high alert if you are in black-rhino territory.

Black Rhino Senses

Black rhinos have a good sense of smell, their hearing is reasonably good, but their eyesight is poor. This is good news about their eyesight because you might be able to avoid detection by standing absolutely still. That is, if you find yourself close and downwind of them.

If you are charged, you may be able to get the animal to deviate from its course by loud shouting and gesticulation. But be prepared, for the chances are pretty good that it will charge repeatedly. The best thing if a charge is imminent and there is a tree conveniently close-by is to climb it quickly! Still better advice is not to let the animal become aware of you; otherwise, you will have trouble with a capital T.

Tracking Hippos

Hippos are not regarded as one of the Big Five, but they should be! Don't track a hippo just for fun. They are extremely dangerous animals, especially when they are out of water. It is said, with enough evidence to substantiate the claim, that hippos have killed more humans in Africa than any other wild animal.

It is important for anyone interested in hiking, canoeing, or hunting to be able to identify hippo sign. If you are aware of the presence of these huge animals, you will be able to avoid them. They spend most of the daytime hours in water with occasional bouts of sunbathing on the riverbanks. See Figure ccch.07.01.43. They have good sight, hearing, and smell. They are very silent and stealthy movers on land and will head for the nearest water if disturbed. Hippos, like buffaloes, once having initiated a charge, are very likely to carry it through to completion. They will only be stopped completely with a brain shot.

Depending on food availability, they will exit the water to feed soon after sunset and return shortly before daybreak. When there is a shortage of food or if they have to walk far to the nearest available grazing, hippos will leave the water earlier and return later than normal. When the food source is in short supply, they will also, on occasion, exit the water to graze on cool and overcast days. They make use of well-established paths when leaving or returning to water, so be alert when traveling along these paths. If the hunter/tracker finds himself in the way of a hippo wanting to return to the water, he had better get out of the way in a hurry, or he will run the risk of becoming one of Africa's statistics.

Hippos can also be a danger to people standing next to water because they will sometimes rush out of the water to attack. However, they feel safer in water and will not be overly aggressive to people standing on the shoreline. Hippos sometimes attack small watercraft and boats. They kill or injure victims by biting them. Hippos swim well and walk on the riverbottom, surfacing every three or four minutes for a breath.

Looking for Sign

Sandbanks are good places to look for sign because hippos are partial to sunning themselves on land. Water is essential to their survival and is not actively ingested but taken in as the animal moves around in the water. They must keep their skin moist to stop it from cracking. Hippos will occupy any body of water deep enough to

Figure CCCH.07.01.43: Hippos are water dependent; they will often lie on the banks of a river sunning themselves for hours. They usually leave the water soon after sunset to feed.

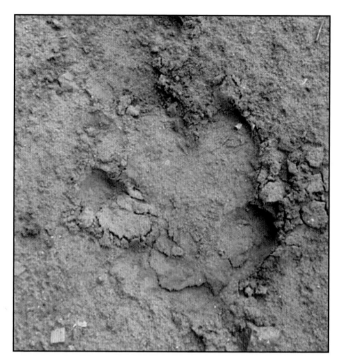

Figure CCCH.07.01.44: A hippo foot and track.

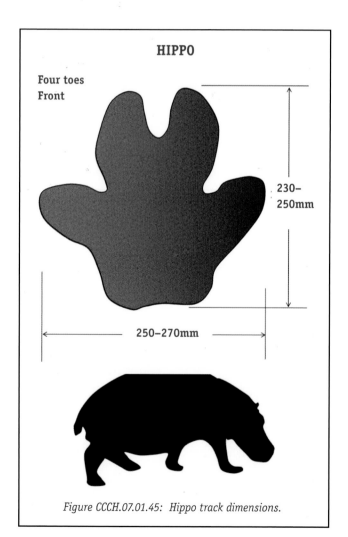

HIPPO

Four toes
Front

230–250mm

250–270mm

Figure CCCH.07.01.45: Hippo track dimensions.

keep themselves covered. Hippos can be found in rivers, dams, lakes, swamps, and even farm reservoirs. See Figure CCCH.07.01.43. In times of drought, they will live in shallow water and even mud pools to try to keep themselves wet and cool; they can be found as far away as ten to twelve kilometers from the nearest water in their search for food.

Tracks

Both front and back feet have four toes. Tracks are about 250mm in length. See Figures CCCH.07.01.44 and CCCH.07.01.45. They make well-worn paths leading to and from their water habitat, and these "tramline" paths are about 20 cm wide, with a distinct *middelmannetjie* (hump). Because hippo and rhino tracks are similar in size and are often found together close to water, someone new to tracking might confuse them. As discussed earlier, they are very easy to differentiate. See Figure CCCH.07.01.46.

Scat

Hippos are nonruminant, single-stomach grazers that feed primarily on grass and fine reeds. Although they feed mainly at night, they will occasionally leave the water to graze on overcast days. Hippo dung is large and shaped like a barrel. Hippos often break their dung up whilst defecating by swishing their tail back and forth. It is also sprayed and scattered onto bushes in areas they frequent. See Figure CCCH.07.01.47. The colour is generally yellowish green. When dry, dung crushed in the hand consists of fine, undigested grass material.

Feeding

Hippos leave feeding "swaths" through grass and also create channels in marshy areas.

Voice

Hippos are very vocal when in water and can be heard a long way off. They make peculiar honking and snorting sounds. When one animal vocalizes, it usually sets off a honking chain reaction. When fighting, they roar and bellow loudly and can be mistaken for lions roaring. They are very silent when out of water and can move very quietly through the bush despite their size. The tracker must be very observant when walking in areas where hippos are likely to be encountered such as along riverbanks or close to water. An unexpected meeting with this species can have dire consequences.

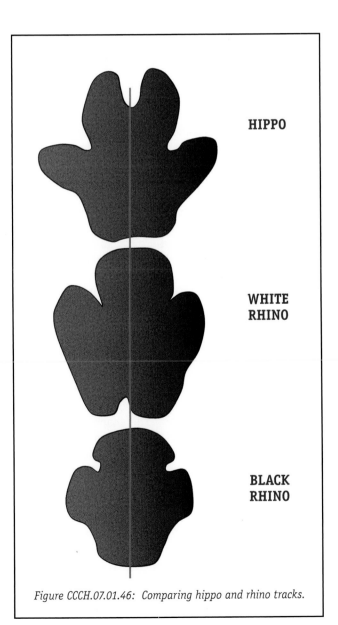

HIPPO

WHITE RHINO

BLACK RHINO

Figure CCCH.07.01.46: Comparing hippo and rhino tracks.

Figure CCCH.07.01.47: Hippo scat consists of digested grass matter. It is often deposited against bushes with the tail swishing back and forth to break it up.

Tracking Buffaloes

Tracking buffaloes can be a risky business. The African buffalo has often been referred to as "Africa's black death." Somewhat melodramatic, but let it be said that this reputation has not been earned by hearsay alone.

Where to Look for Buffaloes

Buffaloes show a wide range of ecological adaptation, ranging from dense forest (preferring secondary growth and clearings) to open woodland. Habitat preference includes an abundance of grazing, shade, and water. Although buffaloes will utilize open grass plains during the cooler hours of the day or during the night, they prefer moving to wooded areas during the heat of the day to rest in the shade. Buffaloes are dark-skinned and their body temperature rises quickly in direct sunlight. When it gets too hot, they will stop feeding and seek out the nearest shade where they will rest and ruminate until it cools down. About 85 percent of the twenty-four-hour cycle is spent on feeding and ruminating. Feeding takes place mostly at night.

Buffalo are water dependent and will generally drink twice a day, generally early morning and at sundown. See Figure CCCH.07.01.48. Looking at water holes for buffalo sign is, thus, a good place to begin or to wait for buffaloes. They are also partial to resting and feeding in reedbeds. They enjoy wallowing in mud, which helps them to regulate body temperature and to rid themselves of external parasites.

In open habitat this gregarious animal may occur in herds numbering in the hundreds and at times in the thousands. These are generally breeding herds made of both sexes and of all age groups. These large herds often split up into smaller groups for a while and then join the large herd again. The larger herds may migrate seasonally in search of water and grazing and might split up into smaller groups to reduce competition for scarce resources. Buffalo herds have fairly well-defined home ranges that can overlap with neighboring herds.

Adult and older bulls often leave the breeding herds to form small bachelor groups of four to ten animals; these and old, lone bulls are often referred to as *dagga* boys. The word *dagga* refers to the mud that often encrusts these old warriors, which they pick up whilst partaking in one of their favourite pastimes, wallowing.

Buffalo Sign

This species leaves behind very clear indications, which makes them relatively easy to track.

Tracks

Buffalo tracks fall under the cloven-hoof category, and their large tracks could only be confused with those of cattle or eland. The front hoofs are larger than the rear. See Figure CCCH.07.01.49. On hard ground the dewclaws will not show up in the track, but in soft sand or mud they will be clearly visible. Large herds of buffaloes trample grass to a significant degree. It is easier when following a herd of buffaloes in grassy areas, where tracks do not show up well, by following the swaths left behind in the grass as the animals move along in file. Figure CCCH.07.01.50 shows track shape and approximate dimensions and Figure CCCH.07.01.51 a typical track.

Scat

The shape of scat is flat like a pancake, which is typical of cattle. It is olive green when fresh and becomes darker with age. Old scat is brownish black. Because buffaloes are browsers, scat consists of fine, undigested grass material. Buffaloes defecate frequently, so it is easy to follow a buffalo herd by following the scat. The odour of buffalo scat is

Figure CCCH.07.01.48: A lone buffalo bull drinks in the late afternoon.

typically bovine. Buffaloes do not make use of middens, and their droppings are scattered randomly. Dung beetles are often attracted to buffalo droppings, and their noisy flight can give the tracker an indication of fresh dung deposits in an area. See Figure CCCH.07.01.52.

Rubs

Buffaloes will occasionally leave rubbing sign (e.g., mud rubbed off after wallowing or to relieve an itch) on rocks and old tree stumps. See Figure CCCH.07.01.53. The choice of these rubbing spots seem to be fairly random and not specific as is sometimes the case with rhinos and warthogs who will return frequently to favourite rubbing posts. The observant tracker will sometimes find hairs stuck in the bark of the tree or squashed ticks.

Bush Thrashing

Dominant bulls are wont to vent their pent-up energy on bushes and small trees by horning them vigorously with their bosses. When this happens, they often shred the bark. See Figure CCCH.07.01.54.

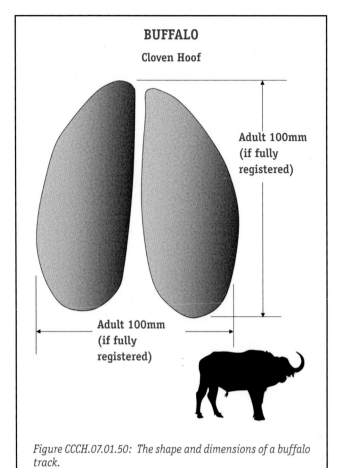

BUFFALO

Cloven Hoof

Adult 100mm (if fully registered)

Adult 100mm (if fully registered)

Figure CCCH.07.01.50: The shape and dimensions of a buffalo track.

Figure CCCH.07.01.49: The cloven-shape hoof of a buffalo.

Figure CCCH.07.01.51: A typical buffalo track.

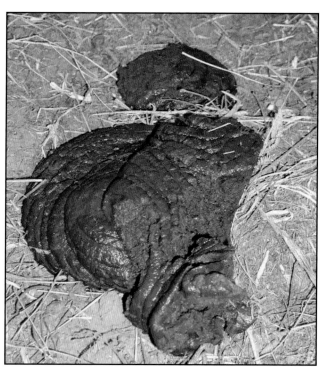

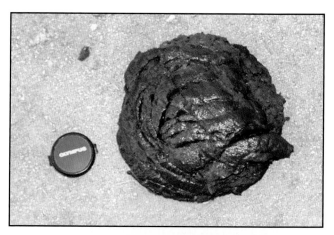

Figure CCCH.07.01.52: Fresh buffalo scat (above and top right) and old (opposite).

Figure CCCH.07.01.53: A buffalo bull relieving an itch on a convenient stump.

Figure CCCH.07.01.54: Bark shredded from a young tree by a buffalo's boss.

Figure CCCH.07.01.55: There is nothing a buffalo enjoys more than a cool wallow on a hot day. (Photo courtesy of A. Brackskovski)

Wallowing

Buffaloes enjoy wallowing in hot weather. See Figure CCCH.07.01.55. They often leave clear signs when walking away from a wallow by dropping mud and depositing it onto vegetation that they brush up against. This is easy to follow and a useful aid in determining whether the sign is fresh or not. They also leave clear signs in mud wallows in the shape of body impressions and tracks. Small bull herds and lone bulls are often found in the sodic areas *(brak kolle)* adjacent to perennial and seasonal streams. In these areas, one often finds seasonal pans and pools of water to which buffaloes gravitate.

Behaviour

Is the bad reputation of the buffalo justified? In some respects no. Buffaloes are generally placid and peace-loving animals and are, in many respects, like cattle. I have had hundreds of encounters with buffaloes whilst leading wilderness trails on foot in the Kruger National Park. Many of these encounters were at close range, walking within fifteen to twenty meters of herds of up to four hundred animals. When approached, bulls form a protective phalanx with the cows and younger animals safely ensconced within the lager.

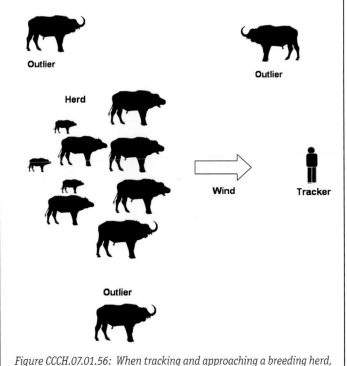

Figure CCCH.07.01.56: When tracking and approaching a breeding herd, always stay downwind and be careful of old bulls hanging around in proximity to the herd. They are easy to miss if you are not on the lookout for them.

Figure CCCH.07.01.57: Buffaloes have a reputation for doubling back and lying in wait for whoever is following them.

The bulls would stare intently at the intruders and, with noses raised to test the air and eyes rolled back, would determine if the intrusion was perceived as a threat. When approaching a breeding herd, the tracker should always keep his senses attuned to detect "outliers," usually old (cantankerous) bulls that hang around on the periphery of, but not within, breeding herds. See Figure CCCH.07.01.56. It is easy to focus all your attention on the herd and miss the hangers-on. This can have dangerous consequences.

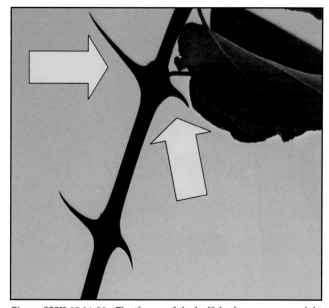

Figure CCCH.07.01.58: The thorns of the buffalo thorn—one straight and the other hooked—were described by old hunters as typifying the behaviour of a wounded buffalo.

Buffalo herds appear to be more nervous and skittish in early morning but are far more content and "approachable" in late afternoon. The small bachelor herds and lone bulls are definitely more nervous and less predictable, and caution is advocated when approaching them. They are definitely more aggressive and often without provocation.

Without doubt, a wounded buffalo is definitely one of the greatest hazards one can encounter in Africa. These animals will usually head for cover when hurt and if followed will often circle back and wait in ambush on the trail for the hunter or tracker. See Figure CCCH.07.01.57. It is interesting to note that the buffalo thorn *(Ziziphus mucronata)* is said to have got its English name from old hunters. The branches have pairs of thorns, one straight and one hooked. They said these thorns aptly described the behaviour of a wounded buffalo: It would run off but then double back and lay in wait for the unsuspecting hunter. See Figure CCCH.07.01.58. Always take extreme caution when following a hurt or wounded buffalo, especially in dense bush.

A charge from a wounded buffalo can only be successfully thwarted with a brain or spinal shot from a large-calibre rifle. Once initiated, a buffalo will not stop its charge until either the buffalo itself or the pursuer has been terminated. A charge invariably begins with a snort. The head is held high with the buffalo peering down its nose at the intended victim. The head is dropped at the last moment to either use the boss as a battering ram or to scoop the victim with the horns. Repeated ramming and goring with the horns will follow, accompanied by trampling with the massive hoofs. Yes, buffaloes can be as dangerous

Figure CCCH.07.01.59: Oxpeckers are helpful in warning the tracker of the whereabouts of buffaloes.

as they are made out to be if you underestimate them and do not afford them the respect they deserve. If you understand them, are cautious, and remain aware of their lethal potential, then they are not the danger folklore makes them out to be. Be especially cautious when tracking old lone bulls. See Figures CCCH.07.01.59 and CCCH.07.01.60. Birds such as oxpeckers will warn you of the presence of buffaloes.

Buffaloes have fairly poor hearing. Their eyesight is reasonable but not good. Their sense of smell is highly developed, making it important to approach a buffalo from downwind.

Resting Areas

Buffaloes lie up in shady areas during the heat of the day and whilst resting at night. They leave clear signs. They will flatten grass around the base of trees and bushes. The positions of where they have been lying, relative to that of the sun and shade at a particular time of day, can also sometimes give the tracker some indication as to when they were there. The smell of their droppings and bodies is also very evident.

Sound

Buffaloes tend, at times, to be quite vocal. As they jostle one another and sort out levels of dominance, they can bellow, grunt, snort, and bash horns together. All these sounds plus the calling of calves can be heard distinctly from a long way off; they should serve warning to the hunter/tracker that buffaloes are in the vicinity. Breeding herds are far noisier than bachelor herds, and lone bulls are generally very quiet. It is easy to stumble unexpectedly upon the latter.

Figure CCCH.07.01.60: These old companions are crusty, cantankerous, and dangerous.

Tracking Leopards

Habitat

Leopards are found in a variety of habitats ranging from arid desert to dense bush, like that found along riverine areas. They are also partial to rocky outcrops from where they can observe the surrounding area from a suitable vantage point.

Habits

Leopards are generally solitary animals found only in pairs when adults come together to mate or when an adult female is found with young offspring. Leopards are predominantly nocturnal but can also be observed during the day, especially on cooler overcast days. Their voice is a hoarse grunt or cough that is repetitive and can be likened to the sound of sawing wood. When hunting, they cover a wide area. They move silently and take refuge in trees or rocky hideouts if pressed. Leopards can be extremely aggressive and dangerous when protecting their young, when injured, or when feeling threatened. They will not hesitate to attack a man given these circumstances and are formidable adversaries when cornered, wounded, or trapped. The tracker should always bear this in mind. If a leopard charges, it will carry through with the charge and can inflict serious injury within the space of a few seconds.

Feeding and Drinking

Leopards are not dependent on water but will drink when it is available. They are very efficient predators and have a wide selection of foods in their diet. They are classed as carnivores but will eat almost anything, including mammals, birds, amphibians, reptiles, fruit, and insects. They feed mainly on monkeys, baboons, impalas, hyraxes, bushpigs, and warthogs and will readily feed on domestic stock such as sheep and goats in farming areas. Their close-set eyes allow binocular vision for judging distance accurately, which makes it a lethal and very successful predator. Prone to kill more than it can immediately consume, leopards often haul their prey up into a tree where it is firmly secured in a convenient fork to keep it away from scavengers; they will return to consume their meal at a later time. The power of these cats becomes evident when you see that they haul fairly large species—often weighing more than themselves—up into trees. If prey has been left on the ground, leopard will hide it by covering it with vegetation. If driven by hunger, leopard will eat carrion.

Records of man-eating leopards, although commonly recorded in parts of Asia, are less common in Africa although attacks are becoming more frequent of late. There have been a number of well-documented cases resulting in the death of human victims. Perhaps death by leopard attack in Africa has been far more common than previously believed. Attacks on man are more common from a leopard that is sick or injured, but healthy animals are also known to attack and kill humans. The large canines of a leopard deliver the killing bite; larger prey species are usually dispatched with a bite to the base of the victim's neck or throat.

Leopards will breed throughout the year, and after a gestation period of ninety to one hundred days will give birth to a litter averaging two to three cubs. The female will hide up in a cave, rocky outcrop, or dense bush to give birth and will keep the cubs hidden for the first two months. The female is dangerous and very protective of her young when they are nearby. Predation on leopard cubs by other leopards and particularly hyenas is very common.

Leopard Sign

Leopards leave a variety of signs behind that betray their presence.

Tracks and Scat

The tracks are very distinctive. The spoor is a paw without claws. Leopards do have claws, but these are generally retracted and do not register in the track. The distinctive features of the track include four toes

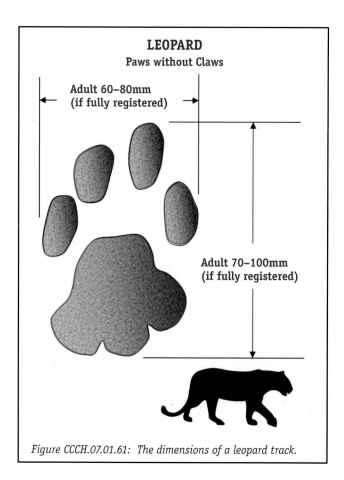

LEOPARD
Paws without Claws

Adult 60–80mm
(if fully registered)

Adult 70–100mm
(if fully registered)

Figure CCCH.07.01.61: The dimensions of a leopard track.

(no claws showing) and a heel pad with two leading edge lobes and a trailing edge consisting of three distinct lobes. The only other animals with the same configuration are genets, lions, servals, African wild cats, and caracals. Because the leopard is a diagonal walker, the rear track will often be superimposed upon that of the front foot. See Figures CCCH.07.01.61 to CCCH.07.01.62.

Leopard scat is described as sausage shaped, segmented, and with a tapered end. The diameter is about 20 to 30mm. It usually contains a large amount of hair and undigested bones, and hoofs are sometimes also present. Leopards, like most cats, are not partial to bundu-bashing and will make use of roads and game paths if available. It is often along these access routes that scat and tracks will be found. See Figure CCCH.07.01.63.

Figure CCCH.07.01.62: Leopard tracks (top and bottom).

Figure CCCH.07.01.63: Leopard urinating (top) and fresh scat (bottom).

Claw Marks

Leopards, like most cat species, like to keep their claws sharp; their presence can be detected from tree scratchings. These are not generally very obvious, and it is only the more observant hunter or tracker who will spot this sign.

Scent Marking

Leopards make use of urine, combined with scratching with the hind feet, to mark territories. When fresh, the urine gives off a pungent, easily discernible odour, and the scratch marks are clearly visible.

Vocalizing

One of the most common ways that leopards betray their presence is by vocalizing. Their sawlike grunting is unmistakable.

Feeding

Another giveaway are the remains of carcasses dragged up into trees (Figure CCCH.07.01.64) or, if left on the ground, covered by vegetation. Also be on the lookout for drag marks that are left behind when a leopard drags its prey to a convenient tree. Signs of a leopard feeding are also the following: The animal is eaten from the buttocks end and the shoulder. Internal organs are consumed, but the stomach and intestines are discarded and often buried under debris.

Figure CCCH.07.01.64: Leopards haul heavy prey up into trees to keep it away from scavengers.

Tracking "Nondangerous" Species

Tracking Impalas

Impalas are one of the most beautiful African antelopes. Because they are relatively widespread, it is a species that is often hunted. Tracking an impala can be fun and a good subject for young, learner trackers to practice on. Because they are so abundant, the aspiring tracker will have ample opportunity to examine different tracks on a variety of substrates and also the variations one may find in a track. An assortment of scat samples will help to ascertain the effects of aging and how diet can change the consistency of dung.

Impala Sense

One of the challenges in tracking impalas is to avoid being detected. These animals have excellent eyesight and a good sense of smell and hearing. Furthermore, those that walk in herds have many eyes, ears, and noses to see, hear, and smell what is going on around them. To track impalas successfully, make sure you remain downwind of them, move as quietly as possible, and make full use of cover to conceal yourself. When you are close enough to make visual contact, keep watching the animals. If their heads are down, they are feeding on a low stage of alert; if the heads are up with ears pricked and they are staring at something, they are on high alert and you should stand dead still until they once again relax. See Figure CCCH.07.02.01.

Impala sign

Impalas leave behind substantial sign to advertise their presence. Throughout their distribution, impalas are associated with woodland, showing a preference for more open woodland communities. They generally avoid open grassland and flood plains but will utilize these areas when there is a flush of new green grass. They are partial to transition zones (called ecotones) between open grassveld and woodland as this suits their diet, being both grazers and browsers. They also tend to avoid montane areas. Impalas are dependent on surface water and cover. Their spoor is often located on game paths, especially those leading to or from favourite drinking or feeding sites.

Tracks

An impala's front and rear hoofs are about the same size, and there is no distinct difference between the sexes. Impala tracks are described as a cloven hoof. See Figure CCCH.07.02.02. They walk on two toes. Figure CCCH.07.02.03 illustrates an impala hoof and typical tracks. The tracks that a tracker must sometimes identify or follow are not always typical and may be weathered by wind, gravity, or rain, be registered on substrate not conducive to recording good detail, be distorted by some movement by the animal, or be partially obliterated by other animals stepping onto them. Figure CCCH.07.02.04 illustrates some atypical impala tracks.

Figure CCCH.07.02.01: Impalas on low alert (left) and high alert (right).

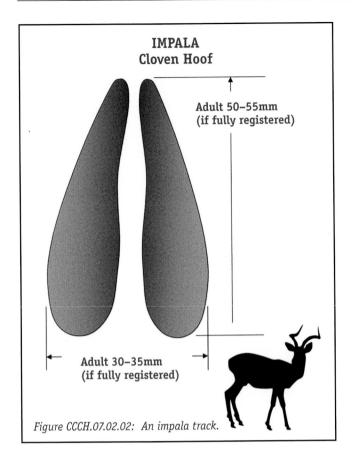

IMPALA
Cloven Hoof

Adult 50–55mm
(if fully registered)

Adult 30–35mm
(if fully registered)

Figure CCCH.07.02.02: An impala track.

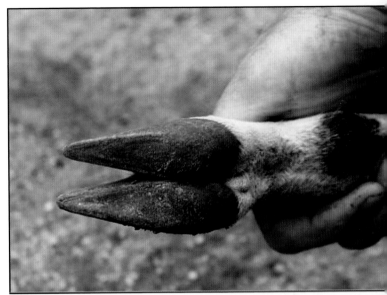

A good tracker should study what tracks look like on different substrates, what they look like as they begin to weather, and how tracks can be distorted. The animals that fall into the cloven-hoof category are numerous, and it may be difficult to differentiate the tracks of impalas from others. These include springboks, common reedbucks, mountain reedbucks, and blesboks, which look similar and are of similar size. To distinguish one from the other, one must use additional tools of reasoning and must ask oneself questions such as:

➤ Do the species occur here?

➤ What is their preferred habitat? Can I expect to find this species in this type of habitat?

➤ What is the social grouping? Do the animals walk alone, in small groups, or are they found in bigger herds?

➤ Are the animals active during the day or night?

➤ What are their preferred feeding areas?

➤ Are they water dependent?

Using questions like these can narrow down the options and help you identify a particular track. Impalas have three social groupings, consisting of lone rams, bachelor herds consisting of young males, and breeding herds consisting of both sexes and all age groups. See Figure CCCH.07.02.05. Impala tracks may be found singly,

Figure CCCH.07.02.03: An impala hoof and typical tracks.

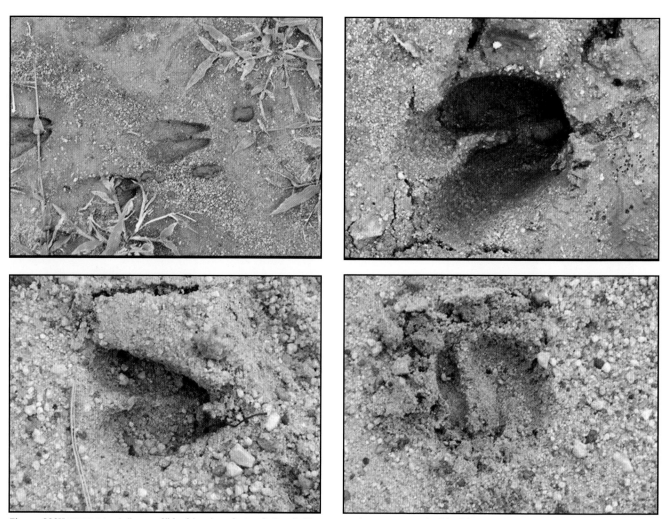

Figure CCCH.07.02.04: A "normal"-looking impala track (top left) compared to some atypical looking tracks. Note a track in soft mud (top right), a distorted track (bottom left), and a track where the animal has swiveled on its foot to the left (bottom right).

in small groups of subadult or adult males, and in herds representative of all age classes. They can survive for short periods without water but usually stay within about eight kilometers of the nearest water and will drink on a daily basis. They are most active by day.

Scat

Their scat consists of cylindrical pellets 12–14mm in length with a "nipple" on one end. See Figure CCCH.07.02.06. Diet determines the consistency of the pellets. During the summer when the grass is green and high in moisture content, the dung pellets can be of an irregular shape whereas when the grass is dry during the winter months the shape of the pellets is well defined. Fresh dung is dark brownish green and becomes dark brown with age.

Impalas deposit their dung randomly and in middens. It is usually territorial males that use middens to demarcate territory during the rutting season, which stretches from April to May. Middens are then "active."

See Figure CCCH.07.02.07. When a male defecates and urinates at the same time, it is done from a standing position and because of the animal's anatomy there is a distance between the urine patch and droppings. Female impalas squat when defecating and the urine patch is superimposed on the dung pellets. Using this knowledge enables the tracker to determine the sex of the animal where he finds a urine and scat patch together. See Figure CCCH.07.02.06.

Bush Thrashing

During the rut, impala rams try to demonstrate their dominance by horn thrashing small trees and bushes. Damage to small branches is another sign that a tracker can look for. See Figure CCCH.07.07.08.

Vocalization

Impalas can be quite vocal and emit a loud nasal snort as a warning. Youngsters bleat like little lambs, and during the rutting season dominant males utter a

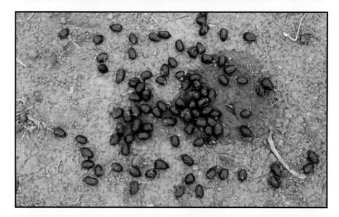

Figure CCCH.07.02.05: The social groupings of impalas.

Figure CCCH.07.02.06: Old droppings are darker (top), fresh droppings on a "dry" diet (next below), a scat and urine patch from an adult female (next below), and fresh droppings on a high-moisture-content diet (bottom).

loud guttural "roar," which can be heard a long way off. The males also snort when chasing each other. These auditory signs can be very helpful to the tracker. Red-billed oxpeckers often associate with impalas, and their presence, detected by their shrill calls as they descend to sit on the antelopes or when flushed from them, can indicate impalas are nearby. See Figure CCCH.07.02.09. Bear in mind that these birds also associate with rhinos, buffaloes, hippos, and giraffes.

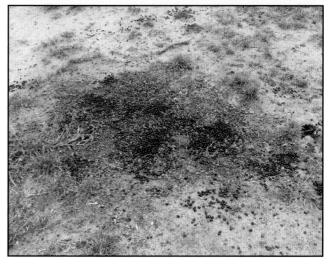

Figure CCCH.07.02.07: Impala middens; the one on the bottom is active.

Figure CCCH.07.02.09: The call and flight of red-billed oxpeckers can indicate the presence and whereabouts of impala.

Figure CCCH.07.02.08: A dominant impala male thrashing a flaky bark acacia.

Tracking Porcupines

Porcupines (I know all about porcupines!)

I once managed a 33,000-hectare reserve that had a lot of porcupines, many of whom tended to see our garden as the local restaurant, and so I spent at least three nights out of every week getting up at the most unearthly hours, torch and stick in hand, to chase porcupines out of our yard or, more specifically, out of my wife's prized vegetable patch. I would give the trespassing porcupines a good thrashing with a stick in the hope that they would be dissuaded from ever returning. Well, either they were slow learners or I was, for I didn't get rid of them. Come to think of it, quite possibly they were new porcupines digging their way in under the fence each night. Doubtful, but perhaps true.

Most people will never even see a porcupine; chances are small that you will see one of these prickly rodents walking around during the daytime. They are nocturnal by nature, but you may be fortunate to spot one in the early evening as they head off on their nightly rounds or early in the morning as they head back for a snooze in an old aardvark burrow. They excavate their own burrows but will also make use of those vacated by aardvarks. Even though they may not be seen by most people, they leave behind plenty of signs to show that they have passed that way.

Tracks

The track made by the porcupine is classified as a paw with claws. The claws are nonretractable and readily show up in the track. In the front track, five oval-shape toes are usually registered with claws that usually show up in all but the smallest toe. Sometimes the animal walks on its toes, and then only the toes and three intermediate pads are visible. The track will be

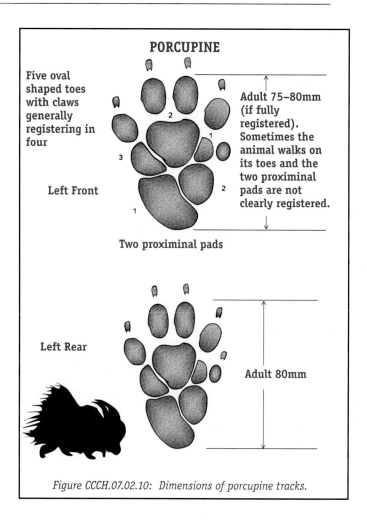

PORCUPINE

Five oval shaped toes with claws generally registering in four

Left Front

Two proximinal pads

Adult 75–80mm (if fully registered). Sometimes the animal walks on its toes and the two proximinal pads are not clearly registered.

Left Rear

Adult 80mm

Figure CCCH.07.02.10: Dimensions of porcupine tracks.

Figure CCCH.07.02.11: Rear track of a porcupine (left) and the front track (right).

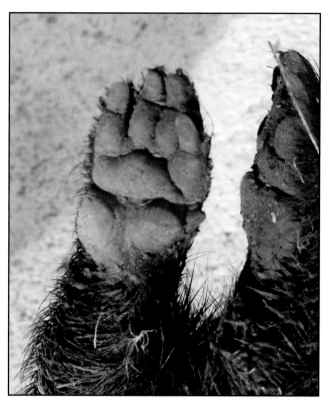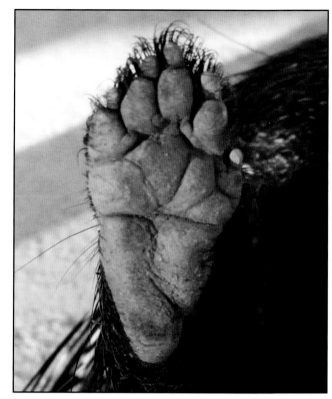

Figure CCCH.07.02.12: The front foot (left) and the rear foot of a porcupine (right).

50–60mm long. If it is walking "flat footed," the track may be between 78–80mm long. The rear track usually registers completely and often five claws can be seen. It is approximately the same size as a fully registering front track but may be slightly narrower. See Figures CCCH.07.02.10 to CCCH.07.02.12.

Excavations

Porcupines are rodents, and their vegetarian diet consists of roots and tubers dug out of the ground, tree bark, fruit, and berries. They may cause a lot of damage to cultivated crops because they are wasteful feeders. When feeding on surface vegetables and plants, they leave distinctive incisor marks. Their excavations may be shallow or deep but never as extensive as those of an aardvark. See Figure CCCH.07.02.13.

Scat

Porcupine scat is very distinctive and resembles short, fat cigar-shape pellets; they average 40-70mm in length. Porcupines drop their scat randomly in clusters of up to twenty pellets throughout their home range and often along roads, game paths, and trails. The scat is characterized by having coarse plant fibres. See Figure CCCH.07.02.14. One of their favourite foods, which is toxic to many other animals, is the bark of tamboti trees.

Figure CCCH.07.02.13: A porcupine excavating for underground food.

Figure CCCH.07.02.14: Porcupine scat is dark brown and often contains undigested bark fibres.

Quills

Porcupine quills are not deeply embedded in their skin and can dislodge quite easily. Quills lying around are also an indication of the presence of the animals. See Figure CCCH.07.02.15.

Quill Scrapes

On suitable substrate one can also verify tracks as those belonging to porcupines by the scrape marks left behind by the rump quills as they drag along the ground. See Figure CCCH.07.02.16.

Bones

Bones are collected by porcupines and gnawed on, most probably to supplement their diet and mineral requirements. See Figure CCCH.07.02.17.

Bark damage

Trees sometimes die as a result of porcupines chewing the bark off around the circumference of the tree. This is known as ring-barking. See Figure CCCH.07.02.18.

Figure CCCH.07.02.15: Shed quills are often one of the most obvious signs of porcupines in an area.

Figure CCCH.07.02.16: The fine scrape marks left on the ground from dragging quills are a good confirmation that the tracks you are seeing belong to a porcupine.

Figure CCCH.07.02.17: Bones gnawed by porcupines are often found in or near the entrance to their burrows.

Digging

Porcupines are not generally deterred by fences and are quick to dig their way underneath. See Figure CCCH.07.02.19.

Under normal circumstances, porcupines are not vocal, but the rustling of their quills as they scurry along can sometimes be heard in the quiet of the night. You might not actually lay eyes on a porcupine, but you sure will find many of this animal's calling cards. See Figure CCCH.07.02.20.

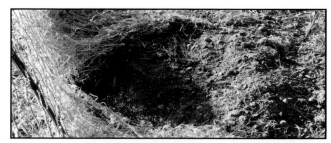

Figure CCCH.07.02.18: Porcupines often ring-bark trees, which will result in the tree dying.

Figure CCCH.07.02.19: Porcupines are excellent diggers. Fences are generally no obstacle to them.

Figure CCCH.07.02.20: Porcupines are most active at night and seldom seen.

Tracking Cheetahs

General Habits

When tracking any animal, it is very useful to know something about their anatomy and their habits. Do they live alone, in pairs, or in groups? Where do they prefer feeding and on what do they feed? How do they feed? What sort of noises do they make, if any? What times of the day or night are they most active? When this sort of information is stored away in a memory file, it helps us to know what to look for and where to find it. We need to listen for distinctive sounds and detect peculiar odours.

Cheetahs live singly or in small parties numbering up to six individuals. These animals prefer open and semiarid savannas and never forested country. They are also found on the fringes of desert country.

This species is predominantly active by day (diurnal) with peak activity occurring around sunset and sunrise. Occasionally cheetahs will be active on moonlight nights. Cheetahs are timid, shy, secretive, and wary. They lie up in thick tall grass or in shade during the heat of the day. There are very few reported cases of a cheetah attacking a human; compared with leopards they are relatively harmless. Although it will snarl, bare its teeth, and strike out with its claws when cornered, it will not readily attack. They are safe and fun to track.

Tracks

Cheetahs have a distinctive paw with claw track in which the nonretractile claws often show up. The track is quite long and narrow and has a double indentation

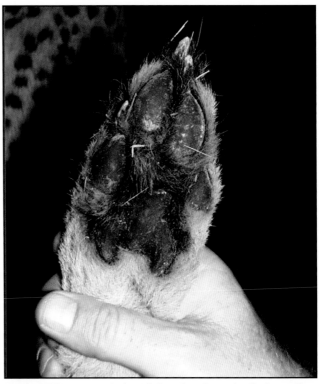

Figure CCCH.07.02.21: A cheetah foot that shows the distinct nails.

on the posterior edge of the main pad. Four toes show up in the track. The pad of the rear track is distinctively elongated. Longitudinal ridges on the pads provide grip and prevent the animal from skidding. The length of the front track is about 85-90mm in length and 75-78mm in width. The track of the hind foot is about 90-95mm long but slightly narrower than the front foot. See Figures CCCH.07.02.21 to CCCH.07.02.24.

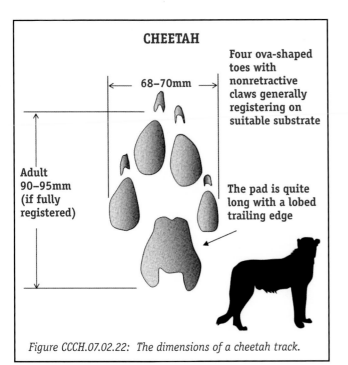

CHEETAH

68–70mm

Four ova-shaped toes with nonretractive claws generally registering on suitable substrate

Adult 90–95mm (if fully registered)

The pad is quite long with a lobed trailing edge

Figure CCCH.07.02.22: The dimensions of a cheetah track.

Figure CCCH.07.02.23: The track of a walking cheetah.

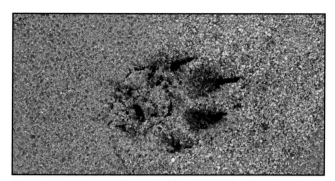

Figure CCCH.07.02.24: The track of a running cheetah.

Figure CCCH.07.02.25: Fresh cheetah scat.

Scat

A cheetah's scat is sausage shaped, segmented, and with one end tapered. See Figure CCCH.07.02.25. Cheetahs often back up against a bush when defecating. In some areas cheetahs use latrine bushes where there is usually a strong smell of urine. Thus our noses can be used to track cheetahs.

Voice

Cheetahs make a chirping, almost birdlike sound when alarmed or when greeting other cheetahs. The birdlike chirp can be heard for a short distance and can warn the tracker of the presence of a cheetah. When feeling threatened, cheetahs will also emit an audible growl and spitting type of sound.

Scratch and Play Trees

The cheetah is averse to entering water and is not well adapted to climbing. Cheetahs will use suitably shaped trees on which to sharpen their claws. The trees will have trunks or branches growing almost or close to parallel with the ground to enable the cheetah to clamber up onto them. Scratch and claw marks will be evident on the bark of these trees. See Figure CCCH.07.02.26. Leopards, unlike cheetahs, can climb vertically up tree trunks.

Feeding

Cheetahs prey mostly on medium-size antelope but have been known to pull down waterbucks and kudus. They will also catch warthogs and smaller prey like hares, springhares, porcupines, guinea fowls, and bustards. Cheetahs will only eat fresh meat and will not touch carrion. They are reasonably independent of water but will drink readily when it is available; thus, water holes are a good area to search for tracks.

Cheetahs kill by strangling their prey. There will be shallow teeth marks about 35mm apart on the neck with minor hemorrhaging. Cheetahs start eating from the rump, move on to the abdomen, rib cage, shoulders, liver, and heart. Large bones are not broken and the carcass is usually dragged into shade.

Figure CCCH.07.02.26: Cheetahs have favourite trees in which they play. They will often sharpen their claws on branches and tree trunks.

Tracking Blue Wildebeests

Blue wildebeests are reasonably easy to track and approach as they do not run away as quickly as other species will do if they see you approaching. They may amble away at a fast walk, slow trot, or run off for a short distance with a rollicking gait and much tail swishing but will generally come to a stop after a short distance to look back.

Where to Look for Wildebeest Sign

Wildebeests leave quite a lot of sign. Blue wildebeests are partial to savanna woodland where there is a ready supply of water. They are also known to utilize open grassland, grass flood plains, open woodland, and open shrub savanna.

Home ranges are dependent on available food and water. They follow favourable conditions that sometimes result in massive migrations. Like many plains animals, they disperse during the rainy season and aggregate during the dry season around available water and suitable grazing. They tend to graze in a scattered formation and are active at all hours excepting during the middle of hot days. Wildebeests have more rigid water requirements than other species that frequent the same areas (e.g., gemsboks, springboks, red hartebeests) and need to drink every day. Water holes and short grassy areas where they prefer to graze are good places to look for signs of wildebeest. See Figure CCCH.07.02.27.

Tracks

The tracks of wildebeests show a typical cloven hoof. Hoofs have low and well-developed dewclaws that will show up in soft substrate but not on hard ground. Their tracks are similar to but wider than those of the red hartebeest; they are about 100 to 110mm in length and 90–95mm in width. See Figures CCCH.07.02.28

Figure CCCH.07.02.27: Typical blue wildebeest habitat is open, short grassy plains.

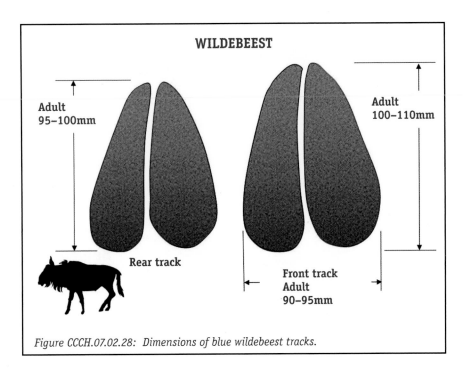

Figure CCCH.07.02.28: Dimensions of blue wildebeest tracks.

to CCCH.07.02.31. During the rut, the territorial bulls can leave knee and pawing marks on the ground when depositing preorbital gland secretions.

Scat

The individual pellets are about 14 to 20mm long and are sometimes clumped when the animal has been feeding on green grass. Bulls will frequently defecate

Figure CCCH.07.02.29: Blue wildebeest hoofs.

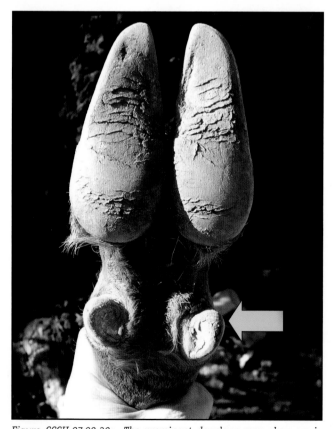

Figure CCCH.07.02.30: The prominent dewclaws may show up in soft substrate.

and urinate on open, elevated patches; otherwise, scat is deposited at random. Fresh scat is dark olive brown and becomes dark brownish black as it ages. See Figure CCCH.07.02.32. Scat pellets may be clumped together.

Territorial Patches

These areas, frequented by a territorial bull, are usually devoid of vegetation and are scattered with their droppings and tracks. One will often find harvester termites, which utilize the grass and dung pellets, in these areas. Wildebeests will scent mark by rubbing their preorbital glands on the ground or on low vegetation. They will paw the ground and deposit interdigital gland secretions. These secretions have quite a strong "tarry" odour, which can also be detected by humans.

Horning

Wildebeest sometimes horn the ground and vegetation and will leave behind sign. Bulls sometimes adorn their foreheads and horns with mud and broken vegetation.

Game Paths

Because wildebeests drink regularly and have the tendency to walk in a single file, they tramp out well-worn game paths that often radiate out from a water hole like spokes on a wheel.

Sand Bathing

They prefer open sandy patches for rolling and dust bathing.

Rubbing

Wildebeests will sometimes rub against trees, which will dislodge pieces of bark or leave traces of their hair behind.

Resting Spots

Herds will choose shady spots to shelter in during the heat of the day. Impressions of their bodies can be sometimes seen on suitable substrates, and the position they choose to lie in relative to the position of shade and sun can sometimes give an indication as to the age of the sign. See Figure CCCH.07.02.33.

Feeding Areas

Look for signs in areas of short grass.

Behaviour and Senses

Wildebeest senses are not as good as other species. Vision, smell, and hearing are pretty average, which makes stalking them easier. If wildebeests have an obvious escape route, they are not dangerous. If they feel trapped or hemmed in, they can be unpredictable.

Figure CCCH.07.02.31: Blue wildebeest tracks.

Figure CCCH.07.02.32: Fresh wildebeest scat (top) and older scat (bottom).

Figure CCCH.07.02.33: Blue wildebeests will rest in shade during the heat of the day and leave sign.

Tracking Burchell Zebras

Like tracking any animal, the key to success lies in knowing and being able to recognize the track and in understanding the biology of the animal. What are its preferred feeding and bedding areas, how frequently must it drink water, how does it respond to danger? When we understand how an animal behaves and "thinks," tracking it becomes a lot easier. If we are looking for zebra sign, it stands to reason to begin looking in preferred zebra habitat. See Figure CCCH.07.02.34.

The Burchell zebra is a savanna species that is partial to open woodland, shrub, and grassland where water is readily available. See Figure CCCH.07.02.34. They avoid dense woodland if possible, and although they occur in semiarid areas, they are not found in true desert country. Their particular habitat preferences and water requirements often result in seasonal migrations.

Zebras are gregarious animals that form small family groups consisting of a stallion, one or two adult mares, and foals of varying ages. A family group size averages seven to ten animals. Stallions that have no mares form bachelor groups or live alone.

Family groups remain distinct even in large aggregations of zebras. There does not appear to be any social organization above that of family groups. Burchell zebras are often seen in the company of blue wildebeests because they both favour areas of short grass. Zebras have loosely organized home ranges and readily move to wherever food and water are available.

There is quite a lot of group interaction and social grooming in zebras. They often lean against each other. Vocal communication is important in this species. When attacked by predators, a breeding herd bunches up. If they run, the stallions hang back or position themselves on the flank to ward off the predators, which they often do successfully. Scarred rumps from unsuccessful lion attacks attest to the effectiveness of their defensive kicks.

Zebras, to their own detriment, tend to be inquisitive, often returning to investigate a source of initial flight. This can sometimes give a tracker a second chance if he has "spooked" a herd. Competition between rival stallions can sometimes erupt into full-scale fights with biting, kicking, and rearing. Burchell zebra are not territorial. Lions and hyenas are the main predators of zebras. Mortalities also occur through disease. Zebra are very partial to

Figure CCCH.07.02.34: Zebras in grassland (top) and open woodland habitat (bottom).

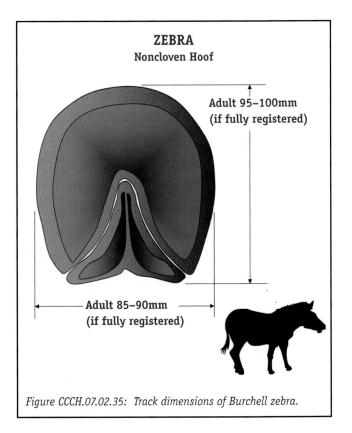

ZEBRA
Noncloven Hoof

Adult 95–100mm
(if fully registered)

Adult 85–90mm
(if fully registered)

Figure CCCH.07.02.35: Track dimensions of Burchell zebra.

taking dust baths, and it is common to find areas within their habitat where they roll in the sand or bare ground. Because lions prey on zebras especially around water holes, they are wary when approaching to drink.

Zebras are mainly grazers, but occasionally will browse on leaves and scrub. They also dig for grass rhizomes and corms during the dry season. They graze on short grass and are able to survive in areas with poor or coarse grass cover. They are very dependent on water and never wander very far from water holes. Zebras require approximately fourteen liters of water per day to meet their physiological requirements but will drink an average of twenty-one liters at a time if forced to go without water for longer than a day. Water holes are good places to look for tracks and scat.

Burchell Zebra Signs

Vocalization

Zebras are very vocal animals and will frequently betray their presence by "barking." Courting stallions "nicker." Animals will whinny or snort by forcing air through their nostrils to warn of danger. These sounds can carry a long way in the bush and can lead you to zebras long before you have a visual sighting. Listen for these signs.

Figure CCCH.07.02.36: The hoof of a zebra showing the frog.

Figure CCCH.07.02.37: An assortment of zebra tracks. The top photo shows the tracks of a zebra mare and her foal.

Figure CCCH.07.02.38: Horse tracks are larger and rounder than those of a zebra.

Tracks and Scat

The tracks of zebras are those of the typical horselike hoof. See Figures CCCH.07.02.35 to CCCH.07.02.37. The general hoof structure is well known and should be familiar to anyone who has seen a horse. The horse family only has one "toe" (the third) on each leg and only the tip of the toe (the hoof) comes into contact with the ground. The tracks of Burchell zebra resemble those of a small horse.

Figure CCCH.07.02.39: Fresh zebra scat (top), old (centre), and broken up by dung beetles (bottom).

Zebras grazing on a green flush after a burn.

The length of the track is about 90 to 100mm with the hind track being slightly longer and narrower. On hard ground only the edges of the hoof and the frog will be visible. The only animals whose tracks might be confused with those of the zebra are horses, donkeys, mules, and other zebra species. Horse tracks are bigger and rounder than those of zebra (see Figure CCCH.07.02.38) and it is unlikely that different zebra species will be found together as they have different zoogeographical distributions.

Zebra dung is kidney shaped with each individual pellet about 50mm in length. It is usually deposited randomly because zebras are not territorial. When fresh, it is olive green and becomes dark brown with age. See Figure CCCH.07.02.39. The contents of scat are composed mostly of fine, undigested grass fibres. The odour is typically "horsey."

Grazing Areas

Areas heavily grazed by zebra are often characterized by trampling and by grass having been cropped fairly close to the ground. Signs of digging with hoofs in search of underground corms and rhizomes can sometimes be observed. Zebras are very partial to green flushes that occur after a burn or following rain, so these are good areas to look for them. See Figure CCCH.07.02.40.

Dust Baths and Rubs

Zebras enjoy rolling in sandy areas, and they leave bare, dusty patches behind. See Figure CCCH.07.02.42. They also sometimes choose a convenient object such as a rock or log to rub themselves on. Hair will be left behind on the object.

Figure CCCH.07.02.42: An area used by zebras for dust bathing.

Figure CCCH.07.02.41: Note the association of zebras with wildebeests.

Tracking Kudus

Kudus are like "ghosts" in the bush. They move silently and slowly, stopping frequently to check their surroundings. When tracking kudus, the tracker must move carefully because these animals have excellent senses of sight, smell, and hearing.

Figure CCCH.07.02.43: Typical kudu habitat.

Habitat

Kudus prefer savanna woodland and are partial to areas of broken, rocky, or hilly terrain, usually in proximity to a source of water. Figure CCCH.07.02.43 shows a kudu in typical habitat.

In arid country they are confined to woodland on the fringes of watercourses, woodland thickets, or in bush tall enough to provide cover. Kudus are not usually found in open grassland except when crossing it to other suitable habitat.

Habits

Kudus are gregarious, occurring in small herds of four to five and seldom more than eleven. Herd size appears to peak during November to January (just prior to calving) and again between June and July during the rut. Adult bulls are usually associated with female herds but can be found alone or in small herds of up to six. Kudus are mainly active in the early morning or

Figure CCCH.07.02.44: Kudus blend in very well with dry bush and are difficult to spot. The cows on the left are very difficult to see, and, if it were not for the horns, the bull on page 221 would also be hard to spot.

later afternoon. They rest in dense cover or woodland during the heat of the day.

In areas where they are harassed, they may become nocturnal. They are shy antelopes, always alert and cautious. They will take a few steps at a time, then stop, look, and listen. With their large, radarlike ears pivoting this way and that and with their nostrils flared and quivering, they test the air. If suspicious or disturbed in open areas, they will immediately take flight to the nearest cover with their white and fluffy tails raised, which is a warning and an indication of the direction of flight to those following. Once spooked, they will seldom look back or stop to determine the cause of their fright. They are less nervous when standing in dense cover and will often "freeze" whilst observing an intruder. When standing still, they can blend in superbly with their surroundings, making them very difficult to spot. See Figure CCCH.07.02.44. Kudus are accomplished jumpers and clear a two-meter-high fence with consummate ease.

Feeding and Drinking

Kudus are predominantly browsers and will eat a wider range of vegetation than other antelopes. They prefer leaves and young shoots but will also eat seedpods, leaves of aloe species, and other plants that are poisonous or avoided by other browsers. Kudus prefer forbs to woody plants. They will drink day or night and require about nine liters of water a day.

Kudu Sign

Apart from visual sighting, the hunter/tracker should look for other signs that will indicate the presence of kudu. Kudus are very well camouflaged in dry bush, especially the females as their colour and vertical pale stripes provide ideal camouflage.

Spoor

The hoof is cloven, typically oval in shape, and 55 to 75mm long. See Figures CCCH.07.02.45 and CCCH.07.02.46. The forefeet of the males are relatively broader than those of the females. Their tracks are very similar to and may be confused with those of nyalas, bushbucks, or reedbucks. Nyala and bushbuck tracks are slightly smaller, and reedbuck tracks narrower and more pointed. Although nyalas and bushbucks may occur in similar habitat to kudus, reedbucks generally prefer flood plains, open grassland marshes (vleis), or montane grasslands.

Scat

Dung pellets are usually about 20mm in length; they are slightly shorter and narrower than that of elands and giraffes but larger than that of impalas. An accumulation

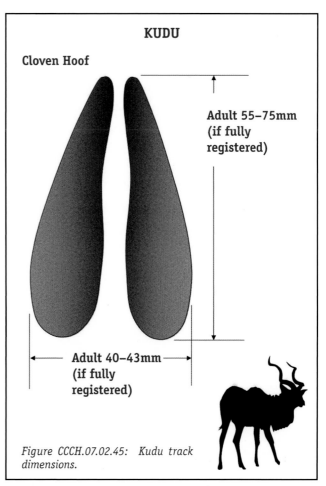

Figure CCCH.07.02.45: Kudu track dimensions.

of pellets may be found in favourite feeding spots. See Figure CCCH.07.02.47. The colour of fresh scat is olive green and turns dark brown with age.

Debarking

During periods of shortage, kudus will use bark as a source of food, using the incisors of the lower jaw to scrape it off.

Horning

Kudu bulls use their horns to break off branches to gain access to leaves normally out of reach. Ground horning, when the horns and face are rubbed in mud or dry ground, is a form of territorial behaviour found in kudus as well as in nyalas, bushbucks, and wildebeests.

Browse Lines

In areas where there are large populations of kudus and/or other browsers, a distinct "browse line" becomes evident in the tree foliage. This is the vertical distance from ground level to the point where animals can extend their necks to reach food.

Vocalization

Kudus emit one to three loud, hoarse "barks" when giving alarm; it is similar to but louder and deeper than the alarm bark of the bushbuck. When a tracker hears this bark, it can mean one of two things. He himself has been spotted, or the kudu has become aware of some other danger, such as a predator or other human, which is also useful knowledge to the tracker.

Figure CCCH.07.02.46: Kudu tracks.

Figure CCCH.07.02.47: Fresh kudu scat.

Tracking Warthogs

Warthogs are reasonably easy to track but are very alert and will take flight if they feel at all suspicious. At the same time, they are inquisitive animals. Approaching warthogs on all fours and making a soft grunting sound can often induce them to come closer to investigate.

Habitat

Warthogs are at home on savanna grassland, *vleis,* flood plains, and open areas close to water holes and pans. They prefer areas where water is readily available in which to wallow but can live in dry areas where water is seasonal. They will utilize open woodland and scrub but will avoid dense riverine vegetation (only moving into these areas to get to water), thick bush, and montane forest. They are attracted to areas of new growth, especially after a burn.

Habits

Warthogs are diurnal animals (active during the day) and retire to large excavated burrows during the night. Warthogs will usually rest in deep shade during the hot times of the day. This species is not water dependent but will drink and wallow regularly when water is available.

Warthogs live in groups called sounders that usually consist of a dominant boar, one or two females, and their offspring. Males associate with the females only during the rutting period and will become solitary or associate in small bachelor groups during the remainder of the year. Maternal groups consisting of females and young will be joined by adult males when females come into season.

Home ranges vary considerably from season to season and may overlap. Whilst not territorial, adult boars may show intolerance to younger males if their paths cross. Warthogs leave scent by rubbing the sides of their mouths against objects, spraying urine, and by smearing secretions from preorbital glands onto objects.

Warthogs have a good sense of smell, eyesight, and hearing. They will stand and stare at any disturbance and the moment they feel threatened will run off at great speed with the tail held straight up in the air. They will also bolt when other animals in the vicinity do so and will quickly respond to the warning calls of oxpeckers, gray louries, and cattle egrets.

Warthog Sign

Tracks and Scat

The cloven hoofs of warthogs are smaller and narrower than those of bushpigs and have a rounded front end. The dewclaws might sometimes show up in soft substrate but are not often seen on hard substrate. See Figures CCCH.07.02.48 to CCCH.07.02.50. Warthogs defecate randomly and do not make use of middens.

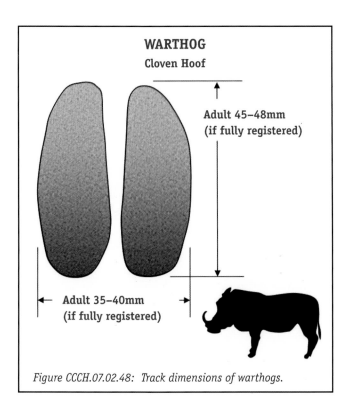

Figure CCCH.07.02.48: Track dimensions of warthogs.

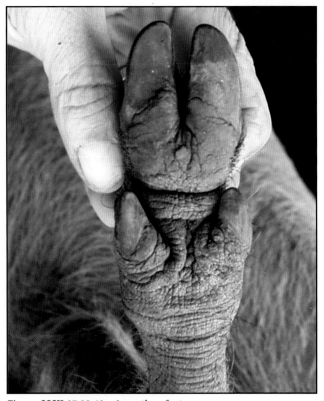

Figure CCCH.07.02.49: A warthog foot.

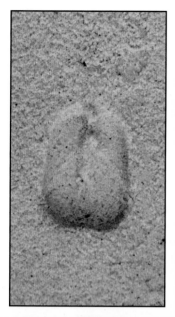

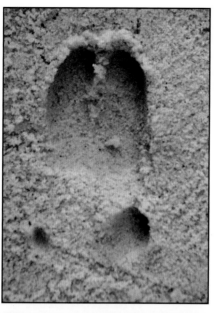

Figure CCCH.07.02.50: Warthog tracks.

Their dung is kidney shaped (similar to but smaller than that of the zebra), less than 50mm in length, and does not crack across the middle. Because of the forbs and herbs in their diet, the dry dung, when crushed in the hand, can have a rather pleasant and aromatic smell.

Feeding Sign

A warthog is primarily a grazer but will browse and eat fruit, seeds, and herbaceous plants. They are partial to rhizomes and roots. They can often be observed down on their front knees, using their snouts to dig up underground food. Areas of turned-up soil show where warthogs have been feeding. See Figures CCCH.07.02.51 and CCCH.07.02.52. They tend to root more during the winter months than in the summer months when fresh green grass makes up the bulk of their diet. Warthogs will sometimes leave clear signs of rooting especially in open *vleis*; in green, post burn flushes; and in areas where there is a supply of underground rhizomes and roots. Signs consist of little furrows 10 to 15 cm deep, overturned earth, a very characteristic smell (given off by damaged root when still quite fresh), and the remains of food material. Warthogs will sometimes return to prime feeding areas and will sometimes eat carrion.

Rubs and Wallows

Convenient rubbing posts are often located around water holes and wallows. These are usually short tree trunks or rocks that become smooth and shiny with regular use. Warthogs will often return to their favourite rubbing posts. Warthogs are very

Figure CCCH.07.02.51: A warthog's feeding sign includes soil turned over from "rooting" (yellow arrows). Warthogs are partial to feeding in areas of new growth.

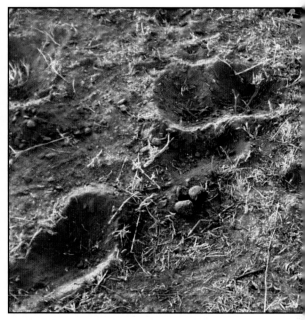

Figure CCCH.07.02.52: Warthog digging.

partial to wallowing, especially in the hot summer months. They will drop small pieces of mud and leave mud sign on vegetation when they move off into the bush after a wallow. Wallowing helps to regulate body temperature and control external parasites. In areas where warthogs are common, many trees around the wallows bear the evidence of mud smears. See Figure CCCH.07.02.53

Burrows

These shelters are usually made by modifying vacated aardvark/antbear/porcupine burrows and provide protection for the warthogs, from inclement weather and predators. Warthog will sometimes remain in or retire to their burrows during stormy or rainy weather. Warthogs reverse into the burrows and emerge "sharp end" first. It is, therefore, not advisable to stand in front of an occupied burrow as a fast-exiting warthog can cause serious injury.

Burrows are changed on a regular basis. At sunset a warthog will look for a burrow. If one is found already occupied, he will move on until another is found. Warthogs make use of vacated aardvark or porcupine burrows. When occupied, there will be tracks entering and leaving the burrow and flies will be present at the entrance as well. The soil at the entrance will be freshly trampled. When the burrow is not in use, there will be no flies or fresh tracks, and the entrance will often have spider webs constructed across it. Soil will be compacted.

Sound

Warthogs are generally silent except when disturbed. Adults will grunt and piglets squeal to communicate. Warthogs grunt and squeal when fighting.

Figure CCCH.07.02.53: Trees showing sign of warthog rubs (top) and a warthog enjoying a wallow (bottom).

Tracking Elands

Habitat

Elands can utilize a wide range of habitats, from semideserts to bushvelds to mountain grasslands. They can be found on the fringes of woodlands but prefer not to frequent dense woodland or open grassland. As predominant browsers, they prefer bushvelds where trees and shrubs are available.

Habits

Elands are gregarious animals that move around in small herds. Large herds made up of smaller units have been recorded. The calving season takes place from October to January. During this time adult bulls will leave the breeding herds to form bachelor groups.

Food preferences, availability, and seasonal rains generally determine movements and migrations. Elands will often move into burnt areas in search of fresh new growth.

There is no sign of territorial behaviour in elands. Hierarchy appears to be based on size and age. When disputes occur, they can result in serious fights and mortalities have been reported.

Elands are fond of rubbing against objects and mutual grooming is commonly observed. Elands are not exclusively diurnal and can often be found active at night. They are generally shy animals and will trot off if approached too closely. They can maintain a steady trot for extended periods if disturbed.

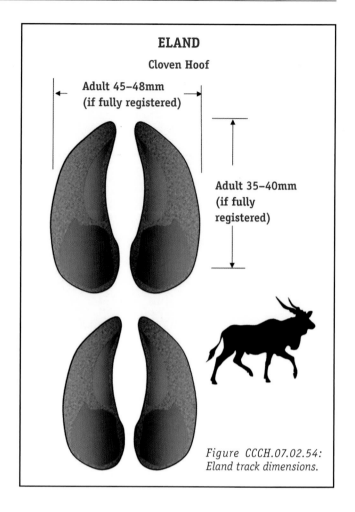

ELAND

Cloven Hoof

Adult 45–48mm (if fully registered)

Adult 35–40mm (if fully registered)

Figure CCCH.07.02.54: Eland track dimensions.

Figure CCCH.07.02.55: Eland tracks.

Figure CCCH.07.02.56: Eland tracks.

Figure CCCH.07.02.57: Eland scat.

Figure CCCH.07.02.58: When an eland eats a green grass diet, this is what its scat looks like. Note how the typical pellet shape is no longer as distinct.

Feeding and Drinking

Whereas they will drink water regularly when it is available, elands can go for extended periods without drinking, by taking in sufficient moisture with their food to meet physiological requirements.

Elands are mainly browsers but show preference for new grass after a burn. Although their diet consists mainly of browse, they will utilize grass in small quantities throughout the year. They use their horns to break branches to get to food and have also been observed using their horns to strip bark.

Eland Sign

Feeding Sign

Keep an eye open for stripped bark and broken branches.

Tracks and Scat

The track is a cloven hoof and rounder at its anterior end than most antelopes. The front track is 45mm to 48mm long and the rear track 35mm to 40mm long. The rear tracks are similar to, but more elongated than, that of the buffalo and domestic cattle. The rear tracks are slightly narrower than the front tracks. See Figures CCCH.07.02.54 to CCCH.07.02.56.

Dung pellets, 25mm long, are spherical and second only in size to those of the giraffe. Because elands are not territorial animals, they do not generally deposit dung in middens. The scat shape can change if the elands are feeding on green forage. See Figures CCCH.07.02.57 and CCCH.07.02.58.

Voice

Elands are generally silent animals but will vocalize occasionally.

Tracking Gemsboks

Habitat

Gemsboks occur in dry, open areas. In South Africa, Botswana, and Namibia they are found in open grasslands, open bush savannas, and open woodlands. They show a preference for sandy dunes with sparse plant life that consists of short perennial grasses and other forbs. They are fairly independent of surface water but will dig with their fore-hoofs to reach water below the sand; they will make regular use of water when it is available.

Habits

Gemsboks are nomadic and aggregate in areas where scattered rainstorms bring on a green flush of vegetation. They occur in family groups, nursery groups, small bachelor herds, and single bulls. They can be found sometimes in large herds during the wet season when food is in abundant supply. As the dry months are ushered in, the herds splinter into smaller groups of twelve or less as they range wider for food.

Territorial bulls are more tolerant of other bulls than are males of other territorial species. Territorial males mark their areas by thrashing bushes with their horns, pawing the ground, and defecating in small piles from a low-squatting position. They have interdigital glands that mark the ground wherever they walk.

They are extremely vigilant animals and because of the open habitat they frequent are difficult to approach without being seen from a long way off. If they become suspicious, the animals will be sure to maintain a healthy distance between themselves and what they perceive to be a possible threat.

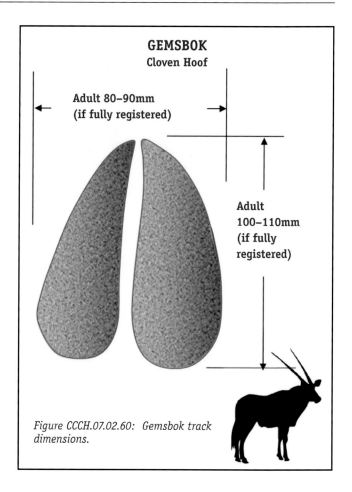

Figure CCCH.07.02.60: Gemsbok track dimensions.

Feeding

Gemsboks are mainly grazers but will browse on bushes and forbs when grass is in short supply. They prefer to graze at night when it is cooler and when the moisture content of vegetation is higher. By producing a highly concentrated urine and allowing body temperature to rise without sweating, the gemsbok is able to survive without drinking. They tend to seek out shady areas during the heat of the day when it is available. They meet body water requirements to a large extent by eating succulent foods such as t'sama melons and wild cucumbers *(Cucumis spp.)*. See Figure CCCH.07.02.59. They like to make use of mineral licks.

Gemsbok Signs

Spoor and Dung

Spoor is characteristically heart shaped. The anterior parts of the hoofs are sharply pointed. The front hoofs are larger than the hind hoofs, and the rear spoor is more rounded. The length of front spoor is about 100 to 110mm and about 90mm wide. See Figures CCCH.07.02.60 and CCCH.07.02.61. The dung

Figure CCCH.07.02.59: T'sama melons are a favourite food of the gemsbok and provides them with much-needed moisture.

Figure CCCH.07.02.61: Gemsbok tracks.

Figure CCCH.07.02.62: Gemsbok scat.

pellets are lozenge shaped with individual pellets being 14 to 20mm long. See Figure CCCH.07.02.62.

Gemsboks, with the exception of rutting bulls, drop pellets throughout their home range. Territorial bulls have a characteristic low crouching posture when defecating. Fecal pellets lie in a small pile and retain their odour longer than if they were scattered. Before defecating, territorial bulls paw the ground to transfer secretions from interdigital glands. These sites may be located along territorial boundaries or randomly throughout the home range. When fresh, the dung is black and shiny. It soon dries and cracks if exposed to heat. Favourite feeding spots, a rolling area and middens, will be indicated by an abundance of old and possibly new spoor and the absence of grass

from trampling. When gemsboks urinate on dry sand, it consolidates the particles to form a "urine table." Signs of grazing may be evident in areas frequented by these animals.

Digging and Feeding Signs

Gemsboks will dig for underground roots and leave behind partially chewed t'sama melons. Look for signs of gemsboks digging for water, especially in dry riverbeds.

Territorial Sign

Signs left by territorial males will include ground that has been pawed and bushes that have been damaged by "thrashing."

Tracking Blesbok

Habitat

Their natural distribution was the eastern highveld grass plains of southern Africa. Subsequent relocations have shown that they are an adaptable species but sweet grass and readily available water are requirements that they need to adapt successfully. They are quite at home in fairly hilly country as well as open plains.

Habits

Blesboks are gregarious animals that are most active during overcast days, early morning, and from sunset until late night. They usually rest up in shade during the warmer hours of the day. They become very lazy when it is hot, and animals can be approached quite closely at times. They are grazers. When moving to feeding or watering areas, they move in single file. This eventually leads to the formation of well-defined game paths. Social groups consist of territorial rams, bachelor groups, and breeding groups made up of a territorial ram and from 10 to 25 adult females. Serious fights sometimes result between territorial rams during the rutting season. They face one another on their front knees and try to inflict wounds with their horns on their rival's flanks. The observant tracker will find gouge marks in the ground where these fights have occurred.

They mark their territories using dung middens, by inserting grass storks into their preorbital glands

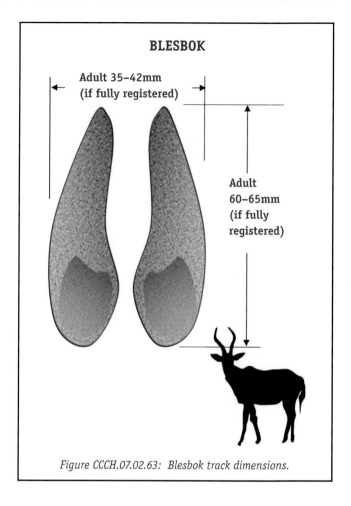

BLESBOK

Adult 35–42mm (if fully registered)

Adult 60–65mm (if fully registered)

Figure CCCH.07.02.63: Blesbok track dimensions.

Figure CCCH.07.02.64: A blesbok hoof seen from below.

to smear them with a secretion, and by wiping the glands across vegetation. This secretion is sometimes transferred to the base of the horns by sweeping the horns across grass stalks that have been marked with glandular secretions. Blesboks also mark territories with secretions from interdigital glands between their hoofs. They can sometimes be seen scratching on termite mounds with their hoofs.

Herds split up during the rutting season but coalesce to form large concentrations during the cold, dry winter months of June to August. They begin breaking up from about September and reach maximum fragmentation by about April.

Feeding

Blesboks are predominantly grazers. There have been isolated observations of them browsing. They are very fond of new grass growing after a recent burn and will move quite a long way, back and forth, between these feeding areas and the closest water. Certain grass species will only be utilized during the early growth stages but will be avoided later on in the winter months.

Blesbok Sign

Tracks

The front tracks of blesbok are noticeably larger than the rear ones. See Figures CCCH.07.02.63 to CCCH.07.02.65. Blesboks have a typical cloven hoof. Tracks are about 60 to 70mm in length.

Feeding Sign and Scat

Look for feeding sign in typical open grassveld areas, under trees and shrubs where they rest, and territorial sign such as middens and pawing on termite mounds. The scat of the blesbok is cylindrical with a small nipple on one end and about 12mm to 14mm in length. See Figure CCCH.07.02.66.

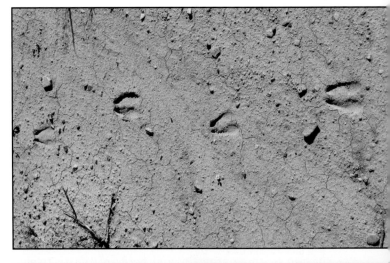

Figure CCCH.07.02.65: Blesbok tracks.

Figure CCCH.07.02.66: Blesbok scat.

Tracking Giraffes

Habitat

Giraffes occur in a wide range of dry savanna habitats. They generally do not occur in deserts and dense forest. They are dependent on trees and large shrubs for food.

Habits

Giraffes have very gentle natures but can defend themselves successfully against large predators like lions by kicking out with sharp and heavy hoofs. Many a lion in Africa has ended up dead or severely injured after having tangled with a giraffe.

Gregarious by nature, they will be found in groups of two to three animals, and herds of ten to twelve individuals are not unusual. Groups of between forty to seventy have been sighted occasionally and reported in scientific literature. Old bulls are sometimes solitary. Giraffes have good eyesight and hear well but authorities differ in their opinions on how well giraffes can hear. It is reasonably easy to get up fairly close to a giraffe due to their inquisitive natures. Males challenge one another and fight by the curious behaviour called "necking." They stand side by side facing in opposite directions. Heads are lowered and swung in the direction of the opponent with blows being directed toward the body or neck.

Feeding and Drinking

Giraffes are primarily browsers. Because they browse high up, some trees take on a curious hourglass shape. See Figure CCCH.07.02.67.

They spend most of the day and part of the night feeding. They will drink regularly if water is freely available but can survive short periods of water scarcity. Because they have to adopt a wide-legged and vulnerable stance when drinking water, they will often stand for a long time carefully surveying the scene around a water hole before committing themselves to this ungainly position.

Giraffe Sign

Suitable Habitat

Search in dry savanna with tall trees of preferred browse. Because giraffe are so tall, they can be spotted from a long distance and are not very difficult to locate in open woodland or savanna. Water holes are good places to wait for giraffe and to look for tracks.

Feeding Sign

Hourglass-shaped trees characterize areas frequented by giraffes.

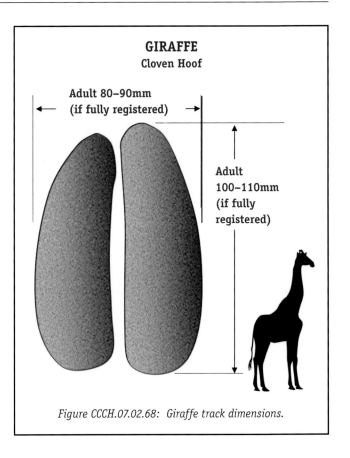

GIRAFFE
Cloven Hoof

Adult 80–90mm (if fully registered)

Adult 100–110mm (if fully registered)

Figure CCCH.07.02.68: Giraffe track dimensions.

Figure CCCH.07.02.67: Giraffe browsing sometimes results in hourglass-shaped trees.

Tracks and Scat

Giraffes have large cloven-hoofed tracks that cannot easily be confused with other tracks of similar shape by virtue of their size. See Figures CCCH.07.02.68 and CCCH.07.02.69. The hoofs are somewhat rounded at the apex, and the length of the tracks are about 110mm long and 90mm wide.

Scat is typical of antelopes, being cylindrical and having a "nipple" on the end. The length is approximately 30mm. Because they are dropped from a height, pellets are usually quite spread and not in a concentrated pile.

Vocalizing

They are mostly silent animals but will occasionally utter moans, snorts, and grunts. Giraffes vocalize infrequently and sounds made by them cannot be relied upon as a means to locate them.

Figure CCCH.07.02.69: Giraffe track and scat.

Tracking Baboons

Habitat

Baboons occupy a wide variety of habitats, including open grassy plains, rocky outcrops, cliffs, riverine bush, and savannah woodlands. They are a highly adaptable species.

Habits

Baboons are highly gregarious and social animals that move together in troops and vary in size from ten to one hundred animals; troops average about forty individuals. Troops form very stable and permanent units with a well-defined social structure. Baboons are highly protective of each other (and especially their young) and will gang together to drive off potential predators. When the troop is resting or feeding, individuals will be put out on sentry duty. A warning bark from the lookout will send members in the troop scattering in all directions with barks and shrieks.

Baboons are terrestrial during the day but will quickly take to tall trees or rocky *krantzes* to escape danger. They can swim and will sometimes do so for the pure fun and enjoyment of it. They are highly intelligent animals and have excellent eyesight and hearing. They are very vocal animals and are most noisy at dawn and dusk. They have a wide range of vocalizations, but their warning bark is very distinctive and can be heard from a long way off.

Baboon troops cover quite a distance during the day as they forage. They will return to favourite resting sites before nightfall, which are usually tall trees or high ground that is difficult for a potential predator to scale. Baboons awake at daybreak but usually descend from their perches only after sunrise. Baboons generally do not appear to defend their home ranges against other troops (there are exceptions that have been recorded). Baboons usually spend the first hours of the morning feeding and will move into shade to rest during the hotter part of the day, and as the day begins to cool, they will resume foraging as they slowly begin to make their way back to their sleeping area. Young baboons enjoy play and spend hours each day occupied in a variety of games including chasing one another, demonstrating their acrobatic prowess, or teasing older animals. Dominant males quickly discipline unruly youngsters.

Feeding and Drinking

Baboons are omnivores. They feed on almost anything, including plant material, insects, and even meat. One researcher said it was easier to list what baboons did not eat than what they did eat! Their diets will adapt according to environmental conditions. They eat seeds, roots, tubers, fruit, leaves, stems, and the flowers of plants. They are partial to locusts, caterpillars, ants, and even scorpions. They will eat birds' eggs and fledglings and are known to catch and eat the young of impalas, steenboks, and klipspringers. Baboons are very dependent on water and will drink daily. They can become troublesome crop raiders.

Baboon Sign

Tracks and Scat

The tracks of baboons are described as "hands and feet." The foot is about 135 to 140mm long and the toe stands out at an angle of about 45 degrees to the foot. See Figures CCCH.07.02.70 and CCCH.07.02.71.

The hand (front foot) is about 80mm in length and the thumb stands out at about 75 degrees. Baboon scat can take on a variety of shapes and forms and is scattered at random throughout their home range. See Figure CCCH.07.02.72. There are usually accumulations of scat under favourite roosts; it gives a very distinctive and pungent smell to the area. Fresh droppings have a thick porridgelike consistency and a roughish surface.

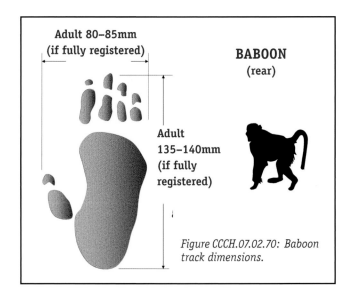

Figure CCCH.07.02.70: Baboon track dimensions.

Feeding Sign

Baboons will often leave signs of feeding in their wake. This will consist of partially eaten wild fruit, or, in the case of crop raiders, maize cobs and oranges. Baboons also damage forestry plantations by breaking off the tips of young trees. Baboons overturn rocks to look for grubs, insect larvae, and scorpions.

Voice

Vocalizing baboons can be heard from a long distance away and can also lead the hunter/tracker to the roosting sites.

Roosting Sites

Roosting sites will have accumulations of dung and will have a characteristic baboon smell.

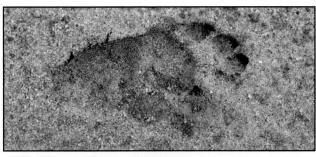

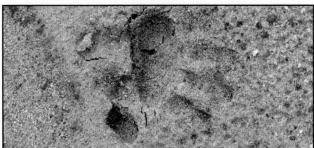

Figure CCCH.07.02.71: Baboon tracks.

Figure CCCH.07.02.72: Baboon scat.

Tracking Caracals

Caracals typically live in arid zones and dry savannas; they prefer arid brush. However, they inhabit a variety of habitats, including plains, mountains, and rocky hills, and venture into open grasslands at night. They seem to need woody vegetation for cover, but they avoid dense evergreen forest.

Habits

Caracals are solitary except when breeding or with young. They are active mainly at night, but also sometimes during the day and at twilight. They usually lie up in cover or in rocky refuges during daylight hours. Because of their secretive ways, not much is known about their habits. They will vigorously defend themselves if cornered and will hiss and spit. Otherwise, apart from purring softly, they are silent.

Feeding

The caracal kills bigger prey animals such as hyraxes, monkeys, and hares by strangling them. It covers its kills with leaves or caches them in trees and returns repeatedly to feed. They also catch rats, mice, and small game birds. They are finicky eaters and will discard the viscera of the mammals they catch; they will partially pluck the fur off hyraxes and larger kills; and they will

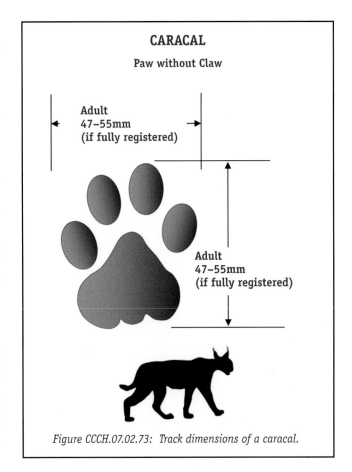

CARACAL

Paw without Claw

Adult
47–55mm
(if fully registered)

Adult
47–55mm
(if fully registered)

Figure CCCH.07.02.73: Track dimensions of a caracal.

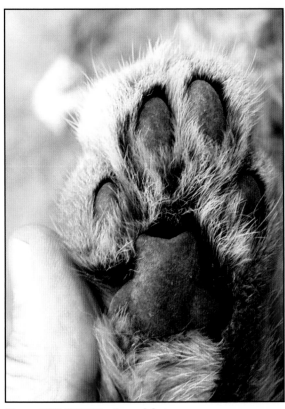

Figure CCCH.07.02.74: Caracal feet.

avoid eating hair by shearing meat neatly from the skin. Yet they will eat the feathers of small birds and are tolerant of rotten meat. They can also catch small antelopes and the young of larger antelopes. They sometimes become killers of domestic stock like sheep and goats.

Caracal Sign

Tracks and Scat

The tracks are classified as paws without claws. See Figures CCCH.07.02.73 to CCCH.07.02.75. They are similar in shape and form to the leopard's but smaller. The normal walking stride is 60 to 80 cm. The claws are kept sheathed during normal walking and will not be seen in the track. When leaping for prey, the claws are extended and may be visible in the track. The scat is described as sausage-shaped droppings, tapered at one end, and usually segmented. See Figure CCCH.07.02.76.

Feeding

If one finds prey that has been killed by a caracal, there are some distinguishing features: In larger prey (small or young antelope/sheep/goats), caracal typically feed on the flesh between the hind legs or on the inside of the hind legs, brisket, and shoulders. See Figure CCCH.07.02.77. They might chew on rib tips, but they never eat the large bones. The kill may be partially covered or cached in a tree to be fed on at a later stage.

Figure CCCH.07.02.75: A clear caracal print in mud (top) and an indistinct print of a caracal running across gravelly substrate (bottom).

Figure CCCH.07.02.76: Caracal scat.

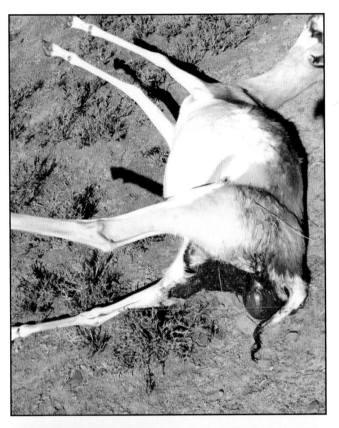

Figure CCCH.07.02.77: A springbok killed by a caracal.

Tracking Springbok

Habitat

Typically they are associated with dry, arid areas and open grass plains. In parts of Botswana and in the Kalahari they are often found associated with pans and dry riverbeds. The factors that influence their choice of habitat include availability of their preferred plants, minerals, and the height and density of the vegetation. They avoid mountainous areas and rocky outcrops, dense woodland, and high grass.

Habitat

Springboks form small herds of twenty to thirty animals during the dry months of the year. Very large herds may form after the rains and when the first green flush appears in localized areas. In the past, researchers have documented mass migrations numbering hundreds of thousands of animals.

Social groupings consist of bachelor herds, territorial males, and breeding herds consisting of adults and juveniles of both sexes. A territorial ram demonstrates his status by urinating and then defecating on top of the urine to form middens at strategic points in its territory. A low back posture, with the belly held close

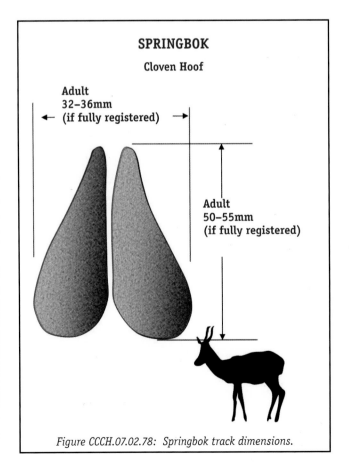

Figure CCCH.07.02.78: Springbok track dimensions.

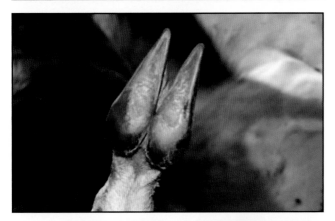

to the ground, is adopted when urinating and defecating for territorial marking and may be preceded by pawing of the ground. Dominant males may also thrash at low bushes with their horns—to the extent that the horns are sometimes stained green. They prefer open territorial areas and also like to make themselves prominent. They attempt to keep breeding females in their areas by actively herding them. When doing this the tail of the dominant ram is held horizontal or even vertically when very excited.

Springboks have two periods of peak activity in the early morning and late afternoon. They can also remain fairly active during the night. They do not look for shade during the heat of the day to the extent that other species do. They move slowly whilst grazing but can run up to speeds of eighty-eight kilometers per hour if disturbed or chased.

The tail of a springbok is in constant motion, switching back and forth. The more excited the animal is, the more the tail moves. Springboks are not very vocal. Two calls that have been identified are a low communicating grunt and a whistling snort of alarm.

Feeding and Drinking

Springboks are grazers and browsers. Browse makes up the bulk of their diet during the dry times of the year and grasses during the wet months. They utilize a wide variety of grasses, forbs, and woody plants.

Figure CCCH.07.02.79: Springbok tracks and hoofs.

Figure CCCH.07.02.80: Springbok scat.

When water is available, they will drink throughout the year at any time of the night or day. They can drink water with a very high mineral content that is unpalatable to many other species. They are very partial to mineral licks. They can, however, during time of drought get by without water, obtaining enough moisture from their food and especially by grazing at night when the water content of grass can rise from 8 to 26 percent.

Springboks are not strictly seasonal breeders but there does appear to be some correlation to the first rains of spring/early summer and a peak in breeding activity. A nutritious and abundant food supply will improve the physiological condition of females and make them come into season when favourable conditions prevail. They can have young at any time of the year.

Females will leave the herds to give birth and will hide young lambs in dense grass where they will "freeze" when danger threatens. The young begin nibbling on vegetation after about two weeks and will then join up with the herd. They are weaned at two months. Young lambs often form small nursery groups within the breeding herds.

Springbok Sign

Suitable Habitat

Springboks are partial to open to semiopen areas. They will avoid dense bush. They can often be found in areas of green flush after first seasonal rains. They are very partial to and will regularly visit mineral deposits or licks.

Territorial Markings

Middens, ground scraping, and damaged vegetation from horn thrashing are some of the signs a tracker can look for.

Tracks

Springboks have a typical cloven-hoof shape that is about 50 to 55mm long and 32 to 36mm wide. Tracks will be plentiful where springbok herds occur and will give a good indication of areas frequented. The hoof is quite sharply pointed. See Figures CCCH.07.02.78 and CCCH.07.02.79.

Scat

Their cylindrical-shaped pellets with a nipple on one end are about 12mm in length. Whilst normally passed as individual pellets, clumped scat can be found when animals have ingested green grass with a high moisture content. See Figure CCCH.07.02.80.

Voice

The bleating of young lambs, the grunting of adults, and a whistling alarm snort can be sounds the tracker should listen for.

Tracking Black-Backed Jackals

Habitat

These jackals occupy a wide range of habitats but tend to prefer drier areas. Where annual rainfall exceeds 1,000mm black-backed jackals tend to be replaced by side-striped jackals *(Canis adustus)*. They are generally not partial to dense woodlands and prefer more open habitat.

Habits

Black-backed jackals are active both during the day and night. When they live close to human habitation, they tend to confine their activities to the hours between sunset and sunrise.

They move singly, in pairs, or small family groups consisting of the parents and young. Larger groups may sometimes be observed congregating around carcasses. They normally trot when moving but will move slowly with ears pricked when hunting. Their senses are particularly well developed, especially their sense of smell. They are sly and cunning animals and are very suspicious of humans, especially in areas where they are persecuted. They have a very distinctive call.

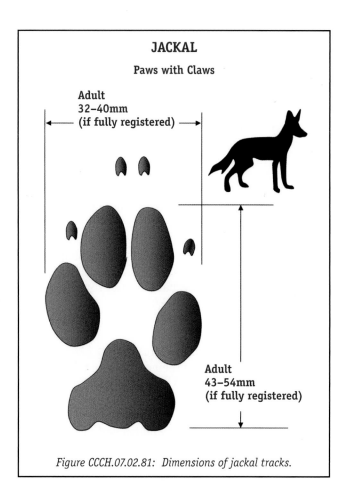

Figure CCCH.07.02.81: Dimensions of jackal tracks.

Feeding and Drinking

They are independent of water but will drink when it is available. Black-backed jackals could be classified as omnivores; their diet includes carrion, insects, wild fruit, small mammals, reptiles, game birds, and eggs.

Reproduction

Males and females stay together for a long time. Gestation is sixty days with litters of up to six pups, which are born underground in abandoned antbear holes. Caves or rock crevices are also sometimes used as nesting sites. The female will not hesitate to move the litter to an alternative site if she feels they are in danger. Both sexes help raise the pups. The adults regurgitate food to feed the pups. Pups make their first appearances from the underground burrow after about twenty-one days and are weaned within eight to nine weeks. They are very vulnerable for the first fourteen weeks of life and have a high mortality rate.

Black-Backed Jackal Sign

Suitable Habitat

Look for signs around old antbear holes and for tracks along game paths and bush tracks.

Feeding Sign

A carcass in a state of smelly decomposition is sure to attract jackals, so setting up a temporary hide at approaches to the carcass might lead to success. Old bones, skin, and hair might be found around burrows.

Tracks and Scat

The front track averages 54mm in length and 40mm in width. The hind track averages 43mm in length and 32mm in width. See Figures CCCH.07.02.81 and CCCH.07.02.82. The track has a distinctive triangular main pad on the front foot and the middle two toes of both front and rear feet extend well beyond the outer toes.

Jackals defecate in prominent places but do not make use of latrines. The scat is sausage shaped and pointed at one end; it has a diameter of 18 to 20mm. Sometimes the scat may have a slightly segmented appearance. See Figure CCCH.07.02.83.

Voice

A sure indication of the presence of black-backed jackals will be the sound of their distinctive call. The call of the black-backed jackal is ascending and descending, whereas that of the side-striped jackal ascends and then breaks off suddenly. Calls are heard just after sunset and at any time during the night and till early morning.

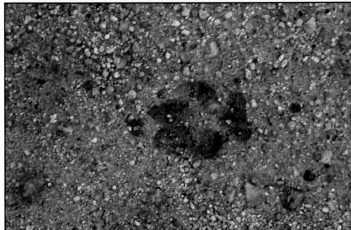

Figure CCCH.07.02.82: Jackal track.

Figure CCCH.07.02.83: Jackal scat.

CHAPTER 8

TRACK, STALK, AND APPROACH

Animal Senses

Most trackers will agree that it is not easy to stalk up close to wild animals. In the wild, it is a case of "eat or be eaten," so it is natural that animals have to be wide awake if they plan on living a full life. All animals are equipped with detection systems to monitor their surroundings. They have five systems: smell, sight,

hearing, taste, and touch. Not all animals, however, have developed all five senses to the same degree. Some have rather poor eyesight, but to make up for this their sense of smell and hearing will be acute. Others will have rather mediocre smelling but will have excellent eyesight and hearing. Each species of animal will have at least two of the five senses developed to the extreme, which they rely on to give them warning of danger.

Sneaking up without being detected is easier said than done!

Most animals have an incredible ability to pick up scent. To make a comparison between us and animals, we can say that we see with our eyes and animals see with their noses. The olfactory ability of animals is something difficult for us humans to grasp. We communicate verbally. Animals communicate to a large degree by smell; consequently, their ability to pick up even the faintest scent and interpret what it means is very highly developed. A finely honed and acute sense of smell is undoubtedly many animals' first line of defense. Most antelopes, elephants, and rhinos appear to fall into this category. The sense of smell in predators, although better developed than that of humans, does not appear to be as well developed as those in the group above.

Wind and air movements assist animals significantly by blowing scent all over the place, and that is why monitoring wind direction is the most important thing we can do when attempting to stalk up close to wildlife. Be assured of one thing as far as animals are concerned: We smell pretty "high." This smell drifts from us in whatever direction the air is moving, and we wipe this

scent off on everything we touch. So the first thing we have got to learn to beat is an animal's nose.

To animals we smell pretty high!

Sight is probably second on the list in terms of detection systems. Many species not only see well but they are also familiar with their surroundings. If you arrived home from work and were headed for your favourite chair, would you not notice it if there was a stranger sitting in it? We are, in a manner of speaking, out of place in the wilds: We don't really look as if we belong. Wild creatures perceive us as strangers in their backyard. So what is it that makes us visible? Shape, shine, silhouette, surface, shadow, and movement make us visible.

Of these, movement heads the top of the list. Pay attention to how people walk and compare this to the way wild animals walk. Wild animals walk slowly. They stop every few steps to observe their surroundings carefully. Their movement is silent and fluid and often if they become aware of something they will "freeze." If you want to learn good lessons in stealth and stalking, watch your cat. Cats are expert stalkers. Their movements are slow, fluid, and deliberate. They can "freeze" in midstride, and they are very, very patient. In contrast we walk too fast, too jerkily, don't stop to observe often enough, and are impatient.

Take some lessons from your cat.

Our shape also gives us away. The upright stance of a human is a dead giveaway and recognized by most wild animals. So somehow we have to disguise our shape. One way we can do this is to make use of camouflage. Another is to always keep a screen of vegetation between us and the animals we are stalking.

Shine is another giveaway. Light can reflect off spectacles, binoculars, rangefinders, wristwatches, equipment, and smooth surfaces. Somehow we have to prevent the light reflecting.

Silhouetting ourselves against a contrasting background is something else we have to avoid, for a silhouette immediately defines the characteristic human form.

We must learn to make use of shadow. When you stand in open sunlight, you are much more visible than if you were standing in deep shade. Our task is to trick the eyes of the animals we're stalking.

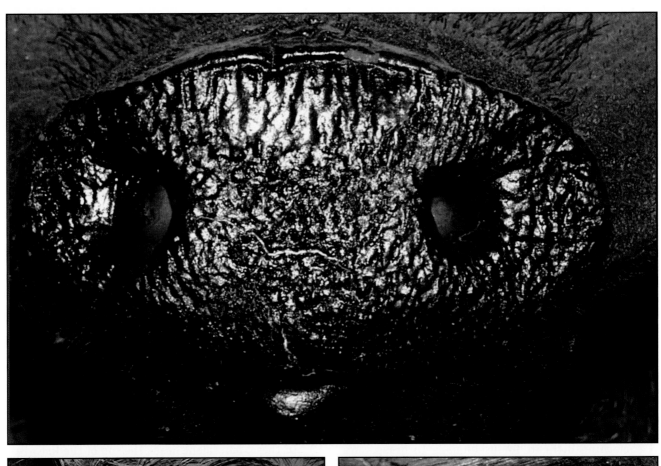

Figure CCCH.08.01.01: Camouflage and stalking techniques are the art and science of learning to avoid detection by an animal.

Many animals have huge ears compared to ours. Roan antelopes, warthogs, kudus, wildebeests, zebras, rhinos, and buffaloes are examples that come to mind. Antelopes, without exception, have large, funnel-shaped and very mobile ears that are constantly turning. Think of them as large radar antennae that pick up and magnify sound. Whereas this might not be an animal's best detection system, it is certainly very effective. They will be quick to pick up any sound—especially if it is a sound foreign to the natural environment. One of the sounds that will be detected very quickly and will generally put animals to flight is a human voice. Noisy or squeaky equipment, the scraping sound of various types of material against vegetation, and snapping a twig underfoot will put an animal on high alert.

The human voice soon puts an animal to flight.

And, so, the third detection system we must overcome is an animal's ability to hear. With perhaps a few exception, it is generally much better than ours.

And then there is the sense of taste. We might well ask how an animal's ability to taste enables it to monitor its environment. Here we must understand that there is a connection between smell and taste. If you don't believe this think back to a time when you had a bad head cold. Do you remember that suddenly your food was very bland and had no taste? To a human the sense of taste refers to substances in contact with taste receptors on the tongue, while smell refers to gaseous molecules dissolving in the mucus lining of the nasal passage.

This separation is highly subjective. The sense of taste, located in the mouth, distinguishes salt, sweet, sour, and bitter. When we speak about the "taste" of food, most of the information is obtained through the nose. The powerful connection between taste and smell is very strongly developed in the animal world. It is, therefore, quite logical to assume that animals with such a strong sense of smell can quite literally "taste" human scent. Taste should quite conceivably rank at the top with smell as a detection system because the two are inextricably linked.

Animals can "taste" human scent.

Many species have a structure situated in the roof of the mouth referred to as a vomeronasal organ. It is a small passage linking the mouth to the nasal passages. When animals test a smell, they lick the substance (such as a female's urine), and then this taste is forced into the vomeronasal organ for a "taste-smell" analysis. You might have seen an antelope or lion curling its top lip upward when doing this. It is referred to as flehmen. So here again is a very effective combination of detection

systems that we have to overcome if we wish to be successful in our walk and stalk attempts.

Lastly there is the sense of touch. Obviously an animal will detect if it is being touched directly. I believe this sense is underrated and, perhaps, not fully understood or appreciated. The skin is the largest organ of the body and is filled with receptors for touch, pain, pressure, and temperature. I would not be surprised if animals can detect humans from a distance with their skin. This should not be surprising since we humans can detect things at a distance with our skin. You have all felt (with your skin) heat radiated at a distance from your campfire (temperature receptors) or the wind blowing on your cheek (pressure and temperature receptors).

Animals appear to have a sixth sense.

I often wonder if the "sixth sense" we attribute to animals is their ability to "sense" human presence with their skin. I have observed animals in the wild from hidden positions. I have been motionless, dead quiet, and most important of all the wind has been in my favour. I have seen an animal come along and suddenly "freeze" as it has somehow become aware of my presence. I cannot explain it, but then again there are many things we cannot explain. With the five, highly developed senses that animals are equipped with, it is a real challenge to stalk them successfully. See Figure CCCH.08.01.01.

Avoiding Visual Detection

The Use of Camouflage

In the early 1980s textile technicians began developing camouflage pattern materials for hunters to use. Some of the early efforts were based on military patterns and were not very effective because they were too dense and the hunter's outline was apparent. Later experiments led to the development of three-dimensional patterns—almost photographic in detail—that were highly effective. These later patterns took the visual laws of binocular rivalry, Ricco's law of distance vision, and the theory of blurred images into consideration and used them to good advantage. To compensate for Ricco's law, patterns became large and bold with neutral background colours and distinctive highlights. To compensate for the phenomenon of binocular rivalry, dark-coloured sticks and branches were introduced into the patterns to draw attention and cause the background to be lost. It is then very difficult for an animal to recognize the shape of the hunter. The pattern induces an animal to stare to try to figure out what it is seeing, and the image becomes blurred, thus making it even more effective as camouflage.

There are many patterns now available based on these ideas. Camouflage has been designed for different habitats—from grassland to woodland to wetland and for the different seasons. Figure CCCH.08.02.01 illustrates a good camouflage pattern based on sound optical principles.

The difference between military-type personal camouflage and camouflage for hunters is that hunters and trackers can be much more selective. Military camouflage must be suitable for a wide range of applications and is not always as effective as it should be. A soldier dressed in woodland camouflage would not be effectively camouflaged in an urban environment. Military camouflage is usually selected for a theatre of operations, e.g., desert or jungle. The hunter can be more specific in his choice of camouflage. Figure CCCH.08.02.02 shows how effective camouflage can be when used in an appropriate environment.

We have determined that some animals are short-sighted whereas others can see well at a distance. There is strong evidence to suggest that herbivores see mainly in shades of gray, blue, and yellow. They do not see reds and greens. Nocturnal animals probably see mostly in shades

A neutral background fools peripheral (ambient) vision, causing the object to blend into the environment.	The distinctive lines "capture" the focal vision, causes boundary disruption, and makes it difficult for the observer to recognize a shape (law of Binocular Rivalry).	Spatial frequencies vary. The disruptive pattern is not uniform or repetitive—this makes it difficult for the brain to organize what it is seeing. The longer the observer stares, the more difficult it becomes to recognize an object.

Figure CCCH.08.02.01: A good camouflage pattern.

Figure CCCH.08.02.02: Appropriate and effective camouflage patterns used as an aid to avoid visual detection.

Figure CCCH.08.02.03: *The principles of good camouflage. Break the outline and then fill in the body with large neutral colours and lines similar to the background. The shape then becomes lost in the background. A good camouflage pattern is very effective at breaking up the characteristic human shape, which is quickly recognized by animals.*

Figure CCCH.08.02.04: *When you are stalking an animal, always look back and try to position yourself against a background that will cause you to become "lost" in it (top). An inappropriate background will make you stand out in sharp contrast—even if you are wearing good camo (bottom). Remember, you do not want to be silhouetted.*

Figure CCCH.08.02.05: *Camouflage always works better in dappled shade. Try to keep in shadow as much as possible and avoid moving or standing in direct sunlight.*

Figure CCCH.08.02.06: Camo leaves stuck into a cap break the outline of the hunter's head (left). The outline of the tracker on the right (in right-hand photo) is better camouflaged by the leafy attachments.

Figure CCCH.08.02.07: Bits of scrim tied to clothing is effective in breaking the human outline.

of gray. Herbivores have a narrow field of depth perception and a wide field of peripheral vision. Carnivores have a wide field of depth perception and a narrow field of peripheral vision. In addition, we know that animals have the ability to recognize the human shape or form. Now how can we put this knowledge to good use when hunting? Let's give some attention to camouflage from a visual perspective.

We don't want animals to recognize our shape. We can assure ourselves of this in two ways. We can break our outline and fill in the body with a pattern that will be lost in the background. Large areas of neutral colour and broken with dark lines are very effective. The eye is drawn to the dark lines, and the rest becomes merged and very difficult to distinguish from the background. These principles are illustrated in Figure CCCH.08.02.03.

For camouflage to be effective, there are a number of rules to remember. Choose an appropriate pattern similar to the background you will be working in. Make sure when stalking or when hiding that you choose a background into which you can blend. If you choose an inappropriate background, you can stand out in sharp contrast and be silhouetted. See Figure CCCH.08.02.04. Try to imagine yourself approaching from the animal's perspective. Look back to see what your background looks like. This cannot be emphasized strongly enough.

Camouflage is more effective in dappled shade than in open sunlight. See Figure CCCH.08.02.05. When you are looking for animals or stalking them, try to keep in dappled shade as much as possible. While observing an

Figure CCCH.08.02.08: *This demonstrates from the perspective of the animal how much less obvious you will be if you use cover to screen your approach and if you learn to observe animals through intervening bush instead of exposing yourself to look around cover.*

Figure CCCH.08.02.09: *This figure illustrates a tracker using good stalk-and-approach techniques.*

Figure CCCH.08.02.10: Light reflecting off spectacles, binoculars, or rangefinders can betray the hunter's presence. Wearing a peaked cap casts a shadow on the face, which helps hide the reflection (centre). An alternative is to wear a see-through face mask (left) that covers the whole face (right). This cuts out all reflection.

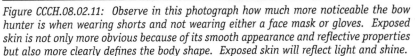

Figure CCCH.08.02.11: Observe in this photograph how much more noticeable the bow hunter is when wearing shorts and not wearing either a face mask or gloves. Exposed skin is not only more obvious because of its smooth appearance and reflective properties but also more clearly defines the body shape. Exposed skin will reflect light and shine.

Figure CCCH.08.02.12: Compare the difference between an exposed hand (left) and a gloved hand (right). The bare hand is far more noticeable.

animal, move from shadow to shadow and spend more time in dappled shade than moving in direct sunlight. Movement is also detected more quickly in direct sunlight. If a camouflage pattern is too dense, it loses its effectiveness (refer back to Figure CCCH.02.04.13, page 30). The earliest personal camouflage patterns made this mistake.

Camouflage is also made much more effective by having loose leaves or material attached randomly to it. This helps break the recognizable outline of the body and also mimics the natural motion of leaves as they are moved by the wind. See Figure CCCH.08.02.06. Artificial leaves are available commercially, which can be sewn onto camouflage garments. Alternatively, natural materials can also be used, such as small leafy branches stuck into headbands or into parts of clothing. Don't overdo this.

Scrim material—lengths of burlap or sacking—tied onto parts of the clothing is also an effective means of helping to disguise the human outline. See Figure CCCH.08.02.07.

When attempting to stalk up to animals, it is important to make sure you have a good background; also try to keep bush or cover between you and your quarry as this helps to further hide you and screen your movements. Learn to look "through" intervening bush without

exposing yourself. See Figure CCCH.08.02.08. Figure CCCH.08.02.09 illustrates good stalking technique.

Surface and Shine

Surface and shine are closely associated because the one influences the other. Sunlight glinting off an exposed smooth or shiny surface can be a dead giveaway. Whether or not animals will associate something shiny with humans is debatable as there are things in the natural world that shine and reflect sunlight, such as water. Something shiny can draw an animal's attention and make it suspicious and more on the alert.

Since spectacles can reflect light, an alternative is to use contact lenses. If there is some condition precluding the use of contact lenses, then using a face veil/net and a peaked cap to cast a shadow over the face will go a long way to prevent unwanted reflections of light. See Figure CCCH.08.02.10. Standing in deep shade or shadow will also minimize the possibility of light reflecting off lenses. Also make a point of not facing the sun, especially in the early morning or late afternoon when the sun is low on the horizon. When stalking or approaching an animal try, if possible, to position yourself in such a way that the sun is behind you.

Rangefinders and binoculars should be covered with some nonreflective camouflage, stick-on material. The lenses can be covered with nonreflective tape, leaving only a small slit through which to observe. The less the lens is exposed, the less chance there is of light being reflected.

Exposed skin can also be a giveaway. Its colour and smooth texture will show up as a lighter patch to an herbivore; it will also show up because of its light-reflective qualities, especially when sweaty. See Figure CCCH.08.02.11. Gloves can be used to cover hands and wristwatches. See Figure CCCH.08.02.12.

Face masks/veils are available in various thicknesses and designs. They are not only good for concealing the skin, but they are also most useful in keeping pesky midges, gnats, and mosquitoes off the face. For those who don't like wearing a mask or gloves, then camouflage paint works well as an alternative. Gloves are available in light, cool, netting material suitable for hot conditions and in heavier materials ideal for keeping the hands warm and hidden in cold weather.

Equipment can also reflect light and betray your presence. Shiny reflective surfaces should be toned down. An excellent way of doing this is to use adhesive backed polar fleece camo tape. Rangefinders and binoculars should be covered with some nonreflective camouflage stick-on material. The lenses can be covered with nonreflective tape that leaves only a small slit through which to observe. The less the lenses are exposed, the less chance there is of light being reflected.

Figure CCCH.08.02.13: Sitting quietly and observing in shadow—even in a place of very little cover—is often a key to success.

Figure CCCH.08.02.15: When cover is scarce, you might have to resort to crawling. Remember to keep watching the animal the whole time so that you can "freeze" if it looks your way.

Movement

Movement is by far the biggest giveaway. Even when a tracker is well camouflaged, movement will immediately attract an animal's attention. Whilst tracking and stalking, you should regularly stand still and observe. Before moving where you can be seen, ensure there are no animals in sight. Then move slowly and cautiously to your next point of observation. Sometimes a small patch of shadow in scant cover works very well because animals will be less likely to expect danger from an area almost devoid of cover. This is where your camo can work well for you to help disguise your shape. See Figure CCCH.08.02.13.

Now we will look at the critical aspects of stalking and approach techniques. You should adopt stalking techniques not only when you see animals but also when approaching likely areas such as feeding areas and water holes. Remember, stalking is a way of moving so slowly and soundlessly that your presence goes undetected.

There are a few cardinal rules to remember with regards to vision when stalking up to animals with the intention of getting closer. (Keeping the wind in your favour is obviously the most important, but it has to do with smell, not vision.)

Figure CCCH.08.02.14: If an animal looks your way, "freeze" until it looks away.

1. Take your time. Once you have located the animals, don't be in a hurry to get closer.

2. Move only when the animals are not watching you.

3. Keep your eyes on the animal you are stalking.

4. Keep your hands and arms close to your body.

5. Avoid any sudden movements.

If the animal you are after is in a herd, try to establish the position of other herd members because they will also give an alarm. It is better to look for an animal on the edge of a herd rather than in the middle. Also notice what the animals are doing, for it will give you an indication of their level of alertness. If they are resting, feeding, drinking, or occupied with social behaviour (grooming one another for example), it is a reliable indication that their level of alertness is low and that you are undetected and can continue approaching. If the animal you are stalking or others in the herd

suddenly stop what they are doing and "freeze," stare fixedly, stamp their feet, snort, or stand very erect, something has disturbed them, and they are in a state of "high alert." When this happens, you too must "freeze" in place and not move until the animals appear to have settled down again. See Figure CCCH.08.02.14.

There are a couple of other tricks that will help if the animals have seen you. Slowly sink down into the grass, crouch, and keep very still. Some species such as the wildebeest, giraffe, and zebra are by nature curious and may even of their own accord approach closer to identify what you are. That might bring them within or close to bow, camera, or rifle range. As you are crouching, make the whistling call of contented guinea fowl.

The sound of their call is difficult to describe in words, so you will need to listen to a wild guinea fowl or an audio tape of bird calls. Learn to mimic it. This call often has a calming effect on alert animals. They seem to think that if the guinea fowls are content,

Figure CCCH.08.03.01: Methods for monitoring wind direction include wetting a finger, dropping dust, putting a feather on a bow, using an ash bag, or observing the flame of a butane lighter.

there is not too much to worry about. Warthogs will also sometimes respond by coming closer to investigate if you crouch down and make a grunting sound.

Continue slowly approaching as long as you have not been observed. Be patient. It is quite natural for animals—even whilst they are busy feeding or carrying on with some other normal activity—to periodically stop, lift their heads, sniff the breeze, and scan their surroundings for possible danger. Wait motionless and silent during these intermittent periods of surveillance and then move slowly when the animal drops its head to resume feeding or looks away from you. In low brush or grass, you may have to crouch, crawl, or even inch forward on your belly. See Figure CCCH.08.02.15. Last, if all else fails, try the "open approach."

Remember we spoke about the wide angle of peripheral vision and narrow field of depth perception in herbivores in an earlier section. Walk openly and at a normal speed at a tangent past your quarry but spiraling in slowly. They will stare directly at you initially, but after a while they will begin looking away to carry on with other activities whilst keeping you in their peripheral vision. Because they cannot perceive depth in their peripheral vision, they will not be aware of the fact that you are getting closer. Using this technique, you can sometimes get very close, but it will require careful stalking techniques for the final few yards of approach. Walking openly also appears to arouse less suspicion. Avoid walking directly toward the animal; this is quickly perceived as a threat and will induce flight. The animal must get the impression that you are walking past it. It is worth a try.

Avoiding Detection by Scent (Smell)

You stink as far as an animal is concerned! You might not think so. After all, you spray half a liter of "Axe" into your armpits twice a day. Nevertheless, as far as the animals are concerned, your body odour is overpowering. The first step in the right direction is to accept this fact.

Your scent carries on air currents—a breeze if it is light and wind if it is stronger. Now the most important lesson you can learn is that there is never a time when there is no wind. Never! What causes air to move from one place to another? The answer is temperature differentials, and there are always temperature differences from one spot to another.

A spot in direct sunlight will have one temperature; a few centimeters away there will be a spot in the shade that will be cooler. This difference in temperature, however slight, will cause air to move and will carry your rather odiferous smell along with it. The breeze might be almost imperceptible, you might not feel it on your skin, vegetation might not be visibly moving, but be assured air is moving from one place to another. Animals constantly monitor the breeze with their wet noses held aloft, and they have an extraordinary ability to smell things we would not even know exist.

The very best thing you can do to avoid animals smelling you is to always stay downwind of them. In other words, whatever breeze is blowing must preferably

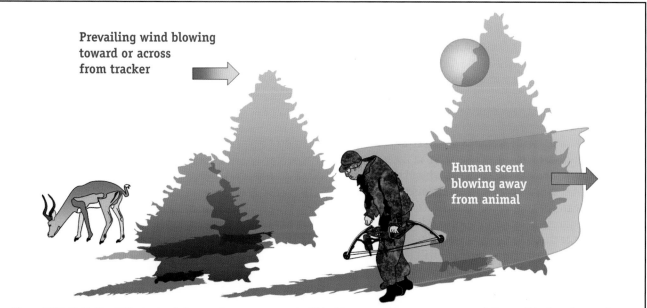

Prevailing wind blowing toward or across from tracker

Human scent blowing away from animal

Figure CCCH.08.03.03: If the breeze is in your favour, your scent will be blown away from your quarry and there will be less chance of being detected.

Figure CCCH.08.03.02: Packing your bush clothes into a plastic bag with local vegetation helps mask your scent by absorbing some of the local natural odours into the fibres of your clothing.

the windward side of your finger will feel cooler. See Figure CCCH.08.03.01.

Again in anything less than a light breeze, this is not a very accurate method. Third, you can pick up some grass or dust and drop it and see which way it blows. See Figure CCCH.08.03.01. This works well even in light breezes but quite a lot of movement is required (such as stooping down), and that can give you away. A "flick of your Bic" is another option as the flame will bend in the direction of even a light breeze. See Figure CCCH.08.03.01. The best way to monitor wind is with an ash bag. A small bag is filled with fine ash from a fire. When flicked, a fine powder drifts in the direction of the wind/breeze.

However, this can be a bit of a schlep every time you want to check the wind and have to reach into your pocket for your lighter. I have also seen some trackers light a match then blow it out straightaway to see which way the smoke drifts. Accurate but again impractical if you have to reach into your pocket every five minutes for a match. The scratching sound of the match against the matchbox can also be a giveaway. Some trackers tie a feather onto a stick or part of their equipment to see which way the breeze is blowing.

The fourth trick to help us win the scent war is to take some local vegetation, bruise it, and pack it in an unscented plastic bag together with your hunting clothes to absorb the natural odours into your gear overnight. See Figure CCCH.08.03.02.

Fifth, avoid eating spiced food (curry, garlic, onions) or using strong soaps, deodorants, and toothpaste before going hunting. This just adds to your already strong smell.

Sixth, if you are prepared to go to the extreme, get some cow dung or buffalo dung that is reasonably but not completely dry and rub this onto the outside of your hunting clothes. Don't use carnivore dung. Remember carnivores spell danger to an herbivore.

Use hunting clothes for hunting only. Do not wear them for working in the garden or on the car or doing other household chores where you might pick up human odours.

Don't wear your hunting clothes in camp or in the car on your way out. Change into them when you arrive, thereby avoiding smoke, exhaust, or food odours.

Urine is a human as well as an animal marker. Use a tightly sealed urine bottle for nature's call if you are hunting from a static position.

And last, you can go the whole hog and get yourself a Scentlok suit, which is a camo hunting overall with an activated carbon lining that absorbs your scent and prevents it from radiating from you. It is reasonably effective but expensive.

Again, the most important thing that you can do in the scent war is to monitor the wind and make sure you stay downwind of the animal you are hunting.

be blowing from the animal to you. That is the first prize. You can get away with a breeze quartering toward you, and you can even get away with a crosswind. If you feel a breeze on the back of your neck and your nose end is facing your quarry, you might as well call it a day because long before you have got within shooting range of bow, rifle, or camera, the animal will have caught a whiff of you and will have taken flight.

So the third thing we can do toward winning the scent war (the first being that we admit we smell, the second being to stay downwind of an animal) is to constantly monitor the wind to make sure we are downwind. When there is anything stronger than a light breeze blowing, you will see vegetation blowing in the direction of the wind; you will also feel it on your skin.

This is the easy stuff, and it is pretty straightforward to judge where downwind is and to make sure you position yourself accordingly. It is when the breeze is so slight that not even grass stalks are moving that you have to pay careful attention. You will then need to use some technique to help you monitor wind direction.

So what techniques can we use to monitor wind direction? There are a number, but I will leave the best till last. First, as already mentioned, you can watch to see in which direction vegetation is bending. This is fine if there is a strong enough wind. It is of not much help in very light breezes. Second, you can wet a finger with saliva and hold it aloft. If there is a slight breeze,

Avoiding Detection by Sound

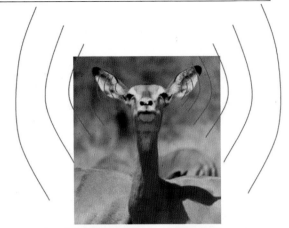

The sensitivity of nearly all mammals' hearing is much better developed than that of humans. This is largely because their external ears are mobile cones that funnel sound waves down their eardrums and magnify sound. See Figure CCCH.08.04.01.

Cat species can hear frequencies of up to 78,000 Hertz (a Hertz or Hz is one vibration per second), dog species hear up to 40,000 Hz, rats and mice up to 100,000 Hz, and in some bats as high as 210,000 Hz. On the other end of the spectrum, elephants respond to sounds as low as 20 Hz. The human range of hearing is between 20 to 20,000 Hz. See Figure CCCH.08.04.02. The type of sound that is most likely to give us away quickly is the sound of human voices.

When we are walking through the bush, the sound of our footsteps and the occasional snapping of a twig might draw an animal's attention to the noise. While they might stop and stare in the direction of the sound, they will not necessarily associate it with humans or danger.

Animals themselves make a certain amount of noise as they wend their way through the natural environment. If you are downwind, hidden, or well camouflaged and standing still—even if you have made some noise like standing on dry leaves and have attracted an animal's attention—wait in a "frozen" position. The animal will soon look away or continue doing what it was busy with before they heard a noise and stared in your direction. This is quite normal surveillance behaviour. On the other hand, the sound of a human voice will immediately cause animals to go into a state of high alert, and they are very likely to run off.

A hunter can also ensure that equipment and clothing are "soundproof." The choice of material for clothing is important. Wool and cotton are the quietest. Avoid nylons as they are noisy.

Figure CCCH.08.04.01: Observe animals and watch how the ears are constantly turning this way and that to pick up any sounds that might warn them of danger.

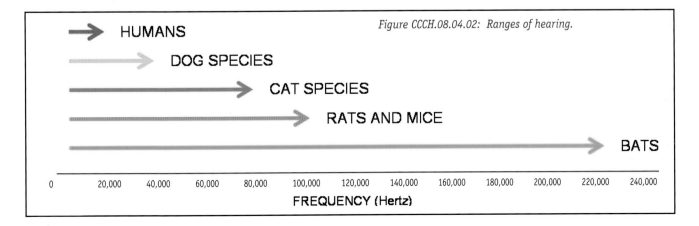

Figure CCCH.08.04.02: Ranges of hearing.

HUMANS

DOG SPECIES

CAT SPECIES

RATS AND MICE

BATS

| 0 | 20,000 | 40,000 | 60,000 | 80,000 | 100,000 | 120,000 | 140,000 | 160,000 | 180,000 | 200,000 | 220,000 | 240,000 |

FREQUENCY (Hertz)

Figure CCCH.08.04.03: To stalk silently, boots are the worst option. Thin-soled "vellies" are better. Moccasins or socks will enable you to stalk most effectively.

You have searched hard to find the animal you were tracking, and now you have to stalk closer. This is the hardest part and the part that we end up "blowing" in 90 percent or more of the cases. Before we go any further, let's look for a moment at footwear. In your final approach you should walk as silently as possible. Whilst heavy-soled boots are good footwear for walking in the bush, they are not good for stalking. With them, you cannot feel twigs underfoot, which could break if you stood on them, or noisy dry leaves. Thin-soled "vellies" or moccasins are a better option, but the best choice for your final stalk is to wear moccasins or thick socks. See Figure CCCH.08.04.03.

As you begin your approach, observe the animal(s) closely. If the animal is on its own, your task will be made easier. If it is in a herd, it will be that more difficult to get close to because there will be more eyes, noses, and ears monitoring the environment for danger.

Look behind you to blend with the environment and avoid being silhouetted on a skyline or by a background that is very different from your camouflage. If you are walking upright, lift one foot slowly off the ground and bring it up alongside the other leg at knee level. Keep the toe pointed downward so that it does not snag on anything. Balancing on one leg, bring the other foot down in a slow movement.

When you place your foot, roll the foot forward slowly from the heel to the ball of the foot or alternatively from the outside of the foot inward. If you feel something underfoot that might make a noise, lift your foot and place it elsewhere. Keep your weight on your rear foot until you are sure there is nothing under your front foot before transferring weight to your front foot. Only when your entire foot is safely and soundlessly on the ground do you shift your weight. See Figure CCCH.08.04.04.

When you are stalking up to an animal, it is very important to "read" and correctly interpret its "body language." You will then know if you must stand dead still or if you can proceed with the stalk.

When animals are relaxed, they will busy themselves with the sort of activities that are "normal" when no danger is threatening them. They will eat, wallow, take dust baths, groom themselves and others, advertise, play, drink, stand, or lie resting in the shade if it is hot or in a sunny spot if it is cold. If in a group, they will often be looking in different directions and be busy with different activities.

If something catches their attention, they will stare or even approach closer to investigate. They may not feel threatened or compelled to run away at this stage. If danger is perceived, a very marked

Figure CCCH.08.04.04: Keep your eyes on the animal and make sure there is nothing noisy underfoot before transferring your weight to your front foot.

Figure CCCH.08.04.05: A good tracker must be able to read and interpret animal body language. In this example an impala on high alert stands tall and alert, ears and eyes are directed toward the source of disturbance, tail is clamped down, and muscles are tense. Compare this to the relaxed impala busy feeding.

change in behaviour will result. If in a group, all animals will exhibit similar behaviour. They usually stop what they are doing and will stare fixedly in the direction they perceive the threat. Animals usually "stand tall" and make themselves as "big" as possible. Ears are generally cocked in the direction of the threat. Muscles become tense and stand out in better definition. See Figure CCCH.08.04.05.

If you are stalking up to an animal and notice any change in its level of surveillance, STOP and stand dead still. Even if it is looking at you, there is a reasonably good chance that it will lose interest within a few minutes or, if you are well camouflaged, will "lose" you as your image becomes blurred. If this happens, it will resume its normal activities, thus affording you the opportunity to resume your stalk.

CHAPTER 9

BIRD, REPTILE, AND INVERTEBRATE SIGN

Birds

Birds, like mammals, leave signs as they go about their daily business, and these give us clues as to the species and their activities. It is difficult, with some exceptions, to identify birds on the basis of tracks alone. You will find that other signs, like nests and eggs, are generally more helpful in identifying birds.

We will give some attention to tracks and some basic information on other incidental signs. It is also important to note that bird behaviour is often a useful tool for the tracker; knowledge of birds and their peculiar habits helps the tracker figure out what is going on around him. A tracker should also be able to identify the calls of local birds and interpret what information they are conveying; this information can include advertising or warning, for example.

We will begin by looking at the types of bird sign, and we will then give attention to the structure of birds' feet, their tracks, and any particular characteristics that will help us to identify the bird. See Figures CCCH.09.01.01 and CCCH.09.01.02.

Visual Sightings and Calls

Visual sightings or calls of birds and proper identification can assist the tracker in a number of ways.

➤ Certain species can lead a tracker to water: These include all water birds (ducks, geese, herons, waders, etc.), seedeaters (e.g., queleas, weavers, sparrows), guinea fowl, double banded sand grouse, etc.

➤ Birds can warn the tracker of potential danger: oxpeckers associate with buffaloes and rhinos as well as nondangerous species. Egrets associate with buffaloes. Alarm calls of birds such as the gray lourie and most other species can warn the tracker of the presence of snakes, predators, or other humans in the vicinity.

➤ Certain species can lead the tracker to potential food: raptor activity in the vicinity of the nests of quelea colonies, greater and scaly-throated honey guides,

and scavengers (such as kites and vultures). Fruit-eating birds can lead the tracker to edible fruits.

Eggs, Feeding Sign, Scat, and Incidental Sign

Eggs can be useful in identifying bird species and are also a source of potential food for the tracker. Eggs range in size from those of the diminutive sunbirds, cisticolas, and other small birds to that of the ostrich egg, which weighs as much as 1.6 kilos and can be as large as 159x131mm. A very useful and highly recommended book is *Nests and Eggs of Southern African Birds* by Warwick Tarboton. Feeding sign can also indicate the presence of certain species and their food preferences.

With the exception of a few species such as the ostrich, some game birds, and owls, it is very difficult to identify bird species from scat because it is often fluid and similar looking. The volume of scat can indicate whether the species is large or small, and the scat of fruit-eating species will sometimes take on the colour of their food. Large

A QUICK REFERENCE GUIDE TO BIRD SIGN

Bird "Sign" Can Consist of the Following

- ➤ Visual sightings
- ➤ Calls
- ➤ Tracks
- ➤ Nests
- ➤ Eggs
- ➤ Scat
- ➤ Feeding sign
- ➤ Incidental sign

Figure CCCH.09.01.01: Bird sign.

Figure CCCH.09.01.02: Examples of bird sign.

amounts of scat in a particular area will indicate favourite nesting, roosting, or feeding sites. Owls regurgitate the undigested remains of their food as pellets. One can learn a lot about the owl's diet by studying its pellets. See Figure CCCH.09.01.03. Incidental signs can include feathers, signs of bathing, skeletal remains, unusual nesting material, scrapes and scratchings, and odours (vultures for example). See Figure CCCH.09.01.06.

Ground birds like guinea fowl, francolin, and quail will often leave telltale signs as they are scratching in the ground for food. See Figure CCCH.09.01.06 and CCCH.09.01.07. Birds like fish eagles, ospreys, herons, storks, and kingfishers will leave behind remains of crabs, freshwater mussels, or fish.

Oxpeckers have a symbiotic relationship with a variety of species with both benefiting from the association. See Figure CCCH.09.01.08. The oxpecker is supplied with food (ectoparasites) and renders a service to the animal by removing them. Their shrill calls also warn animals of potential danger. See Figure CCCH.09.01.09. The tracker should also be aware of these calls and, in turn, will be warned of the possible proximity of dangerous species such as the rhino and buffalo. Bird calls are an extremely useful way of identifying the bird species, so the good tracker should become familiar with those occurring in his area of operation.

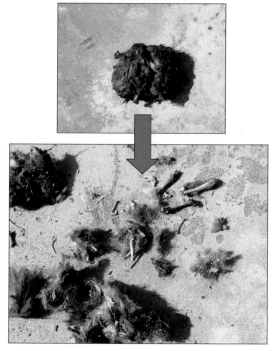

Figure CCCH.09.01.03: Feeding signs of an owl. The pellet of undigested material (bones, hair, feathers, keratin) is regurgitated. Investigating the contents can lead to some very interesting discoveries and give a good indication of the owl's diet and favourite foods. Note the large bones from small mammals. Figures CCCH.09.01.04 and CCCH.09.01.05 illustrate more examples of bird scat sign.

Figure CCCH.09.01.04: Fresh guinea fowl droppings (top left), below roosting site of mourning doves (top right), below favourite roost of an owl (below centre), fresh droppings from Natal francolin (below left), and from spurwing goose (below right).

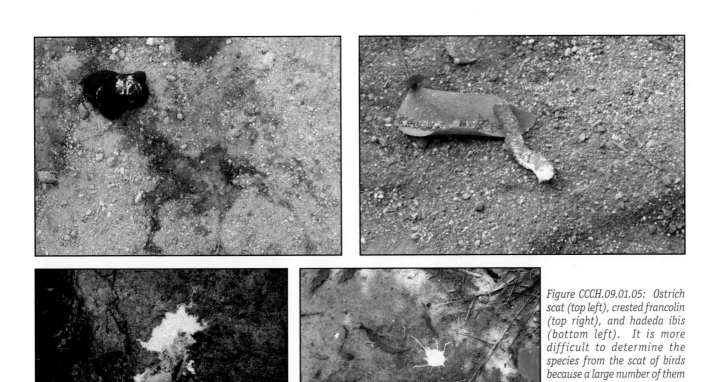

Figure CCCH.09.01.05: Ostrich scat (top left), crested francolin (top right), and hadeda ibis (bottom left). It is more difficult to determine the species from the scat of birds because a large number of them have no real form or shape and end up as an unidentifiable "splat" (bottom right).

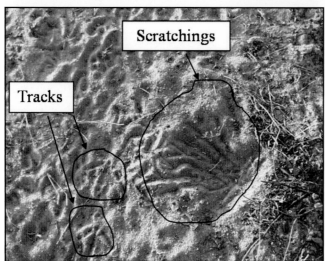

Scratchings

Tracks

Figure CCCH.09.01.06: Incidental bird signs include a hornbill wiping its bill on the ground (top left), guinea fowl scratchings (bottom left), and the remains of a dove killed by a little goshawk (above). Note scat circled.

Figure CCCH.09.01.07: Francolin and guinea fowl will leave behind telltale scratch marks on the ground as they forage for food.

Figure CCCH.09.01.08: Oxpeckers associate with a variety of animal species including the buffalo, rhino, and hippo.

Figure CCCH.09.01.09: Cattle egrets and red-billed oxpeckers associate with buffalo. Visual sightings or calls can warn the tracker of the presence of these potentially dangerous species.

Nests

To a tracker, nests mean a number of things: a place to respect, a place for potential food (eggs and fledglings), a place to find material to start a fire (down feathers, grass, dried moss, etc.), a place that will indicate direction, and a place of potential danger (often frequented by snakes).

Nests vary widely in size, location, and method of construction. Some are very methodically constructed or woven whereas others are little more than a scraping on the ground. Building materials can consist of feathers, grass, dried moss, lichen, spider webs, mud, twigs, or leaves. Often bits of manmade material, such as bits of string, cloth, or shiny objects, will be included.

Location is often species specific. You will find nests in tall, flat-crowned thorn trees, under the eaves of houses, overhanging water, on riverbanks, in naturally occurring holes in trees, on cliff ledges, and so on. The size of the nest can vary considerably—from tiny nests weighing a few grams to the massive nests of social weavers and hammerkops. A quick reference guide to bird nests is shown in Figure CCCH.09.01.10 a through c.

Figure CCCH.09.01.11: The communal nest of the red-billed buffalo weavers is a rather untidy nest made of small twigs (top). The large nest of a hammerkops (middle) is usually built in proximity to, and often over, water. The woven nest of spotted-back weavers (bottom) is neat.

BIRD, REPTILE, AND INVERTEBRATE SIGN

QUICK REFERENCE GUIDE TO BIRD NESTS

MUD PELLET NESTS

Top Entrance, bowl shaped
➤ Cliff swallows

Bowl shaped with entrance tunnel
➤ Greater striped, mosque, and red breasted swallows

Open cup shaped
➤ Pearl breasted, white tailed, and white throated swallows and rock martins

NESTS IN HOLES

Large Dome shaped nests
➤ Sociable weaver and hammerkop

Natural holes in trees
➤ Hoopoes, rollers, hornbills, parrots, some owls, oxpeckers, tits, and glossy starlings

Self excavated in trees
➤ Woodpeckers, barbets, and tinker barbets

Holes in river banks
➤ Kingfishers, pied starlings, martins, and bee eaters

Self excavated holes in the nests of tree ants
➤ None in South Africa

FLOATING NESTS

➤ Dabchick, grebes, jacanas, and red-knobbed coots

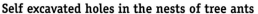

NESTS WOVEN INTO SMALL BALLS

Felted with short side spout
➤ Penduline tit

Nest with a long entrance spout
➤ Redheaded and spectacled weavers

Nest with a short entrance spout
➤ Lesser masked and golden weavers

Nest with a very short entrance spout
➤ Spotted-backed, yellow, and brown-throated weavers

Coarse but tidy nest with top entrance
➤ Sunbirds, bishops, prinias, queleas, apalis, and cisticolas

Untidy nest with top or side entrance
➤ Sunbirds, bishops, prinias, queleas, apalis, and cisticolas

Finely woven nest with top or side entrance
➤ Waxbills, firefinches, and some sparrows

NESTS COMPRISED OF LARGE TWIGS AND STICKS

Large stick nests on the crown of trees
➤ Marabou and saddle-billed stork, secretary bird, lappet-faced vulture, and tawny eagle

Untidy mass of twigs in trees
➤ Red-billed buffalo weavers and wattled starlings

Medium to large twigs and sticks in the forks of large trees
➤ Many raptors, some vultures, crows, and herons

Figure CCCH.09.01.10 (a), (b), (c): A quick reference guide to bird nests (adapted from A Field Guide to the Tracks and Signs of Southern and East African Wildlife by Chris & Tilde Stuart, 1994).

THE COMPREHENSIVE GUIDE TO TRACKING SKILLS

QUICK REFERENCE GUIDE TO BIRD NESTS

NESTS COMPRISED OF LARGE TWIGS AND STICKS *(continued)*

Small purselike nest suspended on reeds, vegetation, or thick grass stalks
➤ Crombec

Small cuplike nest in the fork of branches
➤ Robins, shrikes, drongos, thrushes, buntings, bablers, white eyes, and
➤ mousebirds

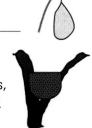

NESTS BUILT ON CLIFFS

With nesting material
➤ Cape griffon and marabou stork

No nesting material used
➤ Barn owls, peregrine and lanner falcons, rock pigeons, spotted eagle owl, and kestrels

GROUND NESTS

Nests on the ground containing nesting material
➤ Ducks, geese, pelicans, cormorants, buntings, larks, guinea fowl, longclaws, francolin, pipits, and quails

Ground nest on substrate surface
➤ Ostrich, bustards, plovers, sandgrouse, coursers, terns, thick knee, pratincole, and some owls

Ground nest with a shallow scrape
➤ As above

QUICK REFERENCE GUIDE TO BIRD TRACKS

NOT WEBBED

3 toes forward—back toe off-centre
➤ Cattle egrets and some herons

2 toes forward—none back
➤ Ostrich

3 toes forward—none back
➤ Plovers, coursers, thick kneew (dikkop), korhaans, Kori bustard, sandgrouse, and some cranes

3 toes forward—back toe angled
➤ Nightjars, guinea fowl, francolin, crowned cranes, marabou, and white storks

3 toes forward—rear toe straight
➤ Includes many species—hornbills, barbets, starlings, doves, sparrows, pigeons, bulbuls, buntings, wagtails, crows, and larks

2 toes forward—2 toes back
➤ Woodpeckers, owls, and parrots

WEBBED

3 obvious toes
➤ Some gulls, shelduck, Egyptian geese, and spurwing geese

3 obvious toes
➤ Cormorants, grebes, pelicans, and coots

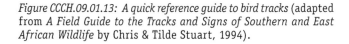

Figure CCCH.09.01.13: A quick reference guide to bird tracks (adapted from A Field Guide to the Tracks and Signs of Southern and East African Wildlife *by Chris & Tilde Stuart, 1994).*

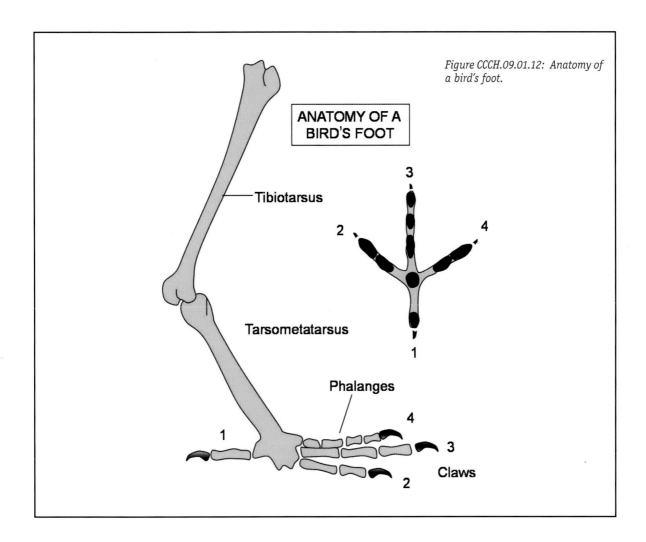

Figure CCCH.09.01.12: Anatomy of a bird's foot.

ANATOMY OF A
BIRD'S FOOT

Tibiotarsus

Tarsometatarsus

Phalanges

Claws

Anatomy of a Bird's Foot

While the feet of each bird species are specifically adapted to suit their lifestyle, the basic structure of the legs and feet is consistent. Each leg is made up of the femur, the tibiotarsus (formed by the fusion of the tibia and proximal tarsals), the tarsometatarsus (formed by the fusion of the distal tarsals and metatarsals), and the four toes. See Figure CCCH.09.01.12. A sesamoid bone (the patella) is found at the knee joint. Depending on the species, there are two to five phalanges on each toe. A bird's foot is adapted for swimming, perching, wading, walking, climbing, or seizing.

Birds walk on their toes; the heel does not generally touch the ground and will only show up on very soft ground. There are four or fewer toes and in most cases the toe terminates in a claw. The claws are strong and well developed in raptors and poorly developed in geese and ducks. Birds that have adapted to a swimming lifestyle will have webs between their toes. The passerines have long opposable first toes that enable them to hold tightly to a perch. Some birds, like woodpeckers, have two toes

at the back that support them as they peck at the bark of trees. Smaller, ground-frequenting birds such as larks, sparrows, and thrushes may move on the ground by hopping and walking. Doves and pigeons are well adapted for either perching or walking on the ground. This is made possible by the wider angle between their outer toes. Birds such as guinea fowl and francolin have a shorter back toe, which is suitable for roosting but not perching. Toes are thick, terminating in thick claws that are suited to scratching on the ground for food.

Tracks

Tracks are the impressions birds register in the soil when they walk on the ground. Let's start off with a quick reference guide to the different types of tracks.

Two Toes Back/Two Forward

This group is made up of woodpeckers, owls, and parrots. Woodpeckers and parrots do not, as a rule, frequent the ground much, and it will be unusual to find their tracks—except maybe in soil adjacent to water where they might come to drink. Woodpeckers clamber around in trees and parrots prefer perching high up. Some species of owls will sometimes sit on the ground. Parrots and woodpeckers are diurnal and owls mostly nocturnal.

Other signs to look for:

➤ Regurgitated owl pellets.

➤ Feeding signs by parrots on fruits and flowers.

➤ Wood chips and bits of bark dislodged whilst woodpeckers are searching for insects.

Three Toes Forward/Rear Toe Angled

This group includes species such as nightjars, francolins, guinea fowls, crowned cranes, marabou storks, and white storks. The angle of the rear toe is variable and the rear toe is short in most species. These species are often on the ground and it should be relatively easy to locate and identify tracks. Most species in this group are diurnal, roosting at night. See Figures CCCH.09.01.14 to CCCH.09.01.18 for examples of tracks exhibiting two toes forward/rear toe angled.

Other signs to look for:

➤ Scratching in the soil.

➤ Large amount of scat deposits under favourite roosting areas.

Francolins are useful to the tracker in that they can provide him with a good source of food, are a good natural alarm clock (early heralds of the morning), and they give a clear warning against danger because they flush with much vocalization when threatened.

Figure CCCH.09.01.15: Take note that the rear toe track of a francolin is not always obvious, so look around at some of the other tracks to confirm what you are observing. Track length is approximately 50mm.

Figure CCCH.09.01.14: Track of a Natal francolin walking. The pads of the track are clear and very little soil has been dislodged. A slight smudge in the soil on the far right indicates where the rear toe has just made contact (top). Clear tracks left by francolin in fine-grain soil with a high clay content, which makes for a good tracking medium (middle). Natal francolin in a hurry (bottom). Note how the claws are leaving a drag mark because the bird is not lifting its feet high. The rear toe is also making clear contact with the substrate.

Three Toes Forward/Rear Toe Straight

This group includes a large number of species such as hornbills, barbets, starlings, doves, sparrows, pigeons, bulbuls, buntings, wagtails, crows, and larks. These species often frequent the ground, and it should be easy to find their tracks. This group consists mainly of diurnal (day-active) birds.

Special sign to look for:

➤ Nesting holes in trees (hornbills).

Figure CCCH.09.01.16: These three pictures show the tracks of the crested francolin. In the top left photo the bird is running across the road.

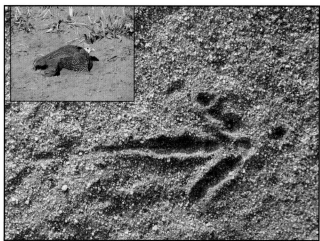

Figure CCCH.09.01.17: A close-up of guinea fowl feet. If you have a good impression in your mind of what the feet look like, it is easier to identify their tracks. This guinea fowl track is about 80mm long. Guinea fowls are also partial to taking a dust bath and will leave signs of having done so.

Figures CCCH.09.01.19 to CCCH.09.01.25 give examples of birds with the three toes forward/rear toe straight.

Vultures also belong to the group of birds with three toes forward/rear toe straight. Vultures can be useful to the tracker by guiding them to kills and possible food. When vultures are circling, they are looking for food. Once they spot food, they descend quickly, and it is this the tracker must look for. They can also warn of the presence of dangerous predators like lions.

Another bird belonging to this group is the greater honey guide, a useful little bird as it guides men to honey. I have twice taken the trouble to follow this delightful little bird and on both occasions I was taken to a hive. It will initiate the process by coming to sit on a conspicuous perch where it will attract attention by an incessant call sounding somewhat like a box of matches being shaken. Once you start to follow, it will fly ahead, stopping regularly to call to you. Once it is near the hive, it will suddenly go quiet. Look carefully, and you are bound to see bees in the immediate vicinity entering or leaving a hive.

Two Toes Forward/None Back

The only bird in this group is the ostrich. The ostrich is a flightless bird, so you will find its tracks in areas it frequents. Everything about this bird is very distinctive. Its size, the size of its eggs, and its foot structure are unique. See Figures CCCH.09.01.26 and CCCH.09.01.27.

The ostrich is one bird that the wise tracker will regard as potentially dangerous. During breeding time, males become aggressive, will readily attack humans, and are quite capable of inflicting serious injury. Their nests and tracks are distinctive as is the volume of their scat.

Figure CCCH.09.01.18: A freckled nightjar has three toes forward/one angled back. These birds are nocturnal and make their presence felt just after sunset with their "whip-poor-will" call.

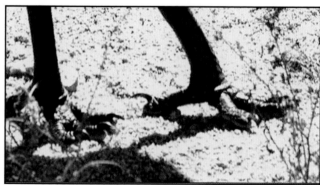

Figure CCCH.09.01.19: Ground hornbills often forage on the ground in search of food, which includes insects, frogs, snakes, and small mammals. They have a deep resonant call that sounds something like the words "How much?" answered by "One pound, two shillings." They walk on their toes, which means the central portion of their tracks do not readily show up on hard substrate. The length of a foot is 130 to 155mm.

Figure CCCH.09.01.20: Ground hornbill tracks.

Figure CCCH.09.01.21: (Right) A yellow-billed hornbill showing the typical foot structure of this group. Yellow-billed hornbills perch well but are often found on the ground looking for food. They generally hop, so their tracks will be alongside one another; their tracks are similar to sparrows. "Walkers" such as doves and southern ground hornbills will have their left and right feet alternating. The track length of a yellow-billed hornbill is 58 to 60mm.

Figure CCCH.09.01.22: (Lower left and right) A red-billed hornbill shows details of its feet and how it perches. Its foot length is 55 to 60mm. It digs in soil and dung for food.

Figure CCCH.09.01.23: A fork-tailed drongo is a diurnal bird that prefers perching but will alight onto the ground to catch food. These birds are quite tame and will allow humans to approach closely. They are often found in proximity to grazing animals, where they will perch on a conspicuous branch close-by as they look out for any insects that are flushed by the feet of the grazing animals. Will sometimes sit on an herbivorous animal. The observant tracker will notice these birds and be looking for the animals that these birds often hang around.

Figure CCCH.09.01.24: Spotted-back weavers nest in colonies suspended in vegetation above water. A typical nest is shown below. Not only are these birds useful indicators of water, but they also mob [gang up and harass potential attackers] snakes, which can warn the observant tracker.

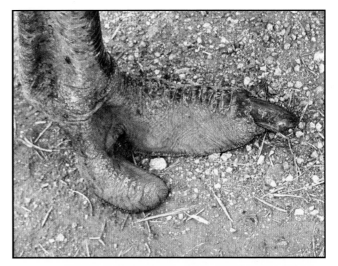

Figure CCCH.09.01.25: The black crake (top) is a small black bird with red legs and a bright yellow beak that forages in the undergrowth on riverbanks. Its deep, growling, bullfrog-type call is not one that a person would associate with this petite bird. The tracks of an orange-throated longclaw is on the bottom. Some of the clues to identifying bird tracks are the type of track, the habits of the bird, and the habitat in which the track is found.

Figure CCCH.09.01.26: An ostrich egg compared to that of a hen's egg.

Figure CCCH.09.01.27: An ostrich foot and track. The length of the track is 165mm.

Three Toes Forward/None Back

This group includes plovers, coursers, dikkops, korhaans, kori bustards, sand grouses, and some cranes. The species in this group spend a lot of time on the ground, so it should be relatively easy to find tracks. Some species are nocturnal (e.g., dikkop) while others are diurnal or crepuscular.

The double-banded sand grouse are very reliable water indicators. See Figure CCCH.09.01.28. At sunset they converge on water from all directions, flying in pairs or small groups. They congregate in large flocks around water holes where they set up a chattering noise that can be heard quite distinctly. The tracker should acquaint himself with its call.

Three Toes Forward/Back Toe Off-centre

This group is comprised of herons and some egrets. These are mostly diurnal birds with a few exceptions such as the black-crown night heron. Herons spend most of their time wading in water or sitting in vegetation overlooking water in search of prey—fish, frogs, small reptiles, and crustaceans. Herons are associated with water, so a wise tracker can use that knowledge to find water. Egrets, as mentioned elsewhere, are often seen in the presence of cattle and buffalo, so their proximity can warn the tracker that these animals are nearby. The track length of herons is 130mm; that of little egrets is 100mm. Examples of this group are shown in Figure CCCH.09.01.29.

Three Obvious Toes/Webbed

This group includes some gulls, shelducks, Egyptian geese, and spurwing geese. A typical example is shown in Figures CCCH.09.01.30 and CCCH.09.01.31.

Four Toes/Webbed

This group includes cormorants, grebes, pelicans, and coots; they are all water birds and can, therefore, lead a tracker to water through visual or auditory recognition of the bird, their calls, or their roosting sites. Cormorants eat fish, frogs, crustaceans, and mollusks. They usually sit on rocks or logs; and their tracks will not always be easy to find. Their presence is made obvious by the white scat that covers their favourite perches. Coots have very strange-looking feet consisting of scalloped webbing.

This concludes this brief introduction to bird tracking. Its purpose was not to be comprehensive but to whet the appetite of the aspirant tracker to get to know birds, their habits, and signs of their passing better. By now it should be more and more evident that tracking must be seen and studied in its very broadest context.

Figure CCCH.09.01.28: Double-banded sand grouses have a track that is 29 to 31mm long. Their flight to water at sunset is so accurate and direct that one can almost set a compass by the bearing of its flight path. You can be sure of finding water if you stay on that bearing. They are mostly active at dawn and dusk (crepuscular).

Figure CCCH.09.01.29: Black-crown night heron (below left) and goliath heron (below right).

Figure CCCH.09.01.30: Example of a "three obvious toes/webbed" foot structure.

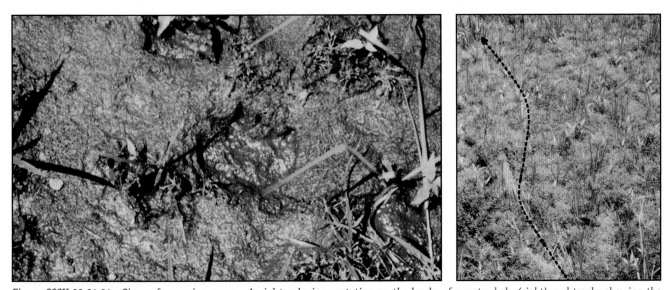

Figure CCCH.09.01.31: Signs of spurwing geese. Aerial tracks in vegetation on the banks of a water hole (right) and tracks showing the three obvious toes with webbing (left).

Reptiles

Reptiles include crocodiles, lizards, tortoises, turtles, terrapins, skinks, geckos, and, of course, snakes. They inhabit all types of habitat, from deserts to tropical rain forests and from oceans to freshwater habitats. The one habitat where they are scarce or absent are places of extreme cold. Being "cold blooded," they are dependent on their environment to regulate their body temperature and metabolism. They cannot survive for long in an environment of extreme cold.

The tracker should be aware of the presence of reptiles and should be able to identify signs indicating they are frequenting a certain area. The most important reason is safety, for some reptiles are potentially lethal. In this overview of reptiles, we will look at some of the most important signs the tracker needs to recognize in order to monitor his environment. A quick reference guide to reptile sign is shown in Figure CCCH.09.02.01.

Visual Sightings

Visual sightings are the most obvious way of knowing reptiles occur in a given area. Correct identification can be of great value to the tracker because certain species can lead a tracker to water. This includes terrapins, water monitors (leguan), and some snakes. Correct identification can also be of great value because the tracker will be warned of potential danger. Once a venomous species is identified, the tracker can take the necessary precautions. Where signs of crocodile are evident, the tracker will be cautious in and around water. Another value in identifying certain species is that they can lead the tracker to potential food: Snakes and lizards often rob nests of eggs and fledglings for food, and in a survival situation, the tracker can utilize the reptiles themselves for food.

Eggs, Feeding Sign, Scat, and Incidental Signs

Like birds, reptiles reproduce by laying eggs. The eggs of most snakes, crocodiles, tortoises, and terrapins differ from those of birds in that they do not have such a hard shell. The shell is more parchmentlike and leathery. Similar to owls and other raptors, snakes often bring up food pellets of undigested material.

The droppings of reptiles are sausage shaped, pointed usually at both ends, and has a hard cap of white or yellowish uric acid. The size of the dropping can vary from a few millimeters to as long as 10 cm in larger species. Snake and lizard droppings are of this kind, but they are seldom found. It is also very difficult to identify a particular species of reptile from scat. Crocodile produce droppings that look very similar to that of hyena when it

A QUICK REFERENCE GUIDE TO REPTILE SIGN

Reptile "sign" can consist of the following

➤ Visual sightings
➤ Vocalization
➤ Tracks
➤ Nests
➤ Eggs
➤ Scat
➤ Feeding
➤ Incidental sign

Figure CCCH.09.02.01: A quick reference guide to reptile sign.

Figure CCCH.09.02.02: Snake skin caught in a bush.

BIRD, REPTILE, AND INVERTEBRATE SIGN

is dried and can be found on riverbanks where they sun themselves. Tortoises produce droppings similar to that of porcupine.

The most common incidental sign left behind by snakes and lizards is skin, which sloughs off at regular intervals. Snake skins are quite often found dangling from thorn trees. See Figure CCCH.09.02.02. The skeletal remains of larger snakes and tortoise shells are found quite often.

Snakes and lizards cannot produce vocal sounds as do other animals. Most snakes and some larger lizards, such as the monitors, can hiss audibly by the forced expulsion of air through the nostrils. Crocodiles also hiss and can also make a deep growling sound. Many reptiles will make a nest during breeding periods or when going into states of torpor during hibernation or estivation. Typical nesting sites are found under logs or rocks, in decaying vegetation, in holes in trees, and in the ground. Tracks and drag marks will often be seen at the entrance to nests. See Figure CCCH.09.02.03.

Crocodiles and some snakes can be aggressive when in the vicinity of their nests during the breeding period. This is especially true of black mambas. A quick guide to the tracks of reptiles is shown in Figure CCCH.09.02.04.

Tortoises are diagonal walkers, so a track will show the feet on the opposite sides of the body alternating. The hind feet usually register over those of the forefeet. Most tortoises have five claws on the forefeet and four on the hind feet. See Figure CCCH.09.02.05.

Some skinks are legless and slide along their bellies in an undulating fashion. Most of them and lizards have legs that show up in the track as well as a drag mark from the tail. See Figure CCCH.09.02.06.

Despite obvious differences in size, crocodiles, lizards, geckos, agamas, and monitors all produce similar tracks—a tramline trail. Individual feet will show with a continuous drag mark. See Figures CCCH.09.02.07, CCCH.09.02.08, and CCCH.09.02.09.

The tracks of tree agamas are not often found, but when they are it will be when they scurry from one tree to another. Geckos have bulbous toes that enable them to walk on vertical surfaces.

QUICK REFERENCE GUIDE TO REPTILE TRACKS

TRAMLINE TRAIL—INDIVIDUAL FEET SHOWING
   Tortoise
   Terrapin

TRAMLINE TRAIL—INDIVIDUAL FEET SHOWING WITH CONTINUOUS DRAG MARK
   Skinks (with feet)
   Lizards
   Monitors
   Crocodiles

DRAG MARKS
   Legless skink
   Snakes
      ➤ Linear
      ➤ Undulating (slow)
      ➤ Undulating (fast)
      ➤ Sidewinding

Figure CCCH.09.02.04: A quick guide to reptile tracks.

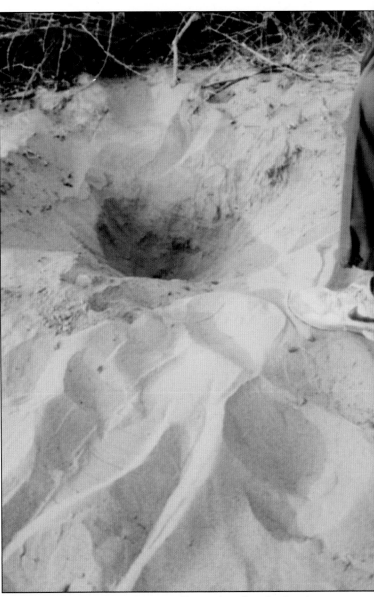

Figure CCCH.09.02.03: In this crocodile nesting site, the female excavated a hole about 500mm deep and deposited her eggs. She then covered the hole up by scooping sand over it with her hind feet. The tail drag marks are evident and even the pattern of the belly scales.

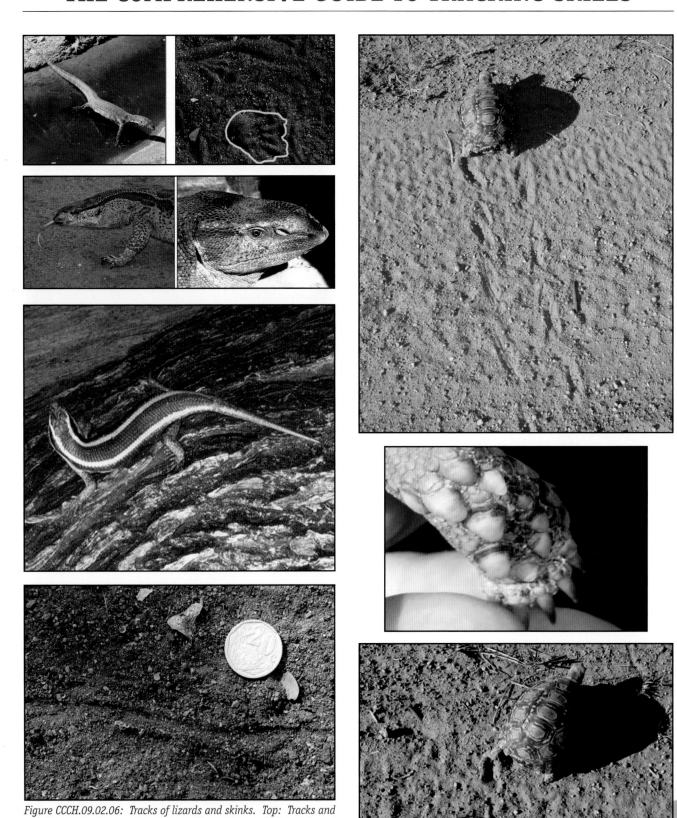

Figure CCCH.09.02.06: Tracks of lizards and skinks. Top: Tracks and tramline trail of a water monitor with continuous drag mark and individual feet showing clearly. Centre: Rock or veld monitor signs will be similar to that of water monitors but can be found far from water. They often shelter in holes, whereas the water monitor takes to water when threatened. Exercise caution when handling these reptiles. Although not poisonous, they can bite and use their tails as whips. Bottom: A striped skink. Although the feet marks are indistinct (but still visible), the tail drag mark is clear.

Figure CCCH.09.02.05 : Tracks of a leopard tortoise. Top: Foot structure of the leopard tortoise showing the five front toes. (Photos courtesy of B. Rossouw)

BIRD, REPTILE, AND INVERTEBRATE SIGN

Being cold blooded, reptiles have to use their environment to regulate their body temperature. In cool weather they will often sun themselves on rocks or on footpaths. When tracking, keep your eyes open on game paths because they are a favourite spot for puff adders.

The cryptic colouration and special adaptations of some species, like flap-neck chameleons, enable these reptiles to blend into the background. Puff and gaboon adders are masters of camouflage. See Figure CCCH.09.02.10.

Figure CCCH.09.02.07: The foot shape of crocodiles is very characteristic and, by virtue of its size and together with the tail drag mark, leaves unmistakable sign. These should warn the tracker of their presence in any body of water. BEWARE OF CROCODILES! These reptiles are deadly predators.

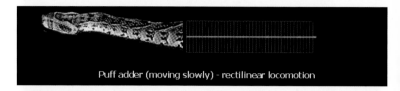

TRACKS OF SNAKE LOCOMOTION

When large, sluggish snakes such as puff adders and python move slowly they move in what is essentially a straight line. This is referred to as rectilinear locomotion. When they speed up the motion becomes more sinuous and wavy. This is then referred to as undulatory locomotion.

Puff adder (moving slowly) - rectilinear locomotion

Puff adder (moving more quickly) - undulatory locomotion

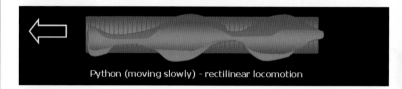

Python (moving slowly) - rectilinear locomotion

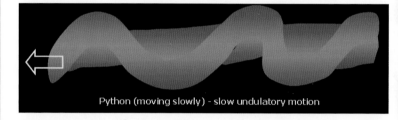

Python (moving slowly) - slow undulatory motion

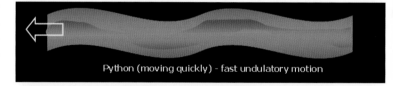

Python (moving quickly) - fast undulatory motion

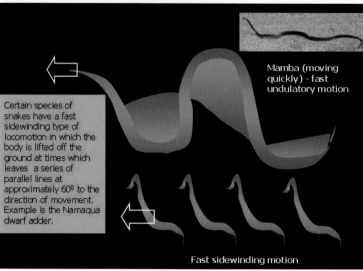

Mamba (moving quickly) - fast undulatory motion

Certain species of snakes have a fast sidewinding type of locomotion in which the body is lifted off the ground at times which leaves a series of parallel lines at approximately 60⁰ to the direction of movement. Example is the Namaqua dwarf adder.

Fast sidewinding motion

Figure CCCH.09.02.08: Patterns of snake locomotion.

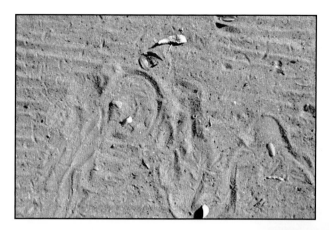

Figure CCCH.09.02.09: Above left: A puff adder was sunning itself and then moved off when it had warmed itself sufficiently. Above right: A snake track registers across a tarred road. Who says you cannot track on hard surfaces? Lower left: The track on the left (probably a black mamba) moving at medium pace. Lower right: A puff adder crossing a track in the bush. Slow movement will result in a rectilinear track. The faster it moves, the more undulating will be the track. A tracker must always keep a wary eye open for snakes and their signs. Tracks of arboreal (tree loving) species like the boomslang, vine snakes, and green mambas will be found less frequently on the ground.

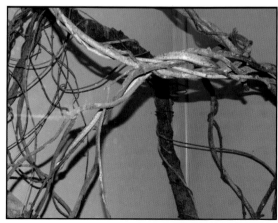

Figure CCCH.09.02.10: Many reptiles are masters of camouflage as seen with the puff adder (left), gaboon adder (middle), and a vine snake (right) in this photo. The tracker must always keep his eyes open.

Insects and Invertebrates

The largest and most diverse group of animals is the invertebrates (animals without backbones). This group includes amongst others insects, crustaceans (crayfish and shrimps), arachnids (scorpions and spiders), mollusks (snails), centipedes, and millipedes. If we could set before us a representative of every species of animal that lives on earth, 90 percent of them would be invertebrates. Of these, about one million would be insects. It is obvious, therefore, that only a tiny fraction of what there is in the world will be presented here.

Invertebrate sign is prolific and easy to find all around us, every day. The buzzing, humming, whining, chirping, rasping sound of insects are invertebrates: bees gathering pollen on flowers, crickets on the lawn, cockroaches in the cupboard, mosquitoes round our ears, fleas on the dogs, spiders in the garden, snails on your wife's best potted plants, and so on. And many of these creatures are extremely important to the tracker as we shall see in some examples.

Arachnids

Spiders, ticks, and scorpions belong to the class Arachnida. If you begin to take notice, you will find spider webs all over the place. Although you might not always see the spider, the web betrays its presence. Not all spiders make conspicuous webs. Some, like baboon spiders, live in holes in the ground, some build communal nests, while others build intricate webs. See Figure CCCH.09.03.01.

What information can a web betray to a tracker? First, it will tell the tracker what kind of spider it is and if it is dangerous to humans. Second, a broken web can supply information. The observant tracker will notice when a web was broken. The tracker will ask himself: How was it broken, when, and by what? Knowing the habits of the spider species in question and how long they take to repair a broken web will give

a fair indication as to when it was broken. The height of the web above ground can give a clue as to the size of the animal (or person) that walked into it. Animals generally walk through webs. People usually stop and take a pace back if they have walked into it. If they see the web, they will generally walk around it.

Another reason it is important for a good tracker to be on the lookout for spider sign is safety. He should be able to identify the venomous spiders in his environment, while bearing in mind that most are harmless to man.

Figure CCCH.09.03.01: The homes of spiders. Top: The nesting hole of a baboon spider. Centre: Intricate webs of the golden orb spider (left) and the kite spider (right). Bottom: Communal spider nests. Even though the spiders themselves are tiny and not easily seen, the web is highly visible. The males are smaller and more brightly coloured than the females. When prey lands in the web, it is killed by a small group of spiders that then drag it into the nest to be consumed by the community.

In southern Africa there are only about six species that are of medical significance to man. Most spiders, even those that have a fearsome reputation, are not venomous to man. See Figure CCCH.09.03.02.

Baboon spiders can be induced to come out of their holes in the following way:

1. Insert a grass stalk into the hole.

2. If the spider is home, it will grab hold of the grass stalk.

3. Gently withdraw the straw, and the spider will be pulled out of the hole.

4. Have a good look, and then leave the spider to return inside its retreat.

5. Don't break the hole. Adult baboon spiders lose digging appendages when they reach adulthood and cannot dig a new one.

Most spiders are too small and light to leave discernible tracks other than in a very finely textured substrate. The horned baboon spider is, however, large enough to leave signs of his passing. See Figure CCCH.09.03.03.

Ticks are ectoparasites that are intermediate hosts of many disease-causing organisms. They can transmit diseases such as tick-bite fever, gall sickness, bilary, heart

Figure CCCH.09.03.03: Very large spiders will leave discernible tracks on very fine substrate.

Figure CCCH.09.03.02: Only six species of spiders are of medical significance to man, with the majority being non- or only slightly venomous. The size of a spider is not necessarily an indication of how venomous it is. This large horned baboon spider (centre), while being able to deliver a painful bite, produces only a mild venom and some local irritation. They live in holes in the ground. The diameter of the holes is approximately 20 to 25mm. A rain spider is on top, and a solifuge or sun spider is on the bottom. The solifuge is not actually a spider.

Figure CCCH.09.03.04: (Top) Engorged ticks have dropped off their host, leaving tracks in fine substrate. (Bottom) Squashed ticks embedded in mud were rubbed off by an animal. This is a good illustration of how effective wallowing can be to remove ectoparasites.

water, East Coast fever, Congo fever, and many others. In Figure CCCH.09.03.04 we see some "tick sign."

Scorpions are more common and prolific than people think. They utilize a wide range of habitats and can be found under the bark of trees, under rocks, logs, rubbish, old plant material, and in holes. The wise tracker knows and understands the habits and preferred habitats of scorpions and will exercise the necessary precautions when collecting firewood, picking up rocks, etc. Scorpions will also crawl into footwear and into clothing, so experience teaches us to check these items before putting them on. Scorpions are mostly active at night. Scorpions will leave tracks on suitable substrates like small-grained sand or clay soils. They consist of a "tramline" set of tightly grouped tracks. The one end of the imprints is pointed and indicates the direction of travel. A scorpion mostly walks with its tail raised off the ground but occasionally will lower it and leave a distinct drag mark.

Millipedes and Centipedes

Millipedes belonging to the lower invertebrates are entirely vegetarian; they feed on decaying plant material (detritus) and fungi. They belong to the myriapoda, which means many-legged. They lack any venomous appendages for offense or defense. When disturbed, they coil themselves and secrete offensive fluids from spiracles along the midline of the body. They release benzaldehyde, which is a chemical irritant to sensitive skin, and highly toxic hydrogen cyanide gas when threatened. They generally have up to only 120 pairs of legs. The millipede pictured is referred to as a "wormlike millipede." See Figures CCCH.09.03.05 and CCCH.09.03.06.

Figure CCCH.09.03.05: Millipedes. The one on the right is almost as long as the author's size-eight foot.

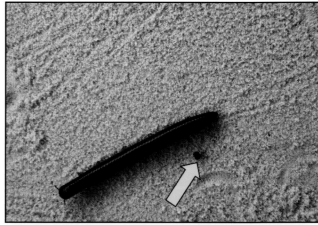

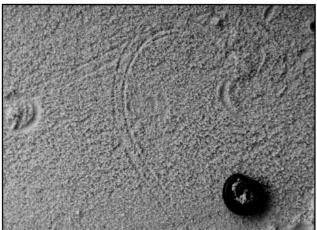

Figure CCCH.09.03.06: Top left: A millipede crosses the tracks of a scorpion. Top right: The tramline tracks are easily visible in these photos. The observant tracker will notice droppings to the left of the millipede (arrow). Bottom: The millipede lays curled up in a protective ball (above) but after a while crawled off to the left, leaving behind a pattern in the soil where it had been curled up.

Millipedes are glossy black or have alternating black and yellow bands. Females lay several hundred eggs the size of pinheads. Young hatch with three pairs of legs, acquiring more each time they molt. They are observed more frequently during the wet months of the year and are one of the preferred meals on the menu of civet cats.

Centipedes also belong to the myriapoda. See Figure CCCH.09.03.07. Unlike millipedes, they can deliver a painful bite. They are usually found under rocks or under tree bark.

A tracker with keen eyesight can pick up signs left behind by millipedes. Find the narrow tramline set of tracks and small droppings in Figure CCCH.09.03.06.

Figure CCCH.09.03.07: A centipede is capable of delivering a painful bite.

BIRD, REPTILE, AND INVERTEBRATE SIGN

Insects

Termites are the favourite foods of many creatures, including birds, frogs, spiders, scorpions, and ants. There are some larger mammals such as the aardwolf, aardvark, and pangolin that live almost exclusively on termites. These species can be present in any given area where termites are available in abundance. Termites make good nutritious eating for humans as well. There are a number of varieties of termites.

Some make large nests above ground (Macrotermes), some make underground nests with ventilation shafts (Odontotermes), and some make shallow underground nests—the so-called harvester termites (Hodotermes). A number of animals shelter in larger termite nests such as the dwarf mongoose, porcupine, warthog, aardvark, aardwolf, and snakes.

Large termite mounds often bend toward the north and can be a useful direction indicator for the tracker. Why do they bend to the north? A plausible answer is that termites build with wet mud. As they extend onto the existing mound, the northern side of the mound gets more sun. This causes the mud to dry and contract more quickly on that side than on the southern side. This makes the tip of the mound tilt to the north. See Figures CCCH.09.03.08 and CCCH.09.03.09.

Figure CCCH.09.03.09: The soldier caste of harvester termites can inflict a painful bite—as the author discovered.

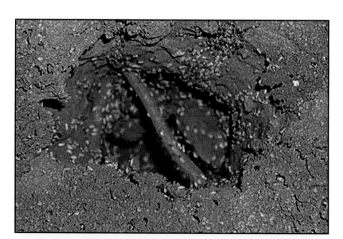

Figure CCCH.09.03.08: Top left: The entrance shaft to a Hodotermes termite nest. Termites are soft bodied and do not expose themselves to direct sunlight. Left bottom: Harvester termite tunnels. Above: A tall termite mound of the Macrotermes variety.

THE COMPREHENSIVE GUIDE TO TRACKING SKILLS

When harvester termites venture out to look for food, they build little tunnels for themselves for protection from the harsh rays of the sun. If these tunnels are broken, it can give the tracker an indication that an animal or person has trod on them or was looking for termites for food.

Antlions are the larvae of winged creatures that resemble dragonflies. Not all antlion species construct pits such as those shown in Figure CCCH.09.03.10. When on the move, antlions move backward with their bodies just beneath the surface of the sand, and this gives rise to trails. See Figure CCCH.09.03.11.

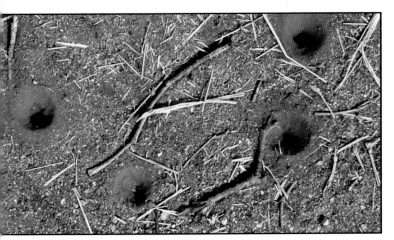

Figure CCCH.09.03.10: Antlion pits.

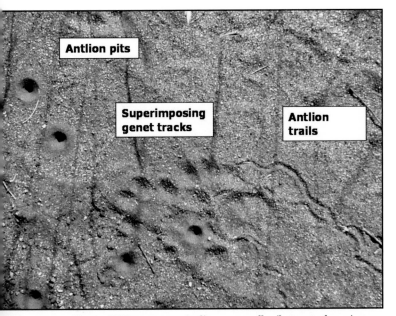

Figure CCCH.09.03.11: Antlions generally (but not always) move about to relocate or build new pits for about two hours after sunset; they leave trails as they move about. When these trails are superimposed by other tracks, this can give the astute tracker an indication of the age of those superimposed tracks.

Beetles comprise a huge group of over 280,000 species that constitute the order Coleoptera. They are characterized by forewings that form a protective shell around the body when the beetle is not in flight. Beetles are also characterized by powerful mandibles and chewing mouthparts. Let's look at just a few interesting insect examples as they relate to tracking.

Poison grub beetles (Diamphidia) can be used as a very effective poison for arrows. It is used by the San Bushmen. The beetle feeds on the leaves of *Commiphora africana* (kanniedood) and lay their eggs on the leaves. When the larvae hatch, they feed on the leaves; they then fall onto the ground where they burrow into the soil and pupate. The pupae of the grub beetle are macerated and applied to arrows as poison.

Dung beetles (below) break down dung and are usually very active around fresh piles, especially that of buffaloes, elephants, and rhinos. Their frenetic activity can alert the tracker to the possibility that these animals might be in the vicinity. See Figure CCCH.09.03.12.

Tenebroid beetles are often referred to as tok-tokkies. They are well known for their delightful (and audible)

Figure CCCH.09.03.12: A dung beetle at work. Dung is collected, formed into a ball, and rolled to a place that the dung beetle finds suitable. Eggs are laid in the dung. The ball is then buried. When the larva hatches, it feeds on the dung and after undergoing metamorphosis emerges as an adult beetle. These beetles perform a vital function in cleaning up the veld and in recycling nutrients.

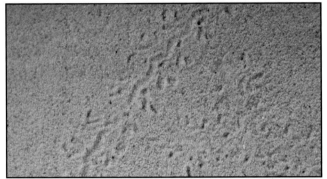

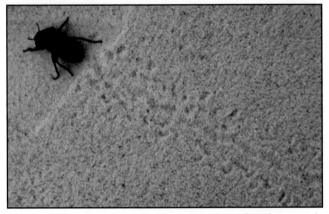

Figure CCCH.09.03.13: Tenebroid beetles, also referred to as tok-tokkies, will leave visible tracks in finely textured substrate.

Figure CCCH.09.03.14: Outer horn material being broken down by the larvae of horn-eating moths (Ceratophagus spp.). The larvae expel their dung out of holes in the horn. This eventually forms tubes (see arrow) out of which the fully developed moth eventually emerges. An increase in fly activity will alert the tracker to the possibility of a carcass in the vicinity or fresh dung deposited by animals as shown below.

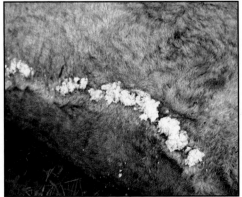

Figure CCCH.09.03.15: The adult blowfly (left) lays eggs on the dead animal (centre). Larvae hatch and feed on the decomposing tissue, after which they pupate and then emerge as an adult (right). The example shown is that of a lioness.

habit of tapping their abdomens on hard surfaces to attract a mate . . . and the attention of a careful tracker. Tok-tokkies can leave visible tracks in suitable substrates as shown in Figure CCCH.09.03.13.

Flies are attracted to carcasses and dung, and blowflies play an important role in causing organic proteinaceous material to be broken down. Even keratin is broken down by the larval stage of certain moths. See Figure CCCH.09.03.14. Blowflies are attracted to dead carcasses and lay their eggs on them. Soon the eggs hatch into larvae, which feed on the carcass and assist in its decomposition and breakdown. See Figure CCCH.09.03.15.

Snails

Snails belong to the group known as mollusks. Most snails live off vegetable matter and carrion, but some are carnivorous and eat other snails and earthworms. Some species such as the giant African snail *(Achatina fulica)* shown in Figure CCCH.09.03.17 can grow to the size of a man's hand. They are more commonly seen during the wet months of the year. A snail also leaves a track of a sort—as unlikely as that may seem. Snails move by means of undulating contractions of their muscular "foot." Mucus is laid down to lubricate their passage, and it leaves a shiny trail. See Figure CCCH.09.03.17.

Figure CCCH.09.03.16: *Food for blowfly larvae. The newly hatched larvae quickly devour the protein component of the dwarf mongoose carcass.*

Figure CCCH.09.03.17: *Snails leave behind a trail of shiny mucus.*

CHAPTER 10

TRACKING MAN

Combat Tracking

Tracking an enemy under operational or war conditions constitutes combat tracking. There are many similarities between combat tracking and antipoaching operations, but there are also important differences, which we will elaborate on in due course. In combat tracking, the tracker is pitted against a possibly well-trained and well-equipped enemy. The goal of this enemy is to kill or maim you; your main objective is to locate the enemy so that he can be killed, maimed, or captured. The enemy might be attempting to evade a contact or can, on the other hand, be leading you and your men into a trap.

Requirements for a Combat Tracker

One of the obvious requirements of a combat tracker is that the individual should have an above-average tracking ability. Combat tracking is physically very demanding. It dictates a very high level of fitness and stamina, for the tracker may be required to stay on a trail for days. The individual must be mentally tough and be able to concentrate for extended periods. An eye for detail and the ability to stay alert are indispensable qualities. Knowledge of the bush, local wildlife, and survival techniques are essential. The tracker, of course, must be a trained soldier. This means a knowledge of small-group tactics, weapons, equipment, and first aid.

Know the Enemy

It is essential for the combat tracker to have as much information as possible about the enemy.

Ideology

What "drives" and motivates the enemy politically, ideologically, and religiously? Has he been forced into combat against his will? Is he very patriotic/zealous? To what extent would he, without any hesitation, offer his life to take out as many of the enemy as possible? A suicide bomber has a very different mind-set and is considerably more dangerous than someone who has been forced into active service against his/her will.

Level of Training

The better trained your enemy, the harder and more dangerous your job will be. Who provided the training? What tactics does the enemy use? How are its soldiers trained? Do they use antitracking techniques?

Equipment

The tracker should be well acquainted with the type of equipment the enemy uses. What do the uniforms look like? Do they wear civilian dress? What type of shoes/boots do they wear and what do the lug/sole patterns look like? Do they operate barefoot? Are they equipped with ration packs, and by whom? (The writing on ration packaging might give away the supplier.) Do they have sophisticated equipment (radios, GPS, vehicles, etc.)?

Weapons

You should know what type of weapons the enemy uses, their effectiveness, and the ballistics. Are their weapons well maintained? Do they have a consistent and reliable source of supply and resupply? A combat tracker must know how to use not only his own weapons but also those of the enemy.

Habits and Tactics

Gather as much information from intelligence reports, patrols, incident and contact reports, police forces, locals, and POWs on the tactics employed by the enemy. Know your enemy's habits. Are they being supplied or living off the land? Are locals sympathetic toward them? What do they do when discovered? Do they split up, bombshell, employ antitracking and countertracking tactics, fight, run, or merge with the local population?

The Level of Morale

The lower the morale, the less inclined the enemy will be to want to fight. The higher the morale, the more he will want to fight. Morale can be affected by poor bushcraft skills. Don't just assume that the enemy has good bushcraft skills. Many guerrillas in Angola, Vietnam, Namibia, Mozambique, Zimbabwe, and other places have been discovered hungry, thirsty, and disoriented because they were not familiar with a particular area.

Equipping Yourself

Travel light and carry only first aid, water, food, ammo, a multipurpose knife like a Leatherman, and a weapon. See Figure CCCH.10.01.01. Additional kit can be brought up by follow-up troops. Wear clothing appropriate for the conditions and environment.

Figure CCCH.10.01.01: A Leatherman multipurpose tool is an indispensable item of equipment.

You can consider the option of dressing like the enemy and using captured weapons. This has its pros and cons. One of the disadvantages is that your own forces could mistake you for the enemy.

You should be in radio contact so as to be able to call in additional troops if necessary, report progress (send SITREPS Situation Reports), or call for casualty evacuation (CASEVAC).

It is useful to carry a tracking stick to point to sign as you go along and to record stride length, straddle, and the foot sizes of individuals.

Learn about local vegetation, wildlife, bushcraft, and living off the land. You need to know where to find water and food; you need to know how to make implements, traps, etc. Take note of local customs and try to pick up some of the language.

Acquaint yourself with and study local weather conditions and patters: day- and nighttime temperatures, months of the rainy season, dry months of the year, prevailing wind directions, and so on. Get to know the lay of the land. Maps, aerial photos, locals, tour guides, police/military units, and patrol reports can provide useful information.

Weapons

There are two main factors to consider when choosing a suitable weapon for operational conditions (war/law enforcement):

➤ Tactical situation

➤ Terrain

As important as the weapon itself is the ammunition you will be using. Most likely it will be of military origin and will probably fall within the choice listed in the table below.

The range at which the enemy is likely to be confronted and the type of terrain will affect the calibre of choice. In open terrain where contacts will occur at long range (more than 250 meters), weapons firing ammunition designed for short-range combat would be a poor choice. These include shotguns firing pellets and pistols/assault rifles firing 9mm Parabellum ammunition. Weapons that fire flat-shooting ammunition designed

Table 10.1: Some Calibres Suitable for Combat Tracking

CALIBRE	BULLET WEIGHT (GRAINS)	VELOCITY (FEET PER SECOND)	EFFECTIVE RANGE METERS
9x19mm (Parabellum)	129	1,100	50
.223 (or 5.56mm)	55	3,200	250
7.62 x 39mm (Soviet)	120	2,400	200
.308 (Win.) 7.62x51mm (NATO)	150	2,850	300

for longer distances would be a far better choice. These include the .223 (5.56mm) or the .308 Winchester (7.62x51mm NATO).

In dense bush, light bullets would be more easily deflected than heavier ones; consequently, the choice would be the heavier bullet. If contacts are likely to occur at short range, the pump or semiauto shotgun can be a devastating weapon when using the correct ammunition: SSG (16 pellets) or a Duplex load made up of a 330-grain slug (for penetration) and 9 No. 3 buckshot pellets (for shot dispersion).

A handgun should never be the principal weapon and should only be used as a backup firearm in combat tracking. The Colt .45 is a good choice. Although limited by the amount of ammunition, shotguns, under the right circumstances, can be devastating weapons. Pump-action shotguns are also good weapons for close contact situations. Some recommendations for assault rifles are shown in Figure CCCH.10.01.03.

Some recommended handguns for the combat tracker are illustrated in Figure CCCH.10.01.04.

High-Tech Equipment

A GPS, or Global Positioning System, is an essential piece of equipment these days, especially when operations are conducted in remote or rugged terrain where navigational skills would be tested to the extreme. CCCH.10.01.05. The old compass/protractor method of navigation, whilst reliable, was slow and not always very accurate. A GPS offers the following advantages to the tracker:

➤ Quickly gives a very accurate position on the ground.

➤ Gives a position day or night, irrespective of weather conditions.

➤ Accurately calculates distances from point to point.

➤ Sets up waypoints to assist in cross-country movement and can guide you back to your starting point.

➤ Calculates elevation.

➤ Has a wide temperature-operating range.

➤ Is lightweight, weatherproof, and of rugged construction.

➤ Uses AA batteries and has a battery life of around ten hours.

➤ Establishes the initial follow-up commencement point, which is essential for the command and control of a tracking operation.

➤ Supplies the command centre with regular updates of the tracking teams' progress.

Figure CCCH.10.01.03: Assault rifles for combat tracking.

Figure CCCH.10.01.04: Suitable handguns as a backup for combat tracking.

➤ Quickly establishes points of tactical importance such as supply caches, temporary bases, water points, visual sightings, contacts, booby-traps, etc.

➤ Guides the tracking team to a specific point for resupply.

➤ Accurately guides the Medevac helicopters/gunships to a specific point.

➤ Enables the tracking team to follow-up quickly when a spoor-cutting team locates tracks.

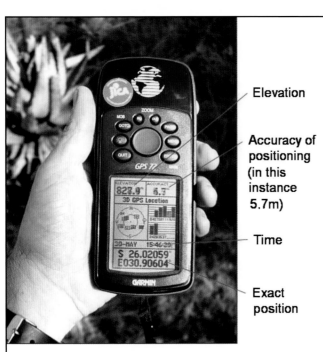

Elevation

Accuracy of positioning (in this instance 5.7m)

Time

Exact position

Figure CCCH.10.01.05: GPS devices can be very useful to the combat tracker.

REMEMBER: A GPS can malfunction and batteries can go flat. Always keep a standard compass and protractor as a backup.

Cellular Phones

The use of cellular phones has become almost universal and during tracking operations a cellular phone can be a very useful communications device. The tracker can quickly be contacted, and he can easily relay information up the command channels. There is no problem with atmospheric interference and static that is common with standard radio equipment. Make sure, however, that the device is switched off when you are in proximity to your enemy. The last thing you want is for your cell phone to ring at an inopportune time. Also be careful that the light emanating from the phone is blocked during night missions.

Sound Enhancement Devices

Human hearing can be limited by extraneous noise (traffic, wind, etc.) or by physiological defects (deafness). There are devices available on the commercial market that can assist the tracker by magnifying ambient sound. This can offer a major tactical advantage to the tracker. See Figure CCCH.10.01.06.

Thermal Imaging Devices

These devices are high-tech equipment that will detect a heat source in open terrain up to a distance of nine hundred meters away and in bush/forest up to four hundred meters away. It works by comparing the heat generated by a heat source (animal/human/fire/engine) to that of its surroundings. See Figure CCCH.10.01.06. These devices work night or day and in all types of weather and terrain, so they are particularly useful in a tactical situation under the following conditions:

➤ When searching through dense bush

➤ In scanning likely ambush sites during follow-up

➤ When contacting the enemy is imminent

➤ When searching for wounded fugitives who leave a blood spoor

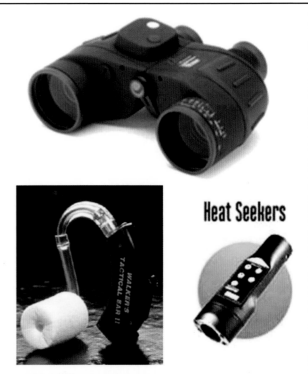

Heat Seekers

Figure CCCH.10.01.06: High-tech devices available to the combat tracker: Centre: multiple-use binoculars (top). Sound enhancement devices (bottom left). Thermal (IR) imaging devices (bottom right).

➤ When locating hidden fires at night

➤ In scanning for latent heat sources as part of lost-spoor procedures

Multiple-use Binocular

A binocular is available that incorporates a compass and rangefinder. This is a very useful tool. See Figure CCCH.10.01.06.

Tactics and Order of Movement

Although formations are determined by terrain and the tactical situation, the formation normally employed when tracking is the "Y" formation. See Figure CCCH.10.01.07.

Flankers or Point Men

They are also trained trackers. They walk up front on the left and right flank and are responsible for forward and flank security. They rotate tracking duties with the tracker when he becomes fatigued. Since flankers are most likely to make first contact, they must remain alert and ready for action.

Tracker

Next in line on the central axis of advance is the tracker. His primary responsibility is tracking and interpreting his findings to the team leader.

Leader

This is the person in control of the trackers and other troops until the time of contact. He relays information to the base and the follow-up troops. He extracts the tracker team when contact is made if follow-up troops are available.

Follow-up Troops

These people can be on foot, in vehicles, or airborne. They need to be ready when called up. When contact is made, they move forward to the skirmish line.

General Rules for Tracking Teams

➤ All members should be trained and experienced trackers.

➤ Four men are ideal.

➤ Keep teams. Members get to know one another. Teamwork saves lives and gets results.

➤ Get trackers onto the trail/spoor ASAP before sign gets old.

➤ The team leader is BOSS until the operation is over. Higher ranks must not be allowed to interfere on the ground.

➤ Team leader relieves the tracker on a frequent basis. Tracking is a tiring, exacting, and high-pressure job.

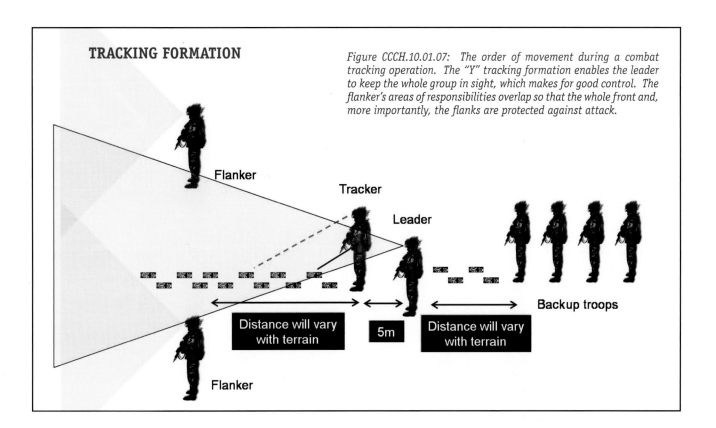

TRACKING FORMATION

Figure CCCH.10.01.07: The order of movement during a combat tracking operation. The "Y" tracking formation enables the leader to keep the whole group in sight, which makes for good control. The flanker's areas of responsibilities overlap so that the whole front and, more importantly, the flanks are protected against attack.

Flanker

Tracker

Leader

Flanker

Distance will vary with terrain

5m

Distance will vary with terrain

Backup troops

Fatigue diminishes a person's powers of observation and alertness.

➤ Avoid verbal communication as far as possible. The sound of voices carries unbelievably far in the bush. Use hand signals or whisper.

➤ Make sure the team rests as often as practically possible (they might be on the spoor for days). Tired men make mistakes.

➤ If a general pattern of movement and direction is established, try leapfrogging. One team stays on the track while the other moves a couple of kilometers ahead. If new tracks are found, shift the tracker team to the new location.

➤ If possible, saturate the area being tracked.

➤ Avoid recklessly fast movement. Move at a consistent and steady pace to keep up the pressure.

➤ Be persistent even if signs look old. Don't give up.

➤ Be aware of trickery and deception. The enemy will use every trick in the book to confuse you or lead you into a trap.

➤ Using a pointer/tracking stick will help the tracker concentrate and stay on a specific track.

➤ Study the enemy's habits at every opportunity.

➤ Check out fruit-bearing trees, water holes, beehives, etc., for enemy sign/activity.

➤ Radio occasional tracking reports of your routes so that a pattern and direction of travel can be established.

Use the code word NDATS (Figure CCCH.10.01.08) when reporting track information:

➤ **N** stands for the number of people you are tracking

➤ **D** is the direction (magnetic bearing as indicated on a compass or GPS) you are headed at the time of the report

➤ **A** refers to the age of the sign (minutes, hours, days)

➤ **T** is for the type of spoor/sign

➤ **S** stands for the speed of travel at time of reporting

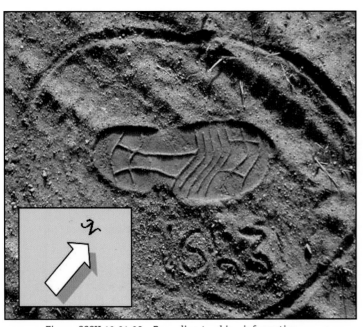

Figure CCCH.10.01.08: Recording tracking information.

Figure CCCH.10.01.09: Flattened grass or cleared areas can be an indication of sleeping or bedding areas.

Identifying and Interpreting Sign

As a combat tracker, you will be looking for signs associated with mostly, but not exclusively, human activity. Think what you as a human do in your daily routine. You eat, you drink, rest, sleep, perhaps you smoke, you wash, cook, walk, run, sit, read, and so on. The enemy you are tracking will be doing most of these things and will leave behind signs of having done so.

Let's live a day with an insurgent/terrorist/freedom fighter, or whatever one would call an enemy, to see what signs we can discover. He wakes up in the early morning. He will have slept somewhere, so look for an area of flattened grass. See Figure CCCH.10.01.09.

Smokers are a liability in a guerrilla war. The smell of tobacco smoke carries far in the bush (something you should always be on the lookout for), cigarettes glow in the dark (a dead giveaway), and, generally speaking, smokers are ill disciplined with their habit. Not only will they "light up" first thing in the morning, but they will also throw matches, cigarette butts, ash, cigarette paper, and bits of tobacco down without thinking. Chances are pretty good that in or close to the area where the enemy camped during the night you will find cigarette butts or matches. See Figure CCCH.10.01.10.

A good tracker can learn quite a bit from cigarette butts. The manufacturer's name on the cigarette might still be visible and could indicate a foreign make. A cigarette butt can indicate the age of a sign. Refer to the section on tracking gardens.

Remember, smoking is an addiction, and the smoker will not be able to go for very long without taking a smoke break. People also tend to smoke more when they are

Figure CCCH.10.01.10: Telltale signs of smokers.

Figure CCCH.10.01.11: Campfire signs. Be on the lookout for burnt pieces of wood or ashes from a fire. Attempts might be made to cover the ashes of a fire with soil. The heat remaining in the ashes might also provide information on how long ago the enemy was there. In addition, the area around a campfire is a good place to look for tracks and other signs.

under stress and become very irritable when they cannot smoke. Look for the signs of a smoker, and you will find a trail of cigarette detritus to follow.

During the night or perhaps during some break during the day, the enemy might make a small fire to heat some food or make tea or coffee or use a fire as protection from wild animals. During some stops soldiers will eat and discard fruit peels, sweet wrappers, and food or drink packaging. Soldiers are trained to bury waste, but often scavengers such as dogs, hyenas, baboons, jackals, civets,

Retained heat of coals / ashes can indicate age of sign.

Figure CCCH.10.01.12: Look for clues around campfires. It is a place around which people tend to relax and become careless.

Figure CCCH.10.01.13: With practice, a tracker can estimate the age of a campfire. (Photo courtesy M. Cowell)

Figure CCCH.10.01.15: Look for signs of fruit and vegetable peelings—especially those out of context. It is possible, however, that the person being tracked might be so hungry that he might eat those as well.

Figure CCCH.10.01.14: Even though attempts might be made to dispose of rubbish by burying it, scavengers often dig it up. Labels on food or drink packaging can often supply useful information, so it's important to read all discarded labels.

Figure CCCH.10.01.16: Toilet areas are sometimes poorly covered or are exposed by animals or weather. Sometimes they are not even covered at all—especially when the enemy is under pressure.

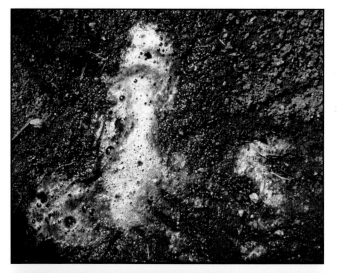

Figure CCCH.10.01.17: The smell of human excrement will attract dung beetles and flies.

and porcupines will dig up the discarded rubbish. See Figures CCCH.10.01.11 to CCCH.10.01.14.

Always evaluate signs in context. Fruit or vegetable peelings lying around in an urban environment might not be that unusual, but in the African bush they will be out of place or out of context. Fruit or vegetables not grown locally could be a sign of your enemy's presence.

Soldiers will wash and carry out daily ablutions, so be on the lookout for toilet areas. Again, most trained military personnel are trained to dig a hole when defecating and then cover it afterward. This is often not properly done and bits of toilet paper might be exposed. Animals might also dig up the toilet. The smell will attract dung beetles. The direction of dung beetle flight can lead the observant tracker to this sign. Be prepared to "smell out" signs of a toilet.

Examine toilet sites carefully. Look for clear tracks where the person has squatted to see if he was barefoot or wearing shoes or boots. Look to see if there is a distinctive tread pattern on the sole. A rock will often be used to sit on and left in position. The person might not have toilet paper and might use a stone or grass/leaves to clean himself. Keep a lookout for these as well.

All humans have to urinate daily, so the tracker needs to look for signs of this very human activity. Fresh urine creates frothy foam that subsides after a few minutes and leaves a wet patch. When this dries out, a filmy residue containing salts (mostly sodium chloride)

Figure CCCH.10.01.18: Determining the freshness of urine can indicate to the tracker how long ago the person was at that specific place. Top: This fresh urine patch is less than five minutes old. Note the foam. Centre: This urine patch is five to ten minutes old. Note the foam disappearing. Bottom: This urine patch is ninety minutes old. Urine takes on a fine crystalline appearance as it dries out. The crystals are made up of sodium chloride and urea.

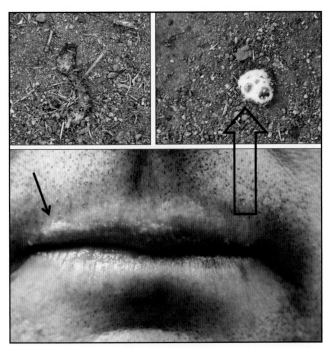

Figure CCCH.10.01.19: *If you are tracking an enemy who is well hydrated and still fresh, spittle sign will look like that shown in the top left. Someone who is exerting himself physically, has become tired and thirsty, will spit out saliva like that shown in the top right. This spittle is white and sticky and dries to a white paste around the edges of the mouth (above).*

Figure CCCH.10.01.20: *Mislaid ammunition can provide valuable intelligence. Check information on the base of the cartridge case. The manufacturer's stamp on the base can supply valuable information to the tracker such as the calibre and country of origin.*

remains. Urine also has a characteristic and quite strong odour when fresh. Butterflies will often be attracted to the moisture in urine patches.

Another human sign that might be left behind by an enemy is saliva (phlegm) or the "products" of a nose blow. Even a well-disciplined soldier will not think twice about hawking and getting rid of saliva or irritating phlegm. The type of spittle can also give an indication of the condition of the person who spat it out. The spittle of a well-hydrated person is bubbly but clear and watery. When a person is physically tired and thirsty, spittle becomes very white and viscous (sticky). The spittle of an individual with severe sinus or chest (lung) infections or a lung or stomach injury can be thick and yellowish or be bloodstained. Blowing of the nose directly onto the ground without using a handkerchief is also not an uncommon practice by some people. Look for fluids (urine, saliva, nasal mucus, blood, feces) when tracking and determine how old the sign is.

Water droplets spilled or splashed when washing, drinking, crossing a stream, filling water bottles, and so on are also useful indicators of the age of sign.

Be constantly on the lookout for equipment dropped or left behind. Clothing, rags, handkerchiefs, and other items of military equipment can be mislaid. Documents, maps, scraps of paper with information, and propaganda leaflets can provide important intelligence. Examine these for valuable information such as grid references of arms or food caches, rendezvous points, call signs, codes, names, places, plans, and so on.

Ammunition is often dropped by mistake. This can provide valuable clues as to the type of weapons carried and the country of manufacture. Always check the base of the cartridge case to determine its calibre and manufacturer. Dropped ammunition can also indicate whether it is of commercial or military origin, which can sometimes (but not always) draw a distinction between a poacher and a soldier. Poachers will often make use of military weapons whereas soldiers will not generally use commercial weapons.

Other signs to be on the lookout for are those indicating that the enemy might be "living off the land" to supplement meager rations. These might include harvesting wild fruit, fishing, robbing hives of honey (often trees will be chopped open with axes), and stealing eggs and fledglings from a bird's nest. If the enemy feels confident and plans on staying in an area for a while, he might even resort to setting snares or traps to catch food.

Always treat items of intrinsic value (watches, money, weapons, knives, compass, etc.) or items of souvenir or tactical value that have been dropped with suspicion, for they might be booby-trapped. Check the area around the item carefully before approaching or attempting to pick up the item.

Figure CCCH.10.01.21: Enemy insurgents, locals, and poachers living off the land may use traps or snares.

Thin wire attached to weapon and hidden from view attached to an explosive device buried under the ground or hidden in a cupboard. When the weapon is picked up, a trip wire detonates the charge.

Explosive device

Figure CCCH.10.01.23: Soldiers collect weapons as souvenirs, but be careful, for a weapon found lying around is likely to be booby-trapped.

Weapons are one of the favourite "baits" used in booby-traps. When the item is picked up, a tripwire leading to an explosive charge causes it to detonate. Take the necessary precautions to avoid serious injury or death. Refer to the section on mine and "booby-trap" awareness.

Washing and brushing teeth can leave telltale signs. The smell of soap, deodorants, and washing powder can carry in the bush, and soapsuds and bubbles can be washed downstream. Soap can also impart a milky

Figure CCCH.10.01.22: If you find items of souvenir, tactical, or intrinsic value, exercise caution. They may be booby-trapped.

Figure CCCH.10.01.24: Toothpaste freshly spat out has a similar look to urine but will have a distinctly different smell.

Figure CCCH.10.01.25: The alert posture of an animal such as that of this impala can warn the tracker of a human intruder or other danger. Note the intent stare at the intruder, the ears pricked and facing toward the intruder, the head held high, the body very erect, the nose lifted to catch scent, and the muscles tense. You can be sure if you see an animal behaving like this that it has seen a human intruder, a predator, or a potential territorial rival of the same species.

colour to water downstream. If someone brushes teeth and then rinses his mouth out, the toothpaste can leave a characteristic mark and smell on the ground.

When the enemy is moving through the bush, local wildlife can warn you of their presence. The expert tracker understands animal behaviour and knows how to interpret it. Let's discuss some of the warning signs.

In the African bush there are a few species of birds that give a clear warning of an intruder. The gray lourie, also known as the "go-away" bird or *kwêvoël,* generally sits on a high vantage point and gives the characteristic kwêêê call when it spots a predator or human. This can be infuriating to a hunter because the call will give your presence away. Guinea fowl and francolin will take raucous flight when disturbed by humans.

Most wild animals will adopt a very characteristic posture when spotting an intruder. Antelopes such as impalas, kudus, and bushbucks and primate species such as baboons and vervet monkeys will often raise an alarm by snorting, barking, or chattering. Foot stamping is also a common alarm signal used by certain antelopes.

Whereas some animals and birds will warn of an intruder by making a noise, other creatures will suddenly

Figure CCCH.10.01.26: This kudu has spotted a human intruder (the photographer). Note the body language that is characteristic of an animal facing potential danger.

Figure CCCH.10.01.27: Baboons and vervet monkeys are quick to give vocal alarms and will stare at human intruders.

become silent. Insects (like cicadas) and frogs will suddenly become silent when disturbed. Frogs and toads are often found concentrated around water and natural pans and are very noisy. If they suddenly become quiet, something has disturbed them.

Crocodiles have very acute senses and will quickly take to water when disturbed. All animals will run away or take flight if threatened. These should be warning signs to the tracker that they have been disturbed. Predator warnings are, of course, also important to the tracker who does not want to lead his men into a pride of hungry lions.

Figure CCCH.10.01.28: Sudden silence of cicadas or croaking frogs or toads can warn the tracker that something has disturbed them.

Figure CCCH.10.01.30: Blood sign includes the darker venous blood (top), brighter arterial blood (bottom right), and bright, frothy lung blood (bottom left).

Figure CCCH.10.01.29: If crocodiles suddenly take to the water, it is a sure sign that they have been disturbed.

Blood sign of a wounded enemy can also provide good information to the tracker. It is fairly easy to follow and can give an indication of the seriousness of the injury and condition of the enemy.

Blood sign can also sometimes give the tracker an indication of how long ago the enemy was there. Human blood clots in about five to seven minutes, so if it has not coagulated by the time you see it, it is a good indication that the enemy has been at that point less than seven minutes previously. The direction in which blood splashes will also indicate the direction the enemy took. The distance between drops can indicate how fast the person is moving. The tracker must be able to extract maximum information from even the smallest clue. For further information refer to the chapter on blood trailing.

One of the most valuable sources of information to the combat tracker are tracks, or spoor, which are defined as the imprint of a foot or footwear registered on a substrate. By being able to read and correctly interpret tracks, the tracker can gain the following information:

➤ the direction of travel

➤ the speed of travel

➤ the size of the person making the tracks

➤ the load a person was carrying (heavy or light)

➤ the number of enemy

➤ the activity at the time tracks were registered

➤ the physical and mental condition of the enemy

➤ the physical characteristics of the person (injured, disoriented)

➤ the thought processes (fear, anxiety)

➤ the position of the head

➤ the time the track was made

and so on . . .

As I've said several times, much information is telescoped through our feet onto the earth. Thought processes are put into action, and the way we stand,

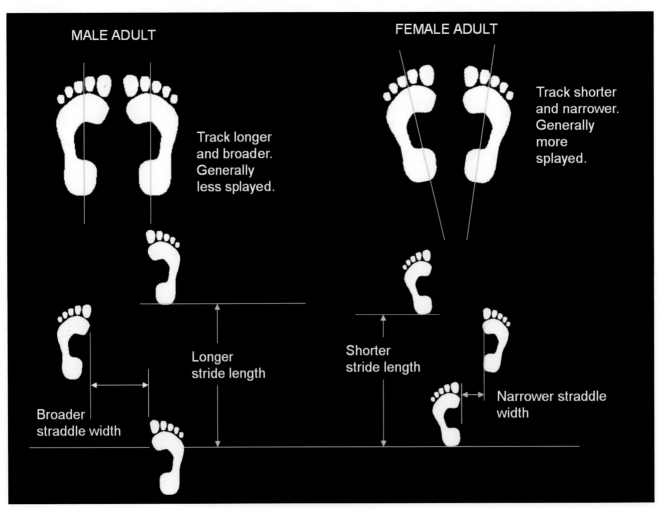

MALE ADULT

Track longer and broader. Generally less splayed.

Longer stride length

Broader straddle width

FEMALE ADULT

Track shorter and narrower. Generally more splayed.

Shorter stride length

Narrower straddle width

Figure CCCH.10.01.31: Difference between male and female adult human tracks.

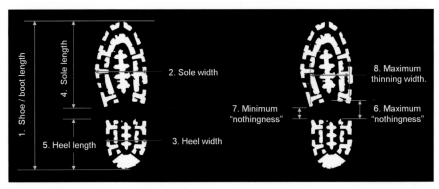

Figure CCCH.10.01.32: Recording track patterns.

walk, crouch, and run is a reflection of not only our physical actions but our thought processes. Let's begin by looking at a single track to see what information we can get out of it.

First, a track will tell us if a person is barefoot or wearing footwear. If barefoot, we will be able to see if the foot is normal or abnormal. Is there a scar underneath or a missing toe? We should also be able to ascertain whether it was made by an adult, youth, or a child; we should be able to see if it was made by a male or a female.

When footwear is worn, the track pattern, shape, and size of the shoe/boot can also supply valuable information. A barefoot track pattern is very distinctive and can identify individuals much like fingerprints can. The tracker should record track information by the process of "foot or track mapping." The information that should be recorded in order of priority is shown in Figure CCCH.10.01.32.

Record the pattern of the sole with a photograph or accurate sketch. Compare it to records of known enemy lug patterns. Indicate wear patterns as follows: Divide the sole and heel each into four quadrants and note down any wear or other abnormalities in each quadrant. Look at the example shown in Figure CCCH.10.01.33.

Walking gait pattern: If the substrate allows, record the stride length and straddle width of the particular individual when he is walking. With this knowledge, you will be able to determine at a later stage if the person is slowing down or speeding up.

Normal Stride Lengths for an Average Adult Man

➤ Walking slowly: 48–52 centimeters (18–20 inches)

➤ Walking normally: 53–59 centimeters (21–23 inches)

➤ Walking fast: 60–65 centimeters (24–26 inches)

➤ Jogging: 65–70 centimeters (27–29 inches)

➤ Running: 112–115 centimeters (44–47 inches)

➤ Sprinting: >115 centimeters (>47 inches)

When jogging, a full track may appear at times but there might also be tracks where the heel is not registered. The faster the jog, the more the person will rise up onto the toes. In a slow jog, the stride length may be shorter than in a fast walk. In a fast jog/slow run, the heel marks will register less frequently. The straddle width narrows. The track will register a disc/crumble. The stride length increases and the straddle width may decrease. The person runs on the toes. The track registers a dish/crumble. When sprinting, the stride length is maximum and the straddle width narrow. This person is running on his toes. The soil is displaced to the rear ("explode off"). The gait pattern can also tell you if the person is injured, lost, stumbling, or tired. See Figures CCCH.10.01.37 to CCCH.10.01.39.

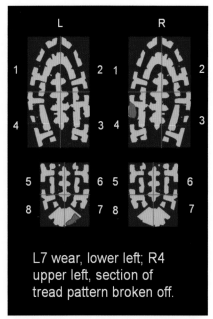

L7 wear, lower left; R4 upper left, section of tread pattern broken off.

Figure CCCH.10.01.33: Recording track pattern details. This means that in the lower left area of quadrant seven of the left foot there is a wear pattern and in the upper left area of quadrant four of the right foot there is a section of lug missing. This information should pinpoint an individual.

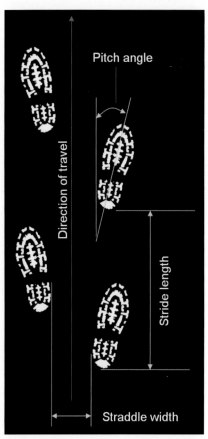

Figure CCCH.10.01.34: Walking gait dimensions.

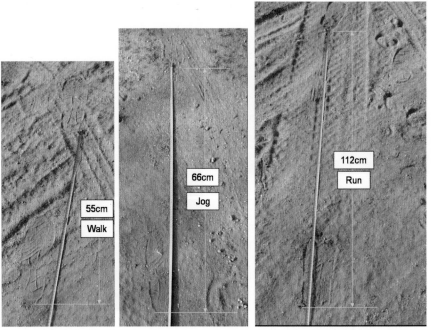

Figure CCCH.10.01.35: A comparison of measurements for walking, jogging, and running.

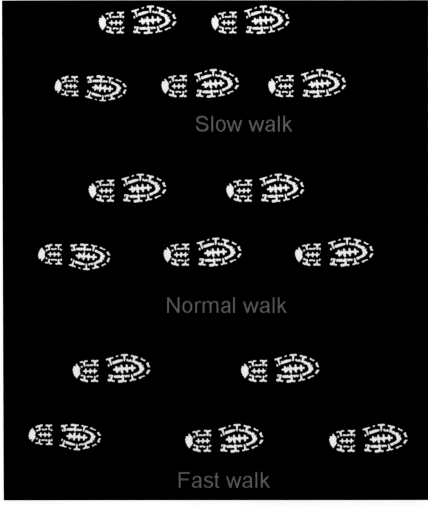

Figure CCCH.10.01.36

You can estimate the number of individuals in the group you are following using the following method. Look for a point in the terrain where the group is channeled into a line, such as along a game- or footpath. Take the length of the average pace and measure it along the ground next to the tracks (about 36 inches). Measure a box 18 inches wide by 36 inches long. Count all the tracks in the box and divide by a factor of 2 to give the number of people you are following. See Figure CCCH.10.01.40.

Resting places: To estimate the number of people being followed at resting spots, count the number of places at that spot and add two. We add two to account for sentries that are usually posted a distance away from where the remainder of the group is resting. Some more examples of interpreting track signs are shown in Figures CCCH.10.01.41 to CCCH.10.01.56.

Unless the substrate is ideally suited to registering tracks such as on a beach, in a dry riverbed, or on soils devoid of rocks or vegetation, the tracker might have to go on less obvious sign such as partial tracks or an occasional single track. If the enemy becomes aware of the fact that there is someone on his trail, he will take great pains to conceal his tracks or backtrack on his trail to ambush you, which is an aspect we will be looking at shortly.

Apart from tracks on the ground, the tracker must also be aware of what is known as "aerial spoor."

Figure CCCH.10.01.36: Comparison of gait patterns in different walking speeds. In a slow walk (top), the full track is shown and the stride length is short. The straddle width is wider than for a person running. The track will show a wave pressure release. In a normal walk (middle), the full track is registered and the stride lengthens. A double wave will be registered in the track. In a fast walk (bottom), the full track is registered and the stride lengthens even more. The heel is often dug in to provide purchase to increase forward momentum. A disc will be registered in the track. See Figure CCCH.10.01.36.

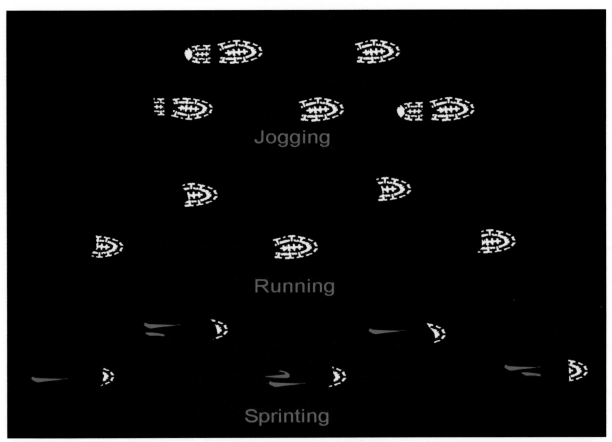

Figure CCCH.10.01.37: Comparison of pressure releases in a jog, run, and sprint.

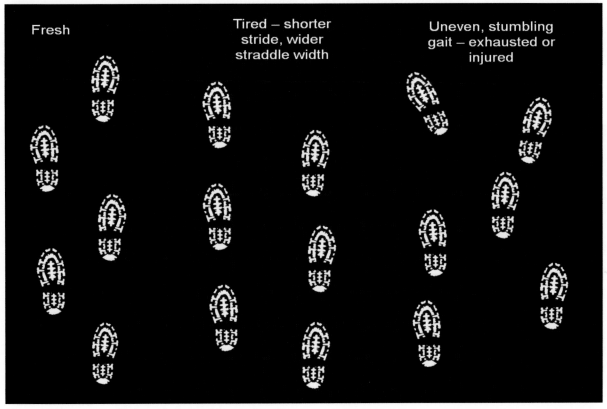

Figure CCCH.10.01.38: Much can be learned from gait patterns.

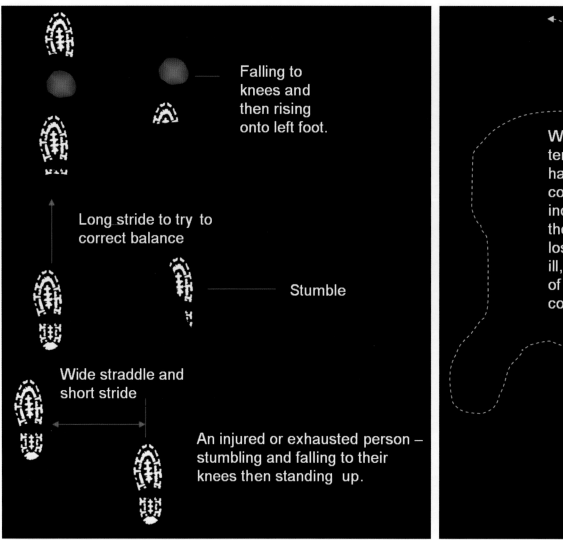

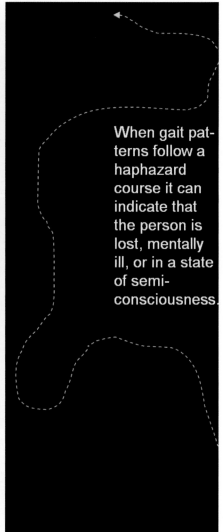

Falling to knees and then rising onto left foot.

Long stride to try to correct balance

Stumble

Wide straddle and short stride

An injured or exhausted person – stumbling and falling to their knees then standing up.

When gait patterns follow a haphazard course it can indicate that the person is lost, mentally ill, or in a state of semi-consciousness.

Figure CCCH.10.01.39: *The gait patterns of exhausted, injured, and lost individuals.*

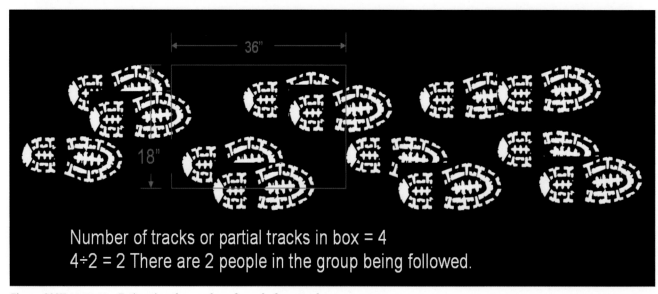

36"

18"

Number of tracks or partial tracks in box = 4
4÷2 = 2 There are 2 people in the group being followed.

Figure CCCH.10.01.40: *Estimating the number of people from tracks.*

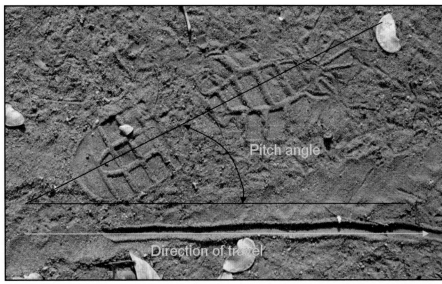

Figure CCCH.10.01.41: The track of a large (rather fat) adult man carrying a heavy load. The foot shows a large pitch angle that is indicative of a large person. The feet also become more splayed when carrying a heavy object in front. The wear pattern is indicated by the half-worn outer L1 and the half-worn outer L8. The heavier the object being carried in front, the greater the pitch angle.

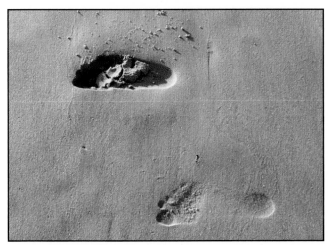

Figure CCCH.10.01.42: This track shows a person changing from a walk (lower track) to suddenly starting to run off. The upper track is deep just behind the toe area and the soil is mounded and displaced to the rear.

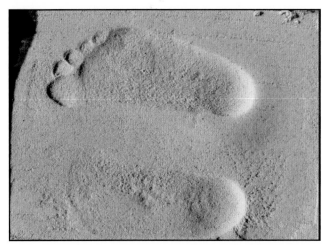

Figure CCCH.10.01.44: Looking up (more weight on the heels) and either carrying something heavy on the right side or displacing weight onto the right foot (as when resting in the standing position) for a moment.

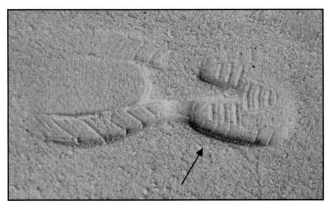

Figure CCCH.10.01.43: The track of someone without a load (right) and carrying a load (left). Note the deeper track impression in the heel area (arrow).

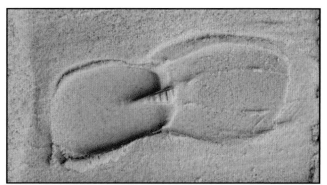

Figure CCCH.10.01.45: This track shows what is referred to as a wobble, which can indicate fatigue or injury.

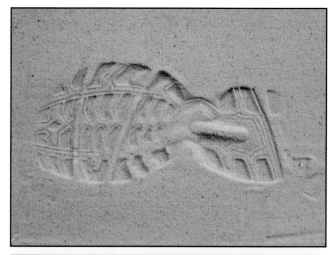

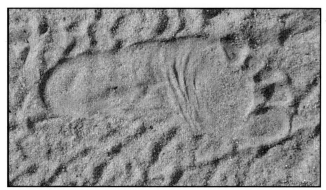

Figure CCCH.10.01.46: To the eye of the experienced tracker, this track indicates indecision.

Figure CCCH.10.01.49: The tracks of the same man, wearing the same footwear, and carrying the same load on different substrates show how the substrate can influence the appearance of the track.

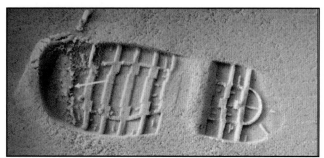

Figure CCCH.10.01.47: A $^1/_8$ disc indicates a slow speed walk. See arrow.

Figure CCCH.10.01.48: A cave-in indicates an abrupt turn to the right.

Figure CCCH.10.01.51: Apart from the tread pattern, this track has a very characteristic indicator known as an "indent." There is a cavity in the sole that is being filled as the track is registered in the soil. It might not be as easy to identify on a hard or nonhomogenous substrate such as gravelly soil or soil with small stones.

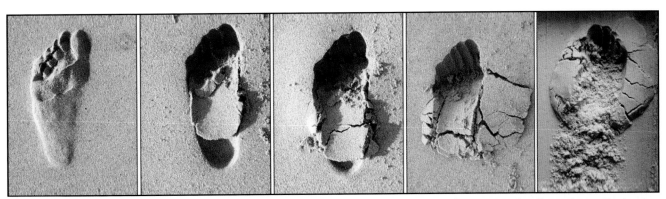

Figure CCCH.10.01.50: Notice in this sequence how the nature and shape of the track changes from a normal walk to a fast walk, slow jog, and run to a sudden "blast off" (left foot only shown). These tracks have been made on an ideal substrate; a more experienced eye will be needed to identify these same patterns on a more difficult substrate.

Figure CCCH.10.01.52: A partial track in grassy terrain.

Figure CCCH.10.01.54: On difficult tracking substrates, you might find few tracks and might have to look for more subtle signs like dislodged stones or small pebbles. The underside of pebbles and stones are usually darker, and they also leave a small crater where they were dislodged.

Figure CCCH.10.01.53: Tracks might not always be that clear to see. Can you see this one?

Figure CCCH.10.01.55: Do you see how easy it is to spot spoor through long grass from a plane?

Aerial spoor is swaths left in vegetation as it bends in the direction in which a person is walking. Aerial spoor is easy to see and generally just as easy to follow because the bent vegetation catches the light in such a way as to make its colour look different from surrounding vegetation. Some examples are shown above and to the left.

Broken spider webs can also indicate that someone or something has passed by. Spiders will quickly set about repairing broken webs, so to find a web broken or being repaired would be indicative of having been recently damaged. See Figure CCCH.10.01.56. Humans, animals, birds, and machines can break webs. Look for associated evidence to confirm that the web was broken by a human; otherwise, you might be led off on a wild goose chase.

Being Aware of Mines and Booby-Traps

During the past twenty years, more than one hundred million land mines have been placed in more than fifty countries, and numbers are increasing with each new local war. Major clearing operations cannot prevent the land-mine epidemic from accelerating. In

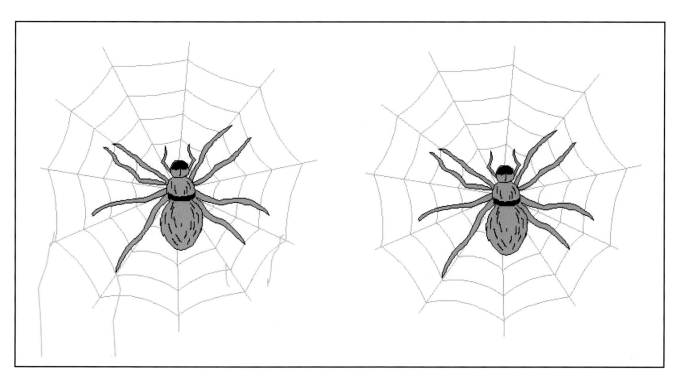

Figure CCCH.10.01.56: Spider webs can be an indicator of passage.

1993, one hundred thousand mines were cleared worldwide, whereas two million more were placed. The population at risk is mainly rural farming families in low-income countries. Surveys in mine-infested countries indicate mortality rates of civilian mine victims as high as 40 to 50 percent, with most fatalities occurring before the victim reaches a hospital.

The typical victims of land mines are local farmers and children. Military personnel are also at high risk during the course of military operations. Whereas antipersonnel mines are designed to incapacitate or cause serious injury by blowing off a foot or hand or being wounded by fragments, about 20 percent die from mine blasts or ensuing complications. About 81 percent of these die at the scene of the explosion. For example, for every 1,000 people injured by land-mine blasts, 200 people will be fatally wounded, and of those, 162 will die on the scene. With these sobering statistics, the operational tracker should be very aware of the dangers of mines.

Mines and booby-traps are designed to kill, incapacitate, slow down, and demoralize. There are basically two types of land mines: those designed to kill or wound people, which are referred to as antipersonnel mines, and those for destroying vehicles, which are referred to as antitank mines.

The most prevalent of the conventional land mines are the so-called blast mines, which are normally buried by hand or placed on the ground. They rely upon the energy released by the explosive charge to harm or destroy their target. The injuries they produce result primarily from the explosion, but secondary fragmentation injuries are possible as the mine casing or surrounding dirt or gravel is blasted at the victim.

Booby-traps are improvised explosive devices. The combat tracker must be especially aware of mines and booby-traps. He must have a knowledge of their workings and how they are employed. We will begin by looking at antipersonnel mines.

The enemy will lay antipersonnel mines at key points, such as along prominent game paths/tracks/roads, at water points, in buildings, and virtually any place where he thinks you are likely to travel. Antitank mines are usually planted on a road or track where the wheels of a heavy vehicle are likely to run over and detonate it. All mines consist of an explosive and a trigger or igniter mechanism to explode the detonator, which, in turn, detonates the main charge.

You Don't Want to Become a Statistic!

Antipersonnel mines cause injury through two primary mechanisms. The first is a blast without fragmentation. (For example, an AP mine such as a PMN that consists of a large charge in a lightweight container.) When the mine detonates, there are few metal or other fragments. Injury is caused primarily due to blast of the explosive charge. The second is a blast accompanied by fragments. (In this case, you might have a smaller charge located in a metal housing—POM-Z.) When this mine detonates, many metal fragments are propelled at high velocity, and injury is caused primarily due to fragments. Some of the most common antipersonnel mines found today are illustrated in Figure CCCH.10.01.59.

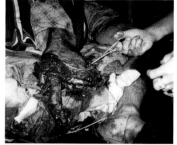
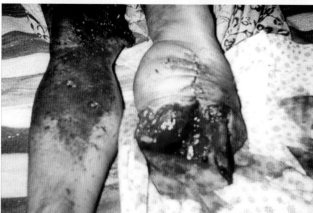

Figure CCCH.10.01.57: Antipersonnel mines are deadly. The combat tracker must be aware of mines and how to avoid them. (Photo courtesy of 0grish.com)

Figure CCCH.10.01.58: Antipersonnel mine injuries. (Photo courtesy of 0grish.com)

Mines and booby-traps can be set off by a number of methods. These include direct pressure, pull, pressure release, electrical, or chemical. Signs to look out for:

➤ Disturbed soil

➤ Signs or sounds of digging

➤ Greaseproof wrappers or packaging

➤ Tripwires

➤ Vegetation or obstacles used to "channel" you in a certain direction.

➤ Objects that might attract your attention and induce you to approach them or pick them up such as weapons, equipment, food, documents, etc.

➤ Marks on trees, marks on the ground, and grass tied in knots all might be signals warning other insurgents of the presence of mines or booby-traps.

Exercise Extreme Caution When:

➤ Walking along bush paths or tracks or on the verge of roads. These are some of the favourite places to plant antipersonnel mines.

➤ Collecting water from an isolated point such as a borehole, dam, well, or reservoir. Again these are favourite places to plant mines.

➤ You feel you are being channeled either by natural vegetation, the lay of the land, or by introduced obstacles to use a certain route.

➤ You become aware of the fact that the enemy knows he is being followed.

➤ You spot objects of interest such as enemy weapons, uniforms, ammunition, or any other equipment. Be careful as this might be the bait used to lure you to a specific point. Approach these objects with great caution using a bayonet or sharp stick to prod under the soil at a shallow angle to check for AP (antipersonnel) mines and be on the lookout for tripwires and scatter mines that might be lying camouflaged on the surface.

Figures CCCH.10.01.61 to CCCH.10.01.71 illustrate some favourite spots for laying mines and setting booby-traps.

Water points are one of the favourite areas to mine or booby-trap, and all paths

The PMN mine contains a large amount of explosive, and the injuries it inflicts are often fatal. It is designed in such a way that it is practically impossible to neutralize. As a safety precaution for those laying this mine, a 15- to 20-minute delay mechanism is activated when the mine is armed. Buried underground.

Originally developed in World War II, the PMD-6 antipersonnel mine is a rudimentary pressure-activated blast device in a wooden box. It has been widely used in Cambodia and Angola. As wood rots, the mine mechanisms may shift, and the device often sets itself off or becomes inoperative. Buried underground.

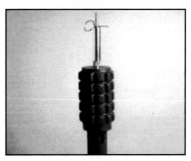

There are numerous varaitions of the PMR-2A or POMZ-2 antipersonnel stake mines, which are generally planted in clusters or rows above ground of at least four units and are set off by an intricate system of tripwires.

This Vietnamese antipersonnel mine is about the size of a tennis ball, and can be mounted on a stake for use above ground with a tripwire or buried just below the surface and set off by pressure.

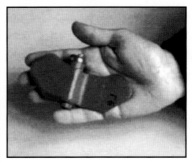

Widely used in Afghanistan, the Soviet PFM-1 scatterable pressure-sensitive blast mine is also known as the "butterfly mine" because of its shape, which unfortunately attracts children who think it is a toy. It has been produced in various shades of brown, green, and white. The PFM-1S version of this mine is one of the rare designs which include a self-destruct mechanism. It explodes 24 hours after deployment. Lies on top of the ground or just under surface litter.

Figure CCCH.10.01.59: Commonly used antipersonnel mines.

The MON-50 antipersonnel mine is a Soviet version of the American M-18 Claymore, a directional fragmentation mine. The curved plate is filled with pellets or projectiles in front of the explosive charge. It can be mounted against a round surface such as a tree or can be placed on a small stand-alone stake. Preformed metal fragments of selected shapes and sizes are shot out by the blast at a high velocity over a predetermined arc. Sometimes described as the military equivalent of the sawn-off shotgun, the widely copied American M-18 Claymore mine contains 700 steel balls and can kill targets up to 50 meters away. Other types can kill people as far away as 200 meters. Directional fragmentation mines are often planted around foxholes or used against convoys, and can sometimes be activated by a simple remote control switch.

The irregular shape and small size (about 9 cm diameter) of the BPD-SB-33 scatterable antipersonnel mine make it particularly hard to locate. A hydraulic antishock device ensures that it cannot be detonated by explosions or artificial pressure. It is also exceptionally light, and can thus be carried and deployed in extremely large numbers by helicopters.

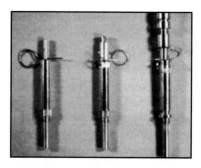

Three types of igniters, which may be used with tripwires or with pressure-activated systems.

The OZM-4 is a metallic bounding fragmentation mine. A bounding fragmentation mine is designed to kill the person who sets it off and to injure anybody nearby by propelling fragments. The cylindrical mine body is initially located in a short pot or barrel assembly; activation detonates a small explosive charge that projects the mine body upward. As it "bounds" into the air, the mine is activated by an anchor cable secured to the barrel assembly which remains on the ground; the cable pulls a pin from the fuse on the mine's body. The resulting blast scatters fragments, some of which may be preformed, over a much wider radius and area than would be possible with a surface or buried mine of similar size.

Figure CCCH.10.01.60: Commonly used antipersonnel mines.

ON BUSH ROADS

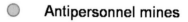

Antitank (vehicle) mines   Antipersonnel mines

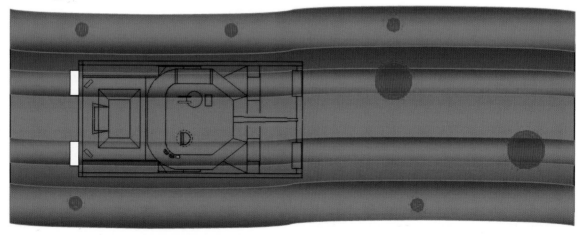

Figure CCCH.10.01.61: Antitank mines are usually planted along the tracks left by vehicle wheels, whilst antipersonnel mines are placed on the verges of the road where pedestrians usually walk or where soldiers will alight from a vehicle.

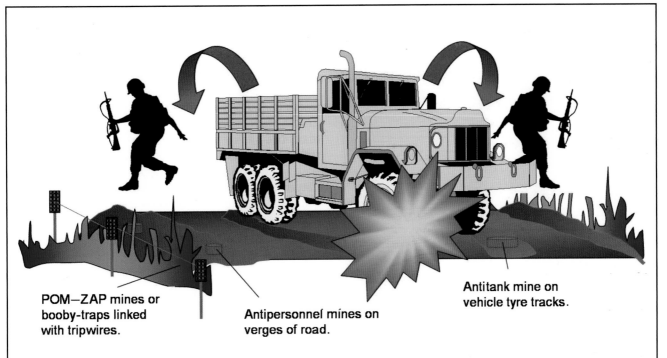

POM—ZAP mines or
booby-traps linked
with tripwires.

Antipersonnel mines on
verges of road.

Antitank mine on
vehicle tyre tracks.

Figure CCCH.10.01.62: Antitank and antipersonnel mines are often used together. If a convoy drives into an ambush or a vehicle detonates a land mine, the soldiers jump off (debus) to take cover. They then detonate AP mines or booby-traps hidden along the verges of the road.

Figure CCCH.10.01.63: Bush tracks are favourite spots for laying land mines.

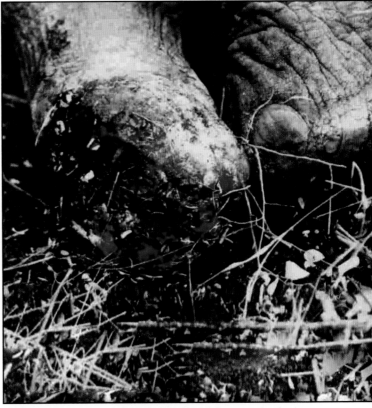

Figure CCCH.10.01.64: Wild animals often fall prey to land mines. The author shot this elephant after an antipersonnel mine had blown off its foot.

WATER POINTS

Figure CCCH.10.01.65: Water is a favourite spot for laying land mines.

leading to and areas around water should be regarded as suspect. See Figure CCCH.10.01.65. Water can also be purposely poisoned or contaminated with human waste or a carcass of a dead animal. Trackers sometimes have to replenish their own water from natural sources, and if they cannot use water because it's poisoned or contaminated, it can delay the tracking operation.

Antipersonnel mines or booby-traps are often placed at doorway entrances (under a mat, buried, or a tripwire strung across the door entrance), under windows, or around walls. If searching for mines in an area, use a bayonet or sharply pointed stick to feel for buried mines. See Figures CCCH.10.01.67 and CCCH.10.01.68.

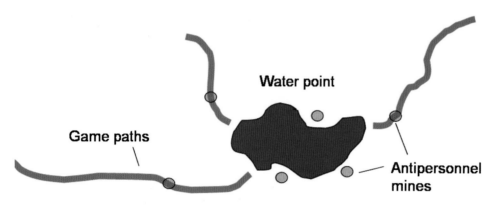

FOOT PATHS AND GAME TRAILS

Figure CCCH.10.01.66: Game paths are very likely choices to bury or scatter mines or for tripwires to be erected above surface mines. In this photo a person is channeled onto the track by the vegetation, irrespective of which direction he approaches (arrows). Mines can then be strategically buried or tripwires erected as illustrated. Tripwires are very thin and are difficult to spot, especially under low-light conditions.

The safest way of clearing or checking an area for mines is with a mine detector. See Figure CCCH.10.01.69. That is if you have one, know how to use it, and know what to do when mines are found. Older mine detectors worked by detecting metal underground. Newer mines are made of plastic, so state-of-the-art mine detectors now work on density as well as metal content. Sometimes a mine detector is a luxury and not always available.

Many booby-traps consist of an explosive charge, an electrical detonator, batteries, and wires to connect it. Observing any of these components should immediately arouse your suspicion. Booby-traps are activated by completing an electrical circuit. Some examples of the "triggers" used to complete a circuit to detonate an explosive charge are illustrated in Figures CCCH.10.01.72 to CCCH.10.01.75.

There Are Thousands of Variations on These Themes

Some examples of improvised booby-traps are illustrated in Figures CCCH.10.01.70 to CCCH.10.01.79. Improvised Explosive Devices (IEDs) can also be set off remotely with radio transmitters and cell phones.

Land mines and booby-traps are one of the scourges of the twentieth century. When army engineers lay mines, they plot the minefields so that the mines can be removed at some later date. Unfortunately, unconventional armies worldwide and some regular forces have sown mines indiscriminately. The result is that civilian casualties have been much higher than military ones. Figure CCCH.10.01.81 indicates the threats posed by land mines worldwide.

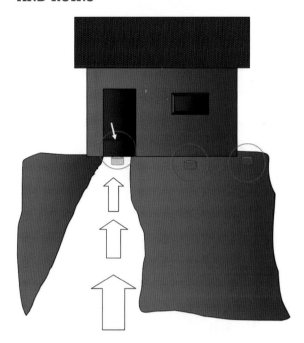

IN AND AROUND HOUSES, HUTS, AND RUINS

Figure CCCH.10.01.67: Always clear a path to an entrance to make sure it is clear of mines—especially if you believe that the enemy knows he is being followed.

Figure CCCH.10.01.68: Searching for mines. Insert a sharply pointed stick at a shallow angle in the soil. If you do not feel anything, move a little forward. Continue. If you feel an object under the soil, STOP! Don't apply force. SLOWLY and carefully remove the soil around the buried object to expose it. If it is a mine or looks suspicious, mark it and leave it for the engineers to come and lift. Don't attempt to do so yourself if you are not trained.

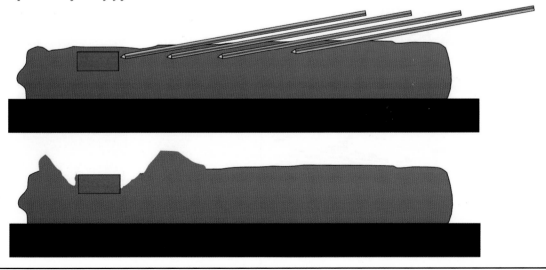

When inside a hut or house, be careful when opening windows, doors, and cupboards. Always check for tripwires. Don't pick up anything alluring or enticing such as food, drinks (which may be poisoned), equipment, and binoculars without checking to make sure that they have not been booby-trapped. Remember that some booby-traps are activated by a pressure release switch, so the mere act of lifting an object can detonate an explosive device.

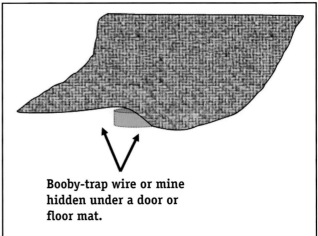

Booby-trap wire or mine hidden under a door or floor mat.

Figure CCCH.10.01.70: If there is a mat at the entrance to the door of the hut or one inside the hut, lift it carefully to check for a wire that might detonate a booby-trap. Check to make sure there is not a mine buried under the mat.

Figure CCCH.10.01.69: Using a mine detector.

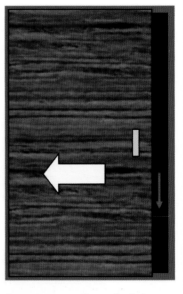

Tripwire visible behind a door opened slightly to check.

Figure CCCH.10.01.71: When opening a door, check for any tripwires before opening it fully.

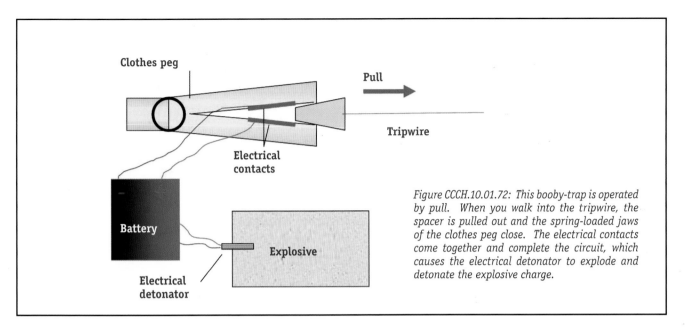

Clothes peg

Pull

Tripwire

Electrical
contacts

Battery

Explosive

Electrical
detonator

Figure CCCH.10.01.72: This booby-trap is operated by pull. When you walk into the tripwire, the spacer is pulled out and the spring-loaded jaws of the clothes peg close. The electrical contacts come together and complete the circuit, which causes the electrical detonator to explode and detonate the explosive charge.

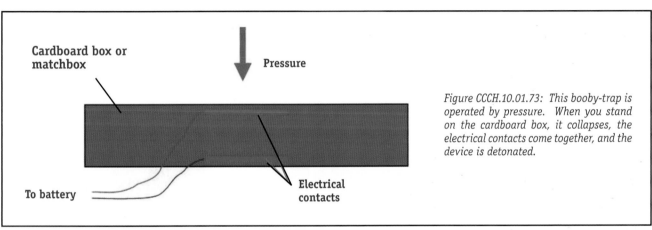

Cardboard box or
matchbox

Pressure

To battery

Electrical
contacts

Figure CCCH.10.01.73: This booby-trap is operated by pressure. When you stand on the cardboard box, it collapses, the electrical contacts come together, and the device is detonated.

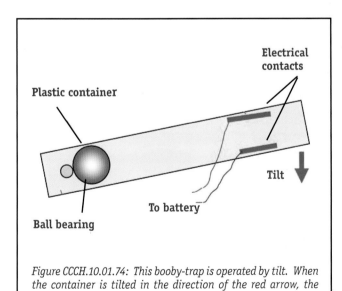

Electrical
contacts

Plastic container

Tilt

To battery

Ball bearing

Figure CCCH.10.01.74: This booby-trap is operated by tilt. When the container is tilted in the direction of the red arrow, the ball bearing runs down the plastic container to make contact with the two contacts. When that happens, it completes the circuit and detonates the explosive.

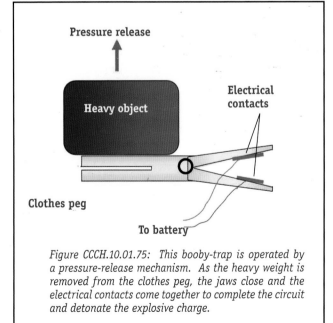

Pressure release

Heavy object

Electrical
contacts

Clothes peg

To battery

Figure CCCH.10.01.75: This booby-trap is operated by a pressure-release mechanism. As the heavy weight is removed from the clothes peg, the jaws close and the electrical contacts come together to complete the circuit and detonate the explosive charge.

USING HAND GRENADES

Tripwire

Grenade inside tin
can or pipe

Cans containing grenades hidden in grass next to path

Figure CCCH.10.01.76: Safety pins are removed, but the levers are kept depressed as the grenades are inserted into empty tin cans or plastic pipes. The tripwire is strung across a path, and when someone walks into the tripwire, it pulls the grenades out of the holders and causes them to explode.

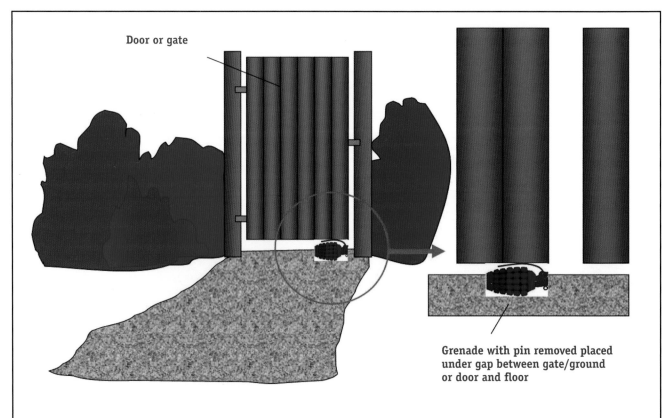

Door or gate

Grenade with pin removed placed
under gap between gate/ground
or door and floor

Figure CCCH.10.01.77: The safety pin is removed from a grenade, and it is then placed below a door or gate with the lever held in place by the door or gate. When the door/gate is opened, the lever flies off and the grenade explodes.

Sharpened stakes are inserted into a hole in the ground. The tips are smeared with excrement. The opening is camouflaged. When someone steps on the "lid" it gives way and the foot is impaled.

In this trap sharpened stakes in the side of the pit make it difficult to withdraw the foot. These simple traps are easy to make but very effective. Materials are readily available.

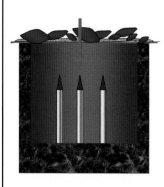

Figure CCCH.10.01.78: Sharpened stakes used as booby-traps.

1.) Electric globe is broken to expose the filament

2.) The broken globe with exposed filament is inserted into a light fitting

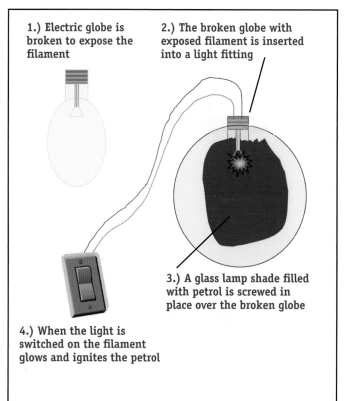

3.) A glass lamp shade filled with petrol is screwed in place over the broken globe

4.) When the light is switched on the filament glows and ignites the petrol

Figure CCCH.10.01.79: The design of a booby-trap is limited only by the imagination of the one setting it. Here an electric light bulb is used as an igniter to ignite a lamp shade filled with petrol.

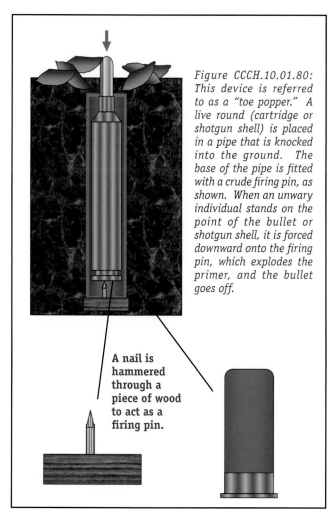

Figure CCCH.10.01.80: This device is referred to as a "toe popper." A live round (cartridge or shotgun shell) is placed in a pipe that is knocked into the ground. The base of the pipe is fitted with a crude firing pin, as shown. When an unwary individual stands on the point of the bullet or shotgun shell, it is forced downward onto the firing pin, which explodes the primer, and the bullet goes off.

A nail is hammered through a piece of wood to act as a firing pin.

Mine Trauma Statistics

➤ Fragmentation mines cause a higher rate of critical area injuries (head and torso injuries) compared with blast mines.

➤ The rate of infectious complications was significantly higher in blast mine injuries compared with fragmentation mine injuries.

➤ Anatomical and physiological severity of fragmentation mine injuries is significantly higher than the severity of blast mine injuries.

➤ Mortality rate is higher and the effect of prehospital resuscitation less for patients injured by fragmentation mines.

➤ Antipersonnel mines result in amputation injuries 44.5 percent of the time (42 percent are upper limb amputations and 58 percent are lower limb amputations).

➤ Fatality rate is significantly higher in amputees with fragment injuries than in amputees without such injuries. In 7.2 percent of amputees with associated fragment injuries, there are deteriorating physiological indicators during evacuation, whereas most amputees without fragment injuries show improved physiological scores during the prehospital transit period.

➤ Fragmentation mines in general cause injuries that are more difficult to treat.

➤ Eighty-eight percent of mine incident fatalities occur before admission to a hospital.

➤ Good first-aid trauma care at the scene of the mine incident can reduce mortality from 40 percent to 12 percent.

The information given so far is more than adequate for combat tracking and for search-and-rescue operations. More detailed information is necessary for "forensic" tracking where one is trailing a poacher or a fugitive from the law. This will be described later on under the relevant headings.

Tracking and Countertracking

A fugitive, whether he is a soldier, poacher, criminal, or terrorist insurgent will attempt to evade his pursuers. Depending on the time he has available and on his level of

skill, the fleeing fugitive will take great pains to delay or throw off his pursuers by hiding signs of his passage and by making it as difficult as possible to follow his trail. Should you ever find yourself in an escape-and-evade situation, you could use some of the following techniques.

➤ Antitracking techniques

➤ Countertracking

➤ Sign reduction

➤ Speed and distance

Antitracking and Sign Reduction

Antitracking uses methods of passive evasion whereas countertracking employs active persuasion not to follow. Let us assume for this section that we are the ones being followed. Put yourself in your enemies' shoes. To make things as difficult as possible for your pursuers, try the following methods. Use your imagination.

Avoid the Obvious

If you do the unexpected, like taking the less likely or less obvious route, the tracker will constantly have to double-check himself, and that will slow him up. It might take you a bit longer to do the less obvious, but it is always more difficult and more time-consuming for the ones following to figure out your choices. See Figure CCCH.10.01.82.

Avoid Regular Routine

If you are predictable, you make the trackers' job easier. Don't always do things at the same time and in the same way. If the tracker can establish that you are sticking to a routine, he can preempt your next move.

Use animals to cover your tracks. Walking ahead of animals, such as a herd of cattle, horses, goats, sheep, or even large herds of wild species such as buffaloes will help obliterate or mask your tracks. See Figure CCCH.10.01.83.

Brush out Your Tracks with Hats, Blankets, Neck Scarves, or Branches

An average tracker will quickly see this ruse. Be careful to eliminate the drag marks of

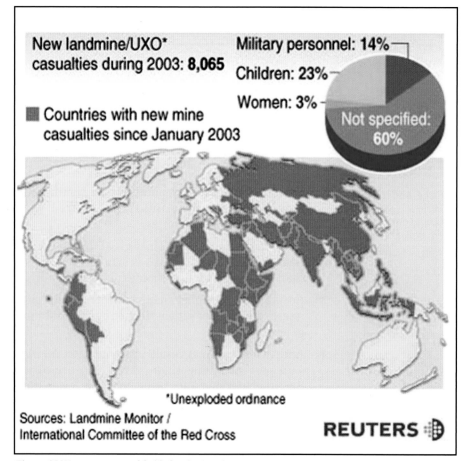

New landmine/UXO* casualties during 2003: **8,065**

Military personnel: 14%
Children: 23%
Women: 3%
Not specified: 60%

■ Countries with new mine casualties since January 2003

*Unexploded ordnance

Sources: Landmine Monitor / International Committee of the Red Cross

REUTERS

Figure CCCH.10.01.81: Worldwide land-mine threats. (Landmine and Cluster Munition Monitor by the International Committee of the Red Cross)

whatever you are using to wipe away your tracks, or you will have created an easy trail to follow. See Figure CCCH.10.01.84.

Use Streams/Rivers/Roadways/Railways to Cover Your Spoor

Walking in streams, small rivers, along the stone bed of railroad tracks, on the tracks themselves, or on tarred roads will cover your tracks. When walking in streams, the bottom, if it is muddy, might be churned up. This will discolour the water downstream with suspended silt. It is better to choose a stream with a rocky or gravel bottom. When exiting the water, the dripping water will create sign, but it will take time for your pursuers to find your exit point, so it will buy you time. Don't use water, roads, or railroad tracks for a long time because these are places the enemy will look for sign. See Figures CCCH.10.01.85 to CCCH.10.01.87.

Choose Rocky Terrain to Walk Across

Walk across stretches of rock, where there is scattered rock, or from rock to rock. A good tracker will circle the rocky area to pick up your tracks, but this will take time and slow your pursuers. See Figure CCCH.10.01.89.

Move in the Rain if Possible

While it's not very comfortable, walking in the rain is an excellent way of washing out your tracks and making it very difficult for trackers to follow you. If you see heavy weather approaching, head for it. The heavier the rain, the better. Try to avoid leaving tracks in deep mud as some of your tracks might remain after the rain has passed. See Figure CCCH.10.01.90.

Hiding Your Scent

If dogs are on your tracks, use tear-gas powder, pepper spray, pepper, or powdered chilies laced with ammonia to hide your scent. See Figure CCCH.10.01.91. You can also walk in water or smear yourself with animal dung to mask your scent and confuse the dog. Walking in rain will wash away your scent.

Avoid using strong scented or strong smelling products. Tobacco products have strong, distinctive smells and will be quickly detected in the bush. Any scented products such as deodorants, shaving cream, aftershave lotions, sunscreens, medical ointments, soaps, and toothpaste can also be smelled a long way off in the wild. See Figure CCCH.10.01.92.

Start a Bushfire

This is a desperate and dangerous option but worth it if your life is threatened. Head INTO the wind and start the fire behind you. The wind will carry the fire quickly toward your pursuers but will move slower in the direction you are headed, which will allow you to move ahead of it. See Figure CCCH.10.01.93.

The easiest and most likely (obvious)

The more difficult and less obvious

Figure CCCH.10.01.82: Don't take the most obvious route if you are being tracked.

Figure CCCH.10.01.83: Walking ahead of a herd of cattle or other animals is an effective way of hiding your tracks.

Figure CCCH.10.01.84: Erasing tracks with branches. (Photo courtesy M. Cowell)

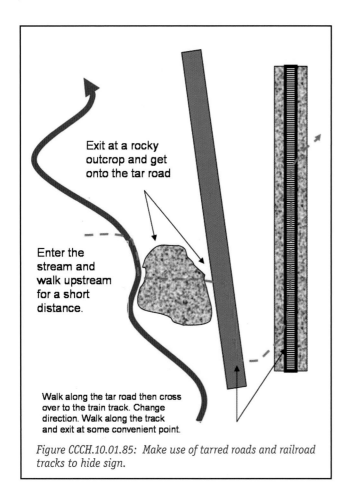

Exit at a rocky outcrop and get onto the tar road

Enter the stream and walk upstream for a short distance.

Walk along the tar road then cross over to the train track. Change direction. Walk along the track and exit at some convenient point.

Figure CCCH.10.01.85: Make use of tarred roads and railroad tracks to hide sign.

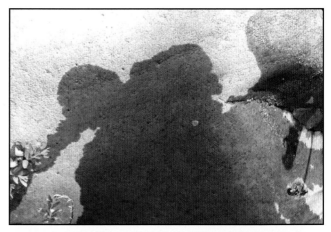

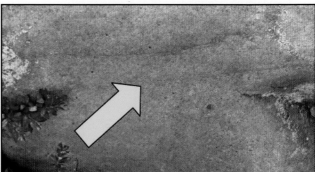

Figure CCCH.10.01.86: If you exit onto rocks from a stream, there will be splashes of water left on the rocks. If your followers are close behind, this will surely indicate your passage. If, however, your followers are quite a way behind, this sign will evaporate quickly on a hot day.

Figure CCCH.10.01.87: This is a good place to cross, and one that will leave little sign. Crossing at the lower waterfall would be dangerous since one could easily slip on the rocks and fall over the edge.

Figure CCCH.10.01.88: Avoid using rivers or streams as an axis of travel as this is one of the areas that the enemy will search for you.

Figure CCCH.10.01.89: It is easier to hide tracks by traversing rocky terrain. Try not to dislodge smaller rocks, for this will leave sign of your passing. (Photo courtesy M. Cowell)

Figure CCCH.10.01.90: Rain helps to obliterate tracks.

Figure CCCH.10.01.93: If you start a bushfire to throw off pursuers, make sure of the direction of the wind.

WIND DIRECTION

YOUR PURSUERS

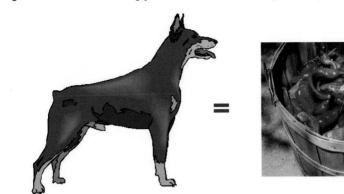

Figure CCCH.10.01.91: Hiding your scent when tracker dogs are on your spoor.

$$= \quad + NH_3$$

Adapt Your Footwear

Use the same boots as your enemy, wear smooth-soled shoes, car-tyre sandals, or if your enemy goes barefoot do the same. See Figures CCCH.10.01.93 to CCCH.10.01.95

Walk on the Side of the Foot or Use Foot Coverings

This leaves no heel or toe marks. See Figures CCCH.10.01.96 and CCCH.10.01.97.

Walk Backward

This will fool an inexperienced tracker for a while. A good tracker will discover the deception fairly soon, but again it will buy you needed time to put more distance between you and your pursuers.

Use a Stick to Bend Grass/Bushes Back after They Have Been Disturbed

When walking through tall grass and vegetation, you leave a visible swath; this is known as an aerial spoor. The vegetation can be bent back to its approximate original position with a stick. This is time-consuming and quickly spotted by a good tracker.

Move through Villages or Densely Populated Areas to Lose Your Tracks

If you can mingle with the local population, do so. The bigger the crowds, the better. It will be extremely difficult to differentiate or even find your tracks amongst all the others.

Abrupt Changes of Direction

This is an effective technique especially if done on hard or rocky ground. A good tracker, using the lost spoor technique, will eventually find the spoor again, but it will result in a delay.

Figure CCCH.10.01.92: Avoid using strong-smelling or scented products.

Figure CCCH.10.01.94: Adapting your footwear. Sandals, made from old car and truck tyres, are a popular form of footwear in rural Africa and are also worn by insurgents and poachers. They are durable, thorn-proof, and weatherproof. In short, they are excellent footwear.

Figure CCCH.10.01.95: Another trick is to tape a shoe sole facing backward onto your footwear, giving the impression that you are walking in the opposite direction. A good tracker will pick this up after a while, but, again, it will buy you time to put distance between you and your pursuers. (Photo courtesy M. Cowell)

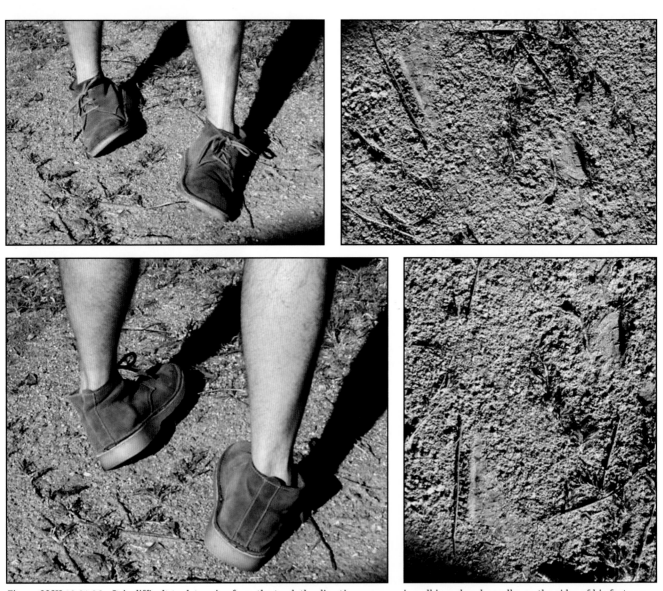

Figure CCCH.10.01.96: It is difficult to determine from the track the direction a person is walking when he walks on the sides of his feet.

Countertracking

Countertracking is an offensive tactic that results in an injury or death (or the fear of injury or death) to members of a pursuing tracking team. It is used against trackers to delay or abort a follow-up. Should a member of a tracking team be killed or injured by a countertracking tactic employed by the fugitive, a medical evacuation will have to be arranged. The benefits to the fugitive include:

➤ The follow-up will slow down or stop all together.

➤ The number of individuals killed or wounded will reduce the strength of the tracking team.

➤ The action will have a demoralizing effect on the pursuers, or it may evoke an angry response that will result in the pursuers becoming careless or making rash decisions.

➤ The person hunted might be able to determine the exact position of the pursuers by the sound of an explosion or the point of descent of a medevac helicopter.

Figure CCCH.10.01.97: Spoor can be made more difficult to follow by wrapping the feet or footwear with cloth, sacking, or animal skins. (Photo courtesy M. Cowell)

Booby-Trap/Ambush Your Trail

When you know you are being followed, you can look for suitable terrain, double back, and ambush your pursuers. See Figure CCCH.10.01.98.

Spoor Reduction Tactics

Split up/bombshell/circle back/gather at RV. If you are in a group and are being followed, you can make things difficult for your pursuers by getting members of your group to split away one at a time or "bomb shelling" simultaneously with each individual heading in a different direction. Arrange beforehand to meet up at a prearranged rendezvous point (RV). See Figures CCCH.10.01.99 and CCCH.10.01.100.

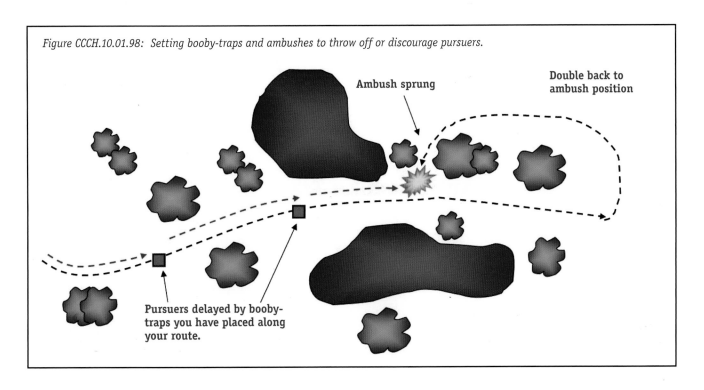

Figure CCCH.10.01.98: Setting booby-traps and ambushes to throw off or discourage pursuers.

Ambush sprung

Double back to ambush position

Pursuers delayed by booby-traps you have placed along your route.

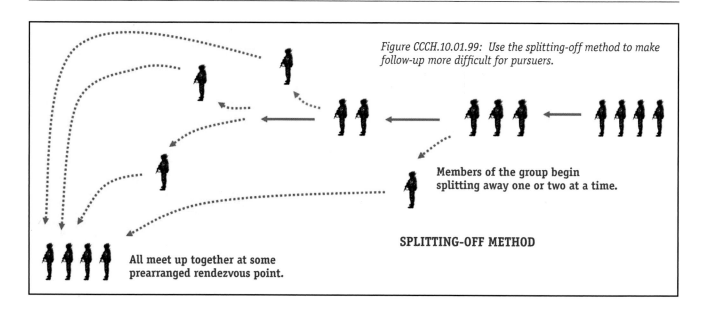

Figure CCCH.10.01.99: Use the splitting-off method to make follow-up more difficult for pursuers.

Members of the group begin splitting away one or two at a time.

SPLITTING-OFF METHOD

All meet up together at some prearranged rendezvous point.

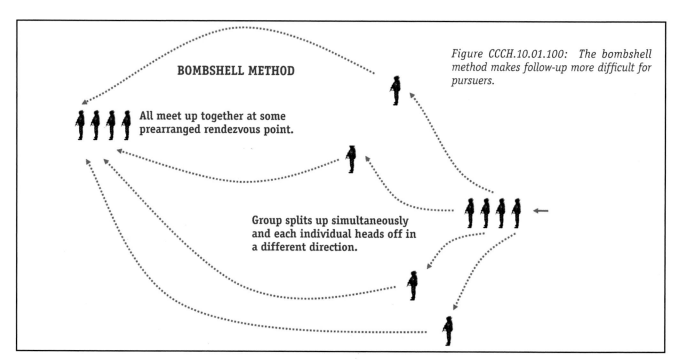

Figure CCCH.10.01.100: The bombshell method makes follow-up more difficult for pursuers.

BOMBSHELL METHOD

All meet up together at some prearranged rendezvous point.

Group splits up simultaneously and each individual heads off in a different direction.

Antipoaching Tracking

Poaching has become a literal war in Africa. We must differentiate between two types of poaching, subsistence poaching and commercial poaching. There are some similarities:

➤ Both types of poacher are cunning.

➤ Both are generally very bush wise.

➤ Both are potentially dangerous.

Subsistence Poaching

Here the term poaching is, perhaps, harsh. A subsistence poacher kills to procure food for himself and his family. He is referred to as a "poacher" because he kills game that does not belong to him. In a different context he would be regarded as an aboriginal hunter who kills animals to obtain meat to survive. **Subsistence hunters are usually poor, without work, and trying their best to survive under harsh conditions.**

Figure CCCH.10.02.01: Strategic spots along fence lines are favourite places for setting wire snares.

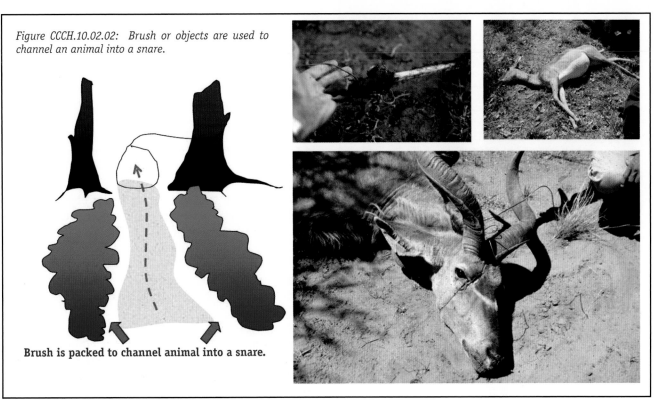

Figure CCCH.10.02.02: Brush or objects are used to channel an animal into a snare.

Brush is packed to channel animal into a snare.

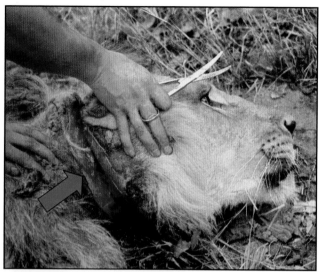

Figure CCCH.10.02.03: *Results of a wire snare.* (Photo courtesy Butch Smuts)

Commercial Poaching

Commercial poachers kill animals illegally to make money from selling meat, hides, or other products such as horns or tusks. Whereas the subsistence poacher will kill when he is hungry, the commercial poacher will kill at every opportunity. The more he kills, the more money he will make; therefore, he will use any means at his disposal to kill as many animals as possible in the shortest time. He is rapacious and ruthless. Commercial poachers are often highly organized groups of well-armed gangs. They are often ex-soldiers who are well trained. This makes them a dangerous foe not to be underestimated.

A new type of commercial poacher is also emerging in Africa. These are ex-rangers or conservation staff who have gained experience in the use of capture drugs and have turned to poaching. There will be more on this later.

Let us now look at the types of signs that will be left behind by subsistence and commercial poachers. Many signs have already been mentioned in the section on combat tracking, so we will not go over this ground again. Subsistence poachers will make use primarily of traps and snares but will also use primitive weapons (spears, bows and arrows, etc.), old weapons such as muzzleloaders, modern firearms, and even military weapons (such as the infamous AK-47). Commercial poachers will have the best equipment available.

Traps and snares

Subsistence poachers are usually excellent bushmen who know and understand animal behaviour. They know the best places to set snares and traps. The most common and deadly snares used in Africa are simple wire or cables fashioned into a noose. They are very cruel, and animals die slow and agonizing deaths. These wire cables are often placed along fences, especially at migrating points. Another favourite spot is on well-used game paths—especially those leading to and from water. See Figure CCCH.10.02.01.

Poachers will channel animals into walking into snares by using natural vegetation or packing brush in such a way as to force animals to take a certain route. Snares are often tied to trees or heavy objects such as logs. When a big animal drags the object, the wire bites ever deeper into the neck or leg. The animal eventually dies of exhaustion, asphyxiation, or from loss of blood. See Figures CCCH.10.02.02 to CCCH.10.02.04. When wire snares are set in the natural environment, they are very difficult to spot and are deadly effective. See Figure CCCH.10.02.04.

A trigger mechanism is sometimes attached to a snare as a means of quickly causing the noose to tighten. A bent sapling usually supplies the "power" to cause a noose to pull tight over an animal's neck or foot. The "trigger" is attached to a tripwire or to a bait. When the

Figure CCCH.10.02.04: *Poachers remove a young warthog from a wire snare.*

Figure CCCH.10.02.05: Wire snares are very difficult to see in a natural environment. In the bottom photograph the poacher has set a cable snare between two trees above a game path.

trigger is activated by walking into the tripwire or taking the bait, the sapling whips up and tightens the noose of the snare. A baited snare can be used to target a specific species of animal. Power snares are illustrated in Figures CCCH.10.02.06 and CCCH.10.02.07.

Poachers also use deadfall traps sometimes, but because they are not as effective as wire snares, they are used far less frequently. They work by allowing a heavy weight to fall on an animal. Spikes are sometimes added to impale the animal. See Figure CCCH.10.02.09.

Commercially bought gin traps are also used occasionally. They normally trap animals with steel jaws that snap closed over a foot. The gin trap is buried under a layer of leaves to make it less visible. It is often

Figure CCCH.10.02.06: An example of a power snare.

Bent sapling

Trigger

Tripwire

Wire noose

Figure CCCH.10.02.07: When the animal walks into this snare, it will activate the trigger and the bent sapling will whip up the wire. (Photo courtesy M. Cowell)

baited to lure animals to it or placed along well-used game paths. Gin traps are usually attached to a nearby fixed object or a heavy movable object that the animal will drag along, leaving an easy trail for the poacher to follow. When the animal is found, it is dispatched with a spear, ax, or similar weapon. Poachers are often accomplished bushmen and trackers in their own right. See Figures CCCH.10.02. 10 to CCCH.10.02.12.

Subsistence poachers in Africa are armed and very dangerous. Commercial poachers are generally armed with military weapons as well as commercial firearms. The tracker should be on the lookout for ammunition belonging to military and commercial types of weapons. See Figure CCCH.10.02.13.

Subsistence poachers will generally make use of an entire carcass. They will eat the meat and sometimes use

Figure CCCH.10.02.08: A ranger inspects a snare (above left). More examples of baited snares and tripwires made of thin twig are shown top and bottom right.

the skin for leather or clothing. Commercial poachers target mostly rhinos (for their horn), elephants (for their ivory), or body parts for *muti*. This is all they will remove from the animal and will leave what remains to rot or be consumed by scavengers. See Figure CCCH.10.02.15.

If you find an elephant or rhino carcass with horns/tusks still intact as in Figure CCCH.10.02.16, there are three possibilities.

1. It has died of natural causes (old age, disease).

2. It was wounded by poachers but got away and died.

3. If the carcass is still fresh it could be that the poachers were disturbed (possibly by an antipoaching patrol) and ran off before they could remove the ivory or horns.

Poachers armed with fairly light-calibre military weapons such as the AK-47 are responsible for the scenario in example three below. A poacher tries to shoot big animals like an elephant or rhino and finds that the limited penetration of these weapons doesn't always drop the animals on the spot. The wounded animal can run for a great distance before finally succumbing through blood loss or infection. Always check a carcass for sign of bullet holes; in addition, use a metal detector to search for bullets in the carcass.

When carcasses of big animals are left in the veld, it will attract large numbers of vultures, marabou storks, and other scavengers such as hyenas, jackals, and even lions. When vultures are sitting in a tree, it is a good indication to the tracker that there is a dead carcass close-by and that the predators might still actively be feeding. The smaller hooded vultures (see Figure CCCH.10.02.18) will always sit in the lower branches closest to the kill. Because they are small, they are low on the feeding order. Once the larger vultures move down onto the carcass, these opportunistic birds dart in to snatch scraps while the predators are feeding.

The stench of rotting meat will carry far in the bush and can lead a tracker to a poaching scene. There will also be increased activity of scavengers, blowflies, and dung beetles in the vicinity. See Figure CCCH.10.02.19.

To deter poachers from shooting rhinos, conservation authorities began dehorning them. This measure has not always proved to be successful. Poachers spend hours and sometimes days tracking rhino with the intention of shooting it for its horn. When they discover a rhino

Figure CCCH.10.02.09: A deadfall trap with spikes.

Figure CCCH.10.02.10: Commercial gin traps. The remains of a baboon hand is still in the trap on the right bottom. Animals sometimes escape from these traps—minus a limb. In this maimed state, few survive.

Figure CCCH.10.02.11: Poachers at work checking tracks.

Figure CCCH.10.02.12: Poachers setting snares.

Figure CCCH.10.02.13: Be on the lookout for empty cartridge cases or whole rounds dropped by mistake by poachers.

Figure CCCH.10.02.14: An improvised trap. Poachers are very innovative and can manufacture "homemade" traps that can work very effectively.

Figure CCCH.10.02.15: Rhino and elephant poachers usually take only the horns and tusks and leave the remains to rot.

has been dehorned, they vent their fury by shooting it anyway! Their logic is that they will not waste time in the future tracking a dehorned animal! Nowadays many conservation authorities that have the funds and the trained personnel implant transponders into rhino horns. In this way they can keep track of the animals and even trace the whereabouts of a horn if it has been removed from the animal. This process is, however, expensive.

Poison. Some commercial poachers use poison. They poison baits that will attract certain target species such as hyenas and vultures. Body parts are then sold to *sangomas* (witch doctors) as *muti*. Organophosphates, strychnine, and various other poisons are used. A poison with the trade name of Temic is popular. A poacher will spike a bait carcass with one of these poisons. When scavengers eat the poisoned meat, they will die, usually in proximity to the carcass. No animal, bird, reptile, amphibian, or insect is safe from the commercial poacher.

Because the struggle against poaching in Africa has taken on the characteristics of a war, the tracker must always be on the alert for the sound of shots. Antipoaching forces and operations are conducted like military operations. An antipoaching tracker will always be on the lookout for signs indicating a poacher's camp. See Figures CCCH.10.02.20 and CCCH.10.02.21.

Signs Often Associated with a Poacher's Camp

- ➤ Smoke from fires
- ➤ Well-traveled footpaths
- ➤ Toilet areas
- ➤ Material associated with poaching, including bits of wire, metal, traps, poison containers, ammunition, etc.
- ➤ Smell of cooking meat/fish

Figure CCCH.10.02.16: A dead elephant with ivory still intact.

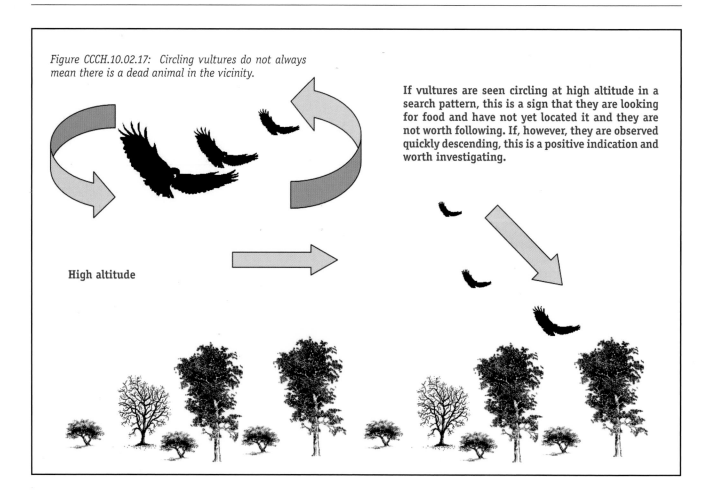

Figure CCCH.10.02.17: Circling vultures do not always mean there is a dead animal in the vicinity.

If vultures are seen circling at high altitude in a search pattern, this is a sign that they are looking for food and have not yet located it and they are not worth following. If, however, they are observed quickly descending, this is a positive indication and worth investigating.

High altitude

Figure CCCH.10.02.18: Vulture indicators of predators in the vicinity of a carcass.

The larger vulture species sit higher up and farther away from the carcass patiently awaiting their turn.

The smaller hooded vultures sit closest to the carcass in low branches.

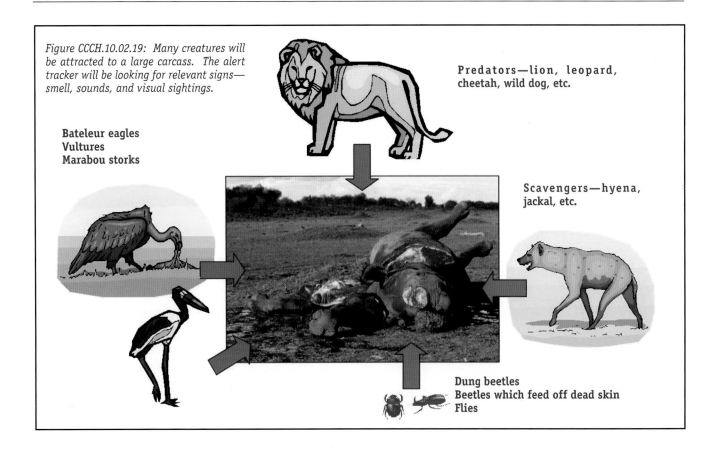

Figure CCCH.10.02.19: Many creatures will be attracted to a large carcass. The alert tracker will be looking for relevant signs—smell, sounds, and visual sightings.

Predators—lion, leopard, cheetah, wild dog, etc.

Bateleur eagles
Vultures
Marabou storks

Scavengers—hyena, jackal, etc.

Dung beetles
Beetles which feed off dead skin
Flies

- Collection of firewood
- Old fires
- Meat drying racks
- Clothing
- Animal remains—bones, skulls, teeth, hair, skins, etc.

Antipoaching Operations

When conducting antipoaching operations, it is important to establish a pattern or the modus operandi used by the poachers. Careful observation and intelligence-gathering will often give clues as to when, where, and how poachers will strike.

- Poaching is of a higher intensity close to border settlements or protected areas.

The antipoaching tracker should give special attention to these areas, but not to the exclusion of others. The poachers also monitor the activities of antipoaching personnel and will look for predictable patterns in antipoaching forces. Poachers sometimes make the tactical mistake of conducting poaching forays deep into protected areas. It is essential, therefore, to monitor wide areas and to adopt unpredictable tactics so that the poacher can never guess when and where you will be operating.

- Poachers can sometimes be identified by the specific methods they use, e.g., the way they tie a wire snare or set a trap.

- Poaching activity may increase during a full and sometimes a new moon.

- Poaching activity increases toward the end of the month. People have more money at this time to buy poached products; consequently, there is a higher demand for meat and other wildlife products then.

- Antipoaching forces rely heavily on information obtained from informer networks. Poachers, however, often have informers of their own who work for conservation organizations. These informers keep poachers up to date on the movements of antipoaching operations. Tight security on planned operations is vital.

- Leaders of antipoaching operations need to keep poachers guessing. Make use of foot patrols, horse patrols, bicycle patrols, ambushes, and listening and observation posts. Don't use regular routes or fall into the habit of a fixed and predictable schedule. If, for example, you send scouts out every Monday morning on a bicycle patrol along a specific route, poachers will avoid this area and operate elsewhere.

➤ Maintaining a presence in an area is one of the best ways to prevent poaching. Poaching activities declined in areas of the Kruger Park that were previously troubled by poaching when walking trails were introduced into these areas.

➤ Proactive operations are better than reactive operations.

When freshly set snares are found, it is not always a good idea to remove them immediately. Clear away signs of your own presence and then set up an ambush at this point and wait. There is a good possibility that the poachers will return to check on their snares, and you will then be able to catch them in the act.

A new form of rhino poaching has emerged in the past number of years. Disgruntled conservation staff who are poorly paid, have been dismissed or displaced, or bear some grudge have begun poaching rhinos for

Figure CCCH.10.02.20: The photograph shows rangers posing in Kruger National Park just before departing on an antipoaching patrol.

Figure CCCH.10.02.21: A poacher's camp. The camp contains all the "tools of the trade." These camps are usually well hidden and are moved on a regular basis to make discovery more difficult. (Photo courtesy M. Cowell)

their horn using chemical darting techniques. These people are often very familiar with the areas in which they poach (having worked there previously) and with the type of antipoaching operations carried out by the organization. They are highly trained and have even been known to make use of helicopters to be able to make a quick strike. They may also operate on foot. After the horn is removed, they will inject the animal with an antidote and release it.

This type of poaching is potentially a big threat as there are a variety of drugs available for either the immobilization or the killing of game. Succinylcholine chloride (Scoline), which has been used for culling elephants and buffaloes by national parks, is an ideal drug for poaching as it leaves no trace in the carcass. Although the use and acquisition of scheduled capture drugs are strictly controlled, there are ways and means of getting hold of them. With either prior experience or the proper training, this high-tech type of poaching will undoubtedly become prevalent in the future. See Figures CCCH.10.02.22 and CCCH.10.02.23.

Action on Finding a Carcass Suspected of Having Been Poached

Don't move or remove any evidence without carefully recording information pertaining to it! See Figure CCCH.10.02.24 for standard operating procedures.

Gathering and recording evidence at the scene. Thoroughly search the area where the incidents have occurred without disturbing/damaging/eliminating any evidence. Sketch the crime scene to indicate any evidence found, to measure distances, and to record track and spoor information. Examine the carcass to determine how the animal died (shot with a firearm or killed with a primitive weapon such as assegai, bow and arrow, or poison). Take photographs, and the more the better. Try to establish the time of death of the animal; look for other signs in the area.

Make sure the exact position of all evidence is recorded before it is collected. When collecting evidence, use gloves and place the evidence in a labeled Ziploc bag. Empty cartridge cases can be picked up by inserting a small stick in the mouth of the case, lifting the case, and dropping it into a plastic bag. See Figure CCCH.10.02.25. If you are not familiar with ways to collect evidence, have the area sealed off and wait for the police or forensic experts to arrive.

Training Regime for Combat and Antipoaching Trackers

➤ Tracking roles and techniques

➤ Sense enhancement exercises to develop skills (sight, smell, hearing, taste, and smell)

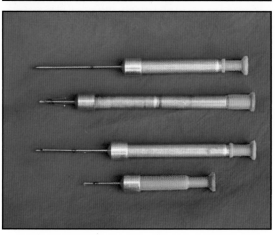

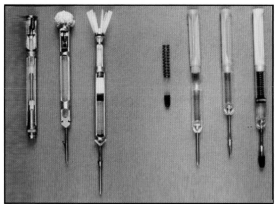

Figure CCCH.10.02.22: Given the training, darting animals is a fairly simple procedure and an ideal poaching tool.

Figure CCCH.10.02.23: There is a variety of highly sophisticated darting equipment commercially available. While the equipment is easily obtained, the drugs are harder to acquire.

➤ Team tactics

➤ Weapon use and employment (sniper training/quick kill/IA drills).

➤ Crime scene investigation procedures

➤ Immediate action drills and battle drills

➤ Navigation skills (map reading/compass/GPS)

➤ Camouflage and concealment techniques

➤ Use of high-tech equipment (thermal sensors, sound enhancement, etc.

➤ Observation and surveillance procedures

➤ Intelligence-gathering methods

➤ Coordinated weapon tactics (covering/reflexive/direct fire)

➤ Helicopter drills

➤ Radio communication and SITREPS

➤ Poaching techniques

➤ Casualty evacuation drills

➤ First aid

➤ Command and control

➤ Mines and booby-traps

➤ Physical fitness

➤ Animal tracks and signs

Search and Rescue Tracking (SAR)

Trackers' Role in SAR Operations

Accomplished trackers are often called in to help find people who have been lost in the outdoors. People exposed to the outdoor environment can become disoriented and soon lose their way. Others might be injured and unable to send for help. Whatever the cause, people lost in the outdoors are vulnerable to adverse weather, wild animals, and thirst. Unless they are quickly found, they often succumb to exposure. Since many people who are lost in wild country have little or no survival training, they are often ill equipped mentally and physically to survive prolonged exposure. It has been proven beyond doubt that skilled trackers can be employed to help prevent deaths associated with being lost in the outdoors.

The tracker should be familiar with the type of tracking involved in search-and-rescue operations and also with the way different people and age groups respond when becoming lost.

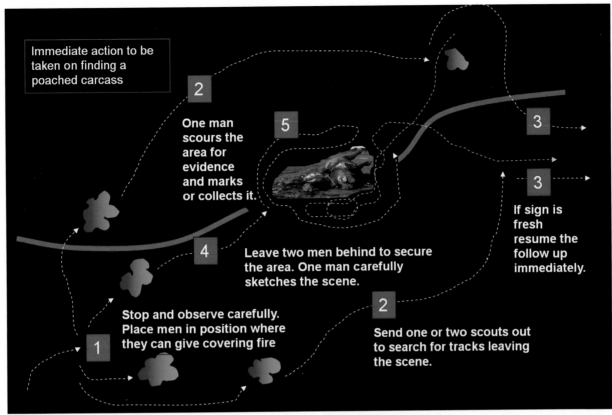

Figure CCCH.10.02.24: *Standard operating procedures on finding a carcass suspected of having been poached.*

Inside figure 3:

Immediate action to be taken on finding a poached carcass

2 One man scours the area for evidence and marks or collects it.

5

3

3 If sign is fresh resume the follow up immediately.

4 Leave two men behind to secure the area. One man carefully sketches the scene.

1 Stop and observe carefully. Place men in position where they can give covering fire

2 Send one or two scouts out to search for tracks leaving the scene.

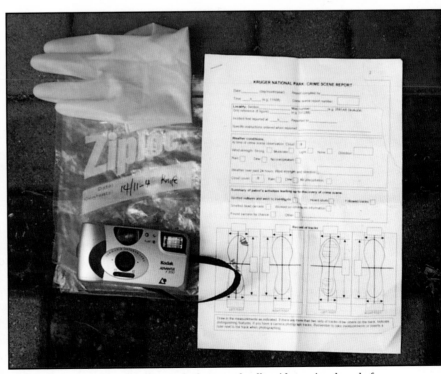

Figure CCCH.10.02.25: *Number and photograph all evidence in place before collecting it (above left). Use gloves when handling evidence (left). A basic poaching incident kit (above right) includes Ziploc bags, digital camera, incident report, and measuring tape.*

Figure CCCH.10.02.26: *If you do not have gloves, collect an empty cartridge case by inserting a stick into the mouth of the case (above) and then dropping it into a Ziploc bag (below). Avoid touching the case with your bare hands/fingers.*

Behavioural Characteristics of Lost Persons

People respond differently to becoming lost in the wilds. Age, sex, cultural background, knowledge of the wilds, and physical and mental condition all influence the behavioural response to being lost. A good article on the behaviour of lost persons was published by the Search and Rescue Society of British Columbia (Doyle, 1995-96) and can give some valuable insights for trackers involved in search and rescue operations. The following guidelines, slightly modified, have been based on these observations.

The tracker must have an understanding of these behavioural traits. The way in which people respond to being lost shows certain trends; thus, people who are lost can be classified according to these trends into seven main groups. In some instances these groups can be subdivided. The main groups are:

➤ Children

➤ Hikers, campers, and climbers

➤ Hunters and fishermen

➤ "Walkaways" include old people who may be suffering from Alzheimer's disease, senility, or a form of mental psychosis.

➤ Mentally challenged

➤ Hopeless and despairing

➤ "Others"

In each of these groups we will consider various aspects of behaviour.

Having an understanding of how people will react to becoming lost will greatly assist the tracker in predicting where to look for a lost person.

GROUP 1: Children
(Figures CCCH.10.03.01 – CCCH.10.03.03)

Children between the ages of 1–12 are in different stages of mental development and understanding and will, therefore, respond in different ways to becoming lost. For this reason this group must be divided into three subgroups: ages 1–3, 4–6, and 7–12.

The youngest group can busy themselves with myriad activities and usually become lost when there is poor or no supervision. They may not even be aware or have the understanding that they are lost and may continue to wander aimlessly about. Some will stay on a game path or trail. If the weather turns bad, they will look for some form of shelter. They will generally not walk farther than about 1 kilometre from their original position as they tire quickly. Most are afraid of the dark and will begin crying as night falls and will continue crying until they fall

Figure CCCH.10.03.01: *Group 1 includes small children between 1 and 3 years old.*

asleep. The tracker should listen carefully for the sound of whimpering or crying. More than 55 percent tend to move downslope, a third upslope, and about 10 percent will stay on level ground. There is more chance, therefore, of finding them in lower-lying areas.

Children in the 4–6 age group are generally inquisitive and are inclined to go exploring. They are often alone but are especially inclined to explore if a friend or house pet accompanies them. There are many things in the wild that will draw their attention: Animals, people, or objects will interest them. This age group is more mobile than the younger age group and will travel farther and faster. At this age, most children understand the concept of being lost and will attempt to return home or to a place that is familiar. More than 50 percent will stay on a track, trail, or game path. They will look for shelter in inclement weather or when they are tired and want to sleep.

As with the youngest group, the main reason they become lost is due to a lack of supervision. They are usually suspicious, even scared of strangers, but will respond quickly to a familiar person or voice. Their movement patterns with regards to walking up or downhill or staying on level ground is very similar to that of the younger group. They are usually found on average a little more than one kilometre from their original position but may travel farther than the younger group.

Children belonging to the age group of 7–12 years are mentally more alert and developed, and understand the concept of being lost. They panic quickly and become confused when lost. As with the 4- to 6-year-olds, they enjoy exploring and will often set off into the bush with a friend or pet. Generally speaking, they have better developed navigational skills and will attempt to return home or to familiar surroundings when becoming disoriented. They have similar fears to that of adults but more pronounced with a greater sense of abandonment/ loneliness/fear/panic/helplessness.

Most make use of bush tracks, trails, or paths and tend to avoid areas of thick bush. Most get lost because they become distracted, but some may intentionally run away if angry, to gain attention, or to avoid punishment. They will look for cover in poor weather, e.g., under a bush or rock overhang, cave, and so on. See Figure CCCH.10.03.04.

If they have run away to avoid punishment, gain attention, or because they are angry, they may decline to respond to efforts to locate them until such time as they become cold and/or hungry. They often will not answer when called. Darkness, however, often brings on a willingness to accept help and to be found. More children in this group tend to travel downslope (58 percent) with 8 percent staying on level ground and 33 percent moving to higher elevations.

They tend to move a lot farther than younger age groups, with a range of 0.14 to 8.00 kilometres with an average of 1.48 kilometres. In youths aged 13–15 years the behaviour is similar to this group. The range of distance walked before being found is 0.4–7 kilometres with a mean of 1.49 kilometres.

Figure CCCH.10.03.02: Group 1 includes young children between 4 and 6 years old.

Figure CCCH.10.03.03: Group 1 includes children between 7 and 12 years old.

Figure CCCH.10.03.04: Lost children taking shelter. (Photo courtesy B. Roussouw)

Figure CCCH.10.03.05: Group 2 includes hikers and campers.

If older children have run away to avoid punishment, gain attention, are defiant, or are angry, they may not respond to efforts to locate them until such time as they become fearful, cold, and/or hungry. They may ignore calls or shouts to locate them. The fears that darkness holds for this age group will often, however, bring about a change of behaviour and a willingness to respond positively to search and rescue efforts. Close to 60 percent of this age group will choose to travel downslope, a third upslope, and about 8–10 percent will choose to stay on level ground. Children in this age category tend to move farther and are found, on average, about one-and-a-half kilometres from their original position.

GROUP 2: Hikers, Campers, and Climbers
(Figure CCCH.10.03.05)

This group is involved in a wide variety of outdoor recreational activities that includes backpacking, different types of climbing sports, and camping activities. There are exceptions, but people in this group are generally in good physical and mental condition but not necessarily experienced or knowledgeable of the outdoors or survival techniques. Ages in this group are variable but most (about two-thirds) are under the age of 30. About 40 percent are generally well equipped for the outdoors whereas the remainder may be questionably or even poorly equipped for wilderness or bush travel and the outdoor emergencies that may occur in these environments. Most people (about 75 percent) in this group generally plan their activities in terms of staying or attempting to stay on marked trails, routes, or drainage lines.

People in this group can become lost for a variety of reasons including the following:

➤ Trails are poorly marked, poorly defined, or become overgrown.

➤ Physical abilities in a group differ and the group/ individuals become strung out and eventually separated. People with bush and orienteering skills are often separated from those who do not have these skills.

➤ Taking shortcuts often causes people to get lost.

➤ Inclement weather, overcast sky, and walking at night often result in people becoming disoriented.

➤ No navigational aids or inexperience as to how to use them.

➤ Failure of navigational aids such as batteries in a GPS going flat.

➤ Misjudging time and distance.

People in this category are generally fit and can cover fairly long distances from the place where they were last seen to where they are found; this can range from between a few hundred metres to as much as 24 kilometres. More than half tend to move downhill, 25 percent move uphill, and the remainder choose to stay on level ground. People in this category respond positively to search-and-rescue efforts and will often assist searchers by making smoky fires, using distress flares, or signaling with mirrors. Climbers who are also grouped into this category may cover a wide range of ages but are generally in the younger-age bracket. See Figure CCCH.10.03.06.

They are, by and large, well equipped and self sufficient and tend to stay on or near climbing routes. The cause or contributing cause(s) of missing climbers can be any of the following or a combination thereof:

➤ Most common causes: Falling, being hit by dislodged/falling objects, exceeding personal abilities, climbing un-roped, personal injury

➤ Common causes: Equipment failure, stranded, inadequate equipment, climbing alone, illness

➤ Less common causes: Becoming separated from a climbing team, darkness, inclement weather, failure to stay on the climbing route

The majority (55 percent approximately) of climbers are killed or injured whilst ascending and about 35 percent when descending. The remainder are killed or injured under different circumstances. Most injuries or fatalities occur in inexperienced climbers.

GROUP 3: Hunters and Fishermen
(Figure CCCH.10.03.07)

Hunters and fishermen are generally intent on their pursuits and often forget to keep themselves oriented. Hunters, who tend to be overconfident and overestimate their abilities, generally go out into the bush prepared for only one day and are often ill prepared for inclement weather or other outdoor emergencies. Most hunters/fishermen are in moderate-to-good physical condition. The age of hunters may greatly vary, ranging from 15 to 60. Most are in good mental condition. About one-third have good experience, with the remainder having limited experience. Most are adequately clothed (for the prevailing weather) and equipped, but more than 50 percent have no survival training. Hunters who are inadequately clothed suddenly become cold when the weather changes. Hunters, in their pursuit of game, often move off the "beaten track," which makes finding them more difficult when they become lost. They will, however, make efforts to reorient themselves when they become lost and attempt to find paths, trails, tracks, or drainage lines.

Some of the most common causes for hunters becoming lost include the following:

Figure CCCH.10.03.07: Hunters often wear camouflage clothing that makes visual detection difficult.

Figure CCCH.10.03.06: Climbers are often reported missing.

➤ Often physically overextend themselves

➤ Lose track of time and are overtaken by the dark

➤ Move into dense bush or rugged terrain away from roads or other forms of civilization and often try taking shortcuts.

➤ Overcast weather makes orientation difficult

➤ Hunt in unfamiliar areas

➤ Have poor navigational skills

➤ Follow wounded animals without taking note of their surroundings

Hunters will usually take shelter during inclement weather or when it turns dark. The distances hunters walk before being found may vary depending on their experience and outdoor skills and may be as little as a few hundred meters to as much as twenty kilometres.

Lost hunters will respond positively to search and rescue efforts by attempting to call attention to themselves with smoke, fire, signal mirrors, distress flares, left notes or signs, verbal calls, or blowing a whistle, all of which makes it easier for searchers to follow. A complicating factor is that hunters often wear camouflage clothing, and that makes visual detection more difficult. A significant number of lost hunters find their own way back to civilization.

Fishermen may be classified in the same group as hunters and often become lost for the same reasons. Their failing to return from a fishing trip is often related to an accident: a boat overturns, swept off their feet by strong water current, etc. They may also walk far looking for help when lost; this could be from a half kilometer to as much as eighteen kilometres from their original point of departure.

GROUP 4: "Walkaways"
(Figure CCCH.10.03.09)

"Walkaways" are people who may be elderly, affected by senility or Alzheimer's disease, or have some form of mental psychosis. Their behavioural characteristics are often similar to those of children. These people are often oriented to the past. Active individuals are inclined to overexert and overextend themselves and are high hypothermia (abnormally low body temperature) risks in cold conditions and high hyperthermia (overheating) risks under hot conditions. They are often poorly clothed

Figure CCCH.10.03.07: Hunters often wear camouflage clothing that makes visual detection difficult.

Figure CCCH.10.03.09: Walkaways are people who may be elderly, affected by senility or Alzheimer's disease, or have some form of psychosis.

and of a suboptimal nutritional status. They are often ill prepared for outdoor conditions. About half will utilize paths or tracks but many will wander aimlessly with no obvious destination in mind. This can make it difficult for the tracker because the lost person often acts illogically. These people are frequently located in densely wooded areas. Some of the most common causes for these people becoming lost are the following:

➤ They can be attracted by things

➤ They can become distracted and so lost in thought that they just wander off without paying attention to where they are going.

➤ Those suffering from Alzheimer's disease do just not have the mental ability to orientate themselves and can become lost even in their immediate and familiar neighborhoods.

➤ Senile people or those suffering from Alzheimer's can become lost due to a lack of adequate supervision.

"Walkaways" respond poorly at times to search and rescue efforts. This problem is often compounded by the fact that individuals falling into this category are deaf or hard of hearing. Fortunately, "walkaways" generally do not walk too far before being found and are usually located, on average, less than one kilometre from where they were last seen. A significant majority tend to walk downhill as they find walking uphill more strenuous. It is often difficult to locate subjects as they are found most in prone positions regardless of weather conditions.

GROUP 5: Mentally Challenged

These individuals have behavioural characteristics similar to that of children in the 6-to-12-year-old category. They do not always have physical challenges or impairments, but they will not help themselves. They can remain in a reasonably small area for days. More than two-thirds of these people will make use of tracks, paths, trails, or drainage lines. One-third are found in areas of dense vegetation. The main reason for becoming lost is the following:

➤ They are easily attracted by visual or sound stimuli and are prone to go exploring, do not have any sense of direction, and are often unable to return to their starting point.

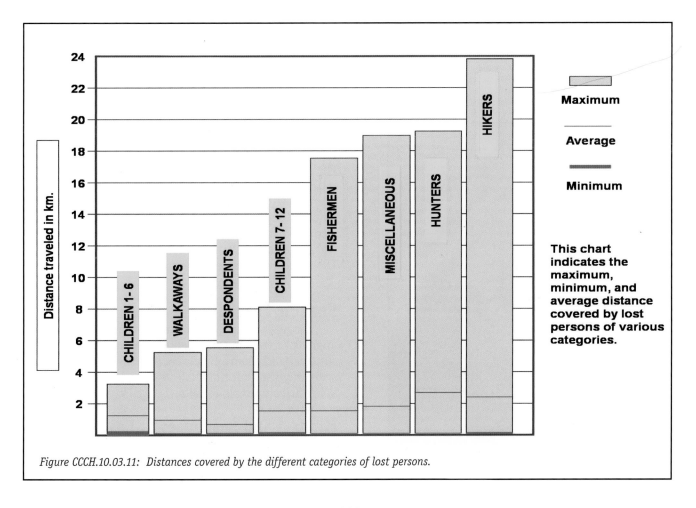

Figure CCCH.10.03.11: Distances covered by the different categories of lost persons.

These people are easily frightened by the dark, noises, weather, and other natural phenomena and will hide away under bushes, behind objects, in caves or holes, and that makes finding them very difficult. Because they are frightened, they do not respond when they hear their names being called. They do little to assist search and rescue efforts. About one-third tend to walk uphill, 8–10 percent will stay on level ground, but most will choose to move downhill. They generally do not walk too far from the place where they were last seen (less than 4 kilometres).

GROUP 6: Hopeless and Despairing
(Figure CCCH.10.03.10)

People with personal problems and who are depressed or need to "get away" to "think things over" are prone to becoming lost. They sometimes have suicidal tendencies and seek solitude. They will use paths and trails until they find a secluded spot, and then they will move off the beaten track but will avoid dense bush and undergrowth. Most tend to walk uphill. The most common cause for these people becoming lost is the following:

➤ To look for solitude
➤ To get away from people
➤ To avoid situations

Once they become disoriented, they cannot find their way back because they fail to take note of their surroundings.

Figure CCCH.10.03.10: Despondents usually seek solitude but may take great pains to avoid being found.

The "hopeless and despairing" are often found within sight and sound of civilization but will go to great lengths to avoid being found. They are unresponsive to searchers and feel intruded upon when teams are sent out to look for them. Many maintain that they were not lost, merely looking for an opportunity to "get away from it all to think." They are often found near prominent or elevated locations with a scenic view. That spot is frequently the first secluded place they find.

GROUP 7: "Other"
This is a high-risk category, and the members do not readily fit into the other groups. They normally are active in good weather and go into the outdoors unprepared for emergencies because they are frequently inexperienced in outdoor and navigational skills and become easily disoriented. Attempts to find their way back leads to greater disorientation, and although they attempt to stay in the area, can end up walking a long way off.

They are generally unfamiliar with the areas they travel into, and they generally carry little or no food, water, or survival equipment with them. About half of this group will make use of tracks, paths, trails, or drainage lines, and two-thirds will opt for downhill travel. Some of the most common causes for members of this group becoming lost include the following:

➤ Disoriented
➤ Poorly supervised
➤ Intentionally separated from group

People in this group will generally respond well to search and rescue efforts and are highly communicative. They will seek shelter during inclement weather. Lost individuals in this group are generally found, on average, within two kilometres or less of their original point of departure. The distances covered by people who are lost may depend on a lot of circumstances, but when statistics are analyzed certain trends emerge. These are summarized in Figure CCCH.10.03.11.

Search Tracking
The normal principles of tracking animals applies to humans as well, but lost people are, in most instances, easier to track than animals because they tend to blunder their way through the bush, leaving behind signs that are relatively simple to follow.

Mindset and Responses of Lost People
People are generally not aware of the fact at first that they are becoming disoriented. The first feelings are vague and somewhat ill defined, with the person

becoming uneasy without really knowing why. When they first ask themselves the question, "Am I lost?" they go into denial. Later on when they grasp the fact that they are, indeed, lost, they are disbelieving and often angry with themselves. "How could I have got myself into this mess?" is a typical response. Close on the heels of disbelief follows panic.

Panic

Panic is a common denominator in all lost people, and it often leads to irrational and unpredictable behaviour. Fortunately, this works to the advantage of the tracker as the fear in a lost person translates into stumbling and forcing his way through vegetation, which leaves a trail easy to follow. Lost people will frequently change direction as they attempt to orientate themselves, and they often end up walking in circles. It is not unusual for lost people to die of psychogenic shock.

Fear of the unknown frequently makes lost people react by actually avoiding detection, believing the searchers to be people that intend harming them. After being lost for one day, many children will not respond to their names being called. This usually happens after two days in the case of adults. Children may remain hidden until discovered by the tracker and may then bolt out of fear. The rescuer might end up chasing them before they become lost again.

The tracker must not only be able to find lost people but must also be prepared and have the skill to deal with the immediate physical and psychological needs of the lost person. It is essential that the tracker carry with him a first-aid kit, basic survival kit, water, and food

(including sweets). You might find the person you are looking for unconscious, dehydrated, hyperthermic or hypothermic (depending on ambient weather conditions and the physiological condition of the individual), hypoglycemic (low blood sugar), or injured and requiring first aid. See Figure CCCH.10.03.12. Frightened children will sometimes have their fears allayed by offering them sweets or something to eat. You might have to make a fire to warm a hypothermic individual.

Attraction to Water

Water holds an attraction for all people; the lost individual will gravitate to water like iron to a magnet. This phenomenon is induced not only because of thirst but also because of the comforting and soothing effect that water has on people. It is a good idea for the tracker to get hold of topographical maps of the search area to look for streams/rivers/bodies of water as likely places to search. The soils adjacent to and bordering rivers/streams are also an ideal substrate to register tracks.

Gradient

Is a person more likely to walk uphill or downhill? Most people would answer "downhill" to that question, but that is not always the case. People will generally choose the easiest route and one that is most suited to their physical build and strength. Children under the age of 6 years will often walk uphill. In the age group 7–12 there is a strong tendency to stay on level ground, and people 12 years old and older will, in the majority of cases, choose to walk downhill.

Figure CCCH.10.03.12: Searchers should carry a survival kit, first-aid kit, water, and food. The person who is being looked for might be in need of medical attention, water, and something to eat.

THE COMPREHENSIVE GUIDE TO TRACKING SKILLS

From a Child's Perspective

The world looks different out of the eyes of a child. If you are searching for a child, bend down frequently and look at the surroundings to get a child's perspective. A dense bush might appear impenetrable to a two-meter-tall adult but might appear, to the much shorter child, as an inviting and protective shelter. Children also have a tendency to shelter, so they will crawl into spaces that would be too cramped for an adult.

Initiating a Search

When you are called to look for a lost person, follow the correct protocols:

1. Determine who you are looking for

2. Determine the place where they were last seen (PLS)

3. Make sure that you have enough equipment and supplies so that you can stay out for 24-48 hours.

Take enough liquids and food for yourself and the lost persons should they be found.

4. Take a first-aid and survival kit along with you.

5. Take maps and navigational equipment (GPS).

6. Make sure you have an effective means of communication. In the absence of radio equipment, cell phones are a practical and viable alternative if there is reception in the area.

7. Take a flashlight, spare batteries, and spare globes so that you can continue the search after dark.

Interviewing Family, Friends, and Eyewitnesses

Contact family, friends, and eyewitnesses to get as much relevant information about the lost person as possible. The following page illustrates a list of questions that should be asked and information that should be gathered prior to setting off on the search. Figure

---

DESCRIPTION OF A LOST PERSON WHEN LAST SEEN

- ➤ Healthy Caucasian male
- ➤ 1.8m
- ➤ 78 kg
- ➤ short, reddish brown hair
- ➤ moustache

Planting stick

Waist satchel (canvas)

Leather belt

Blue denim jeans (long)

Calf high lace up boots (size, Vibram sole, make, tread pattern, wear pattern)

Red safety helmet

Black, red, and white plaid shirt (flannel)

Jewelry (watch, rings, neck chains)

Yellow calfskin gloves

Figure CCCH.10.03.13: Description of a lost person when last seen.

PERSONAL PARTICULARS

Name:

Nicknames:

Sex: Age:

Height: Weight:

Physical build
(slender/well built/overweight/obese)

Hair
(colour type and length):

➤ **Smoker (cigarette/pipe/cigar) or nonsmoker:**
  › Brand:
  › Does the person use a lighter or matches?

➤ **Description of clothing worn when last seen**
  › (headgear, jersey, jacket, sleeveless pullover, shirt, trousers, shorts, dress, handkerchief, socks, underwear, etc. Get an indication of colour and type of material as well)

➤ **Jewelry and accessories**
  › (hair clips, watches, neck or wrist chains, earrings, rings, spectacles, contact lenses, etc.)

➤ **State of health and any medical conditions**
  › (diabetes, hypertension, a bleeder, wears glasses, etc.)

➤ **On any medication and, if so, what type and dosage**
  › you might have to take this medication along with you)

➤ **State of physical health when last seen**
  › (well, sick, vomiting, had a temperature, injured, etc.)

➤ **State of mental health when last seen**
  › (normal and stable, depressed, suicidal, angry, mentally ill, etc.)

➤ **Right or left handed**
  › (left-hand people tend to circle to the left because they take a longer stride with the right foot and right-handed people tend to circle to the right because they take a longer stride with the left foot)

➤ **Past injuries**
  › (e.g., broke the right leg and walks with a pronounced limp)

➤ **Footwear worn when last seen**
  › This is a very important bit of information as it is likely to be the first tangible evidence to present itself (tracks). Find out the type of footwear worn (boot, sandal, running shoe, dress shoe, barefoot). Colour, size (dimensions), type of fastening (laces, studs, Velcro), wear pattern (from other shoes), and track pattern (if you know the model of the shoe you can get a track pattern from a shoe store)

➤ **Hobbies and interests**

➤ **Equipment and supplies carried**
  › Firearms/knife/ backpack/fanny pack/ sleeping bag/bow and arrow/first-aid kit/survival kit/water/ food/ etc.

➤ **Where and when last seen**
  › (Very important)

➤ **Activity when last seen**
  › (rock climbing, hunting, hiking, fishing, playing with friends, etc.)

CCCH.10.03.13 gives an example of a description of a person when last seen.

This background information will greatly assist you in your search, for it will help you to get to "know" the person. You will also know what and who you are looking for, how well they are equipped to deal with an outdoor emergency, and it will provide you with a specific location where to begin the search. You will also be prepared to assist the person physically and mentally. It might help if you can get hold of an old shoe belonging to the individual as the wear pattern

on a shoe can often give an indication as to how the person walks (pronates or supinates). See Figure CCCH.10.03.14.

Sketch or photograph the wear patterns as shown in Figure CCCH.10.03.15. (This is a more simplified form as opposed to that required for forensic recording of wear and tread patterns.) If you know the make and model of shoe/boot, you can sketch or photograph the track patterns from an example at a shoe store. The way this wear pattern is described is illustrated in Figure CCCH.10.03.15. It indicates that the person lands on the outside of the heel and pushes off with the inside toe. Only the left shoe is described on the following page.

Search Procedures

After planning, teams begin searching from the place last seen (PLS). Begin by using the "lost spoor technique" to locate sign. That means to spiral the PLS in ever-increasing circles until a sign is found. An alternative is to use the binary search technique where the area is bisected by cross-tracking. Walk close to maintain voice contact, walk slowly, and search systematically for sign. See Figure CCCH.10.03.16.

When tracks are found, you need to age, measure, study, and confirm them to be those of the lost person. Findings are communicated to the coordinating team. The tracks/signs are marked clearly with some bright, easily visible material. The trackers begin following the trail using standard tracking techniques and procedures. Tracking is conducted under operational conditions with one main tracker walking on the axis of travel and two flankers walking up ahead to the left and right of the axis to look for signs of the subject having deviated from the line of travel. If direction appears to be constant, additional trackers can leapfrog ahead to look for fresher signs. Any evidence found (e.g., sweet wrapper, cigarette butt, resting site, etc.) should be logged with a GPS reference point and reported to base.

Whereas the main objective of search tracking is to locate the lost person as soon as possible, the tracker must be able to interpret track and gait patterns so that he does not miss important information. He should also be able to interpret signs registered by body parts such as fingers, hands, buttocks, knees, head, and elbows. When search trackers are being trained, they should be taught to identify the following track patterns:

➤ Speed and direction of movement

➤ Limp

➤ Stagger

➤ Stagger and fall

➤ Stagger and recover

Figure CCCH.10.03.14: If you can get hold of another shoe belonging to the lost person, look at its wear pattern, for it will give you an indication of how the person walks.

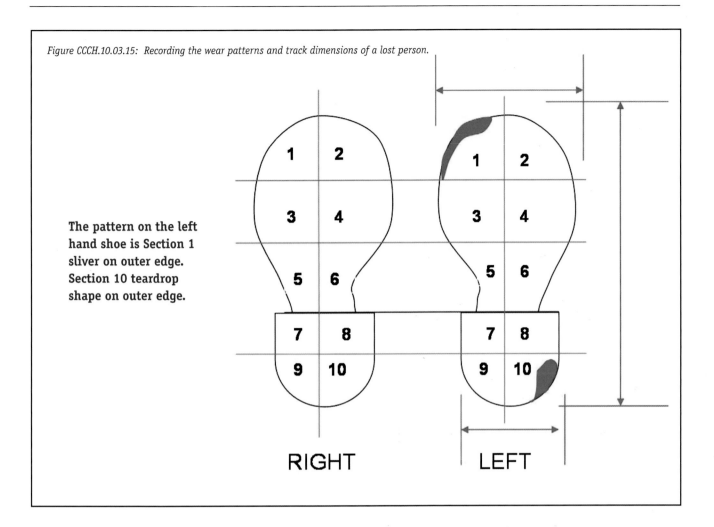

Figure CCCH.10.03.15: Recording the wear patterns and track dimensions of a lost person.

The pattern on the left hand shoe is Section 1 sliver on outer edge. Section 10 teardrop shape on outer edge.

RIGHT

LEFT

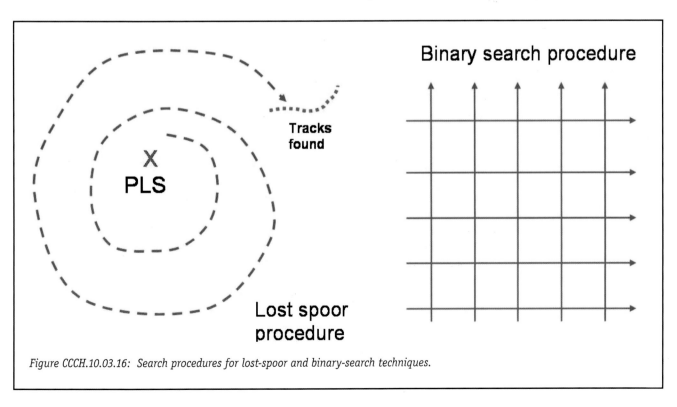

Binary search procedure

Tracks found

X

PLS

Lost spoor procedure

Figure CCCH.10.03.16: Search procedures for lost-spoor and binary-search techniques.

➤ Trip

➤ Trip and fall

➤ Trip and recover

➤ Sit down

➤ Kneel

➤ Lying down

➤ Injury

➤ Panicked gait

When searching for a lost person, call his/her name frequently and blow on an emergency whistle. Be on the lookout for the sight and smell of smoke/fire. Listen for calls for help or the blast of a whistle. Look for emergency signals that the lost person might be using to communicate with the searchers. These include marks, notes scratched onto rocks, soil, or tree bark, signal flares, and so on.

Fugitive Tracking

The difference between tracking a fugitive and tracking someone who is lost is obvious. The fugitive wants to escape detection whereas the lost person wants to be found. In all likelihood the fugitive will resort to violence in order to escape.

If the fugitive has some knowledge of escape and evasion techniques, he is likely to make use of antitracking and countertracking techniques; this will make tracking him more difficult. If the fugitive has little knowledge of bush lore, he will lay an easy trail to follow, but he must be regarded as dangerous, especially if he is armed. When tracking a fugitive from the law, use the techniques discussed for combat and antipoaching tracking.

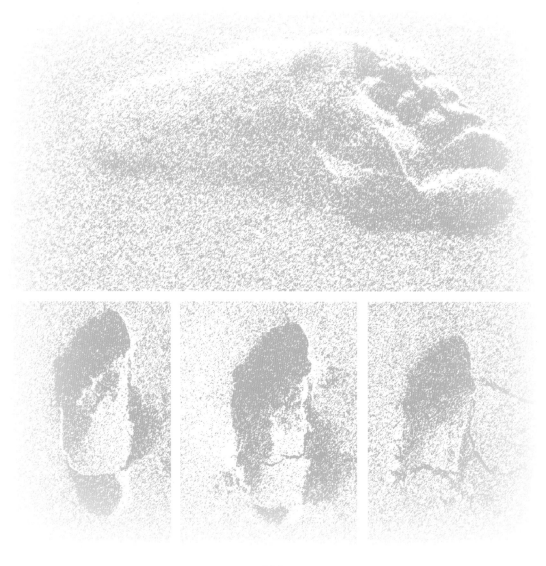

CHAPTER 11

DANGERS OF THE BUSH

The tracker, to function optimally, must have a thorough knowledge of the natural environment. One of the stark realities of the wild outdoors is that it can be unpredictable and dangerous. Dangers come in the form of adverse weather conditions, animals, insects, spiders, scorpions, and reptiles. The more that is known about these potential dangers, the better one is equipped to predict, identify, deal with, or avoid them when and where necessary. While "on the spoor," the tracker must always be aware of other potential dangers.

This chapter is not a comprehensive treatise on survival, merely a reminder to the tracker of the potential hazards he may face in a bush environment. The lesson to be learned is that size is not always in proportion to potential danger. A person allergic to a bee's sting can die within minutes from anaphylactic shock. One must always exercise the necessary precautions; the adage "prevention is better than cure" is both appropriate and pertinent. A competent tracker should be trained to deal with injuries and medical emergencies resulting from wildlife or environmental conditions.

Insects, Spiders, and Scorpions

Most insects, spiders, scorpions, and centipedes have some form of self-defense or attack. Some (like the predatory ground beetle or "oogpister") squirt noxious or irritant excretions, some bite without venom being injected (like the large baboon spider), some inject venom through stings (like scorpions, bees, wasps, and hornets), and some (like spiders) inject venom through mouth parts during the process of biting.

Some insects can pose a serious threat to life. Being attacked by a swarm of bees, wasps, or hornets can be fatal. Even a single sting can kill a person. A person in anaphylactic shock will have severe respiratory distress and eventual respiratory failure because the airways become occluded (closed off) due to swelling. One of the signs of severe allergy is intense itching all over the body and raised welts called hives. See Figure CCCH.11.01.01. Avoidance of bees, wasps, and hornets is a wise option. Antiallergy medication should always make up part of a first-aid kit for the bush.

One of the most dangerous insects, which has killed more humans than all animals and reptiles put together, is the ubiquitous mosquito of the anopheles species. It is the carrier of malaria, which is potentially fatal. It is wise to minimize the risks of being bitten by sleeping under a mosquito net at night, using effective insect repellents, wearing long-sleeved shirts and long trousers,

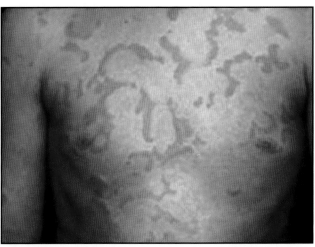

Figure CCCH.11.01.01: Hives caused by severe allergic reaction to a bee sting.

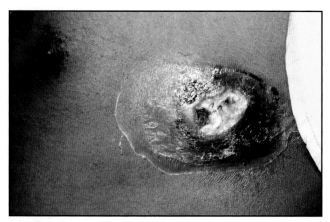

Figure CCCH.11.01.02: The cytotoxic venom of the violin spider can cause severe tissue necrosis, which is difficult to treat and takes a long time to heal.

using a face veil, avoiding (if possible) being out of doors just after sunset and just before dawn (the most active hours for mosquitoes), and getting medical help at the onset of flulike symptoms. Taking malaria prophylactics is also an option, but the pros and cons of taking such medicine should be discussed with your physician.

Tsetse flies deliver a painful bite and can be responsible for spreading diseases such as trypanosomiasis. Fleas can also spread diseases.

The violin or brown recluse spider is definitely one that the tracker should be able to identify, for a bite from this species can be serious. See Figure CCCH.11.01.02. The bite from sac spiders causes tissue necrosis. See Figure CCCH.11.01.03.

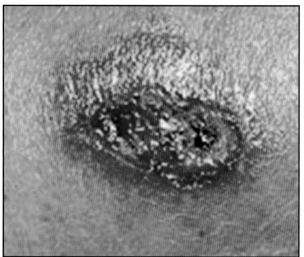

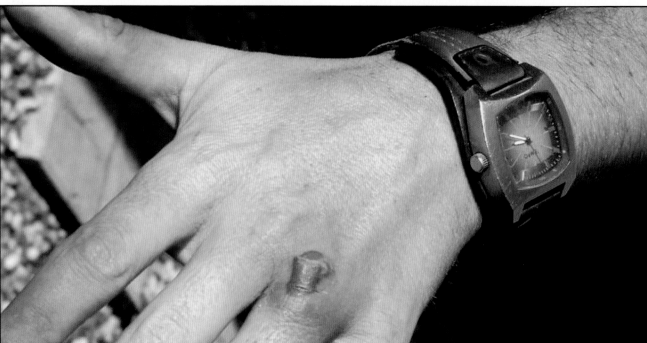

Figure CCCH.11.01.03: The bite from a sac spider also causes tissue to become necrotic. (Spider photo courtesy of N. Larsen)

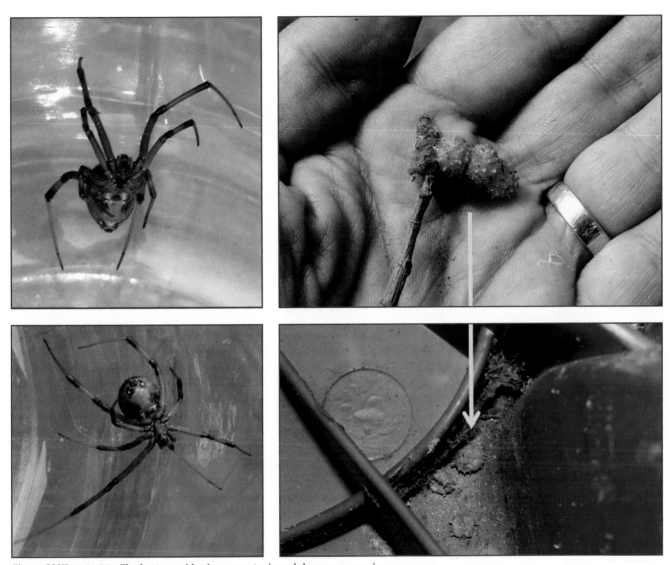

Figure CCCH.11.01.04: *The button spider is a neurotoxic and dangerous species.*

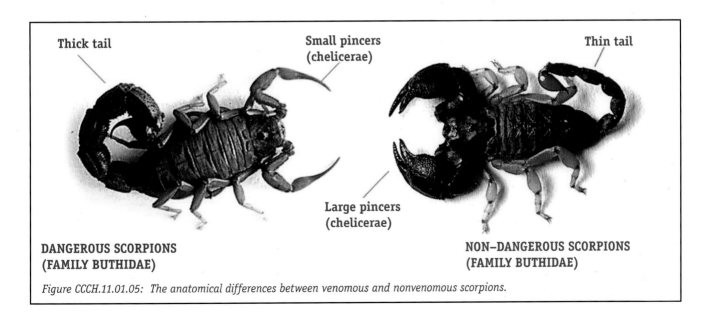

Thick tail

Small pincers
(chelicerae)

Thin tail

Large pincers
(chelicerae)

**DANGEROUS SCORPIONS
(FAMILY BUTHIDAE)**

**NON–DANGEROUS SCORPIONS
(FAMILY BUTHIDAE)**

Figure CCCH.11.01.05: *The anatomical differences between venomous and nonvenomous scorpions.*

Figure CCCH.11.01.06: Some examples of highly venomous Parabuthus spp. *scorpions (top) and mildly venomous scorpions (below). Note the difference between tail thickness and size of pincers.*

The tracker should keep his eye open for the button spider. Button spiders belong to the group known as comb-footed spiders. The black button spider is one of the most dangerous in southern Africa. It has a neurotoxic poison that affects both heart and respiratory function. The site of the bite is painful, and symptoms appear within half an hour. These include severe chest and abdominal pains, anxiety, changes in body temperature, cold skin, and severe headache. Although the symptoms can appear frightening, few deaths have been reported, and the person, although quite sick for a while, generally recovers. These spiders are far more common than people realize. Their round egg sacs are commonly found in old logs and under garden furniture. See Figure CCCH.11.01.04.

All scorpions have a painful sting, but the members of the family Buthidae are the ones that should evoke the most caution. Members of the Scorpionidae family are less poisonous. All scorpions are venomous, and the difference between the more or less dangerous is the quantity and composition of venom they can introduce with a sting. All scorpions carry neurotoxic venom that affects the nervous system of their victims and gives rise to respiratory problems. Of the many thousands of cases of scorpion stings reported in southern Africa each year, only three or four prove to be fatal, and these are usually in old people or young children. How does one differentiate between dangerous and nondangerous scorpions? See Figures CCCH.11.01.05 and CCCH.11.0106.

Reptiles

The tracker must know how to identify potentially dangerous snakes, know what type of venom they have, and how to treat snakebite. It's important to have a knowledge of the preferred habitat of the various snakes, their responses to alarm, and their times of peak activity. It's also important that clients listen to the tracker and do what he says. Tell them not to move if they suddenly come across a snake, and to wear appropriate clothing such as long trousers and boots. Over 80 percent of all snakebites in southern Africa occur below the knee.

Snakebites often occur when handling snakes, stepping on them by accident, or when picking up firewood or rocks. See Figure CCCH.11.02.01. Snakes can be grouped into groups that include cytotoxic venom that attacks the tissues (adders and vipers), neurotoxic venom that attacks the nervous system (mambas and cobras), hemotoxic venom that affects the blood by preventing clotting factors so that hemorrhaging occurs (boomslang and vine snakes), and nonvenomous snakes such as house snakes and pythons. See Figures CCCH.11.02.02 through CCCH.11.02.05.

Figure CCCH.11.02.01: Handling snakes is unwise and is one of the main causes of people being bitten by them. Keep your eyes open for snakes on trails and game paths. Unintentionally stepping on a snake is one of the most common causes of being bitten.

Figure CCCH.11.02.02: Examples of cytotoxic snakes include the gaboon adder (top) that has both cytotoxic and other venom, and a puff adder (bottom).

Figure CCCH.11.02.03: Puff adders have large fangs that fold back into the mouth when closed. When the mouth opens, the fangs become erect and inject venom deep into the tissues. The cytotoxic venom causes severe blistering and tissue necrosis.

Figure CCCH.11.02.04: Examples of neurotoxic snakes include the black mamba (top), snouted cobra (centre), and green mamba (bottom).

Figure CCCH.11.02.05: Examples of hemotoxic snakes are the boomslang (above left) and vine or twig snake (top right).

Monitor lizards

Monitor lizards are not venomous but use their tails to whip potential aggressors; they can inflict a painful bite with their conically shaped teeth. See Figure CCCH.11.02.06.

Crocodiles

Crocodiles are dangerous predators. Always be on the lookout for them and signs that betray their presence. This is especially true when you are close to bodies of water. During dry periods crocodiles can sometimes be found far from water, so pay attention for their signs away from water as well. They are in their element in water but can also move quickly on land.

Figure CCCH.11.02.06: When monitors bite, they are like bulldogs: They don't let go!

Wild Animals

All wild animals are potentially dangerous, especially if injured or if they feel trapped. Serious incidents with dangerous big game involve a number of variables, but there is one common denominator to all: proximity. If you get too close and an animal feels threatened or hemmed in, it will attack. The art of tracking is to get yourself or the people you are tracking for up close enough to the animal without it being aware of you.

While viewing potentially dangerous game, the tracker must constantly be monitoring the situation. This should include the mood and position of the animal(s), the direction of the wind, and the behaviour of clients. As soon as there is an indication that safety is about to be compromised, the tracker should initiate procedures to move the group away from the animal(s). Try to avoid confrontation. Back off while facing the animal at all times. See Figure CCCH.11.03.01. If the animal continues approaching, stand your ground. Shout at the animal, wave your arms, and throw stones at it to try to chase it off. This works in many instances. If this does not work and the aggressive intents escalate, determine a threshold point on the ground at which point you will decide to shoot. See Figures CCCH.11.03.02 and CCCH.11.03.03.

The dangers from wild animals have been dealt with in more detail elsewhere in the book. Figure CCCH.11.03.04 shows injuries to a tracker that was attacked by an elephant, and Figure CCCH.11.03.05 shows a bite inflicted by an African wild dog.

Environmental Dangers

When we think of environmental dangers, we think in terms of weather-related phenomena that can give rise to intense heat or cold, drought, severe storms resulting in thunder, lightning,

Figure CCCH.11.03.01: If possible, try to avoid confrontation by backing off slowly while facing the animal.

Figure CCCH.11.03.02: The author had to shoot this white rhino when it charged.

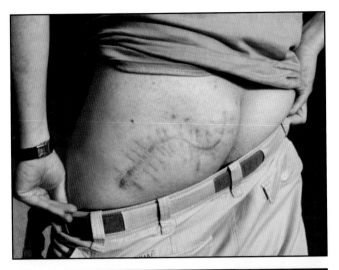

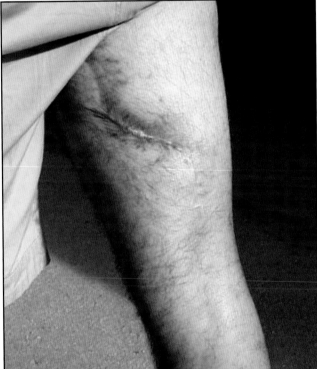

Figure CCCH.11.03.03: *This elephant had to be shot when it charged the author.*

Figure CCCH.11.03.04: *The tracker in the three pictures to the left was fortunate to survive an attack by an angry elephant.*

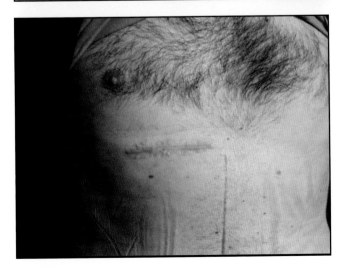

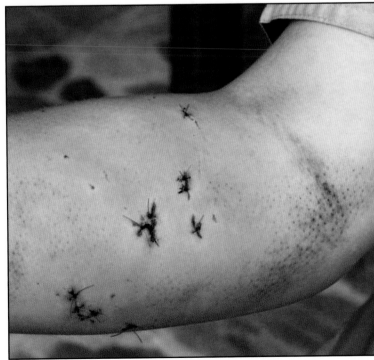

Figure CCCH.11.03.05: *This person was bitten on the buttocks and on the arm by an African wild dog.*

flooding, snow, wind, hail, rain, blizzards, tornadoes, hurricanes, and so on. All have the potential of causing not only discomfort but also death.

Any weather-related phenomenon that results in high ambient temperatures (>35 degrees C) or very low temperatures can be dangerous because of hyperthermia (abnormally high body temperature) or hypothermia (abnormally low body temperature). Tracking in Africa often takes place in hot and, sometimes, humid conditions. Heatstroke and heat exhaustion are two very dangerous conditions that occur in people who are in poor physical condition, overweight, or poorly acclimatized to exercise in tropical Africa. See Figure CCC.11.04.01

The tracker, who is usually reasonably fit and well acclimatized, must remember that others may be neither fit nor well acclimatized. He must, therefore, set the level of pace and exposure to what the others can handle. Generally speaking, if the tracker is maintaining a pace or walking under conditions that are making him tired, clients may become exhausted and some might even be on the verge of collapse. Keep a constant check on clients, and if they start showing signs of overheating (excessive sweating, skin flushed, hot and dry, aggressive, etc.), take immediate and appropriate action.

Thunderstorms

Approaching thunderstorms can usually be seen as a massive buildup of cumulonimbus clouds. These give rise to thunder, lightning, high winds, hail, torrential rain, and possible flooding of waterways. See Figures CCCH.11.04.02 and CCCH.11.04.03. Lightning can be lethal, and if a severe storm is seen approaching, the tracker must take the following appropriate precautions: Head back to camp if you think you can reach it before the storm hits or head back to a vehicle. Stay off high ground and away from fences and tall objects where lightning is most likely to strike,

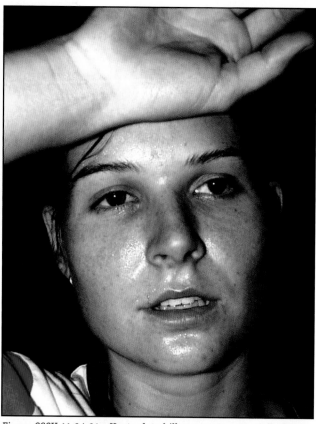

Figure CCCH.11.04.01: Heat-related illnesses are potentially fatal.

Figure CCCH.11.04.02: Lightning kills many people around the world each year and is an environmental hazard.

Figure CCCH.11.04.03: A river in flood after torrential rains.

and stay out of drainage lines where flash flooding may occur. If you cannot reach a vehicle or camp in time, find shelter in a cave, rock overhang, or under low bushes. Hail can also prove to be life-threatening if you find yourself exposed to the elements. Being washed away and drowned is a possibility if you are caught in a flash flood.

Bushfire

There are times of the year when the grass and bush is tinder dry. If the vegetation is set alight by lightning (usually at the end of the dry season with the first thunderstorms), the resulting fire can move at frightening speed. See Figure CCCH.11.04.04. The intensity of the fire is increased with the fuel load and by wind. Bushfires can move so fast at times that one cannot outrun them on foot. A few years ago more than twenty people burned to death when they were caught in a bushfire in the southern region of the Kruger National Park.

The first signs of a bushfire include the characteristic smell of burning vegetation, sounds of crackling fire, and smoke or flames. Immediately move your group away from the direction of the fire and into an area of safety. Areas of safety are large rocky outcrops that are not close to combustible material and areas of very short or no grass, such as trampled areas around water holes, bodies of water, dry sandy riverbeds, and roads. Get away from areas that have dense bush and grass. If the fire appears to be approaching fast and you are worried that you will not be able to reach a place of safety in time, find a small patch of short grass and initiate a back burn. Once a patch has been burned this will be a reasonably safe place to move into until the big fire has passed.

Confrontation with Armed Poachers

The possibility of suddenly coming across armed and potentially dangerous poachers is highly unlikely in some places and quite possible in others. There are a number of scenarios: You see the poachers without them having seen you, the poachers spot you before you see them, or you both see each other. The outcome will be largely determined by one of these three scenarios and if the poachers are armed.

CCCH.11.04.04: A raging bushfire can be terrifying and is potentially lethal. (Photo courtesy B. Rossouw)

If You See the Poachers without Them Having Seen You:
1. Assume they are armed, even if you cannot see weapons.
2. Move your group away from the area immediately. (Your clients are your first priority.)
3. Report the incident and locality (with an accurate grid reference) as soon as you can to the local ranger or police.

If the Poachers See You before They Themselves Are Spotted, They Will Probably Hide or Run Away:
There is always a possibility that they might fire at you, but this is unlikely. Most times they will not want to attract attention to themselves.

Spotting each other is the most dangerous situation, for the poachers might be tempted to open fire at you. In a case like this, get your group under cover immediately and return fire aggressively. Usually three or four rounds accurately placed will be enough to send poachers running. As soon as the firefight ends, move your group away from the area and report the incident and grid reference as soon as possible.

This is good reason for you and your backup to carry ten rounds each. If you operate in an area where coming across poachers or armed insurgents is a good possibility, carry a handgun and fifty rounds of ammo with you in addition to your rifle.

If You Come across a Poaching Scene after the Poachers Have Left:
Secure the area and don't allow people to walk around the scene, pick up objects, or approach the poached animal. They can destroy valuable evidence. If you are in radio contact, report the incident and grid reference as soon as possible and stay at the scene until the police or the section ranger arrives.